VICTORIAN CHILDHOOD

VICTORIAN CHILDHOOD

Themes and Variations

Thomas E. Jordan

State University of New York Press

Published by
State University of New York Press, Albany

© *1987   State University of New York*

All rights reserved

Printed in the United States of America

No part of this book may be used or reproduced in any manner whatsoever without written permission except in the case of brief quotations embodied in critical articles and reviews.

For information, address State University of New York Press, State University Plaza, Albany, N.Y., 12246

Library of Congress Cataloging-in-Publication Data

Jordan, Thomas Edward.
  Victorian childhood.

  Bibliography: p.
  Includes index.
  1. Children—Great Britain—Social conditions.
2. Great Britain—Social conditions—19th century.
I. Title.
HQ792.G7J67 1987   305.2'3'0941   86-30184
ISBN 0-88706-544-9
ISBN 0-88706-545-7 (pbk.)

10 9 8 7 6 5 4 3 2 1

CONTENTS

CHAPTER FIVE

Learning 148

CHAPTER SIX

Social Life 193

CHAPTER SEVEN

Cities 222

CHAPTER EIGHT

Virtues and Vices   259

CHAPTER NINE

Advocacy and Reform   305

PREFACE

In development of this manuscript I have drawn on the resources of a number of libraries, and I express my thanks to the University of Missouri, the Church of Latter Day Saints of Jesus Christ, Washington University, the Library of Congress, the British Library, the Royal Society of Health, the Reform Club, and the Royal Statistical Society. I wish to express my thanks to John Anthony Newland for suggesting helpful resources. K. Peter Etzkorn, Kate Jones, Harry H. Bash, Charles P. Korr, Harvey Goldstein, and James Walvin gave helpful, careful suggestions for which I am grateful.

I particularly wish to acknowledge the assistance of Mary Ellen Heckel, who reads Linear B and typed the tables and manuscript.

Thomas E. Jordan

INTRODUCTION

In the late twentieth century, the place of childhood, if not individual children, seems secure. Despite the cataclysms of two world wars, the world seems unified in its respect for childhood and for the need to create a full and happy life for the young. This positive attitude prevails despite the widespread plague of drugs, the emergence of violence even in schools, and the ever-present image of life presented in less than uplifting form by the media and the world of entertainment. On occasions, the sum of these influences on childhood (compounded by a rising disrespect for life) leads to a sense of worry, and to a sense that we have left behind a Golden Age of childhood, one unencumbered by sophistication and undesirable models for development of a sense of personal identity.

Of course, there has been no Golden Age, and, in fact, the reverse is probably true. We are more enlightened than our ancestors, at least in the sense that we do not tolerate child labor, and we realize the importance of literacy and child health to national progress. Just how Western society arrived at this consensus is a question of great interest. On examination, it appears that it was the nineteenth century which made the transition from the enabling propositions of the eighteenth-century Rationalists to national programs of child care. Even Third World countries, of which Sri Lanka has been an outstanding example, engage in collective welfare; this is the element which the nineteenth century contributed to child welfare.

To examine the question of how progress in concern for children came about requires examination of childhood within the contexts of social forces. In no other country was the matrix of change so evident as in Great Britain. As water power and steam occurred in its towns, weavers and similar operatives were dislocated. There is evidence of this early connection in the 1792 painting by Wright of Derby called *The Iron Forge*. In it, small children play with the forge being worked by a family group. In this painting domestic and industrial themes combine to influence the lives of young children. On the larger scene, Waterloo established the long peace lasting, despite circumscribed outbreaks, until 1914. Victoria Regina held sway, if sometimes absentmindedly, as red became the prevailing color on nineteenth-century maps of the world.

More analytically, the pattern of culture evolved so that there were discernible trends across the century. Cattell (1953) applied factor analysis to the years after 1836, reducing forty-eight data elements (high national debt = 1, N typhus deaths = 48) to seven factors. In the tradition of statistical factor analysis he named the four complexes he inferred from the data *cultural pressure, Emancipation vs. vigor, enlightenment,* and *slum morale vs. cultural integration.* Each of these terms summarizes a subset of his forty-eight elements for the years of 1836–1899. The trend for cultural pressure, meaning social crises and personal stress, grew steadily after 1855, while war stress vs. ease of living rose and fell in minor waves. Emancipation, meaning the participation of ordinary people in government, grew across the years studied by Cattell. This exclusively statistical study, to be added to more literary and inductive formulations, suggests a world of dynamic events.

That world is a remote age to many and its public issues and private moralities are only distinct and fading echoes. The war of 1914–18 was the great watershed, and whatever occurred before it seems a minor problem of an Arcadian age. On closer examination those times become more recognizable; we discern the specificity of situations and perceive that any given day began like those of our lives, with the weak light of morn and the certain sense that it would have its good and bad moments. It would differ, however, in the rhythm of work, for those who toiled on any given day in Britain's cities included hordes of children. The work force was not a restricted age-segment of the population, but a broad swath of humanity ranging from the very young to those on the verge of unemployability in old age. In some sectors of life, children displaced adult workers, being more tractable, cheaper, and at hand in

In contrast to their presence was the absence of major elements in today's world. Health facilities were few and schools, above all, were scarce. It is the contrast with our own times which makes the nineteenth century interesting. Victorian Britain is especially informative to students of the human condition because it was the furnace in which the industrial age, now receding, was forged. It is within this context that I inquire into the nature of childhood and its evolution in the nineteenth century. A powerless minority, exploited and then cast aside, came to enjoy schooling and the protection of effective, enforced legislation by the end of the century. I examine the themes of children's lives—death, work, education, the family—and also address the discontinuities which caused progress to be fitful.

The implicit theses of this work are two; first, that there existed in nineteenth-century Britain what we today would call an oppressed minority, a substantial group of human beings who were neglected, exploited, and subject to arbitrary and excessive restrictions on their opportunities for personal growth; second, that while collectively indifferent and negligent to a morally culpable degree, individual Victorians could be aroused to correct specific abuses. In both of these propositions is a social discontinuity which itself is the essential construct of this work.

The first discontinuity is the comparative neglect of the young within the overall trend to political awareness and liberalism. It is comparative because there were improvements in the lot of children, such as timid efforts at education. But schooling as a national responsibility probably came later in Britain than in the rest of the Western world; when it came it was not only a means for child development and liberation of the human spirit, but also it was a way to discipline a national work force so that the mills of industry would run smoothly and public order would be maintained.

The second discontinuity is the exclusion of children from the general process of emancipation by law and by religious precept which protected the dignity of the individual adult. People saw their prerogatives as citizens broadened, consolidated, and expanded. So pervasive was this that by the end of the century the habilitating functions of local philanthropic groups had become part of the national agenda. It became government's responsibility, not that of voluntary and amateur efforts, to address a social agenda of ways to protect ordinary men and women from the grasping, exploitive, and ignorant excesses of the times. As this general trend of the polity flowed, the welfare of the young did not such programming despite their economic problems. As I have shown elsewhere (Jordan 1981) Third World countries provide a glimpse into conditions of childhood quite similar to those of First World countries in the nineteenth century. The significant difference is that they approach the welfare of children from a virtually preindustrial economic base employing a late twentieth-century valuation of childhood. In their value system, the welfare of individual children is inseparable from national, advance proportionately, despite the passage of laws referring to the young at a rate of approximately one per year from 1800 to 1865 (Index 1973).

In the early decades of the nineteenth century, legislation designed to protect child-workers was piecemeal. Laws addressed apprentices but ignored the majority of children not in apprenticeships. They also addressed factories dealing with a particular raw material and ignored other sites employing different materials. In the 1840s, the prerogative of who was to educate the young was fought over by the churches to the extent that general progress on education was delayed as the price of temporary sectarian advantage. In a trend covering much of the century, law dealt with aggregations of child workers of a size which left those in cottage industries and small "manufactories" (of which canal boats and brick-making are prime examples) quite beyond the effective reach of the law.

In this work I present evidence on the general question of a discontinuity between material and spiritual improvement in the lives of adults and in the lives of children. Here are materials from the lives of children, in some instances from their own mouths, to examine the propositions that children were an unliberated minority culture, and that collective society was perniciously slow to effect reforms, although individual consciences were aroused by specific acts of barbarism.

The explicit mechanism connecting the condition of society to the lives of individual children is *stress*. At the extreme, stress led to death in the form of communicable diseases such as diptheria or cholera. At a less evident level, there was the unremitting stress of long days as a child worker or "slavey" below stairs. Frequently, the two were combined as overwork and ill health aged young mothers long before their time. The themes of this work provide examples of stress and its unremitting demands on children, and on the small, pale adults they evolved into.

Implicitly, there is a second mechanism which pervades the themes of this work. It is the process of socialization by gender. To the Victorians, the sexes were polarities of gender; boys and girls were reared in modes mediated by their sex, and the role expectations for them were quite separate. The relationship between the sexes was important to the Victorians, and they sought to inculcate sex-specific expectations of life, as their ancestors did before them. The difference which emerged was the unprecedented scope of the new opportunities presented by a dynamic, evolving economy. That is, life offered no precedent to guide society, or for individual families to draw on, when machinery replaced muscle in the workplace. At the end of the nineteenth century, the relevance of higher education, the vote, and control of conception began to erode the caste-like role specifications for socialization of the sexes. The slow process of improving the minority status of girls and women began in earnest in the years of Victorian childhood.

While it is obvious that the subject of our inquiry is children, there is some question of which children to consider, in the sense that Victoria's realm had several domains. I choose to avoid the anachronism of treating Ulster alone when examining childhood in Ireland. In the nineteenth century, Ireland meant all four provinces. For that reason, I attend to the situation in Ireland as a whole and discuss childhood in Victorian Britain as a topic arising in England, Wales, Scotland, and Ireland.

Our matrix is the social history of Victorian Britain. Whenever possible, I identify real children and present their words and personal lives. Also, I identify their benefactors and spokesmen, presenting their array of motives and the point of privilege from which they sought to reform their inferiors. Explicitly, the Victorian view of poverty and its metaphysical burden of immorality and unworthiness receives attention. To the reformers (i.e., Dr. James Kay-Shuttleworth, who designed the engine of education for the masses at mid-century), children were, *prima facie,* incipient infidels whose parents were not trustworthy. To Dr. Thomas Barnardo, the children of the poor were to be rescued and protected in a high-handed if altruistic mode. Within the nineteenth century are the Dickensian richness of Victorian days, the scruples of John Wesley's Methodism differentially conceived by master and workman, the rise of central government, and a sense of collective responsibility mediated by preservation of the privileges of class and birth.

With respect to the variety of themes, each constitutes a chapter. Some sources not previously presented elsewhere provide empirical data at various points (for example, data derived from reading the records of ships engaged in transporting boy felons to Australia, and information taken from contemporary accounts of the Famine in Ireland and its effects on children). A temporal sequence is adhered to whenever possible, and a child-development frame of reference guides treatment of specific topics.

1.

DEVELOPMENT AND HEALTH

Data on Children's Growth

The nineteenth century presented a panorama of events; against a background of peace and industrial innovation begun by steam power, there appeared a parade of literary, military, and social leaders in Great Britain. Across the canvas of history strode the Iron Duke, Charles Dickens, and Karl Marx. In more shadowy guise moved ordinary people arrayed in the social ranks which perplexed continental visitors such as Flora Tristan (Palmer and Pincetl 1980) and Gustave d'Eichthal (Ratcliffe and Chaloner 1977). To these observers of the scene, Victorians appeared slaves to social conformity and to prejudices of all kinds in their relationships.

However, particular lives, on closer inspection, had individual rhythms, entrances, and exits. It is to the earliest years of those varied life cycles that this work is addressed. For, however lofty, or obscure their destiny, in Burnett's phrase, Victorian lives began with the mewling of the infant who faced a precarious existence. Medical knowledge was limited to a grasp of anatomy, glimmerings of physiology, and few effective remedies. Accordingly, the characters and personalities we associate with the nineteenth century are the near-random consequences of

1

chance. For one infant, destiny meant malnutrition or early death; for another, life was an alternating series of illnesses (probably traceable to contaminated water) and convalescences. At the least, the processes of human development set the stage for the influences exerted by social factors. Accordingly, exploration of Victorian childhood and its themes begins with the fundamental consideration of children's health and how well such children grew within the circumstances faced by their parents and family.

In his mature years Robert Blincoe, who had also been known as Robert Parson (Brown 1832), was described as being a little man in height with crooked legs. Blincoe's condition was attributed to the life he led as a child worker in Lancashire cotton mills. There, he was overworked, ill-fed, poorly housed, and subjected to punishment that can be accurately represented as torture. The boy survived and reared his own three children with attention to their welfare. However, all through his surprisingly long life—he died at age sixty-eight in Macclesfield— Blincoe bore visible scars which were physical evidence of his ordeal. The fact of survival indicates a sturdy physique in the earliest years of the nineteenth century. It is only by recalling children one by one in that period that we can perceive the state of health and ill health in the young.

To the modern mind, an obvious way to consider children's health is to study their comparative height and weight. The problem is that this empirical approach presumes that we think there is an issue to be studied, an awareness not really evident in the public mind until well into the nineteenth century. A second aspect of the matter is that measuring people other than military recruits received little attention until the Belgian, Adolphe Quetelet, published his first major work in 1836. Even then, children were not the focus, and it was not until the 1880s that systematic studies of the growth of children began. As examples of the genre, we cite the work of Yeats (1864) in Peckham, Roberts (1876) in three North of England Counties, Bowditch (1872) and West (1893) in Massachusetts, Porter (1893) in St. Louis, Geissler and Uhlitzsch in Freiburg (Porter 1894), Boas (1897) in Toronto, and Arkle at Port Sunlight at the turn of the century (Unwin 1918).

The studies beginning with Roberts were models of diligence and organization; however, they lack specification of what we now call covariates or secondary influences, of which social class is an example. Also, the good studies come late in the nineteenth century and leave the early decades quite unrevealed. Prior studies are unsophisticated and in the spirit of the earliest surveys which were censuses conducted to assess potentials for tax revenue. Early surveys of physique were also tied to the welfare of the state, but in the form of assessing the human potential for recruiting into armies. In that vein, we have the 1817 report from Scotland on the heights and chest and head measurements of men in various regiments (Statement 1817). In that survey, the most frequent interval of height in 931 men of the First and Second Argyll Militia was from sixty-seven to sixty-eight inches, which was a good height for the time.

In 1833, Samuel Stanway prepared tables of measurement from Manchester children for John W. Cowell (1833) to present to the Factory Inquiries Commissioners. The data report age by birthday, so that children are grouped between, for example, the ninth and tenth birthdays. The method adopted by Stanway presents obvious problems for the adolescent years since the age-point summary is roughly correct, but the dynamics of adolescent growth are lost in the heights and weights. In the same vein, one reads nineteenth-century studies with care because the words have different meanings. Roberts's report of 1876 draws on measurements of ten thousand children and is impressive. The careful reader learns that the mean is not the arithmetic mean but what we call the mode "at which the greatest number of observations occur." This confusion reappeared in the important anthropometric report of Galton's committee in 1883 (Galton 1884); there were peculiar uses and interpretations of standard error of measurement in Porter's studies of child development a decade later (Porter 1894). To Porter, the arithmetic mean was the average. Of course, our criticisms are anachronisms in relation to Roberts's and Stanway's diligent, empirical approaches. Questions for which there are no answers include what the term "not-factory children" in Cowell's report of 1833 embraces. It is probably Sunday School groups, since such gatherings of children under evangelical auspices were well-established at the time. Also, the size of the total nonfactory sample is half that of the factory children, and the sample sizes of each stratum of age are quite different. Stanway also recorded data on factory and nonfactory girls. In the case of boys, Stanway provides a mean height for four hundred boys of 55.28 inches, which is below that of nonfactory boys by .28 inches. For girls not employed in factories, the mean height exceeds that of the factory girls by only .03 inches.

Jelinger Symons reported to the Commission on the Employment of Children the height of boys working near Halifax in 1842 (First Report 1842). Illustrating the characteristics of early data Symons added up all the heights of all the subjects: "By taking the first ten collier boys, and the first ten farm boys, of ages between twelve and fourteen we find the former measured in the aggregate 44 feet 6 inches in height and

274½ inches around the breast. . . . In girls there is a difference in the height of those employed in farms compared with those in collieries of eight and a half percent in favor of the former."

The Commissioners were told about children working in Wolverhampton (Second Report 1843). The Parliamentary report states: "Lads of fifteen and sixteen years of age are the size of ordinary English boys of twelve and fourteen, but not as strong or healthy. Many of the manufacturing girls of fifteen, sixteen, and seventeen presented none of the external developments corresponding with commencing womanhood. . . . There are many instances of retarded puberty in both sexes."

It is in adolescence that interesting and informative differences in mean height usually appear. From study of records in a variety of sources it appears that at age sixteen years nonfactory youths were 1.60 inches taller than those at work, a trend that persists in the data until, at age eighteen, the nonfactory lads were 6.47 inches taller than the factory boys' mean height of five feet three inches (63.32 in. vs. 69.89 in.). A set of eighteen-year-olds who average five feet three inches is certainly an unwelcome and unwholesome finding. The effect of child labor in factories on the physical welfare of boys was clearly harmful, and the consequences persisted for generations.

A set of data from the period 1837 to 1846 exists in the form of ships' records on boy felons transported from London to Point Puer in Tasmania. In 1832, the *Frances Charlotte* carried 140 boys, and the practice ended in 1846 with 141 boys transported on the *Samuel Boddington;* 1841 was the peak year with 385 boys transported. In the case

TABLE 1.1
HEIGHTS AND WEIGHTS OF BOYS AND GIRLS IN 1873[1] and 1965[2]

	HEIGHT (cm.)				WEIGHT (kg.)			
Age	Boys		Girls		Boys		Girls	
	1873	1965[3][4]	1873	1965[4]	1873	1965[4]	1873	1965[4]
8.5	118.11	128.90	118.05	127.80	25.00	26.20	23.97	26.40
9.5	123.19	134.30	123.03	133.50	27.32	28.90	25.92	29.30
10.5	128.27	139.30	126.69	139.50	29.56	31.90	28.38	33.00
11.5	133.35	144.70	131.42	146.10	31.83	35.50	29.21	37.70
12.5	135.89	150.30	135.18	152.50	33.57	40.00	35.11	43.10
13.5	140.97	156.80	—	157.90	35.70	45.50	—	48.60

n.b. one pound = 2.2 kg., and one inch = 2.54 cm.
[1]Roberts, 1876
[2]Tanner, Whitehouse and Takaishi (1966)
[3]Chinn and Rona (1984) have reported a secular trend to slightly greater height, especially at age eight years and in Scottish children
[4]Fiftieth percentile

of the boy felons sent to Australia on the *Frances Charlotte* in 1832, their height was diminished by several inches in late adolescence (Jordan 1985a).

Roberts's (1870) data on fifty thousand children is important because he studied large groups at each age; more importantly, he went beyond presenting height and weight separately (see Table 1.1 for a summary and a contemporary comparison) and developed tables showing the proportions of the body, and the relationship between age, weight, height, and chest circumference. He rejected the supposition that age could be derived from weight and height, although he thought teeth potentially useful between the ages of eight and fourteen years in order to establish children's level of maturity.

In Dr. Boulton's prospective ten-year study, reported in 1880 in *Lancet,* we see a critical approach to the study of height and weight data. Boulton (1880) presents the mean weight for specific heights and does not give means for particular ages. The brief report in *Lancet* is tantalizing, for Boulton clearly reports that he has ten-year prospective data from "average children of well-to-do parents . . . giants and dwarfs being excluded." Boulton's research is the first to address the velocity of growth (that is, the annual increment in growth), especially in adolescence. Galton's report of 1883 stratified a sample of 2,862 boys by social class, a construct phrased at the time as *media.* The report summarizes the major finding at ages eleven and twelve by stating that "a difference of five inches exists between the average statures of the best and worst nurtured classes of children of corresponding ages. . . ."

There is a degree of relevance in Danson's (1862) study of height of men aged eighteen to thirty years in the Liverpool jail, and it shows that growth extended well into the twenties. At age eighteen, the average height of one hundred convicts was was 64.34 inches. Only in men aged twenty-eight and older is height over sixty-five inches. Danson pointed out that "it is obvious that the results here do not indicate a progressive increase in height." In fact, the minimum height in the series is higher for older than for younger men. Among the men aged twenty-seven to thirty, a set of 433 subjects, minimum height was less than sixty-one inches. Among men aged eighteen to twenty-two there was only one instance of the minimum heights reaching sixty-one inches; and the minimums in the eighteen- and nineteen-year-olds are both fifty-nine inches or less. Criminals are not a representative group but probably represent a substantial subgroup of the poor, since Liverpool had a large criminal class (De Motte 1977).

For our major interest in the welfare of children in the nineteenth century, the chief question is the matter of the secular trend; that is, what happens to data on height and weight of young people as the decades of the century pass. We wonder if children are getting taller and heavier, or whether the data show the opposite, or present gains and losses for age groups in different years. The age at which adolescence appears (e.g., menarche—the onset of menses in girls) is an empirical question. Of course, the problem lies in the scarcity of data for answers. In the case of menarche, it seems quite likely that the onset of menses came later than today, the average age in London girls in 1966 being 13.0 (Eveleth 1979). In the nineteenth century it came later, the age decreasing only after child factory labor ended.

In the case of weight the evidence is a little better because of Roberts's (1876) research. At that time, Roberts had gathered and analyzed a large number of measurements taken in 1873 (see Table 1.2). The research led Roberts to conclude that the increment in the weight of children was such that the nine-year-old of 1876 had the weight of a ten-year-old forty years before.

TABLE 1.2
AVERAGE WEIGHT IN POUNDS

SUBJECTS	AGE LAST BIRTHDAY			
	9	10	11	12
Factory children, 1873	58.56	61.55	66.68	70.57
Factory children, 1833	51.76	57.00	61.84	65.97
Difference	6.80	4.55	4.84	4.60

(Roberts 1876)

> From these figures it will be seen that a factory child of the present day of the age of 9 years, weighs as much as one of 10 did in 1833, one of 10 now as much as one of 11 then, and one of 11 now as much as one of 12 then; . . .

Tanner (1981) reported Norwegian data analyzed by Kiil which begins in 1769. Recognizing that these data draw on a different genetic pool, for Norwegians are still slightly taller than Britons according to Tanner, one learns that the early Norwegians were five to six centimeters below the heights of today's Norwegians. Tanner reports that the peak for velocity of growth was probably as late as age seventeen years and that maximum height was probably attained at age twenty-five. Supporting that conclusion with Scottish data was Professor Forbes's (1837) report that maximum height was "barely attained at the age of 25," a view shared by Bowditch (1872) in Massachusetts. In Galton's (1884) data, males completed growth at about age twenty-three and females at about age twenty.

In considering the secular tend for growth in children, it is helpful to add to the evident picture of an increase in stature over the full course of the nineteenth century. Within the century there was a sharp decrease in the general health of poor children which we call later in this chapter, the "degeneracy problem." Throughout the era of great social reforms in sanitation and factory life, children looked like little old men, and men were dead by age fifty (Jordan 1983). Reviewing the health of the poor in Manchester, Dr. Morgan, according to Henry Rumsey (1871), was struck by the "singular want of stamina." Morgan went on to say that

> the instances in which the muscular system is fully developed or well strung are rare. Cases of deformity, accompanied by actual distortion are not uncommon, while minor physical defects, denoting constitutional ailments, are deplorably frequent.

Flat feet occurred in 70.9 per 1,000 factory children, compared to an incidence of 17.1 in farm children, according to Dr. Bridges and Mr. Holmes (Roberts 1876). Bad teeth in children living in factory towns were common. Roberts reported an incidence of bad teeth of 35.6 per 1,000 in nonfactory towns, but 89.1 per 1,000 among children living in factory towns, which is two to three times greater.

In the earlier decades of our period, the Parliamentary reports are full of horrifying accounts of crippled children and adults. Children working in mines (frequently half-naked girls working in dark, wet tunnels far underground, often with no light), were deformed and brutalized by their labors. The subsequent secular trend to better health and stature can seem so inevitable from the viewpoint of one hundred and fifty years later. It was not inevitable, because the profit to be wrung from child labor was substantial. The Ten-Hours Bill and other piecemeal reforms were vigorously opposed; unscrupulous men found ways to work children in two shifts and so denied them the protection intended by the Ten-Hours Bill. Happily, there was a secular trend to better height and weight over the decades. At Port Sunlight it was possible for Dr. Arkle of Liverpool to demonstrate what an enlightened approach to housing and schooling could produce. In Table 1.3, the key comparison is with the three council schools; and the comparison for weight of fourteen-year-olds at Port Sunlight with "Higher (social) Grade" boys is impressive. Dr. Arkle's specification of the "higher grade" of a school exemplifies the

TABLE 1.3
HEIGHT AND WEIGHT OF BOYS AT PORT SUNLIGHT
AND FOUR OTHER SCHOOLS—1906*

Schools	Height in Inches Age in Years			Weight in Pounds Age in Years		
	7	11	14	7	11	14
Higher Grade	47.4	55.5	61.7	49.3	70.3	94.5
Council Schools (a)	45.3	53.1	58.2	44.1	61.4	75.8
(b)	44.8	51.8	56.2	43.0	59.0	75.9
(c)	44.0	49.7	55.2	43.0	55.5	71.1
Port Sunlight	45.7	52.4	60.7	50.3	65.9	105.0

*Unwin (1918).

sense of experimental design and sampling which, when lacking in earlier studies, allows only illustrative use of data; comparison and inference in the early studies is done very cautiously. At the moment, further increments seems unlikely. Menarche is at an early but stable age, and malnutrition in the Western world is rare. And yet today's strong and healthy children come from the gene pool of small, light children of one hundred and fifty years ago. Man's potential for development is remarkable, and contemporary levels of physical attainment reflect the rise in levels of nutrition since the nineteenth century.

Nutrition

The health of Victorian children depended on their nutrition to resist infections and to build sturdy bodies for a lifetime of work. The quality and level of children's nutrition depended on how well they were fed, and that situation reflected the family's situation. Income was strictly a matter of work by the parents, augmented by children's earnings in many cases. The reports of various Parliamentary inquiries record the earnings of families and how they spent their weekly allocations. Some families would raise a pig to be slaughtered in early winter, and few paid income tax, a levy introduced in 1842. As an element in the national economy, wheat came from the countryside, and its price was protected by the Corn Laws of 1815, which were not repealed until 1846. Some food came from Scotland, and Ireland was still exporting food to England when its population was starving in the late 1840s, according to Gallagher (1982).

The history of family budgets tells us how much discretion families had in the purchase of food as contrasted with rent and clothing. The earliest detail for the beginning of our period is provided by the French historian Braudel (1975), who analyzed the weekly budget of a Mason living and working at the end of the eighteenth century in the modest Prussian town of Berlin, whose population was about 140,000 people. The unnamed Mason spent 14.4% of his weekly income on rent, 6.8% on heat and light. Over three-quarters of the weekly budget went to feed the family of five people; bread absorbed 44.2% of the weekly budget.

In his study of the poor in Manchester, Dr. James Kay (1832) (to be known a decade later as Kay-Shuttleworth) found that workers in cotton mills spent a good deal of money on food and drink. The food of the very poor was a monotonous diet of potatoes, flavored with bacon, at intervals, since they ate little meat. In that regard, we see the decline in living standards which the Industrial Revolution had wrought. The Report of the Commission on the Employment of Children contains many examples of weekly budgets, and the place of food within them, from England, Scotland, and Wales. In the case of British workmen's families, the Factory Commissioners of 1834 learned that a Bolton family had a weekly income of £1.8.5., of which slightly over £1 was spent on food. The money was spent to buy thirty pounds of bread, twenty pounds of potatoes, and three pounds of flour. Of the total income, 3.5s went for rent. A typical budget of £1.6s. was as follows:

Expenditure per week

	£.	s.	d.	%
House-rent and coal		3	6	15.0
Flour, 20 lbs. at 2¹/₂d.		4	2	18.0
Cheese, 6 lbs., at 7d.		3	6	15.0
Butter, 1¹/₂ lbs., at 1s.		1	6	6.6
Bacon, 2 lbs., at 8d.		1	4	5.9
Butchers' meat		2	0	8.8
Sugar, 2 lbs., at 9d.		1	6	6.6
Tea, 3 ozs., at 6d.		1	6	6.6
Salt, 1 lb., ¹/₂d.; pepper, 1d.		0	1¹/₂	1.0
Potatoes, 12 lbs., at ¹/₂d		0	6	2.2
Soap, 1¹/₂ lb., at 8d.		1	0	4.4
Candles, 2 lbs., at 8d.		1	4	5.9
Tobacco, 2 ozs.		0	7¹/₂	2.7
	1	2	7	

Less well-off was another Welsh family of ten persons whose income was £1.2.6.

Expenditure per week

	£.	s.	d.	%
50 lbs. of flour		9	2¹/₂	28.9
2 lbs. of butter		1	10	5.2
1¹/₂ lbs. of cheese		1	0¹/₂	3.2
Animal food		4	0	12.5
3 ozs. of tea		1	11	6.0
1¹/₂ lb. of sugar, at 8d.		1	0	3.1
Soap and sundry small articles		1	10¹/₂	5.8
House-rent, &c.		3	1¹/₂	9.8
Expenses, including clubs, ale, &c.		2	0	6.3
Drapery		6	0	18.8
	1	12	0	

Some did better than others. The unmarried Collier, Griffith Daniel, who lived in lodgings near Llangennech, earned 20s per week. Mr. R.W. Jones the Commissioners' agent, reports, "Surplus 9s. 6. Is supposed to spend it in beer; very little attention being paid to his dress." Young Griffith allocated his money as follows:

Weekly Expenditure

	£.	s.	d.	%
12 lbs. of flour, at 2¹/₂d.		2	6	24.5
1¹/₂ lbs. of cheese, at 4d.	0		6	4.9
1 lb. of butter	0		11	9.0
1 lb. of bacon	0		10	8.1
1 lb. of sugar	0		8	6.5
1 oz. of tea	0		6	4.9
1/4 lb. of salt	0		0¹/₄	1.0
12 lbs. of potatoes	0		3	2.4
1/2 oz. of pepper	0		0¹/₂	1.0
1/2 lb. of soap	0		3¹/₂	2.8
1¹/₂ lb. of candles	0		10³/₄	3.0
4 ozs. of tobacco		1	3	12.3
	0	10	2	

From the perspective of a century and a half, we hope that the 9s. 6d. Griffith spent so freely brought him a little relief in a life of unremitting stress.

Mr. R.W. Jones provided the weekly budget of a Welsh farm laborer, Thomas Jones, aged forty, who had a wife and six children ranging from two to fourteen years. Eight people lived on his earnings of 12s. plus his wife's 2s. and a boy's earnings of 6s., for a total of £1 per week. Mr. Jones adds that Thomas Jones is "a steady man, and his family all tolerably well clothed."

Weekly Expenditure

	£.	s.	d.	%
50 lbs. of barley flour, at 1^1/$_2$d.		6	3	49.0
10 lbs. of cheese, at 4d.		3	4	26.0
1 lb. of butter		0	11	7.2
2 lbs. of sugar, at 8d.		1	4	10.4
1^1/$_2$ oz. of tea		0	9	5.8
1 lb. of salt		0	0^1/$_2$	1.0
1 lb. of oatmeal		0	2^1/$_2$	1.6
^{1}/$_2$ lb. of soap		0	3^1/$_2$	2.3
^{1}/$_2$ lb. of candles		0	3^3/$_4$	2.4
1 oz. of blue		0	1	1.0
1 oz. of starch		0	1	1.0
Rent		0	0	7.8
1 oz. of tobacco		0	3^3/$_4$	2.4
		14	11	

About the time that Mr. R. W. Jones was reporting his findings, the Mayor of Manchester, William Neild (1841), reported to the Royal Statistical Society the expenditures of families in 1836 and 1841, gathered by his partner, Mr. Graham (Neild 1842). The Neild-Graham data have the advantage of being reported consistently by category. We have combined the 1836 data for several families in Table 1.4. The Stoveman had seven dependents and a total income of £2. 17s. in 1836. By 1841, his income was the same but his expenditures had risen by eight shillings. The Labourer had a family of four people and an income of £1. 10.0. in both 1836 and 1841. His expenditures rose over five years by 3s. The powerloom Weaver had two dependents and earned £1.1.6. in 1836, a sum which dropped to 14s. 4d. in 1841, with expenditures rising from 16s. ½d. to 17s. 4½d., as the Hungry Forties began. We

TABLE 1.4
PATTERNS OF WEEKLY EXPENDITURE IN MANCHESTER, 1836
(after Neild and Graham)

ITEM	Stoveman				Labourer				Weaver			
	£	s	d	%	£	s	d	%	£	s	d	%
Rent		5	0	15.5		3	5	18.3		1	10	17.8
Flour or bread		7	9	24		3	9	2		1	11	18.7
Meat		6	3	19.4		2	11	15.6			4½	4.0
Bacon			8½	2.2							8½	7.6
Ham												
Oatmeal												
Butter		3	0	9.3		1	6	8.0			9	8.0
Eggs											3	2.7
Milk						2	0	10.7			10½	9.3
Potatoes		2	0	6.2			6	2.6			5½	4.9
Cheese		1	0	3.1								
Tea		1	5½	4.5			9¼	4.0			6	5.3
Coffee		1	2	3.6			8	3.5			3	2.7
Sugar		1	8	5.2			8	3.5			5½	4.9
Treacle												
Tobacco			9	2.3								
Soap			9	2.3			8	3.5			4	3.5
Candles			6	1.5			8	3.5			1½	1.3
Salt			2	1.0			6	2.6			½	1.0
Coal							8	3.5			6	5.3
	1	12	2			18	8¼			9	4½	

choose this example from Neild's report because it shows falling income in an occupation with a sad history. Neild's analysis yielded the percentage of budgets allocated to various classes of purchases. In 1836, the typical Manchester family spent 13% to 16% of its budget on bread, about 19% on rent, coal, candles, and soap, about 22% on foods, and about 8% on tea, coffee, sugar, treacle, and tobacco. Neild's categories leave something to be desired, but we can see that about 48% of the expenses were for food, and something under 8% for drink, for a total of about half the expenditure. That was in 1836; and five years later things were more expensive in the face of stable or lowered income, leading to a decline in the standard of living. By 1841, discretionary income, what Neild called "Going back into the World per Week," had dropped by over two-thirds in Manchester.

When we look at these budgets from the point of view of nutrition we see that the pattern is very different from that of our generation.

There is a little tea, and that is not surprising if we keep in mind that the duty on tea was always heavy, according to Burnett (1979). He goes on to list the consumption of tea which rose, per capita, from one and a quarter pounds (1.28 lb.) to one and a half pounds (1.16 lb.) between 1820 and 1850. By the latter date, tea was drunk by people everywhere in Great Britain. In 1962, McKenzie analyzed the food purchased by the Manchester families studied by Neild in 1836 and 1841. The major deficiency was protein, and the value of the food consumed appeared to yield about 2,400 calories per day. That is not much for people to live on, especially when they work long hours, and, in the case of children, need nutrition to assist growth, not merely to work. Burnett (1979) compared Neild's data from 1836 to 1841 to current nutrition standards. The diets of the 1841 Manchester families are low in protein, but satisfactory in calories. Iron and vitamin C are markedly deficient, on the average.

In Scotland and the extreme North of England, oatmeal and potatoes were at the heart of the diet, supplemented with fish when available. Rumsey (1871), with his great interest in declining health of the population, thought that oatmeal was responsible for the comparatively good health of the Scots. Levitt and Smout (1979) supplemented their analysis of the 1844 Poor Law Report in Scotland with the interesting report of Mr. David Stuart of the purchases of "a hired servant, with five dependents," at Dryfesdale, in Dumfrieshire. Stuart reported that

> the yearly consumption by a family of oatmeal and barley meal is seventy five stones (1050 lb.) . . . or three pounds per day. Their dinner is constituted principally of potatoes, of which they appear to consume nearly one cwt. (112) lb. per week, or fourteen pounds per day. At dinner, along with potatoes they may use occasionally a little milk, or herring, or a little ham, or inferior meat . . . not above 8d or 9d a week.

When we look at an income of £26 per year, we find it composed of:

ITEM	£.	s.	d.	%
Rent	2			7.6
Fuel	2			7.6
Oatmeal	5	17	6	22.6
Barley meal		16	8	3.2
Potatoes	2	18	4	11.2

Milk	0	10	0	1.9
Tea, sugar, ham, etc	2	0	0	7.6
Whiskey		3	0	1.0
Tobacco		12	0	2.3
Clothes—man	2	15		10.6
—woman	1	15		6.7
—bairns	1	15		6.7
Other (including school fees)	2	2	0	8.0

The total for food is £13. 17s. 6d., which is just one-half the total annual income. The interesting item is the reference to school fees, a commitment which the Scots had, commendably, displayed in the eighteenth century.

In Ireland, nutrition was a persistent source of stress. Typical of the desperate plight which dependence on the potato produced twenty years before the Famine was the episode in Galway in 1822 recorded by the correspondent of a London relief committee.

> This morning a poor woman called at my house, entreating food for herself and her famished children, one of whom was much exhausted; while my wife was getting some butter-milk for them, the children set up a shriek, and on enquiring the cause, it appeared that the poor little sufferer, who was about ten years of age, had expired, . . (Report 1823).

In the early 1840s the potato crop was the central element of the diet. When the crop was blighted by Phytophthora Infestans in 1845, large segments of the population starved. Indian meal had been introduced from North America several decades before, but it was used largely to feed poultry. Crawford (1984) reports that it was incorrectly ground and then improperly cooked causing pain to the hungry. By the 1860s, however, it was more widely used. Dr. Smith (1864) reported that it was 15% by weight of the diet in a Galway family and 20% by weight of the diet in a Tipperary family. Excessive reliance brought the risk of pellagra due to a deficiency of the B-complex of vitamins. Crawford (1984) identified a high incidence of the eye disease, xerophthalmia, in Irish children at mid-century traceable to deficiency of vitamin A. At Trim, the Workhouse Union distributed an uncertain supply of oatmeal to its outdoor dependents. For persons under age fifteen the total contribution was a half-pound of oatmeal per day (Papers 1847). Little wonder that at Ballina the Poor Law inspectors found the Geraghty children lying on the floor of their cottage too weak to come to the workhouse to collect food; Mr. Geraghty was dead from hunger and lying amidst his children (Papers 1847). Elihu Burritt spent three days at Skibbereen in February 1847. In his account of the Famine he recorded an encounter with two children and their mothers in a hovel.

> The cold, watery-faced child was entirely naked in front, from his neck down to his feet. His body was swollen to nearly three times its usual size, and had burst the ragged garment that covered him, and now dangled in shreds behind him. The woman of the other family, who was sitting at her end of the hovel, brought forward her little infant, a thin-faced baby of two years, with clear, sharp eyes that did not wink, but stared stock still at vacancy, as if a glimpse of another existence had eclipsed its vision. Its cold, naked arms were not much larger than pipe stems, while its body was swollen to the size of a full-grown person. Let the reader group these apparitions of death and disease into the spectacle of ten feet square, and then multiply it into three-fourths of the hovels in this region of Ireland, and he will arrive at a fair estimate of the extent or degree of its misery (Burritt 1847).

Of course, our interest is in the nutrition which fires the engine of life. Above the level of starvation the problem of nutrition is complicated by tastes, the quality of food available, and its freedom from adulteration. The taste for white bread was established in Southern England by 1801, according to Collins (1975), with the Welsh eating barley followed by oats rather than wheat; oats followed by wheat and barley was the pattern in the North of England. The introduction of white bread came quickly, and with its advent came the decline of home baking in favor of purchased bread or use of the baker's oven to bake the housewife's dough. A positive aspect of the decline of rye was reduction of the chance of convulsions and death traceable to ergot, a disease to which rye was vulnerable. Green vegetables were conspicuously absent from the purchases, although fruit in season was used. By the 1850s, green vegetables were sufficiently established for a Vegetarian Society to flourish. The British Medical Journal (1862) could report the theme of vegetarians, "Why, then, should men obtain nutriment at second hand, alloyed by the impurities of the animals through which it had passed?"

In the case of children too young to work, nutrition was quite haphazard. To the Health of Towns Commission, Dr. Strange of Ashton under Lyne reported that

> it was no uncommon thing to be consulted about emaciated children with extreme mesenteric disease, and an enquiry to find that the food consists in great part of bacon, fried meat and salt potatoes, when the

child has not perhaps two teeth in its jaws to masticate it (Second Report 1845).

Dr. Greenhow, writing for the Privy Council in 1861, reported that

> children left by their (factory) mothers . . . are fed in their absence on
> artificial food . . . unsuited to their digestive powers. The mothers being
> able to nurse them only at night. Pap, made of bread and water, and
> sweetened with sugar or treacle is the sort of nourishment usually
> given. . . . In several instances little children, not more than six or seven
> years old were seen preparing . . . this food.

There were experiments on diet for children. In 1880, Dr. Boulton reported to the *Lancet* that the residents of a boy's home at Regent's Park were not thriving to his satisfaction. By changing their diets he promoted increments in height of two to three inches and more than six pounds per year.

One source of food was the practice of growing a kitchen garden in which a few vegetables, rarely much beyond potatoes, were grown. A pig could be kept in the cities, although its supreme sacrifice was usually to raise cash rather than to be eaten. Some food could be gathered. The weaver of Clitheroe, John Ward, reported in his diary for 1860 that he found a pint of mushrooms. That would have supplemented his new potatoes at 1d. per pound in the summer, with beef and mutton nine times more expensive than potatoes. In the case of meat there was always the question of spoilage. Walker (1981) has documented the high proportion of diseased meat sold in Edinburgh in 1857, adding that contemporary estimates put the proportion of all livestock which was diseased on the farms at one-fifth to one-quarter. Potatoes would keep for a long time, and, provided a grown man or working youth consumed about six pounds daily, proved, as in Ireland until the Famine, a certain source of nutrition for young and old. For city dwellers, eating tended to be more eclectic. Mayhew (1851), in one of his marvelous pieces of reporting, tells us a street sweeper kept body and soul together at a per diem of 6 ½d. He took bread and butter with coffee for breakfast and paid twopence. His midday meal was a saveloy (sausage) and potatoes, a fried fish or a pudding for 2 ½d. For tea he had the breakfast menu at the same price. On Sundays things improved with a piece of mutton or liver—"if the old 'oman was in a good humour"—plus a pint of beer without fail. About the same time, a miner's wife in Staffordshire told one of the *Morning Chronicle's* correspondents, a group which included Mayhew, about her husband's evening meal. She said, "My husband's dinner is usually half a pound of bread, half a quartern of potatoes, and a piece of meat—bacon very often" (Special Correspondent 1850). On that slim base the miner recovered after a day of hard labor at the coalface. Burnett (1979) also cites 1863 data gathered by Dr. Edward Smith and made extant by Professors Barker, Oddy, and Yudkin in 1970 but not published. Compared to 1965 standards, the caloric value of diets of families of "indoor workers" in 1863 were satisfactory. Proteins were slightly below a 1965 norm and fats were markedly low. Carbohydrate and iron were above 1965 expectation, but calcium was low.

Of course, nutrition is not the whole story, for nutrition interacts with the prevalence of disease, the culture of the home, and the physical circumstances of life. The combination of these factors progressively depressed the overall health and growth of many children. In the early decades of the nineteenth century, thoughtful men and women viewed the deterioration of human stock from social stress with mounting alarm.

The Degeneracy Problem

The concept of "race" in nineteenth-century Britain was a muddled combination of pre-Mendelian genetics, ethnicity, and localism. It was clear that human traits were inherited and that the generations shared some characteristics while also demonstrating new traits. The degree of determinism had yet to be formulated for the sweetpea flower by the Austrian botanist Gregor Mendel. Some sets of people in various locales were consistently fair or dark, short or tall, but how this came about was unclear. Throughout the nineteenth century the pre-1066 Saxon population was a matter of continuous interest, as it had been to Thomas Jefferson, for example, in the eighteenth century. One reads of the virtues of the ancient Briton, of the Scandinavian influence on the stock in both language and physique. The anthropologist John Beddoe (1870a and b) believed that until the migration occasioned by the Industrial Revolution the racial composition of Lancashire had been stable since Norman times. In 1871, he wrote of the men of Berwickshire that "a number of the pure breed averaged 5 feet 11 1/4 inches in height, and 199 lbs. with clothes. The prevailing physique types may be referred to the Anglican and Scandinavian . . . intermixture of blood, may have an unfavorable influence on the physical development of the next generation."

Within the hazy concept of Scandinavian, Cymric, and Norman as racial groups there were interacting elements of language and custom.

All were predisposed towards acquisition of new characteristics and all were evident in the declining stature of the population of factory towns. Even among the informed credulity prevailed; the Belgian statistician, Adolphe Quetelet, cited a contemporary account of acquired degeneracy provided eight years before by Professor Waitz.

> In 1641, and following years, Irishmen were driven out of Ulster and south of Down into the forest by the English. When they were again found, at a later period, they seemed quite altered, only five feet two inches high, big-bellied, features distorted, open mouthed, and projecting teeth (Quetelet 1871).

On to the background projected by this level of discourse, long before 1871, was the certainty that the health and habitus of workers in the new factory towns was declining. The ominous and indisputable fact of falling stature, widespread ill health, and the haunting thought that these newly acquired traits of the human stock were the provenance of future generations. Walker of the Graveyards (1839) concluded that the survival of "weakly children . . . every year" would lead to progressive deterioration, ". . . unless proper means are taken to fortify the constitution in manhood, the relative vigour will not increase in the same ratio as the population." In the case of unhealthy, marshy districts, Dr. Arnott's testimony in 1840 to the Select Committee on the Health of Towns the same observation was made. R. A. Slaney, the Chairman, asked, "The race will continue degenerating?" and was told, "Yes, to a certain extent" (Arnott 1840).

As early as 1817, data were available on the question in the form of the health and stature of army recruits. Scottish recruits were assessed by "a gentleman of great observation and singular accuracy." The chief finding was that there was considerable variation in young men's height, head and chest circumference by county of residence (Statement 1817). One year later, in 1818, the House of Commons noted that "Manchester, which was used to furnish numerous recruits for the army . . . now wholly unproductive in that respect" (Debate 1818, 1959). Interestingly, statistics on soldiers were a prime source of evidence in several countries throughout the nineteenth century. For the French army, Chadwick reported a height minimum of 1.56 meters (61.5 inches) in 1842, pointing out that fifty years before, in the French wars, the minimum height had been sixty-four inches. Chadwick went on to quote statistics gathered by Villermé on the proportion of men meeting health standards for the army in Amien. Among the poorest classes, 29% were acceptable; and within "classes in better circumstances," the proportion was 52%.

Among would-be recruits to British regiments the proportion of men rejected in the period 1835–37 was 32.7%; by 1864–66, it had risen to 38.7% (Rumsey 1871). To those statistics we add that Irishmen constituted 42.2% of the army in 1830, and the proportion was still 14% in 1891 (O'Tuathaigh 1985).

Of course, we cannot be sure that recruitment standards went unchanged over the span of three decades, but it is clear that more English lads were rejected than Scots or Irish. Rumsey quotes Morgan to the effect that in English manufacturing districts in the 1860s, four out of five applicants to the recruiting Sergeants were rejected. George Sala's humorous account of army recruiting in 1857 shows two excellent pictures of recruiting in public houses for the cavalry and for the infantry. The principal difference is that the height gauge is ignored for the infantry. Military data were convincing to those who inquired; perhaps the attribution of success in the Franco-Prussian war to physical education in Prussia's schools was the most effective use of military statistics to influence national policy towards improving children's health (Brabazon 1887).

We turn now to the question of how sturdy and healthy people were in the nineteenth century. As early as 1818, the elder Robert ("Parsley") Peel had observed that children were simply not growing to full size. In Figure 1.1 are data from several decades on the growth of boys in the nineteenth century. The groups are males from several periods living in Britain and the United States, and a group of boy convicts leaving Britain for transportation to Point Puer in Tasmania (Jordan, 1985a). The curious aspect of the data is that slave boys in the United States were taller than British boys. In that regard, it is informative to recall the remarks made by a West Indian slave-owner to Michal Oastler in the 1830s; he said that he and his fellow slave-owners would never treat their slaves as badly as the mill workers he visited in Yorkshire. Long hours, nutrition poor in quantity and quality, and adverse living conditions all conspired to reduce progressively the health and stature of Victorian children, especially those not born into the middle and upper classes.

Reverting to Figure 1.1, we address the lowest line. The data are the heights of boys transported as convicts to Tasmania. There, at Point Puer, a term was to be served after a period of prior training at Parkhurst. The series consists of ninety-five males at or under age eighteen, the youngest being fourteen. The data are taken from the log of the ship, **Lord Goderich**, which made several trips to Hobart Town, the site of Point Puer. The records of convicts in various ships are quite inconsistent, but those of the ninety-five boys described in Figure 1.1 tell us a little about them. The group which reached Tasmania on June 26, 1841,

Figure 1.1
**Heights of Boys in the Nineteenth
Century: Lancashire Factory Boys
(1833), American Slave Boys (1829-49),**
Lord Goderich **Boys (1841), and British
Boys (1876, 1884, 1896, and 1965)**

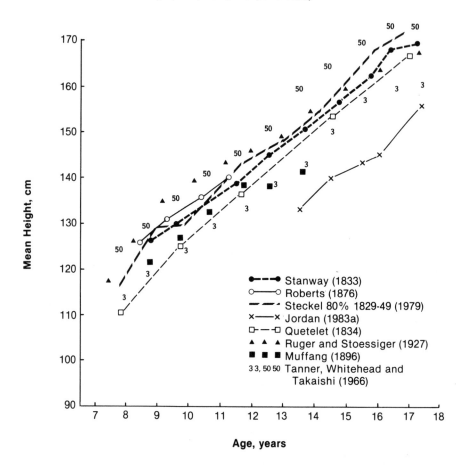

came from a variety of places. The typical ship had convicts segregated
by sex but not by age. In the case of the **John Brewer,** which reached
Hobart on April 6, 1842, the bulk of the boys were Irish, with a majority from Dublin; other boys came from Manchester, Stockport, and
Buckinghamshire.

In considering the manifestly low heights of the **Lord Goderich**
boys, it is helpful to compare them by ages. Each line connects a series of

data, and it does not describe a pattern of growth horizontally. The accurate way to look at the several data lines is to look at the average scores by age in a series of vertical comparisons. By that process we can understand the anomaly of the sixteen-year-olds whose height is markedly below that of other boys of the same age. We can say that those twenty-one boys born in 1825 constitute a most unique group even in reference to other socially disadvantaged boys of the same age. For purposes of clarity, the boys at five ages have heights of 132.69 cm., 139.69 cm., 141.27 cm., 144.11 cm., and the eighteen-year-olds top out at an average of just over five feet, at 153.61 cm. In passing, we note that the ships' logs frequently refer to tattooing, and we are left with the impression that those are not boys who stole the Squire's apples but young men with histories of serious offenses.

For purposes of comparison Figure 1.1 gives contemporary British norms for the fiftieth and third percentiles according to Tanner, Whitehead and Takaishi (1966). The fiftieth and third percentiles represented by numerals are very similar to observed values in St. Louis, Missouri (Jordan 1986) and in Dunedin, New Zealand (Jordan and Silva 1987). It is clear that average heights from 1833 to 1896 were below the mean, or fiftieth percentile, for modern youngsters. Much the same observation may be made about girls, although such data were less frequently gathered in the period under consideration. The same observation applies to data on weight.

When we appraise growth across the decades of the nineteenth century, it is evident that the secular trend of growth in height was negative for a considerable period, so that by 1843 the height of the average man was about sixty-four inches. Around the average—that is, across the full range of social classes—the distribution of heights was wide. The children of the poor and rich of the same age were several inches and several more pounds apart. The Children's Employment Commission of 1843 was told that boys of fifteen to sixteen frequently looked like twelve-year-olds (Second Report 1843), and puberty was quite delayed. To clarify this by contrast with our own period, we note that menarche has been reached at increasingly earlier ages in recent decades. This gap in physical development based on socioeconomic factors was still evident after the end of the Victorian epoch in the data gathered by the *Interdepartmental Committee on Physical Deterioration* (1904), and in the report of the City of Edinburgh Charity Organization Society's *Report on the Physical Condition of Fourteen Hundred School Children in the City* (1906).

In the gross sense, the cause of the deterioration of successive age cohorts of the population was the times. The Industrial Revolution, "the

Moloch of Steam Power," as Rumsey (1871) termed it, was the prime cause in the expanding factory towns. Such expansion without planning led to overcrowding and disease, and planning itself was a soporific on a small scale (even, for example, in the model towns such as Saltaire, near Bradford). In a more diffuse way, which we treat later in this chapter, the adulteration of food in general, and the mindless pursuit of profit through adulteration, also affected the health of both the urban and rural population.

Of course, the more reflective Victorians sought more specific, analytic explanations. To Dr. Morgan (1865), the causes of degeneration of the health of succeeding age cohorts, a secular longitudinal trend, were three: vitiated air (that is, air that was unhealthy by reason of air pollution), temperature, or a lack of ventilation. In the case of vitiated air, one example was given by Ritchie (1844). He found that linen and calico were dried at 150° F, and that temperatures in rooms where fabrics were printed were usually 80°–90° F. Morgan put syphilis in second place and abuse of alcohol was third. To the anthropologist John Beddoe the cause of physical degeneracy was the "increasing concentration of the working class in towns." Beddoe asserted that "it may be taken as proved that the stature of man in the large towns of Britain is lowered considerably below the standard of the nation" (Beddoe 1870). He went on to add selection and elimination by nature, occupational risks, and habits developed in youth. To Dr. Rumsey, writing in 1871, the sorry state arrived at through preceding decades was due to poor food and drink, conditions of employment, and poor housing. Of course, there were other proximate causes, and alcohol and tobacco were frequently condemned. In the case of tobacco, Beddoe was joined by Thomas Reynolds, who solemnly advised the National Association for the Promotion of Social Science, in 1870, that, "in proportion to the increase of revenue from tobacco, there has been an increase in lunacy, and that general paralysis rarely occurs except as a result from smoking." The error, according to Mr. Reynolds, lay in abandoning clay pipes for fancy pipes and cigars!

A second question for which the times had a less complete answer was the matter of the mechanism by which the secular trend to low heights and weights came about. In the early years of the nineteenth century very little was known beyond the obvious about human reproduction and the transmission of genetic elements. Indeed, it is with the opening of the nineteenth century that we encounter recognizable works in biology, of which a prime example is the research of Isadore Geoffroy St. Hiliare. As late as the 1860s, Dr. Langdon-Down, author of the unfortunate paper on the trisomy syndrome of the chromosomes in which a fortuitous and superficial relevance to Asian peoples was bruited, could offer only gross explanations. Degeneracy of the body was continuous for Langdon-Down with specific forms of mental retardation. This lead Langdon-Down to ask, in 1865, "How, moreover, can it be expected but that the mother . . . should propagate an enfeebled race?" (Langdon-Down 1865). By this Langdon-Down meant that once the trait was evident in the form of mental retardation it would follow that the mother would have other limited children. In many treatises, a prominent chin was offered as a stigma of degenerating stock.

The importance of these propositions should not be underestimated. From the 1870s until well into the twentieth century, the specter of an enfeebled race has been raised with regularity in a misguided version of what, in retrospect, we call "the Eugenics question." This topic was to lead many people astray, and led Karl Pearson, the statistician, to intemperate observations. The progeny of the Jukes were studied around the turn of the century, and the pseudonymous Kallikaks are another expression of amalgamating genealogy with genetics and poverty with transmissable limitations. It takes no less than a careful sense of evidence and awareness of experimental design to avoid the errors of reasoning and deduction when distinguishing the role of poverty from that of race, class, or a damaged nervous system.

Mutatis mutandis, the topic appeared in the 1960s with the assertion by rootless environmentalists that there were no limited children but only limiting environments. In retrospect, the naiveté of latter day social determinists seems less tolerable than that of their nineteenth century ancestors who worked with far less information and no less insight. For the Victorians were right, in the sense that poverty bred poverty. Each generation saw an ill-prepared proletariat dissolve its problems in drink, socializing its children into values which reflected the circumstances of life. They were to avoid delaying gratification and to act out impulses, within the limits of an authoritarian social structure. And yet, we are our forefathers' descendents, and most of us find humble people on the Victorian branches of the family tree. Literate, and sometimes less than that, they gained increasing control over their lives and absorbed notions of amelioration for their own lives and those of their children. We are not awash in a sea of mental deficiency, and the height and weight of recent generations has been remarkable. For example, Meredith and Meredith (1944) showed that between 1893 and 1939 the average nine-year-old in Toronto grew taller by three inches.

The process by which children became generally indistinguishable in physical development across social classes began in the nineteenth century. As with the decrease in infant mortality, it depended less on specific medical innovations than on a general rise in the standard of living. In turn, better nourishment and welfare produced healthy would-be mothers and better informed parents. Parents thrived and their children thrived, although class differences and parental occupation set the stage for differential patterns of growth. By 1876, Roberts could report to the Royal Statistical Society that there had been a gain in weight in the fifty years from 1833 to 1873 amounting to one year's growth for children at ages nine, ten, and eleven. On the occasion of the fifty-third meeting of the British Association of Stockport in 1883, Frances Galton, cousin to Dr. J. H. Langdon-Down, could report a positive trend (Galton 1884). However, it was only a trend; and two years later Dr. Cantlie (1885) received wide publicity for his views, which included the observations that he could find no Londoners with London-born grandparents. He went on to describe three young people, aged eighteen to twenty-one, all of whom were short and had disorders of the mouth and eyes. Dr. Cantlie thought "none-ozonised air" of towns to be the mechanism of degeneration, and that cycling, tennis and gymnastics were the best modes of regeneration for the species. Schools became the chief social agency for the promotion of health. The curriculum expanded to include physical exercise—which was linked to aesthetic education on one side and to military preparedness on the other—and, by the end of the century, the problem of drink.

In the case of physical exercise, the emphasis was connected to the apparent relationship between it and the success of the Prussian army in the war of 1870. It was reasoned that the French were defeated, in part, in the schools of Prussia, where the soldiers of the time had been children and had received formal training in physical development. The lesson was apt, because the trend of 1883 reported at Stockport was only that, and there was much to be done to secure the quality of the race if Nation and Empire were to be manned. The Boer War of 1899 revealed that the problem was not yet solved, for a handful of Boer farmers showed themselves quite capable of drubbing an army of young Britons. Seebohm Rowntree's (1901) analysis revealed that about a quarter of all would-be recruits in the Northern manufacturing cities of Leeds, Sheffield, and Manchester were unacceptably short. Of those accepted out of 33,600 volunteers, nearly a third could be considered suitable only with special notation. More alarming was the fact that the Army had to drop its minimum height for recruits in 1901 to sixty inches (Gilbert 1969). Half a century before, recruits had to be six inches taller. In the period just after the turn of the century the Boer war remained an enigma, but there was no doubt about the rise of the Kaiser, who, despite his Anglophilism and connections to Queen Victoria, was itching for a chance to exercise his military resources. The Condition of England question of the 1830s had progressively assumed a more serious, less philanthropic aspect in the next fifty years. In the decade before the lamps were to start going out all over Europe, the health and welfare of children forced itself onto the Nation then groping towards civic efficiency as a political, international question. It was not enough to keep children out of work and in school; they must be properly nourished and exercised in order that the pool of young manpower be sufficient unto the day.

Walvin (1975) has shown that soccer was encouraged as a remediation for the poor physical condition of urban children. Elsewhere (Walvin 1978), he identified soccer as a partial solution of the middle and upper classes for the "Condition of England question." Sport would exercise young proletarians, but on an organized basis it also would instill discipline, loyalty, and piety of a muscular type. In addition, it would organize the young for supervision and channel their spare time into worthy outlets. To some extent this approach worked, although differentiation of health and stature among children of different social backgrounds has persisted well into the twentieth century. One thing is clear; namely, the trend to deterioration was reversed. The cause was a complex of factors: better community services; a rising standard of living; and a conviction that child health was a component of the public interest to be advanced, consolidated, and protected. The task was daunting since waves of infectious disease, of which cholera is the prime example, confounded the best efforts to promote individual health through the collective measures we call public health.

Epidemics and Child Health

One of the predictable hazards of the nineteenth century was the outbreak of communicable diseases threatening the lives of children and rendering them very ill, at the least. In our day of worry about nuclear annihilation we believe that the end of human life is without precedent. This is not so, and mankind has experienced the extinction of life in entire communities. We do not wish to underestimate the nuclear holocaust with threat to most things in the biological domain. However, in terms of the human condition, epidemics have destroyed communities, and our ancestors lived with an existential dread of diseases we do not know, although AIDS may revive that fear. In our day epidemics are confined to mild childhood disorders; however, polio exists in Central America and the Caribbean and is a potential source of epidemic for North America due to the brief flying time to Florida and cities on the

Gulf of Mexico, and also to Europe. In the nineteenth century, disease was slower to move but it was widespread, and children were at serious risk for all diseases. The possible exception was smallpox, for which Jenner's inoculations were a protection if taken before an epidemic.

As limited protection was man-made, so was the communicability of disease. I have spoken earlier of water-borne disease from infected wells. To that I add the density of living and the anomaly of the window-tax. From 1696 until 1803 there was motivation to close-up windows and doors since a house owed an annual tax of two shillings, a house with ten or more windows was taxed four shillings, and twenty windows cost eight shillings (Creighton 1894). Skylights, cellars and passageways were also taxable, and there was every inducement to shut up openings, and so restrict the free passage of air as well as light. After 1803, windows were no longer a problem for new dwellings, but this was no invitation to open windows long since closed up. In typical nineteenth-century style, an abuse was stopped, but there were few positive steps far-sighted enough to undo harm already done.

To some extent, populations of selected towns were more vulnerable than other groups. Creighton (1894) concluded that smallpox was more fatal to children in Edinburgh than the children in other towns in the early years of the nineteenth century. Limerick was a dangerous place for children in the 1830s (Griffin 1841). In the same period, Leeds was spared the impact of typhus and scarlet fever. Whenever mortality was high among children, smallpox was the cause, for the disease appeared with regularity. In 1883, William Guy plotted the years and incidence per one thousand cases of death due to smallpox in London. In the years 1840 to 1880, the peaks of incidence were about four to five years apart until about 1870, when they became less frequent. However, 1871 was a very bad year for smallpox deaths. It was followed by a peak of above average size in 1877, with an incidence of thirty smallpox deaths per thousand deaths from all causes. This last incidence resembles that of 1844. Generally speaking, the peaks of incidence showed a secular trend to lowered death rates from 1844, with the exception of 1871.

For other communicable diseases the pattern was one of slow change, and mortality rates declined. Mitchison (1970) reports declines in mortality rates in the last half of the nineteenth century as follows: tuberculosis −47.2%; typhus and typhoid −22.9% (these two diseases having been discriminated in 1837 by William Gerhard, according to Le Riche and Milner [1971]); and scarlet fever −20.3%, a change Mitchison attributes to a mutation in the infectious organism. Unfortunately, we cannot report that this improvement was shared by all children, having reviewed death rates for ages 0–4, 5–9, and 10–14 between 1838 and 1900. In Mitchell and Deane's (1962) compilation of statistics, the rate for the youngest group of children was 70.7 per K (1000 subjects) in 1838 and 63.4 per K fifty-one years later in 1889. The picture is better, eventually, for the 5–9-year-olds, ranging from 9.1 per K in 1838 and generally remaining below 7.0 after 1872. In the case of the 10–14-year-olds, the 1838 rate of 5.3 deaths per K dropped below 4 cases in 1873 and was below 3 cases, finally, by 1883. On the other hand, the life expectancy of children rose, slowly but steadily, in the nineteenth century. In his inaugural address as President of the Royal Statistical Society, Dr. R. Giffen (1883) pointed to an increase in life expectancy in the preceding decades of 2 years for males, to 41.9 years, and of 3.5 years for females, to 45.3 years.

The slow gain in life expectancy and the slow drop in a fatal outcome of disease in young people was paralleled by slow progress in understanding disease as more than treatable or untreatable symptoms. Modes of infection were described (e.g., water-borne as opposed to sputum droplets) and infectious organisms, including Cholera's vibrio and pneumonia's streptococci, were identified. Vectors of disease expanded to include insects and animals. In drawing these observations to a conclusion, we point out that vectors of disease and characteristics of young people led to illness. Creighton (1894) reported an infection in 1824 which prostrated all forty girls at a school near Charlotte Bronte's home at Haworth, some of whom died at home. Creighton reported the observations of Dr. Batty, who believed that the unsuitability of the house as a school and the meager diet of the pupils were conducive to the infection attacking every girl.

Asiatic cholera was the great plague of the nineteenth century. In India it had been expected at intervals of years, but it became an annual epidemic by 1817, according to Ramasubban (1982). Historically, the disease had migrated after the great fair at Hardwar, in northern India, which was held at intervals of twelve years. In 1817 the disease spread more extensively than before and, according to Creighton, reached the mouth of the Volga by 1823. It appeared in Eastern Europe in 1829, and arrived in Sunderland by the summer of 1831.

The nature of the disease was as significant as its communicability and dispersion. Those who contracted the disease became very ill quickly, and they died quickly. The whole course of the disease shocked relatives by the intensity, speed, and fatality of the episode.

A Keelman named Wilson, who lived with his wife in a decent room in the High Street, and had attended the Methodist chapel on Sunday was seized with Cholera at 4 a.m. on Monday, and died the same afternoon at three (Creighton 1894).

In 1832, cholera appeared in Ireland, most frequently among the crowded poor in the largest cities. Twenty people died in one house in Dublin over the course of a week. With these accounts, the port of London was closed to traffic from selected towns, and this mechanism proved effective for a time. Eventually, cholera was identified in the metropolis, at Rotherhithe on the river, in a man who had had an apparently minor contact with a ship from Sunderland. By June 1832, the disease was clearly in London, with a fatality rate approaching 50% among about ten thousand cases in three warm months. The most severe outbreak was near Wolverhampton, at Bilston, brought, apparently, not from Sunderland but by itinerant German broom-sellers. Creighton says that the outbreak left over 450 children orphaned. Thus, cholera was an indirect as well as a direct threat to the welfare of children. The disease continued to appear throughout the nineteenth century, having reached Canada and the United States in 1833. Today, we are not immune to cholera in those parts of the world visited by catastrophes such as flooding and earthquakes. The year 1961 saw a pandemic which started in the Celebes.

In 1848, cholera occasioned one of the great investigations of disease. Dr. John Snow mapped the exact places in London's West End where victims of cholera became ill. By this process, he traced the disease by time and place of onset to Golden Square. There, setting aside the preliminary but impressive fact that brewery workers did not contract cholera, he pressed on to distinguish the sick by their use of a particular water pump. In a classic of social action, consumption of water contaminated by the *vibrio* (whose existence had yet to be established by Koch in 1883) was ended by removing the handle from the pump.

One of the milestones in child health in the nineteenth century was William Little's monograph "On the Influence of Abnormal Parturition . . . ," which dealt with the condition we now call cerebral palsy (1862). Today, we are inclined to add developmental failure in utero to the list of causes enumerated by Little.

About the same time, John H. Langdon-Down was attempting to catalog syndromes of mental retardation as recapitulation of racial types, the Mongolian being a regression from the "advanced" Caucasian. We have presented this paper elsewhere (Jordan 1966), and generally regret that Down's views have become the basis for naming the pattern of chromosomal error. In 1865 Down asserted that retarded persons "lose a large amount of intellectual energy in the winter, go through, in fact, a process of hibernation, this mental process being always directly as the extreme temperature." Lest we seem too dismissive we add that Langdon-Down disassociated himself from the notion that the condition was a form of Cretinism. More constructively, we find the work of Edouard Seguin in France, and later in the United States, bringing positive benefits to the mentally retarded. Sequin emphasized "moral treatment," as opposed to physical coercion, to influence retarded children.

Other developments in the health of children occurred through clinical study of pediatric diseases. Jacob Heine differentiated paralysis due to poliomyelitis from spastic paralysis, Parrot described the syndrome of syphilis in infants. Semelweiss explained the steps to prevent puerperal fever after delivery, and appendicitis was differentiated from general, untraceable, inflammation of the abdomen. However, it should not be thought that progress in therapy was without its setbacks. Immunization was a step which occurred in the absence of knowledge of virology. The concept of creating defense through activating the body's immune system was not known to Victorian physicians. It was thought that immunization (or 'engrafting') would always work, and those who opposed it, wholly or in part, were adjudged to be cranks. Mrs. Mary Hume-Rothery (1871) acquired such a reputation. Her objection to injecting syphilitic material into the healthy seemed a reactionary position at the time and earned her the enmity of the medical profession. Undoubtedly cranky were the Peculiar People, a sect living in Plumstead, who refused medical assistance, according to Conley (1984) on the grounds that faith would be sufficient. Unfortunately, two children of the sect died in 1872 during an outbreak of smallpox.

Adulteration of Food and Medicine

Just before the Industrial Revolution, Dr. Samuel Johnson had observed, with his usual acuity, directed in this instance to nutrition, "Sir, a man who does not mind his food, will scarce mind anything." John Bull has always taken his food seriously, and the value of Dr. Johnson's advice was as high in the nineteenth century as it had been in the days of "the Great Cham." For one could not afford to take food for granted, and the twin problems of quantity and quality both merited attention.

It is helpful to place the problem in perspective. The tradition of food in times of plenty and in times of want was the only one our ancestors knew. As with the changing of the seasons, people expected that natural disasters, wars, and economic trends would increase and decrease the availability of food. On the one hand, nature was fickle; and on the other hand, food priced out of reach by economic processes was no less unavailable. The average family and its children could count on little to help them except local private charity and the vagaries of public assistance and the Poor Laws. The lack of attention to social questions by the central government was evident in many ways, one of which was the absence of attention to food supplies.

The tradition of the market was to charge what the traffic would bear in food prices. An obvious way to maximize profit was to sell more than nature provided. Flour was flour, and if it could be extended by incorporating ground peas, the profit would rise. If tea leaves from India and the East were expensive, why not gather the leaves of the beech tree and dry them, for they would all taste about the same in the tea pot. Speaking of veal pie to the apple of his eye, the elder Sam Weller, in the *Pickwick Papers,* observes, "Wery good thing is weal pie, when you knows the lady as made it, and is quite sure it ain't kittens!"

Frederick Accum, a German who lived in London for nearly a quarter century, was the first person in the nineteenth century to approach adulteration of food systematically. In his *Treatise on Adulteration of Food and Culinary Poisons . . .* (1820), citing the Old Testament verse that "there is death in the Pot," Accum listed in detail the adulterations of specific foods. While becoming the public's protector, he aroused the antagonism of merchants and manufacturers and returned to Germany. In 1857, Odling examined two-pound loaves from thirty-five bakers in Lambeth, the district for which he was Medical Officer. Odling reported to readers of the *Lancet* that there were ashes and alum in eighteen of the loaves, and that seven contained traces of copper which he thought an accidental contaminant. To bakers, the use of alum to blanche brown grains for the firmly established white bread made sense. Today, people use many additives in food, but the differences are two: first, they state on the package what is put in the product; second, they do not add materials which are other than guaranteed safe to the customer. In the early nineteenth century such scruples did not always prevail. According to Burnett (1979), beer was artificially aged by using sulphuric acid, and oyster shells would rejuvenate beer whose shelf-life, as people phrase it today, had expired. For another beverage, coffee, chicory became a useful adulterant based on the availability of this common weed. In this instance, we have the anomaly of the adulteration persisting; to this day, visitors choose either of two styles when dining in New Orleans, whose residents like chicory in their coffee.

In reference to children, the matter of safe and pure milk was always a problem. Today, cows in a dairy herd must be certified as free from tuberculosis and other diseases. In the nineteenth century, no such guarantee existed. When milk was available it was too expensive for children of the poor, and Rumsey (1871) reported that country children saw buttermilk fed to the pigs. When a family could afford milk, there was little guarantee that it was milk. The Pall Mall Gazette of April 17, 1871, described an embezzlement based on adding an element called "Simpson" to milk, which turned out to be water. This allowed the milkman to effect the liquid equivalent of the loaves and fishes by drawing more milk from the container than the cow had provided. Ignorance contributed greatly to undernourishment; Horn (1974) reports that children in Wiltshire were fed "frogwater" made by pouring hot water over blackened bread crusts. In Wiltshire and North Warwickshire, wheat flour, and warm milk were combined under the graphic names "bang belly" and "Lumpy Tom." The obvious consequence was stress; children's nutrition was weakened, and Burnett (1979) thought this sufficiently widespread to have contributed to the degeneracy problem of the nineteenth century.

One of the differences between the world of our ancestors and today is that milk can be fed to children safely. It is an excellent nutrient, and parents feed it to children secure in the knowledge that it is pure. In nineteenth-century Britain, the only reasonable presumption of the city dweller was that milk was dangerous. Cows were kept in sheds in Golden Square that were filthy, and which smelled to a degree considered unusual even by the low standards of the time. Cows were repositories for diseases, such as tuberculosis, which was transmitted through their milk. In the days before Pasteur, it can be safely speculated that cows' milk teemed with bacteria. The animals themselves were not immune to epidemics, and Drummond and Wilbraham (1939) reported that a severe plague of rinderpest struck London cows in 1863. As a consequence, London came to draw its milk from the country, and Drummond and Wilbraham state that by 1866 two million gallons of milk went to London each year by the new railways. Not the least problem for growing children was that the milk they received was probably half water. Neale (1964) thought that the adulterating water probably came from the wells themselves possibly being contaminated by sewage. The crime of watering milk was compounded by the risk at which the water additive placed children.

In the late 1970s, the sale of prepared milk-equivalents became a scandal in Third World countries. It became a status symbol to feed babies canned products rather than to breast-feed them. The status products were touted by unscrupulous salesmen in laying-in wards, and uneducated mothers adopted the manufactured products. The hazard was that water was the additive, and when water is contaminated, a common state of affairs, the infants received bacteria from the water in which the nutritive material was suspended. Had the infants been fed at the breast, no problem would have arisen. In this instance, the pattern of prepared food for use in advanced countries presupposes the infrastructure of safe water, and it also presumes that mothers are sufficiently educated to evaluate food for infants in terms of health rather than status. This necessary level of education in women is frequently absent in emerging nations, with consequences which go beyond nutrition of infants into other aspects of national life (Jordan 1983).

So far we have spoken of additions which, while non-nutritive, are not inevitably harmful. Even today, there are accidents in which unintended harm is done by oversight or error. Some events occurred in the nineteenth century also. Elliott (1982) records an accident in Bradford in 1859. A maker of peppermint lozenges killed eighteen people and caused two hundred people to become ill by accidently introducing arsenic into his peppermints.

Another type of adulteration was that in which benign medications were extended by means of inert materials. The picture in the early nineteenth century is not clear to us, despite Accum's early writings. In the work of Dr. Arthur H. Hassall, who began microscopy studies of drinking water around mid-century, we see the beginnings of systematic scientific exploration. Stieb (1966) says that Hassall was struck by the discrepancy between shopkeeper's descriptions of their wares and the product actually for sale. His 1850 paper on adulteration of coffee was his first major contribution. It came none too soon, since adulteration of food was widespread. When the founder of the *Lancet*, Thomas Wakely, became interested, progress began to be organized and the problem of adulterated medicine came under scrutiny. Hassall's work was helpful, for Stieb reports that only one of forty samples of powdered opium examined by Hassall, for example, were genuine. With the *Lancet* leading the way, a series of Parliamentary inquiries began in 1856 with a Select Committee. Inquiries leading to legislation also followed in 1874 and in the following decades. However, it was not until the twentieth century, in the 1914–18 war, that final control over opiates was attained. In Stieb's view, the failure to prosecute and convict people who adulterated drugs was an important reason. Of course, the connection still exists between crime and pharmaceuticals, although in different ways. Today, people can be reasonably sure that medication for adults and children will be more than alcohol or opiates. Much of the problem has migrated from the pharmaceutical houses as abusers to consumers.

Today, in developed countries, protection from the manufacturer is not a real problem when compared to reckless consumption of ethical drugs by unthinking consumers. Licensing of manufacturers after clinical tests remains an effective safeguard. For food, we have the practice of manufacturers testing their products and recalling them when study reveals them to be contaminated. Few examples of responsibility are evident in the nineteenth century to protect children and adults from deliberate adulteration or accidental contamination of food. Collective remedy presupposed an aroused and indignant public, plus informed and responsive government.

Food and the Public

The family is the context within which children, then and now, have usually been fed. However, there is another aspect of the matter, because nutrition of children is part of a broader picture of food as a public issue. On the one hand, there is the matter of tariffs on the import of food and protectionism as a policy directly affecting the welfare of children and adults. On the other hand, there is the social consequence of problems surrounding food and popular responses in specific places. Both formulations are valid, but the second is more relevant to our presentation here.

There have always been periods of want when the food supply is reduced and children go hungry; the most graphic account in recent decades is that of the siege of Leningrad, which lasted for nine hundred days. In that period, the welfare of infants suffered because pregnant women were malnourished and delivered small babies, many of whom died (Antonov 1947; Salisbury 1969).

In some places the problem of food, which usually turned out to be the problem of prices, was not manageable. Stevenson (1979) says that there were attacks on food shops in Manchester in 1826, in the potteries in 1842, and in Liverpool in 1855. However, in other places it was not retailers but millers who were attacked by rioters. In such instances the core problem was probably more than price and included distribution. Flour available in a quantity likely to depress retail prices to an accessible level might move to markets whose profits were higher. Women and boys played active roles in food disturbances, and sometimes men dressed as women.

Just prior to our period the French Wars had created distress, known as "the Great Immiseration," and food was not imported from the

Continent. After Waterloo there was economic depression and families went hungry. *The Morning Chronicle* for January 4, 1817, carried an appeal from a committee led by Mr. Samuel Woods for funds to clothe, feed, and house six thousand families in Spitalfields. The committee was spending £1,530 per week from its offices at 53 Brick Lane in the form of seven thousand quarts of soup each day. Uncooked food was distributed in the form of cod, herring, and rice. The public was responsive, and we can trace the scope of public reaction and support over several weeks in *The Morning Chronicle*. Mr. A. Rees, 28 the Strand, subscribed £6.18. 6d.; a set of philanthropists who gathered for therapeutic purposes at the White House, banded together as the "Happy Britons" and subscribed £3.13s. The "ladies at Wandsworth" provided one hundred sets of clothing for women, including stockings, "Lindsey-Woolsey Upper Petticoats," and shawls. "A little Boy" gave 7s. In this instance, we are probably seeing distress among silk-weavers since Spitalfields was a center for the trade. Also, the resources of the metropolis were available through the newspaper, and those untouched by the depression of business were informed and were willing to help.

In the case of the famine in Ireland created by the potato blight, evident in England a few months before it appeared in Ireland, the response to the need for food came from the well-to-do as well as the general run of the population. The élite who founded the Reform Club had an eye for quality beyond Barry's design based on the Villa Farnese, and they summoned Alexis Soyer to cook for them. The kitchen employed gas for cooking nearly half a century before gas ovens appeared in houses. When the problem of starvation became evident, Soyer's genius for organization asserted itself, and he prepared soup for the poor at a cost of three-farthings per quart (Correspondence 1847). With the full support of the Reform Club, he plunged into the welfare of the starving Irish and went to Dublin. There, he organized food kitchens and devised nutritious meals for twenty-six thousand people per day from available materials (Crook 1973). Time has not been kind to the assessment of nutrition in Soyer's dishes, but he acted on behalf of the reforming élite for the welfare of the destitute. We note, in passing, that Soyer undertook public education on preparation of food for the middle classes. Harrison (1971) thought that most of Soyer's writing on daily menus was for "Mrs. B. of St. John's Wood." Soyer published *The Gastronomic Regenerator* and the *Modern Housewife* for the middle classes, and for the poor he wrote *Shilling Cookery*. In a period of public distress, he organized about eight thousand meals per day in Farringdon Road, London, for the poor.

Fairness requires that we record Soyer's work as more than food for the poor. During his reign at the Reform Club, he produced *Cotelettes de Mouton à la Reform,* and his *Sauce à la Reform* was acclaimed. His ability to combine quality with quantity was evident in his banquet menus. Woodbridge (1978) recorded the bill of fare on the occasion of the dinner in 1846 of Ibrahim Pasha from Egypt. The courses began with four soups, and there were eleven entrees to choose from. This material illustrates the range of nutrition in the nineteenth century, ranging from exquisite gastronomy to starvation, a span indicative of the quality of bodily sustenance available to support the stress of work faced by Victorian children and adults.

Work and Health

It is clear to most people that children should not work in factories or otherwise be used as adults in the processes of manufacture. The proposition has the ring of self-evidence, but it merits close inspection. Farmers' sons frequently drive tractors long before they are licensed to drive. The farmer believes he is providing moral as well as vocational training when he requires his youngster to conform to the rhythms of the working farm. Even today's farms need some help, and a boy of ten can contribute his labor, a step in the interest of the family he belongs to.

The history of child labor in the nineteenth century has much the same quality. People agreed, in general, that children should not work, but then they began to recite the exceptions. It was parents who frequently introduced their children to the workplace, not some grim-faced capitalist. Ashton's (1925) analysis of the records of William Stubs's pin manufactory in Warrington in the years 1814 to 1821 shows that parents frequently borrowed against the future earnings of their children. Children frequently welcomed the emancipation of the workplace and the opportunity to spend money they were occasionally allowed to keep. The resulting picture is one in which there were a lot of good general reasons why children should not work and a lot more specific reasons why this child should work at that job. One of the notable examples of premature labor was the introduction of Charles Dickens to Warren's Blacking Factory at Hungerford Stairs, Charing Cross, on his twelfth birthday. The impact of the rats, dirt, and noise on the sensitive and imaginative boy is evident throughout his writings.

The early history of work in the nineteenth century is one of unremitting hazard to the health of children. It begins with the example of chimney sweeps and continues long after laws to end the practice had been passed. In the case of chimney sweeps, the practice of using boys (and occasionally girls) small enough to climb chimneys was very old. It was intolerable because of the accumulated soot in the narrow flues and because places to put hand and foot were unknown to the tiny children forced to climb into dark and dangerous places. Children fell and were injured. One such example, which illustrates how unexaggerated many of Dickens's anecdotes were, is that told to a Parliamentary inquiry by George Reveley (1817).

It appears that the chimney of the Stricklands in East Yorkshire needed cleaning in 1804. The climber, a boy about age four, fell and by his injuries came to the attention of the family. The boy had been sold by an old woman near Bridlington for eight guineas to the sweep. From his accent he was clearly not a Tyke but came from the south of England. George Reveley reported that

> on seeing a silver fork he was quite delighted and said, "Papa had such forks as these." The housekeeper showed him a silver watch . . . he then pressed the handle and said, "Papa's watch rings, why does not yours?" The account he gave of himself is that he was gathering flowers in his mamma's garden. . . . The woman who sold him put him on a horse. He had no recollection of his name or where he lived. His dialect is good and that of the south of England (Reveley 1817).

What makes this story fascinating is that forty years later one of the Yorkshire supporters of Lord Shaftesbury and his efforts at social reform of all kinds was one of the Stricklands of Boynton. There could not be too many Stricklands in their forties in the 1840s; perhaps the little sweep lived out his Great Expectations and repaid his deliverance as a supporter of Shaftesbury and reform in later years.

Unfortunately, very few climbing boys had such prompt and effective deliverance. Abrasions, falls, and burns were their lot, and occasionally death. Strange (1982) has given a full account of the death and memorialization of young Valentine Gray at Newport, Isle of Wight, in 1822. Laws were passed, but the practice of using little boys (depicted by Charles Kingsley in *The Water Babies*) to clean dirty flues continued long after it was officially considered ended. For those who remained associated with the trade, even the hazards were not over long after they became too big to climb. Pott's disease is the form of cancer associated with soot, and it constituted the occupational hazard for sweeps who survived the perils of childhood climbing. The entire episode of controlling this particular form of child labor and risk to young children is a sorry example of reform. Legislation passed in 1788 banned the use of little children, but the practice persisted for a hundred years. The Hammonds (1923), in their biography of Lord Shaftesbury, report harrowing details of climbing boys; six was considered a "nice, trainable age," they went unwashed for years, and in the sale of boys those from Nottingham were especially prized. What is surprising is how close the era of boy chimney sweeps is to our own. Turner (1966) reported that the last known climbing boy, Joseph Lawrence, died in 1949 at the age of 104.

In the case of factory work, the hazards to children were many. The most obvious was the long hours which children worked. The second was that the Industrial Revolution had moved the child worker from the family circle into the world of adult factory life. In that regard, the child worker conformed to the regimen prescribed for adults, including, at its extreme, night work. The conventions of the period saw little wrong with twelve-hour days for workers of all ages; such days began before the winter sun rose and ended after early sunset. George Oldfield recalled his working days near Huddersfield.

> We had to be up at 5 in the morning to get to factory ready to begin work at 6, then work while 8, when we stopped ½ an hour for breakfast, then work to 12 noon; for dinner we had 1 hour, then work while 4. We then had ½ an hour for tee, and tee if anything was left, then commenced; work on again to 8:30. If any time during the day had been lost we had to work while 9 o'clock (Unwin 1906).

In the case of spinning works, the long hours were spent monitoring machines, work became more specialized—in the sense of narrow—and could be performed by children at wages below those of adults. The earliest days of the nineteenth century saw efforts to legislate the working day and there was an effort in 1803 to manage the "health and morals of apprentices." Sixteen years later Josiah Wedgwood recalled that the law "never had the slightest effect of any kind upon our manufactory" (Report 1816). In many respects this form of legislation, piecemeal in its specification of workplaces and categories of people, was to persist through several decades of the century. The result was that children worked very long hours in all manner of places. One of the last worksites to yield to control was the brickyard. Charles Shaw recalled that in 1840, at the age of seven, he worked as a mould-runner from five to six in the morning until seven or eight at night (Burnett 1982). In the 1860s, young Will Thorne of Birmingham also worked in the brickyards. When he was nine years old he was making four to five hundred bricks a day with his uncle for seven shillings a week. In his memoirs (Thorne 1925) he recalled that each brick weighed about nine pounds so that in the course of a workday which began at six in the morning young Will carried several tons of clay. Eventually, his mother decided that he was becoming hump-backed and insisted that he give up the job. After several weeks' relief from the loads and the eight-mile walk, round trip, which began at 4:30 A.M. each day, the nine-year-old's mother thought him fit to look for other work. In 1870, looking back on his childhood from the perspective of a self-made man, George Smith recalled his early working years. As a child of nine he had worked thirteen hours a day. He had carried forty pounds of clay at a time on his head, a practice still possible in 1871 in brickyards employing less than fifty people. The harmful effects of such labor for a day of any length is enormous, and the effects of thirteen hours would be ruinous.

To consider night work is to think of a practice which adults, today, approach with reluctance and with expectations of extra compensation. In the early nineteenth century, the night shifts and the day shifts were fine-tuned so that Fielden could report in 1836, "It is a common tradition in Lancashire that the beds never got cold," referring to children. Ward (1962) further reports that seventeen girls who were locked in for night work at Atkinson's Mill, Colne Bridge, all perished in a fire.

The employment of children and women in mines excavating all kinds of minerals, tin, ironstone, and especially coal, was a brutal, stressful business. In the case of women, it led to sexual exploitation and debauchery, and they also ran all the risk of physical danger which men faced. Out of economic necessity women worked until shortly before delivering children and returned to work two or three weeks later.

In the case of children, the picture is worse because they were deformed physically by the duties they performed, and they were deprived of education, for the most part. Reporting to the Commissioners on employment of children in 1842, Mr. S. S. Scriven was so struck by "a very extraordinary development of some of the muscles of the body" that he measured 220 boys and youths and found that ninety-six boy miners met his criterion for being "muscular" and "very muscular." The investigator for Lancashire, Mr. J. L. Kennedy, probably came nearer to the truth in speaking of muscles "developed to a degree amounting to a deformity." This observation on boys was a forecast of what was to come. J. C. Symons, also reporting to the Commissioners in 1842, said of Yorkshire Miners that after "they are turned forty-five or fifty they walk home from their work almost like cripples, stiffly stalking along, often leaning on sticks, bearing the visible evidences in their frame and gait of overstrained muscles and overtaxed strength." Dr. Uriah Bradbury wrote to the Commissioners that "their knees never stand straight like other people's." However, the sum of the physical distortions was more than the list of symptoms. The investigator of mines in Staffordshire, Dr. Mitchell, discussed the health questions with miners. They believed that a man was finished as a miner by age forty-two. At that age he no longer had the strength to work productively. In 1838, an investigator in Bradford assembled eighty crippled workers. "They stood or squatted before me in the shapes of the letters of the alphabet. This was the effect of prolonged toil on the tender frames of children at early ages" (Hammond and Hammond 1923).

Apart from the accumulated effects of mine work over a lifetime, there were the hazards encountered every day. Mr. J. Fletcher (1842) examined the records of a coal mine at Oldham, Lancashire, owned by Messrs. Chamber and Werneth. The record of accidents to children under age twelve in one year was as follows:

> one of his fingers cut off; crushed by a waggon in the brow; fingers crushed between two waggons; fingers broken by waggon against the roof; leg fractured by a stone falling from the roof; thigh fractured and other bruises; leg crushed by roof falling.

To these seven instances we add another sixteen if we move the age up from twelve to seventeen.

Speaking to the House of Commons in 1842, on the occasion of introducing reform legislation, Anthony Ashley Cooper, Lord Shaftesbury, described the method by which little girls and boys in mines drew heavy carts by use of the girdle and chain. "The child, it appears, has a girdle bound around its waist, to which is attached a chain, which passed under the legs, and is attached to the cart. The child is obliged to pass on all fours, and the chain passes under what, therefore, in that posture, might be called the hind legs; . . . it appears that the labour is exceedingly severe." Robert North says, "I went into the pit at 7 years of age. When I drew by the girdle and chain, the skin was broken and the blood ran down" (Shaftesbury 1842).

One of the jobs in mines was to open and close vertical trap doors allowing wagons to pass, and generally controlling the flow of air in the passageways. The doors were placed at intervals throughout the extensive system of excavations running miles from the main shaft to the coalface. These passageways were no taller than they had to be and were not illuminated by more than the occasional candle or oil lamp. In the dark, the squeak of rats and the drip of water were constant companions. In a South Wales mine, opening a trap when bidden was seven-year-old Mary Davis. The 1842 report states in terse language what the Commissioners' representative found. "A very pretty little girl, who was fast asleep under a piece of rock near the air door below ground. Her lamp had gone out for want of oil; and upon waking her, she said the rats or someone had run away with her bread and cheese, and so she went to sleep." The reaction of the mine owners, who probably had not set foot below ground, was denial. Lord Londonderry responded to such anecdotes by stating that

> the trapper is generally cheerful and contented, and to be found, like other children of his age, occupied with some childish amusement—as cutting sticks, making models of wind-mills, waggons, etc., and frequently in drawing figures with chalk on his door, modelling figures of men and animals in clay, etc. (Hammond and Hammond 1923).

Children died in mines, and we can calculate the hazard from two sources. In coal mines, the proportion of boys to men was three to ten (Commission 1842). A report (Accidents 1862) put the number of deaths at 1,152 in 1857, a date by which some reforms were in place, so that the figure given would be no less in previous years. It appears, if we use the 1842 proportions, that approximately one hundred children died annually in mine accidents in the early decades of the nineteenth century.

Children like George Oldfield and little Mary Davis also ran the risk of being beaten by supervisors. George Smith, who started work in 1838 at the age of seven, recalled, "I myself have seen, over and over again, the black eye, the unhealed sore, the swollen head, the bruised body, in little, very little children . . ." (McCleod 1966). Even younger was Thomas Townsend of Batley, erroneously sent to work in the mine at age five (Finnegan and Sigsworth 1978). Additional information in graphic detail is available on child mine workers in Pollard's (1984) eloquently titled book, *The Hardest Work Under Heaven*.

The workplace itself was a hazard to the health of children and young people. Apprentice knife grinders shared with the journeymen in Sheffield the grave probability of lung congestion. Ritchie (1844) recorded that the age of death for knife grinders was at least eight years below that of agricultural laborers. Millinery workers and others in the clothing trades worked very long hours in cramped quarters. A Coroner's jury ascribed the death of a young woman in 1863 to "working long hours in a crowded work room" (Pitter 1864).

Machinery was a source of danger to young and old, and children working with spinning machines and flying looms were in danger even when not fatigued by the length of the working day. There were mill owners who protected their young workers. Reporting to Commissioners, the tireless Leonard Horner (Horner 1956) cited the safety provisions of Horrocks and Miller's factory at Preston, and that of Wood and Walker in Bradford. Horner thought it reasonable to prohibit "the cleaning of dangerous machinery while in rapid motion, and to fence off dangerous machinery."

So far, we have spoken of factories, for the most part, but it is only fair to add that rural worksites were no less stressful to children. The straw-plaiting industry was a family affair with children set to little tasks early. Farm laborers' children were expected to chase off crows at an early age. The anonymous author of the 1861 "Autobiography of a Navvy," recalled that he began tending sheep as a child of seven.

Farms, mines, factories, and brickyards were obvious places of employment for the young. An invisible class of workers, whose problems have persisted well into the twentieth century, were the girls engaged in manufacturing clothes. Some were engaged in production of "slops," or ready-to-wear clothes, while others fabricated dresses for special orders. The latter were subjected to very long hours when dresses had to be produced on short notice for special occasions, a condition which arises even today. The first public call for reform is probably the letter signed "C," addressed to The Times in 1817. "C" reported that young seamstresses worked eighteen-hour days in the busy season. A reformer of labor and drink, whose Dickensian name gave a false impression of his zeal to help "the Slaves of the Needle," as he called them, was Ralph Barnes Grindrod (1844). He estimated that there were one hundred thousand females ". . . most of whom are of tender age . . ." working to produce clothing. Grindrod noted that their vision was usually harmed by ages twenty-five to thirty. More seriously, he observed and sketched lateral distortions of the spine in the Slaves of the Needle caused by crouching over the materials they sewed. Grindrod ended his survey of the "Distressed Condition Moral and Physical . . ." of the girls by denouncing the ladies of fashion whose whims, as he saw it, led to enslavement. He does not seem to have seen the other aspect, namely, that without work orders there would be no work, creating problems of a different kind. Four decades later, in 1883, the Reverend Andrew Mearns described graphically the wages and hours of young seamstresses in the years before Mr. Singer's sewing machine.

> Women, for the work of trousers finishing (i.e. sewing in linings, making button holes and stitching on the buttons) receive 2½d. a pair, and have to find their own thread. We asked a woman who is making tweed trousers, how much she can earn in a day and are told one shilling. But what does a day mean to this poor soul? *Seventeen hours!* From five in the morning until ten at night—no pause for meals. She eats her crust

and drinks a little tea as she works, making in very truth, with her needle and thread, not her living only, but her shroud. In St. George's-in-
the-East large numbers of women and children, some of the latter only
seven years old, are employed in sack-making, for which they get a far-
thing each. In one house was found a widow and her half-idiot daughter
making palliases at 1 $^3/_4$d. each.

Five years later, in 1888, Beatrice Potter caught the strain of life in the
needle trades in her "Pages from a Work-Girl's Diary." Told in the first
person, the pages tell how she walks the streets of the Hackney looking
for piece work. One of her fellow-workers, a girl of nineteen, "looks at
least thirty" to Beatrice, who traces the girl's appearance to the exhaus-
tion of long hours and related pressures. In appraising the abuse of
needlewomen, it is informative to note that much of the work of the
garment industry was performed in small shops—units which invariably
defy the efforts and control of reformers and bureaucrats. Turnover of
young workers was considerable. The welfare of the Slaves of the Needle
has continued to be a problem down to the present day. Of course, the
hazards are reduced, but the tradition of the sweatshop in the needle
trade is an old one which has yet to be solved fully. We credit Victorian
reformers for beginning the end of the more flagrant abuses of young
people earning their living with needle and thread.

Several comments are in order regarding the evidence we have cited
on the workplace as a hazard to children's health and welfare. The first
is that the corpus of relevant materials only deals with hazards to children. Situations in which children were not at risk were not interesting to
reformers. The result is that we read testimony of evils and, by implica-
tion, of evildoers. And yet there were factory owners who were solicitous
for the welfare of these child-workers, such as the Grants and the Ash-
tons. It was economic necessity or greed within the family which put
children to work originally, and risk of injury or abuse was the consequence.

A picture of child abuse was essential to the propaganda of reform,
so investigators sought out and recorded the most flagrant instances.
Reform has always presented opportunities to more than the reformer.
When Lord Shaftesbury was at the height of his evangelical zeal he supported the life style of Robert Dodd, "the Factory Cripple." Dodd's history is informative on the matter of Shaftesbury's credulity and on the
opportunities which Dodd saw for his nimble mind and fluent pen.
Dodd travelled at Shaftesbury's expense, sending lurid accounts of appalling situations to his humorless but zealous patron in London. By the
power of his pen he provided propaganda for Shaftesbury, whose credi-

bility was reduced when weaknesses in Dodd's background came to the attention of opponents of reform. However, propaganda was based on abuse of children and adults, and the facts, although overstated, were not really in dispute. Dodd and Shaftesbury presented the afflictions of crippled children as a way to influence the hearts and minds of the uninformed but morally attentive public. In the full course of events, they were highly effective.

Handicapped Children

It is likely that the streets of Victorian towns saw many handicapped children. Some of the disabilities were those we know today, but there were others we do not see. The prime example is probably rickets, the deficiency of vitamin D, whose principal effect was to soften bones of growing children, leaving them with bow-legs; in addition, the spleen and liver were enlarged. Rickets expresses malnutrition, and this century has seen adults whose bow-legs and rolling gait were lifelong consequences of poor nutrition as a child in the late nineteenth century. That cohort has now died out, and with it, a link to the problems of child health in the last century.

There were probably many instances of chronic otitis media, infections of the middle ear whose glue-like excretions can lead to conductive deafness. Preceded by intense earaches, such problems are still not easy to treat even with antibiotics because reinfections occur readily. A study from New Zealand of chronic otitis media by Silva (1982) revealed an incidence of forty-seven cases in which both ears were involved among just under nine hundred children. The incidence would be higher for involvement of either ear, and the incidence of the disease among nineteenth-century children could easily have been twice or three times the contemporary rate due to the frequency of colds among malnourished children. Table 1.5 lists the incidence of handicapping conditions in the last half of the nineteenth century.

Although probably not so labelled, there would have been cases of poliomyelitis; children like Tiny Tim in "A Christmas Carol" got around with the aid of a crutch. To the present generation polio is a term comparable in vagueness to smallpox and referring to a long-gone illness, like the Black Death. However, the conditions still exist, and our Victorian ancestors were subject to epidemics which persisted until a few decades ago.

Visual disorders were common, especially those minor but disabling conditions for which prescription of glasses, and today's contact

TABLE 1.5
HANDICAPPED PERSONS BY AGE PER MILLION OF THE POPULATION 1851–1901*

Year	Sex	Blind				Deaf and Dumb				Insane	
		All Ages	<5 Years	5–10 Years	10–15 Years	All Ages	<5 Years	5–10 Years	10–15 Years	All Ages	<15 Years
1851	Both	1073				704					
1861	Both	1023				782					
1871	Both									3039	583
	Male	1029	189	294	401	566	152	662	714		
	Female	876	180	223	317	451	137	517	617		
1881	Both									3253	581
	Male	953	172		312	563	167		627		
	Female	809	161		263	464	116		523		
1891	Both									3358	509
	Male	874	168	204	309	548	131	619	749		
	Female	748	142	172	272	434	106	461	549		
1901	Both									4078	629
	Male	835	151	214	352	524	114	457	613		
	Female	725	108	169	292	417	491	354	416		

*Census 1911 (1917).

lenses for adolescents, is an entirely satisfactory response. There was more blindness, legal and absolute, because treatment of infections was not very effective. Consideration of a Third World country's visually handicapped is probably an apt analogy for understanding the scope of childhood diseases in Victorian times.

There is a class of handicapped children the Victorians probably did not encounter. Today, we have chronically ill children who live because of effective medical care. In the nineteenth century, and well into the twentieth, many conditions shortened life abruptly. Infants who were delivered before the end of gestation and those who were delivered at full term but were small probably died quickly. Children with congenital heart defects—the "blue babies," for example—died from conditions we have learned to repair. Down syndrome babies, who frequently have heart problems—Fallot's tetralogy—probably also died at an early age.

There was a class of children the Victorians encountered but we do not: the workhouse children. In a letter to the *Cork Constitution,* Mr. C.B. Gibson of Monkstown described the condition of children who had lived in the Cork workhouse for an average of five years.

> There are 104 children ranked as healthy. Some of these should not have ranked thus. There are, for example, some very bad eye cases, which must render reading or writing painful. These must soon be transferred to the sick list. Of these 104 ranked as healthy, there are fully two-thirds, and from that to three-fourths, who have been sick, principally with scurvy, the marks of which are still visible, but not being a medical man I cannot speak with perfect confidence.
>
> Ranked as sound, 104; in the lazaretto school, 46; and in hospital, 22. Total, 172. Of these there are 68 sick and maimed. If to this 68 we add the two-thirds (we might say three-fourths) of those ranked as sound, who have been sick, and bear the mark of scurvy, we should have been 34½ of the whole number, (that is of the 172), who have escaped. Now 34½ will go into 172 five times and a fraction over.
>
> I asked how many of the male children there were who had grown from childhood to manhood. I was told sixteen! "Here is one of them, sir." I looked in the direction pointed out, and saw in the distance, (judging from the figure), what I thought was a boy about twelve years of age. He approached, and I found he was a man! But how shrivelled and deformed! In the hospital, a boy about twelve was brought before me, panting like a bird. I took him at the distance (judging from his face), for an old man. What a look of orphaned desolation marked that child's face! It was aged by want and sorrow. Here I must stay my pen. The boy was evidently dying on his legs (Gibson 1859).

Today, experts recognize psychiatric stress in children knowing that emotionally disturbed children come out of the stress of pathological parenting. Given the distortions of family life produced by the early factory system, it is likely that there were many children with damaged emotional lives and disturbed self-concepts. There certainly were many abused children, and Dickens gave us Dotheboys Hall in Yorkshire, a reflection of a harsh reality. One of the code-phrases in newspaper advertisements for boarding schools was the statement that there were no vacations. That made virtual abandonment respectable. For younger children and infants, there was the emotional and physical wasting of baby-farming, group child-care in which little attention was paid to even physical need; marasmus, or wasting away, was a common pattern of physical and mental decline.

The nineteenth century saw much reform in Britain, for there was much to reform. The physical and mental welfare of children as a generation was ravaged by the factory system. Beginning with attention to chimney sweeps at the end of the eighteenth century, reform slowly made its march. Successive waves of reform improved conditions of life and work, and the standard of living began to rise, especially in the second half of the century.

2.

THE FAMILY

Ellen Augusta Hall, born in 1822, was "beautiful, one of the sweetest and prettiest girls in Jersey" at age sixteen, and the middle-class families of St. Helier held her in high regard. In 1838, her diary was in one of the earliest of its sixty years (Sherrard 1966), and in it she records a young girl's interest in the opposite sex. At the series of weekly lectures known collectively in St. Helier as the Athanaeum, she had received sugar plums from Mr. Smyth; and she recorded later, of another admirer, "how the man does stare." Indeed, during the course of a long and comparatively happy life, with a few crises in the early years, Ellen Augusta Hall remained attractive to men. Canevari's portrait when she was fifty-two and her diary's record of admirers show that Ellen had an active social life in West Wickham; curiously, neither she nor her older sister, Emily Mary, born in 1819, married. Yet all around them young men pressed their suits. Emily recorded the case of Adolphus Turner, whose older brother sought the hand of Eliza McNeill. When Adolphus learned that his financially secure brother, a Colonel, pursued Eliza, he fled St. Helier; but he returned impetuously when he learned Eliza had spurned the well-situated elder brother. In a burst of uncharacteristic speed, Lord

Aberdeen had granted Adolphus's request to become Consul in Monte-video at £1,800 per year. With both professional and amatory agendas hurtling to a climax, Adolphus proposed and "was not refused," in Emi-ly's terms. Adolphus was delighted and showed it, while his intended, Miss Eliza McNeill, is reliably reported to have spent the evening in tears. Jane Austen would have understood exactly, even if Colonel Turner might have followed developments with mixed emotions. Subsequently, Colonel Turner wished to marry Ellen Hall, who wrote that she thought "very highly of him but do not love him." With regard to Adolphus and Eliza, it is not clear how things went on the Rio de la Plata, but we can be reasonably confident that one more Victorian family was established.

Surely one of the oddest marriages was that of young Hannah Cullwick, born in Shropshire in 1833. A country girl, she held a variety of servant jobs. At the age of twenty-one she met Arthur Munby, a well-known figure in literary circles. Nineteen years later she married him and continued to work in menial positions, unacknowledged as his wife until long after. Hannah wore a padlock and chain around her neck and kept a diary at Munby's request. Through the diary, begun early in their relationship, we can glimpse life through the eyes of a servant. Appar-ently, the purpose was to provide grist for "Massa's" journalistic mill, and the entries give excellent detail of conditions of work (Stanley 1984).

No less exploitive was the liaison of Friedrich Engels and an Irish girl, Mary Burns, in Manchester. After Mary's death, her sister Lizzie, who had kept house for the couple, took her place. She remained in that liaison until Engels returned to Germany.

Robert Blincoe acquired his wife Martha, according to his biogra-pher John Brown, in 1819, almost on a dare. At a christening, Blincoe was teased about being a bachelor and joked that he would marry Mar-tha the next day. Martha immediately agreed to have her younger suitor, and side bets were made. On the appointed day they married, and they appear to have lived happily ever after. No less informal in its nature, but probably less happy in its outcome, was the practice of wife-selling. Menefee (1981) believed the practice was confined to the south of En-gland and the Midlands, but noted that an instance occurred in North-umberland in this century.

Of course, the establishment of the Victorian family depended on specific and local circumstances. The actions of the Blincoes, Mr. and Mrs. Munby, the Misses Hall and Burns, the brothers Turner, and Eliza McNeill expressed the values of their station in life. Ellen and her friend Eliza had a lively interest in young men. Statistics from the last half of the century show that the interest was reciprocated, and most women in England and Wales (more than three out of four) had married by the

TABLE 2.1
PROPORTION (%) OF WOMEN MARRIED 1851–1901*

Age	Year				
	1851	1861	1871	1881	1891
15–25	17	18	18	18	15
25–35	64	67	67	68	65
35–45	76	76	76	76	76
45–55	71	72	71	71	71

*Census of England and Wales 1911.

time they reached age forty-five (Table 2.1); the rates in Scotland were slightly lower.

The first child generally arrived seventeen months later, according to Duncan (1866), to be followed by others in a period which usually lasted about twelve to fifteen years. The eventual size of the family was mediated by social factors, especially the appalling death rate of infants and children under age five in the factory towns. Had the inexpensive

TABLE 2.2
ESTIMATED BIENNIAL REPRODUCTION RATES
FOR WOMEN OF ALL AGES IN ENGLAND AND
WALES AND IN SCOTLAND BY DECADE PER K WOMEN*

Biennium	England and Wales	Scotland
1850–1852	2.19	—
1860–1862	2.26	2.27
1870–1872	2.35	2.29
1880–1882	2.28	2.26
1890–1892	2.04	2.00
1900–1902	1.72	1.86

*Glass (1940).

rehydration therapy developed for use in Third World countries been available in the nineteenth century, many children would have been spared death from the diarrhea and dehydration of "summer fever." For the most part, the number of children per mother dropped in the last half of century, as Table 2.2 shows.

The Victorians viewed marriage as a tremendous undertaking in which the heart might run its course, but only after the proprieties were fully observed. When they were not, as in the case of Copland vs. Child, the consequences were not trivial. Mr. Child, son of a prosperous grocer in Norwood, took Miss Copland for a drive in February 1853, proposed, and was accepted. On 29 March he married another woman and planned to sail with her to Australia. Despite a spirited defense by Mr. Sergeant Wilkins, Lord Campbell and the jury found for the plaintiff, Miss Copland, and awarded her seventy-five pounds (Breach 1853). The reasons were many, but they all expressed the core concept of the family as a permanent institution, a linkage of lives and of families, of kith and kin. However, contemporary views of life can lead to errors of interpretation. Our view of the formation of a family is inextricable from the times, and perhaps the decade, in which we live. Family is a concept, but there is also the term *household,* conveying that people beyond parents and children may live together. We think of a household in the stereotype of a male and female, married, with two or three children. Currently, there are alternatives, for there are one-parent families, widowed parents with children, grandparents living with children and grandchildren, and so on. Students of the family point out that children in the centuries before our own lived in households which included more than blood relatives. Young William Lancely left his widowed mother's cottage at age sixteen to live with a rich local squire in 1860 (Burnett 1974). The household was well-provisioned by the squire, and William was so comfortable that he found a three-day holiday spent at his mother's cottage quite long enough. Young William had left home, but he appears to have found a home and developed a role which was agreeable to him, to the squire, and to others. Put in the Squire's perspective, the household contained his wife and children, and existed within a larger household of servants plus family. Obviously, the size of the household varied with circumstances.

In the prosperous year of 1871, a family in Chelsea was most likely to have servants in the household, and five times out of six they would be females. In Shoreditch, in contrast, there would be few servants by virtue of poverty; and the few servants known were even more likely to be female, by about twenty-five to one. In their didactic, methodical way, our ancestors provided guides to the emerging middle class on the number and type of servants a household might employ in view of the annual income of the paterfamilias. Similarly, the Silver Fork novels showed how the well-to-do live. Burnett (1974) has summarized the prescriptions in an 1824 guide to domestic economy. At £250 per annum, a couple could employ a maid at an annual cost of £16. At £1,000, they should have three maids and two men servants. At the £5,000 level, a handsome sum in an age of little inflation and no income tax, nine female and thirteen male servants were called for.

Of course, the obvious form of expansion of a household is the birth of children. Biologically, the process began later in the nineteenth century because girls achieved menarche at a later age than they do today. However, the years in which women are capable of producing children are finite, and early marriage began the process sooner. In 1871, Dr. Mathews Duncan calculated the fecundity of women in London's East End, at St. George-in-the-East. Table 2.3 shows that the women marrying youngest had twice the number of children borne by women marrying at the latest ages. The latter group had fewer years remaining until menopause and the end of conception. In the face of the great winnower, the mortality rate for infants and children under age five, households of young couples had the greatest potential for growth. As the social level of the family rose, so the mortality rate fell and the rate of household expansion grew.

TABLE 2.3
AGE OF MOTHERS AT MARRIAGE AND THEIR MEAN
NUMBER OF CHILDREN, LONDON EAST AND HOSPITAL*

Marital Age	N	Mean N Children
15–19 Years	730	9.12
20–24 Years	1418	7.92
25–29 Years	630	6.30
30–34 Years	115	4.60

*Duncan, M. *Fecundity, Fertility, Sterility, and Etc.,* Edinburgh, A. and C. Black, 1866.

It seems likely that household growth was exponential among the privileged, because more children probably meant a disproportional increase of servants as household roles became more specialized. Occasionally, the poor thrived; the marriage of Joseph and Mary Thurman in 1794 produced eleven children, and only one died in infancy (Levine 1979). Table 2.4 shows that the average family consisted of just about five people from 1820 to 1890, and that the size peaked at mid-century and then fell in a process which has continued to this day.

Among the poor in factory towns mortality was above average among children. The result was that the number of children in factory town families was exceeded by the size of families in suburban and rural

TABLE 2.4
CHARACTERISTICS OF FAMILIES IN THE NINETEENTH CENTURY

Approx. Year[1]–4	Populat.[1] U.K. in K[2]	Reproduct.[2] Rate per	% Married[3] Women CA 15–44	N Marriages (K) Religious	Civil	Persons[1] Per Family	Birth Rate %
1820	10.18					4.81	
1825							
1830	11.68					4.77	
1835							
1840	13.06					4.5[5]	
1845				128[4]	3.4[4]		3.52
1850	13.37	2.19	47.33	148[3]	6.8[3]	4.83	
1855							3.55
1860	14.06	2.26	49.13	157	11.3	4.5	3.58
1865							
1870	15.30	2.35	49.64	171	18.5	4.61	3.57
1875							
1880	16.97	2.28	49.14	171	25	4.73	
1885							3.35
1890	20.10	2.04	47.07	195	30	4.62	3.14

[1]1821–91   [2]1850–52 to 1890–92   [3]1851–91   [4]1844   [5]Manchester (Adshead 1842)

manufacturing areas, and by those in nonfactory towns and the country-side; the latter site had a mean family size about one-fourth above that of the factory towns in Roberts's (1876) data.

Conventionally, boys and girls grow to adulthood and marry, the girls being younger than the boys at the time the household is estab-lished. In the period 1850–1900, for which we have the best data, males under age twenty-one provided fifty to eighty grooms per one thousand grooms of all ages, a rate rising briefly to eighty per thousand in the 1879s. This rate of 5% to 8% means that over 90% of males who married were over age twenty-one. On the other hand, the proportion of brides under age twenty-one was never less than 15% (in 1850), and peaked at about 23% at the same time as the young males' rate also peaked. Brides were likely to be under age twenty-one about five times more frequently than their new husbands. Their weddings, incidentally, were overwhelmingly church affairs, although the proportion of civil ceremonies rose from about one in thirty-two in 1845 to one in six by 1890 (see Table 3.4). In the last four decades of the nineteenth century, only about 15% of women had never married by the end of the child-bearing years, roughly speaking.

Another form of growth in nineteenth-century households was the result of economic stress and poverty. In working class homes a lodger was a common phenomenon, so that family income grew, but at the price of overcrowding. Another bulge in the household occurred when a young couple married and moved in with a set of parents. Lack of money created that strategy, and it was effective until the time came when a young couple's earnings enabled them to establish a separate household.

In general, the establishment and growth of households expanded and contracted as servants came and went, grandparents took up resi-dence, and children grew to maturity. Adolescence saw emancipation of young workers in London, according to Mayhew (1851), and the same phenomenon occurred in the factory towns, as young people began the cycle of family development initiated by their own parents and begat children.

Family Planning

Charles Esam could recollect his earliest years at Thornton Heath, Surrey, where, as a tiny child, he would creep into his parents large bed. This ritual was abruptly ended, Burnett (1982) records, when his father angrily sent him back to his own bed. From that time on, the big bed

TABLE 2.5
REPRODUCTIVE TRAITS OF PRIVILEGED FAMILIES

Family	Sex	$\overline{M}$ Age At Married	$\overline{M}$ Family Size	Generation Reproduced	Survived Reproductive Years	$\overline{M}$ Death Age
Burke's Landed Gentry	Male[1]		5.3			63.57
Ducal Families	Male[2]	30.0	3.0	.96	64	
Ducal Families	Female[2]	24.2	4.0	1.33	78	
Peeresses	Female[3]		4.9			

[1]Beeton, Yule and Pearson (1900).
[2]Hollingsworth (1957).
[3]Duncan (1866).

was full, with no room for young Charles. Eventually, all parental beds became full, as did the household, whether the children numbered eight (in the case of Robert Owen in the early years of the century) or one (in the case of young Charles Esam). There came a time when a decision was made that there would be no additional children. The means to that end ranged from separate beds for the most conservative to active physiological steps for the more progressive. The decision was the same, only the methods varied according to the religious and moral convictions of the parents. These values were also determined by social class (fertility being inversely related to social class). Ducal and other privileged families tended to be small and did little more than replace the preceding generation (see Table 2.5)—a phenomenon aided, comparatively speaking, by a longer span of life. In contrast, a poor child had many brothers and sisters, but mortality among them in their earliest years could be a frightful thing. Indeed, it lead to a convention for asking about the prospects for survival in the form of responding to the news of birth by asking if "the little one has come to stay?"

The Victorian family viewed from afar consists of Papa, Mama, and a number of children. On close inspection, the children tend to be more numerous in the early decades of the nineteenth century and decidedly fewer in the last two decades. In the last half of the century, the number of children in families evolved from a number frequently beyond accurate prediction by parents to the predictable outcome of rational decision making by all but the most conservative parents. There were many reasons for the evolution of parents' thinking, including a rise in the level of education, mass publication of manuals on how to run a household, and recognition that raises in income could be wiped out by extra mouths to feed. The stage was set long before the change came about by the essay of the Reverend Thomas Robert Malthus, who saw that overpopulation, malnutrition, and poverty were connected. Malthus saw little relief except by the mechanism of self-denial, a technique not common among people who seldom had the chance to look beyond tomorrow—the urban poor.

The variability of the gross reproductive rate in the nineteenth century varied by locality. In 1850–52, the biennium for which we have the first good data (Glass 1940), children were born in Staffordshire at a rate of 2.26%, while in Cardiganshire the rate was only 1.90%. By 1890–92, the rate in Staffordshire had risen to 2.48% and the rate in Cardiganshire had dropped to 1.56%. During this latter period, the county with the highest gross rate of reproduction was Durham, at 2.5%, and the lowest was Sussex, at 1.49%. A more fundamental trend was the change in the net rate of live births per thousand of the population. Using 1870 as the peak year and an index value of 100, the net live birth rate per one thousand of the population of England and Wales dropped to 96 in 1880–82, to 87 in 1890–92, and to 81 in 1900–02 (Glass 1940). The overall picture is one of the birth rate rising to a peak and then beginning a process of decline for the next century.

The phenomenon of an increasing population and a falling birth rate merits attention. Chadwick's reform and a greater sophistication in urban government acted to reduce child mortality, and yet the birth rate fell. Fecundity was greatest amongst poor families (Census 1911) and fewer children was the pattern among the privileged classes. There were clear differences between the classes on the prospects of dying as a child, but they were more alike in the capacity to conceive and deliver. Accordingly, one looks to the social context within which parents viewed family planning for an explanation of family size.

The last column in Table 2.4 shows how much fertility dropped in sets of two decades. Innes (1938) pointed out that the drop in nineteenth-century fertility was quite proportional to the level of social class. The Registrar-General's data report this quite clearly, with occasional anomalies.

In the earliest decades of the century, poor families had an interest in not restricting family size because they needed to offset the predictable rate of child mortality. They also needed the marginal income of child labor to offset the low or declining wages of the head of the household. In the case of weavers, children played an active role in the cottage industry. A weaver's children were so many productive, if small, hands. Once better times set in, after the Hungry Forties, the economic incentive waned. Parents' roles evolved into specialization, and women recovered a little of their former specialized, domestic role. At the same time, the spread of schooling—even the "Half-timers"—developed the native shrewdness of working people. We point out that domestic home management did not figure largely in schooling. Well-educated women tended to approach marriage schooled in French, piano, and needlework, but quite unprepared formally to care for children and supervise a household. Rising wages offset by expanding food bills left a Micawberish picture which the working man grasped readily. The Reverend Mr. Thomas Malthus's scenario suggested postponement of marriage and other moral options. More concretely, the 1820s had seen the rise of family planning in the form of handbills from which the literate learned of techniques by which conception might be avoided. The writings of Charles Knowlton and Dr. George Drysdale contributed to the matter, but the net birth rate continued to climb until 1870. The real change came with the 1877 trial of Charles Bradlaugh and Annie Besant, who created an incident in order to create propaganda for their cause. They lost, and therefore they won in the larger court of public opinion.

We can only speculate on the dynamics of change within nineteenth-century families. Women and men found that the new technology of family planning gave a freedom to their lives. While substantial, it probably fell short of the radical alteration in women's lives which late twentieth century changes, especially oral contraceptives and attitudes to abortion, have yielded. In some parts of the world, recent change has extended into male and female roles, a degree of mutation the Victorians did not reach, but which probably gave a higher degree of control over their lives to women in the twentieth century.

In the broader sense, the freedom of middle-class women to schedule or plan their children was a note of rationality in the hitherto unpredictable, if generally expected, appearance of particular children. Rationality grew as women and men attempted to communicate this finding to others. Even in the face of conventions and fairly traditional wisdom about the family was added the insight accruing to those who saw family life as a teachable, improvable set of skills. The flow of books and pamphlets was immense. The literate working-class woman was implicitly urged to act as if she were much better off, a consequence of how little the middle-class authors knew of the crises and unpredictability faced by working-class women. The Colonel's lady and Judy O'Grady had a one-sided relationship in which Judy might know a good deal about the Colonel's household and his children, but not vice versa.

The young Isabella Beeton, who died at a quite early age, offered her crisp observations on household management. The great Alexis Soyer published menus for ladies with managerial challenges to be faced in Kensington, Belgravia, and Orpington. At the same time, the rise of domestic service provided an informal education for young women in what freedom from poverty could mean for children and adults. Young domestics saw how a household was organized, dusted beautiful vases, and acquired a sense of contemporary middle-class aesthetics before they left domestic service to establish their own modest household. It was no wonder that young William Lancely was in no hurry to spend his rare holiday away from the Squire's house and in his mother's country cottage. As it turned out, William married and seems to have combined his in-house duties with an external family. Presumably, he applied his acquired sense of values to his own family and attained the Victorian goal of respectability by educating his children to prize that virtue.

Family Education

Viewed from a distance, the early nineteenth century was a period of innovation in Western society. Napoleon had gone for the second time, but nascent republicanism and a demotic sense of the need to change and improve persisted. In the absence of the radical changes installed in France between 1789 and 1815, the structure of British society remained as it had, leavened by a glimpse of reform possible in the institutions of society. Only slowly did such change come, except as a local response by individual philanthropists who started schools or as a response to the growing tension between evangelicals and the established church to control education. Apart from these innovations, life for the individual did not improve greatly. Of course, the economy expanded; and as jobs expanded and wages rose, families achieved a temporary stability. What was lacking was anything beyond custom and convention to prepare couples for married life.

It was generally the case that the first child arrived about a year after marriage. Up to that point the young wife in a factory town might work and so raise the joint income. Such a young woman probably read but wrote little in the early decades before compulsory schooling took hold. However, schooling was for literacy not for living; in the case of a better-off girl, the purpose was to appear cultured and refined in order to catch the eye of Jane Austen's Mr. Darcy. Unless she was the child of an exceptional woman married to an exceptional man, a working-class girl was ill-prepared for managing a family. In similar fashion, her husband would have been equally ill-prepared. His preparation for manhood was, at best, vocational. An apprentice to a good master would learn his trade, but he would also learn what drinking was.

From the 1820s there grew the tradition of books to help mothers manage their children and households. In 1825, Esther Copley published *Cottage Comforts,* and there followed a stream of books on diet and care of the household. The eponymous Mrs. Beeton was a young woman when the first edition of *The Book of Household Management* appeared in 1861. A relatively unknown but perceptive adviser was Dr. J. T. Conquest, who published *Letters to a Mother . . .* in 1848, in which he provided advice on the health of children. Considering the quantity of misinformation abroad, this step was wholly salutary; the use of opium derivatives for newborns who had yet to show any problem is an example of more than ignorance. All through the nineteenth century, physicians and sanitarians denounced the use of "farinaceous" foods for infants. In 1863, a Manchester physician, George Greaves, pointed out that premature introduction of solids was a significant cause

TABLE 2.6
NINETEENTH CENTURY GUIDES TO
CHILD AND FAMILY WELFARE

Copley, Esther, *Cottage Comforts,* 1825

Cobbett, William, *Cottage Economy,* 1830

Conquest, Dr. J. T. *Letters to a Mother on the Management of Herself and Her Children in Health and Diseases . . .,* 1848

Copley, Esther, *Cottage Cookery,* 1849

Soyer, Alexis, *A Shilling Cookery for the People,* 1855

Household Tracts for the People, c. 1860 (Series)

Smith, Dr. Edward, *Practical Dietary,* 1864

Beeton, Isabella, *The Book of Household Management,* 1861

—*How I Managed My Children from Infancy to Marriage,* 1865

Blackwell, Elizabeth, *Counsel to Parents on the Moral Education of their Children,* 1878

The Mother's Handbook: A Book for Her Own and Her Children's Management with Hints and Helps for Everday Emergencies, 1879

Francatelli, C. *A Plain Cookery Book for the Working Classes,* 1882

of infant deaths. In such instances, Manchester's children survived diarrhea and other perils only to be fed indigestible food by ignorant mothers. Alexis Soyer's *A Shilling Cookery for the People* (1855) attempted to teach preparation of nutritious and economical meals (see Table 2.6).

All of these didactic works, like the Silver Fork novels, addressed literate, book-buying people. They were often hortatory to a degree which bordered on the ludicrous, addressing what ought to be if the reader really wished to live like the most enlightened of the rising middle class or the aristocracy. The guides to domestic management offered examples of the size of household and the type of servants one could expect to maintain, and probably ought to in order to appear respectable at a given station in life. In this regard, the young upper-class woman would be brought by marriage to instant command of a large domestic staff; short of being shrewd enough to have observed her parents' household and digested the procedures, a young matron needed all the help she could get. Compounding her responsibility was the appearance of the first child, a challenge in the second year of married life likely to

TABLE 2.7
HOUSEHOLD TRACTS FOR THE PEOPLE (c. 1860)

For Young Men and Women

Are You Thinking of Getting Married?

Going a-Courting, Sweethearting, Love and Such Like.

For Parents

How Do you Manage the Young Ones?

How to Make the Most of Things

Peace in the Household

For Young Men

Young Men in Great Cities

Men Who Have Fallen

How to Take Care of Number One

On Health

The Work of Fresh Air

The Secret of a Healthy Home

How Do People Hasten Death

For Working Men

When to Say "No"

Working Men's Hindrances

For Servants

My First Place

Kind Words for the Kitchen

(Twopence each)

daunt all but the most resourceful. Accordingly, the guidebooks to care of household and children were welcomed. What they left out was the third element of the trio, the husband. In that regard, the guidebooks tended to offer generalities and pious injunctions, but little that was specific, or informative in the delicate areas of Victorian life. The tone of middle-class authors did not compensate for their lack of insight into what a nonprivileged or working mother could do to make ends meet. However, by the end of the 1850s there began to appear publications dealing with the problems of life. In Table 2.7 we list the titles of several in the *Household Tracts* series.

About the same time advice in verses began to appear, sponsored by the Ladies Sanitary Association. By 1860, thirty thousand of their didactic, painless books had sold at twopence each.

The Sick Child's Cry

Open the window, mother,
I can't breathe in this stifling room;
Open the window, mother,
and let out the weight and gloom!

It seemed like an angel breathing—
Now mother I've said my prayer—
I think I can sleep a little
Thank GOD for the blessed air.

Fresh Air

Do you wish to be healthy?
Then keep the house sweet;
As soon as you're up
Shake each blanket and sheet

Do this, it's soon done,
In the fresh morning air;
It will lighten your labour,
And lessen your care.

The Neglected Child

See the neglected child,
He drags himself along,
Staring with dull and listless gaze
at the quick bustling throng.

In the still night or dawn
His father stumbles in,
In drunken rage or low abuse,
From his dark haunts of sin.

So days and nights pass on,
Yet life keeps strong within;
For God is caring for the child,
In his dreer home of sin.

The Baby

If baby holds his hands,
And asks by sounds and signs
For what you're eating at your meals,
Tho' mother's heart inclines

To give him what he wants,
Remember, he can't chew;
And solid food is bad for him,
Tho' very good for you.

Other poems are titled, "Tidiness," "The Young Mother," "Soothing," "Vaccination," "Clean Clothes," "Cooking," and "Tight Lacing."

Sex education and family planning were essential but hard-to-manage topics for the Victorians. The son of Robert Owen wrote *Moral Physiology; or, A Brief and Plain Treatise on the Population Question*, in 1830. The work, written at New Harmony, sold well in Great Britain and in the United States until the later decades of the century. Girls came to menarche, on the average, between their fifteenth and sixteenth birthdays (Duncan 1866) and frequently were unprepared for the event or for the later connection between affection and pregnancy. Nevertheless, the

Victorians managed, for the birth rate fell from a peak of 3.58% in 1865 to below the rate of 3.52% for 1845 to 3.14% in 1890. In that year the average number of persons per family was 4.62, well below the average of 4.83 in 1850.

Perhaps the most desirable element, a place for family education in the elementary school curriculum, came slowly. Given a system hard put to create a literate, numerate population, it is not surprising that domestic science seemed a frill for many years. Schools teach what people want taught, and vice versa; Victorian education was the vehicle for improving health through physical training. The corollary that a well-nourished, well-cared for body was a prerequisite was not so evident. Even today, there are people who prefer ornamentation of the growing mind through Greek grammar to inculcating a grasp of how one's growing and changing body works. The Victorians were at an additional disadvantage, because knowledge of nutrition and the body were imperfect. Equally, a detached view of human relations within the family was not prevalent, there being consensus that sex roles were quite distinct and should remain so. It took time for the utilitarianism which produced a literate, disciplined work force through schooling to yield a broader curriculum in which care of the household was inculcated in girls whose mothers were not quite Mrs. Beetons. In some respects the rise of the cooperative retail movement represented mass self-education by working-class families who benefitted from the lower unit price generated by purchasing in bulk. Domestic purchasing in bulk remains, however, a highly calculated strategy for even the middle class. Even today, male adolescents resist domestic instruction, feeling it is not quite manly; although a degree of self-sufficiency in this area of life is not without merit. For the Victorians, schooling for literacy and morality on a mass scale was a great step forward. Domestic science on a modest degree and some degree of attention to rational family life were eventually introduced. Copelman (1986) has pointed out the apparent paradox to the Victorians of married women teachers working outside their own homes advocating a domestic role for girls.

Bringing Up Baby

In the "Autobiography of a Navvy" published in 1861, the author described his childhood of several decades before near Saffron Walden. Six of eleven brothers and sisters survived on the father's earnings of seven to nine shillings a week. Young Bill was sent out to beg for turnips but could not extract them from the frozen ground. Each day was long and filled with the rhythms of nature at her best and worst. To such a child, the world seemed much as it did to his rude forefathers in the country churchyard. The pace of village life, and the squalor of tied cottages no less stressful because they sat amidst pretty scenery, were an unchanging reality. The cycle of the rural calendar, beginning with Plough Monday and its celebrations, was unchanging. The country child ate of Bagehot's "cake of custom" and acquired the values of his ancestors; Man lived at the mercy of the weather in the long run, and at the mercy of the Squire in a shorter perspective. A country child's values expressed the unchanging mode of living, because technology came slowly to what we now call the agriculture business. A Lancashire weaver, John Ward, saw his first mechanical harvester when he was age fifty in the early 1860s. Not surprisingly, child-rearing in the country changed little, being touched only late in the century by sanitary reforms, enfranchisement, and innovations in technology.

In contrast, William Knowles, John Ward's grandson born in 1863, grew up in Low Moor near Clitheroe and acquired a set of values which expressed the circumstances of his family quite certainly. He would live close to his widowed grandfather, and the neighbors in back-to-back houses would have been an extended kinship of children to play with and elders to guide him. His values-training began with his baptism, and he probably acquired one of the several versions of Methodism. Such children grasped early the centrality of work at "t' Mill" in their lives. An enlightened version of this ethic was the work of Dr. Samuel Smiles, who probably spoke the words "Thrift, Work, Diligence, and Zeal" in italics, as it were, signifying that these cardinal virtues were the road to acquiring capital and joining the ranks of self-made industrialists. Above all, there was clear consensus about morals and conduct. Sex was taboo, formally, and the all-too-common public drunkenness was roundly condemned. A lad should aspire to join his father, brothers, and cousins in the mill. From the mill flowed wages when times were good and outings in Wakes Week. A young lad could try his wings in Blackpool as he could not at home in Colne. He might flirt, get drunk, and engage in all the things Chapel folk denounced—but he would do it out of town on his rare holidays. Through such explorations, he might go as far south as London to the Crystal Palace, being surprised by the density of pedestrians and amused by their local dialect far different from his own Chaucerian sounds. Such contrasts came as a shock and led to introspection as the train hurtled towards Crewe and home.

The world of the child worker was, implicitly, instruction in geopolitics. As the War Between the States raged in North America, so Egypt's and India's cotton supplied the raw material requisite for employment.

John Ward followed the Civil War in America quite closely, knowing the generals and the sites of battles. In his diary he recorded the burning of Atlanta, and he must have speculated in his shrewd way on the effect it must have on the supply of raw cotton and its price, and so on his prospects for keeping his job.

To the middle-class child, a condition of life whose separation from poor children was so marked as to resemble the impermeable boundary between castes, the Victorian world was a pleasant place. The professions had not quite achieved respectability, but education and brass could open many, if not all, doors. The prime advantage of being born into a middle-class Victorian family was the prevalence of a sense that things can be better and that positive action was a virtue. Accordingly, the middle-class baby had a greater chance of living to his or her fifth birthday and of living far longer than poorer children. Provision of hygiene and insistence on cleanliness kept at bay all but the inevitable illnesses of childhood. Roger Langdon recorded that, in 1825, his cradle was placed next to the bed of a boy dying of smallpox so that he might be immunized. In the end "old Nanny Holland" did the job with a darning needle; Roger lived until 1894, when he died at the age of sixty-nine. The value of healthful living was paralleled by the middle-class insistence on education for their children. Mercantilism demanded a grasp of geopolitics, and life in the manufacturing center of the world brought realities beyond the Channel to one's doorstep.

The middle-class child was more likely to be "Church" rather than "Chapel," reflecting the identity of the established Anglican church with the prosperous, for the most part. Working-class people, when churchgoers, usually attend Methodist and Baptist chapels. The values to be inculcated evolved with the times. Patriotism, piety, and style had their place, and a girl was led towards becoming marriageable through her command of the pianoforte and French. An anomaly of the Victorian period was the emergence of the cult of the little girl. Our ancestors developed an apparently sexless valuation of girls in an ideal form. In this value complex, adult males fantasized the clear skins and smooth limbs of preadolescent girls. Charles Ludwidge Dodgson gave us Alice in his writings as an abstraction from his feelings towards little girls. Our sophisticated century brushes aside the "innocence" projected on to Victorian girls and considers the fantasies to be quite sexual.

There is evidence for a sexless orientation before and, indeed, within marriage in the lives of some Victorians. Such a state of affairs we may label, clinically, "psychosexual immaturity," conveying an arrested state of development. Inspection of Victorians besides Dodgson conveys the existence of the condition. It is quite possible that Thomas Carlyle and Jane Welsh did not consummate their marriage (Rose 1984). In the case of John Ruskin, we have his own account in *Praeterita* (Volume III) of meeting the nine-year-old Rose la Touche in 1858 and of her visits to Denmark Hill. Ruskin fervently wished to marry her and awaited her majority when a favorable decision might be forthcoming. However, it was not to be, and Rosie turned down "St. Crumpet." Her mental and physical health waned as her evangelical enthusiasms waxed. In 1848, Ruskin had wed Effie Green, only to lose her to John Millais, the painter, after failing to consummate the marriage.

For boys, always more valued than girls because of their potentials for achievement, the goal was an education which would inculcate a sense of class identity and a sense of self-confidence. Dr. Arnold of Rugby systematized the values and prepared young men to go forth and run an empire. The system worked well and perpetuated itself in the form of new Public Schools. In the Victorian years, education beyond the secondary level was not an intellectual enterprise as much as an interlude for broadening and polishing, and taking a degree was not essential. Even so, the linkage between the Universities' curricula and that of the Public Schools was narrow, a condition from which British education suffered well into the twentieth century. Public School boys made the transition fairly easily, and then "came down" from Oxbridge well-equipped to make their way in the world. Perhaps the striking feature of this stratum of Victorian society was its homogeneity. Within the household it was an accepted value that father was in charge and that children obeyed. Children should not be "spoiled," a uniquely British concept even today, and that a certain spartan quality to their lives should be preserved.

On the other hand, family life resists generalizations. There were tyrants—like the fathers of Frederick Delius and Elizabeth Barrett—and there were indulgent parents; there were incompetent and fluttery mothers and there were chatelaines who managed large domestic establishments with drill-like precision. There were cold, distant people—like Lord Shaftesbury—who could bleed for mankind in general but found it hard to relate to individuals, including their own children. However, there were children who challenged their parents and provoked tension: Mintz (1979) has given an example in Robert Lewis Stevenson's conflict over religion with his father. Analyzing 168 memoirs of Victorian childhoods, Roberts (1978) found that upper-class fathers were recalled as remote, sovereign, but benevolent. Many parents were warm and stimulating. Mary Vivian Hughes (1977) recalled with pleasure and thanks how she and her brother had access to their parents' books in the 1870s. They were read to and observed their mother's skill at water-colours.

This singular woman discussed matters with her children and encouraged them in their pursuits. A similarly stimulating home much lower down the social scale, but a very interesting place, was the home of Aneuran Bevan. Both parents worked, rising before five o'clock in the morning to start the long day. Mr. Bevan is reported to have been a lover of books and of music who found time for civic affairs. Beyond her own work as a tailor, Mrs. Bevan ran an efficient household and was deeply loved by her large family. The family ate together at unchanging mealtimes and generally radiated a glow of mutual affection even under economic stress.

Victorians, like people today, prepared for getting married but not for being married. They were not always prepared for parenthood, a condition undoubtedly complicated by the comparative prevalence of ill health in children. Before twentieth century medicine, people who got sick stayed sick; recovery was slow and a formal period of convalescence was common. How they coped with the birth of retarded, deaf, or chronically ill children is not clear. We can hypothesize that some children fared well despite limitations, while others languished in nonsupportive homes. In such circumstances, as I have documented elsewhere (Jordan 1976), stress between parents can rise, and other children are harmed as the triangle of parents and handicapped child works out its dynamics. The resources available to the family in stress were few; social work did not exist, and hospitals were dangerous places; families could only turn to a clergyman or a wise and supportive member of the family. In 1862, Dr. John Little gave a good description of cerebral palsy which at least objectively described characteristics of some children with neurological and physical handicaps (Jordan 1966). Others, of whom John Langdon Down is the prime example, imposed nonvalid interpretations on relatively superficial aspects of development, thereby confusing matters for decades. On the other hand, there were schools for handicapped children to which parents could turn, especially when children were deaf or blind. Such schools helped parents, if only by providing a brief respite from the burdens they bore. In such matters we recognize that a family can be frozen in the cycle of development, the handicapped child being a permanent, youngest, dependent member of the family. Victorian families had handicapped children and frequently chose silence as they coped with what was largely a personal, private tragedy in an age before social services.

Not all parents who were comfortably off chose to deal as personally with the children as Mrs. Hughes. A feature of middle-and upper-class households was the presence of parent-surrogates—nannies and governesses. Nannies took care of the infants until they were ready for school, and indeed, continued as mother-surrogates to all when there were several children. McBride's (1978) study of nannies indicates that they were a distinctive group. Around mid-century they tended to be under age twenty, at the bottom of the wage scale, and expected to work a seventeen-hour day. Not surprisingly, turnover was high and the average tenure was about one year. Of course, there were exceptions, but the position was not held in high esteem, if wages are an index. Many girls employed as nannies came from the country. Their mode of child care was probably traditional, and there is an account of a young woman who was surreptitiously fed opium derivatives for many years by an ignorant servant. Governesses provided formal education at home as well as supervision of the children in general. Their situation was anomalous; being qualified by their level of education, they were not quite servants, but they were not quite family. Meals could be handled by having them eat with the children when still young. As the age span of the children spread out, the Governess might be a passive attendant at some social occasions. In the case of both nannies and governesses, a good character was considered indispensable. The emphasis was on conformity to the public standards of conduct. For such women, especially governesses, the prospects for marrying and caring for their own children were ambiguous. The nanny, as a servant, could always seek another type of domestic service. The governess had fewer choices. On the positive side, the governess might travel when the family took a holiday. The nanny was more likely to be left to care for the baby so that mother could meet her social obligations.

In both instances, the most precious possession of parents, their children, were turned over to others for care. In the case of the governess, the situation seems a reasonable alternative, because education was not a public monopoly in the nineteenth century. In the case of nannies, as with wet nurses, care was taken by responsible parents to pick them carefully. In both relationships, however, parents placed the fate of their children in someone else's hands, even when not essential. This style of detached child care was benign and relatively orderly. It may be contrasted with the care of children living in congested surroundings. Lady Bell (1907) reported that in the working-class culture of Middlesborough poor living conditions were so routine that mothers were suspicious of the health prospects for a child who disliked dirt and tried to keep clean.

Canal Boat Families

An invisible group of children living in conditions of great adversity were the canal-boat children. Their advocate, George Smith, estimated their number in 1876 at one hundred thousand, a figure perhaps two or three times their actual occurrence, according to McCleod (1966). The English system of canals was extensive but narrower than that in other countries. The result was that the boats were small and had space for little more than cargo amounting, according to Smith (1876), to twenty-five tons. Smith, who was an extremist in his campaigns on behalf of children in brickworks as well as canal-boats, was incensed by the existence of

> men, women and children living, working and floating on our rivers and canals in a state of wretchedness, misery, immortality, cruelty, and evil training that carries peril with it. Not 5 percent of the men, women and children can read and write, and nine out of ten are drunkards . . . and two parts out of three of the men and women living as husbands and wives are unmarried . . . an average seven or eight men, women, and children live, sleep, and die in these wretched holes . . . (Smith 1876).

> Utterly ignorant, as a very large proportion of them are, of all religious knowledge, wholly without instruction, coarse and brutal in manner, and entirely given up to the vilest debauchery and the grossest passions, can we expect, without extraneous assistance, that the children of such parents are ever likely to grow into anything better? I have often and often had occasion bitterly to deplore such sights as I have seen among young boat-children, and have pondered how an improvement in their condition, and in that of their parents, was to be brought about (Smith 1875).

Eventually, Smith's efforts attracted the attention of Factory Inspector Baker; and one of his people, Factory Sub-Inspector Bowling, reported from Birmingham as follows:

> When at Amington yesterday, a case was brought under my notice by a very energetic school visitor, which as it bears on a subject that has engrossed a good deal of public attention lately, it will be as well to give it to you in detail.
> A canal boatman residing in the district is the father of nine children; two of them as infants attended a National school; but all these five children on attaining the age of seven or eight years, and before they could even read, have in turn been taken away from school, and gone to work, either with the father in the boat, or with the coal carts at the colleries. The children, with their father in the boat, have to trudge along the towing-path driving the horse, and my informant tells me they have already become most demoralized, their manners being course, and their language being very foul (Redgrave and Baker 1877).

To Smith and the people whose attention he aroused the disorganization of life in the tiny, squalid dwelling quarters of canal boats was the central problem. Small children managed large towing horses and worked for long hours. Hanson (1975) reported that one of the more obnoxious practices was that of occasionally selling or giving away children to work on other boats. Cut off by travelling from other people, city life, and schooling, canal children remained a problem for decades.

Largely due to George Smith's co-option of Factory Inspector Baker, public attention was drawn to the problem. In 1877, an Act regulating use of canal boats as dwellings was passed, and "Smith of Coalville" turned his energies to the welfare of Gypsy children, several thousand of whom lived in various "Paradises" around London. Smith put the number of children around the country at fifteen to twenty thousand who "live like pigs and die like dogs." He thought a suitable model for legislation to protect Gypsy children was the 1877 Act protecting canal-boat children. With regard to the efficacy of the 1877 Act, we turn to Frank Hird at the end of the century. He listed canal boats amongst "certain British Industries in which children are iniquitous employed" in his book, *The Cry of the Children* (Hird 1898). However, the problem of canal-boat families persisted well into the twentieth century. One of the works still cited on the effects of unwholesome environments is Gordon's (1923) study reporting an average IQ of 74.5 for canal boat children, whose IQs dropped steadily with the passage of the years. Gordon's research was conducted half a century after Smith's pioneering work, indicating, as at the beginning of the nineteenth century, that passage of laws does not automatically cause social problems to go away. Some problems have their origins in the privacy of personal affairs.

Wrong Side of the Blanket

Convention sketches a scene in which the youngest son of an upper-class family, a bounder, seduces the upstairs maid and is sent abroad as a remittance man for a few years. The mother-to-be is dismissed as immoral and as corrupting the tone of the establishment. She bears her child in ignominy, and it is reared by a good-hearted, childless couple beholden to the lord of the manor in some unexplained fashion. That sort of scenario was begun but not completed in the life of Hannah Cullwick. Having missed a ride from Shrewsbury, she accepted a lift from two former officers. As if by cue, the driver went on when Hannah got down about a mile from home. The other gentlemen tried to kiss her, but two laborers came around the corner. Subsequent inquiries led the postman to tell young Hannah that she had met up with one of the worst rogues in the district.

Illegitimacy in the nineteenth century, as today, is the expression of several antecedents, some of which for a time and place may be quite conventional. Some children are sought by young women as the object of a liaison, fantasied as a kind of super-doll to play house with. In that scenario, the role of the male is not that of seducer of the innocent but that of temporary, and perhaps inconvenient, means to the end of motherhood. In contrast, the nineteenth century had its scenarios of which our preceding vignette is the stereotype. One of them was that parenthood was a diffuse, multiperson complex of roles. That is, the children of poor, young, unmarried women were reared jointly by the mother and grandmother; the biological grandfather was father to all, and the latest arrival played the role of youngest in the single household. Another variant was that fertility was too important in a marriage to be left to chance. In that style, marriage was approvable only after the girl showed that she was capable of bearing children. At that point, bride and groom were churched, and marriage sanctified the fertile union.

Our grasp of the scope of illegitimacy in the last half of the nineteenth century is due to the work of the statistician G. Udney Yule (1906), whose concepts are still drawn on today. He abstracted and set out the comparative numbers of legitimate and illegitimate births. In 1850, the legitimacy rate was thirty-two babies per one thousand (K) of the population; it peaked at just under thirty-five per K around 1878, and then declined in the form of a secular trend. The illegitimacy rate in 1850 was about four babies per K of the population; from 1850 the rate declined until it levelled off at about two to three babies per K. Among unmarried women between the ages of fifteen and forty-four, the birth rate in 1851 was 18.8 per K. It peaked in 1865 at 19.2 per K, and then descended steadily to 14.1 per K by 1880. The drop was swifter than for legitimate births, according to data compiled by Innes (1938). Thus, the trend in the last half of the nineteenth century was a secular decline in illegitimacy overall. Within the trend were regional differences.

In his account of a visit to Great Britain in 1833, Alexis de Tocqueville (Mayer 1968) was struck by an anomaly of the system of justice which he observed. Establishment of paternity was settled for the most part by the testimony of the mother under oath. This led de Tocqueville, ever a shrewd observer, to identify the civil procedure as

> an infallible way of diminishing the consequences of her error and (she) even has a way to make it profitable. Thus in England a girl of the peo-

ple who has illegitimate children generally marries more easily than a chaste girl.

We add that de Tocqueville had domestic matters on his mind during his tour of England and Ireland; one of the objectives of his five-week visit was to review his acquaintance with Miss Mary Mottley of Birmingham; they married in 1836, de Tocqueville having visited again in 1835 for four months. Reverting to illegitimacy, we note that the pattern in Scotland was different. In 1871, the *Pall Mall Gazette* thundered about casual ways in Scotland where

> upon the whole, more shame would be attached to the fact of being caught listening to Secular music on the Sabbath than to being the father or mother of an illegitimate child (Assistant Commissioners 1871).

The editorial writer went on to record that the state of affairs existed among Scots who were "well paid, well fed, healthy, intelligent, fairly educated, and religiously inclined." The Sheriff of Berwickshire is reported to have said that "there seems to be no notion among the young women in this country that there is anything improper in receiving men in their bedrooms at midnight."

In Ireland, the situation was quite different; there the rate of illegitimacy was traditionally low, Ulster's rate being the highest at mid-century (Robins 1980). People married comparatively late in life, and pre-marital relations were a gross violation of Catholic morality. We add that abortion and infanticide were equally low and were products of the same moral code.

In the last analysis, the status and concept of illegitimacy was a matter of blameless children, victims of other people's actions rather than violators of moral codes. In the case of Irish children born out of wedlock, they probably presented living proof of a girl's mistake but not the man's. In Scotland, at least in Berwickshire, illegitimate children were, perhaps, no more visible than other children with the run of the village whose paternity was recognized. In the factory towns such children faced a grim future, because they contributed to the rate of infant mortality to a high degree. Waugh (1890) recorded that the death rate among illegitimate children was twice that of children born to married parents. Of course, the baby had to be delivered intact in order to become a dry statistic of the Civil Service shortly after. Among unscrupulous midwives there were two prices for professional services; the higher price was for children born dead. If illegitimate children survived, their unwelcome presence was mitigated by consignment through a third party to a baby farm where death was virtually inevitable through neglect and starvation (Jordan 1986). Indeed, this aspect of illegitimacy formed a minor industry, as women became known as brokers for the evil trade. It goes without saying that the fees were high when the child was guaranteed to be no further problem. Waugh (1890) records a fee of five pounds for the poor and two hundred pounds for the rich; that is, the rate was as much as the traffic would bear. The procedure was institutionalized to the extent that there were advertisements in the newspapers whose benign language was a legally careful offer to dispose of an unwelcome babe.

And yet some illegitimate children thrived. The Swedish Nightingale, Jenny Lind, became a great success, as did Sarah Bernhardt. In such cases there was usually a middle-class father who acted as a patron even when not acknowledging paternity. Such a father provided support and guidance, if not directly, for the child-victim. In the absence of such sponsorship, life itself was at risk and the future bleak. Abandonment was common, and the child street-sweepers of great cities represented, very often, a core of survivors of unions not formalized by marriage.

A few illegitimate children were a source of income for wet nurses, women who breast-fed other people's infants. The inexorable relationship between supply and demand meant that the favored infant got the wet nurse's breast milk, leaving precious little for her own child, under most circumstances. Weaning came quickly, frequently prematurely, so that the wet nurse's child was like the mariner with water everywhere, nor yet a drop to drink. The condition was more than irony, it was tragedy; in place of breast milk, the "farinaceous" foods (bread soaked in water or milk) and a sedative were the lot of the wet-nurse's child.

Social Groups

Among the hazards for all but the more fortunate Victorian families were the inevitable crises of family life: loss of income, a burial to be paid for, and fees to be paid for care during illness. The mechanism for coping with these events was the fraternal and benevolent society. In these clubs—whose function was "mutual assistance," in the phrase of Thomas Wright, the "Journeyman Engineer" (1867)—the working man's family placed its trust in probability theory to guarantee a large payoff for a small weekly contribution. The theory worked, assuring that families could cope with the money aspects of life crises. Wright's account of the Oddfellows shows that the society did more than protect the welfare of the worker's wife and children, it provided him with a sense of belonging to a group beyond family and neighborhood, and allowed him to cultivate a little prestige among his fellows, Odd or not. The former beggar-boy James Dawson Burn recalled in his autobiography of 1855 that his Oddfellow-ship provided him with jobs on several occasions through a network of lodges in England and Scotland. Wright (1867) reported on the elaborate ritual of knocks which led to peepholes opening to admit by a secret phrase—in this case, "Brother Jones without the word." Wright was admitted, still not quite ready to disbelieve "the tales about red-hot pokers and other instruments of torture necessary to the initiation of members." After the Noble Grand had admitted him by requiring repetition of a long promise not to reveal the club's secrets, he was expected to buy a round of drinks for all the Brothers. This step was facilitated by convening the meeting in a pub. The result was that "Brother Bloggs of our Lodge, than whom sober there is no quieter or civiler man breathing . . . becomes pugnaciously quarrelsome . . . while Brother Jones, our oldest member, has to be roused from the sleep of the drunken. . . ."

According to the *Morning Chronicle* in 1851, few towns matched Birmingham in the profusion of clubs. There were the fraternal orders, but there were endless series of excursion clubs, goose clubs, and a club to pay for a group visit to the Great Exhibition. In relation to the drinking mentioned by the Journeyman Engineer, it is interesting to note that the building societies met in temperance halls and hostels rather than drinking establishments. The correspondent goes on to point out that such groups provided the service that banks would not offer to poor people. John Ward (1862) made an investment in a cooperative weaving factory by taking a five-pound share, feeling "there is every likelihood of it prospering." Ward, who was a trustee of the Weaver's Union, recorded going to the committee rooms and the formality of procedures, probably intended to impress on all the serious obligation with regard to members' money. This sense of ritual extended to the grave, with a respectable funeral being the alternative to perceived disgrace. The Burial Society provided this, although the aggressiveness of some societies corrupted the value in the form of insuring infants whose survival become proportionately less probable.

Clothing

We live in an age of man-made fibers and machine-based economies in the fabrication of clothing. To the Victorians, clothing was not taken for granted, for it was expensive and children generally looked shabby and unkempt except for the well-to-do and for ordinary children on special occasions. Photographs of children from Victorian times (for example, those gathered by Horn) show them wearing hand-me-downs in the form of adult clothing, not just the outgrown clothing of bigger brothers and sisters. Reports of the time show that the lack of clothing kept parents from sending children to school. Villages frequently had voluntary committees which provided clothing and bedding, and today's gifts for baby is not without an element of historical necessity as well as the contemporary note of a present on a happy occasion.

A Victorian practice unlike our own was the practice of keeping boys in petticoats for several years. Charles Esam is reported by Burnett (1982) to have recalled his "breeching" at age two, the rite of passage from infancy when he received breeches and abandoned his skirts. A more concrete example is James Northcote's portrait of John Ruskin in petticoats at age three and a half (Cook and Wedderburn 1908). Horn (1974) records that Victorian boys in Juniper Hill, Oxfordshire, stayed in petticoats until they were age six or seven. In the north of England, the transition from shorts to long trousers marked, roughly, entry into adolescence or precocious height, and it generally occurred later in the North.

Footwear was always a problem, because boots and clogs were handmade until the end of the century, when effective sewing machines brought the price down. It is interesting to recall that in Victorian times shoes were not constructed for the left only or the right foot, but for both. Wear gave a shoe its laterality, not the bootmaker or cobbler.

In the early decades of the century, style consisted in producing adult designs in child-like sizes. With the possible exception of headgear (for which boys used caps) and some public-school uniforms (which persist today with an anachronistic charm), the child appeared a miniature adult in dress.

3.

LIFE AND DEATH

Early Development

Recalling her childhood in the 1880s, Sylvia Pankhurst wrote of a little brother, Henry Francis, and the joy she felt when allowed to share her bed with him. For the Pankhurst family in their big house in Russell Square he was a double pleasure; in fact, he was the second Henry Francis, having been born ten months after diptheria carried off the first to bear the name (Pankhurst 1932).

Implicitly, it seems, we think of health, happiness, and growth when childhood is mentioned. For us, modern medicine reduces all but the worst episodes of ill health to predictable and manageable episodes of transient anxiety.

We can approach the welfare of children with confidence, knowing that the typical mother is fairly sophisticated about health matters. She knows that the unborn child can be damaged by her own pattern of nutrition, and she is freed from the burden of thinking every surprise or stress is a potential influence on her baby. In addition, she understands that there are vaccines to prevent childhood diseases, although the notion of prevention is itself a radical and modern concept of child care. The Victorian mother knew of effective vaccination against smallpox, but the idea was limited to that single, terrible disease. Quite without other pediatric support, she faced a virulent form of scarlet fever, and there was always the problem of "summer fever" carrying off infants for what today is a largely preventable reason—dehydration and loss of elements we call electrolytes. Death of infants and children was a theme of life in Victorian Britain, a reality faced by people in all stations of life.

The Victorian mother and child lived in a world of personal misinformation, and the knowledge of basic disease in children that we know as Pediatrics was quite primitive. Only in 1851 was the movement to establish the Hospital for Sick Children at 49 Great Ormond Street, begun; Lord Ashley chaired the organizing committee, and Charles Dickens and Queen Victoria gave their support (History 1862). Apart from that mid-century innovation in London the medical care of children was rudimentary, although clinical observation was probably acute in that generation when sick children abounded. The level of scientific knowledge was not high, so that the welfare of children at all stages of development was never assured.

Gestation. To begin with, there is the question of when in the developmental span of life the first events occur; we place that at conception. Its relevance arises in the question of who is alive biologically and so who exists for the purpose of describing events of childhood. A problem is that our culture tends to view the nine months of gestation equivocally. Pregnancy is an occasion of joy, but those who are informed and experienced temper joy with caution, knowing even today that much can happen in 270 days of gestation. I use this last term, rather than pregnancy, since it suggests the condition of the conceptus.

The fact is that we are an inefficient species when it comes to reproduction. Our offspring have a comparatively long gestation, and they are dependent for a comparatively long time after delivery. They are generally singletons, with twins occurring once in eighty-six deliveries. One part of our incompleteness is the high wastage of conceptions. From the Hawaiian (Kauai) studies of Werner, Bierman, and French (1971) we know that it took thirteen hundred conceptions known at one month to produce eleven hundred live births, in the middle of the twentieth century and in a place with comparatively good health care. The number of concepti lost spontaneously in the first month and described retrospectively as missed periods is unascertained. It is probably high and would raise the rate of fetal wastage above current levels. Beyond the first month the wastage rate is substantial even today. Progress on this matter has taken the form of better prenatal care for women. For the fetuses, it has taken the form of improvements to keep alive children who would otherwise die. In general, pediatricians consider 2,500 grams or 5.5 pounds, to be a desirable birth weight. As childrens' weights fall below 2,500 grams the risk to life rises in a curvilinear fashion. A birth weight below 1.500 grams puts an infant at substantial risk for survival. Today, tiny fetuses whose delivery came quite prematurely, with birth weight at 2 to 3 pounds for example, survive. However, the probability of neurological damage is high (Hack, Fanaroff, and Merkatz 1979). As a final note, low birth weight is refined today so that clinicians speak of babies whose weight is low but proportionate to a briefer gestation. We distinguish them from babies who are "small-for-date," that is, of low birth weight even when the gestation has gone to full term. The former may be an abrupt but spontaneously ended delivery, while the latter is a process of child development which is inherently below average, for a variety of causes.

Fetal Loss. While it would be helpful to apply these concepts to gestation and subsequent development in the nineteenth century, it is not possible. The concepts are comparatively recent and reports of 100 to 150 years ago tend to be summaries of relatively gross events. To be sure, there are early accounts of specific aspects of development. Forbes (1971) reports from the parish records at Aldgate in 1589 that someone recorded the delivery of a "chylde stillborne beinge but a span long" (9 inches). The first study on fetuses was executed by de Montbeliard in the eighteenth century. His later studies of his son's height—in the premetric units, pieds, pouces, and lignes—were eventually published in a work by Sonnini in 1799. However, de Montbeliard's work had virtually no influence at the time. We get an indirect glimpse into the situation just after the Napoleonic Wars in a report from the Westminster General Dispensary in 1818, quoted by Farr (1865). One hundred and twenty-eight women had 305 miscarriages over the years. One hundred and eighty-five of the 305 were in the first trimester of gestation. The same women had 556 live children. The ratio of spontaneous abortions to live births was 3:5.6; that is, for every two children delivered, a third child was lost through what we call today fetal wastage. Dr. A.B. Granville reported belatedly in 1860 on deliveries to twelve thousand women (N = 12,478) in the years between 1818 and 1828. The stillborn rate was 1:45 for these "Females of the Industrial classes in the Metropolis" who, like Farr's cases, were delivered at the Westminster General Dispensary.

In 1844, Edwin Chadwick reported to the Health of Towns Commissioners on fetal loss. He reported that he had focused inquiries on a group of one hundred families. Over the years they had experienced 251 deaths and a still greater, but unspecified, number of spontaneous abortions.

The end of gestation and the process of delivery posed another crisis for the unborn child. Obstetrics in the nineteenth century saw the introduction of refinements in forceps. Queen Victoria's acceptance of weak chloroform at the delivery of her eighth child, Leopold, from Dr. John Snow did much to increase its acceptance. At the time, 1853, there were moralists—undoubtedly male—who insisted that childbirth was necessarily painful in conformity to a biblical injunction. Actually, there was a better case than the religious, because a soporific given to the mother crosses the placenta and reaches the fetus. That connection, however, was not made at the time of Victoria's confinement in 1851. It became fashionable to accept "Chloroform à la Reine" (Miller 1978). Anesthesia popularized a degree of oblivion during an act in which today's young women often participate as active and cooperative partners. Not the least benefit is that sedation avoided by the mother is also avoided by the infant; introduction of anesthesia undoubtedly helped mothers but may also have depressed vital functions in babies. In either case, the risk to babies at delivery was enormous. One-sixth of those interred in the small cemetery at Quarry Hill, in Leeds, were reported by Dr. Baker in 1842 to be stillborn. As a national index of health the picture is blurred, however. Lord Shaftesbury spoke of at least sixty thousand stillbirths annually as the national rate (1858). Thirteen years later, Dr. Farr put the annual rate that thirty at forty thousand stillbirths in England and Wales (Hewitt 1975).

It seems likely that the hazards of delivery increased the death rate among those who were healthy in utero. A prime example is the occurrence of multiple pregnancies. We know little of such deliveries beyond twins; numbers above that seem not to have survived. In 1860, Charles Dickens recalled from his own childhood in "Dullborough" being taken to see dead quintuplets. Apparently, the phenomenon was of an order to lead the family to exhibit the infants and solicit donations from strangers. Death was a common experience, but death of children on such a scale became a public event. The Sara Gamps of the nineteenth century, in the lady's own words, went to a lying-in or a laying-out with equal relish. For many children, the terms had quite the same meaning, for life and death occurred in substantial numbers.

Statistics

In the case of statistical concepts to study the phenomena of development, they remained little more than counting on a large scale until the end of the nineteenth century. Following the original work on the

Bills of Mortality by John Graunt in 1662, Edmund Halley presented to the Royal Society in 1693 some statistics from Breslau. In that paper Halley gives the death rate for children under one year as 28%, and for children from one to six years as 44%. By age six, the proportion of a birth cohort still alive was only 56%. Turning to the Bills of Mortality a century after John Graunt (and also William Petty, according to John Aubrey), Thomas Short in 1750 introduced a slightly narrower focus into his descriptive statistics. He reported that in the period 1728–1743 children under two years died more frequently in September and October. For children between two and five years, the peak months were March to May, and September. Short also reported child mortality data from Breslau. In the first six years of life, mortality was 56%. Between the first known lecture on statistics at the University of Helmstadt in 1660 (John 1883) and the work of Fisher in the early decades of the twentieth century quantitative methods evolved in scope and in scale rather than in powers of inference. The first statistical bureau in Prussia started in 1806 under Professor Hebart, who apparently managed actuarial studies. Demography was popularized among scholars by Bertillon, who is generally remembered for his work on fingerprints and scientific criminology. Until the 1890s, the volumes of the *Journal of the Royal Statistical Society,* as it was by then styled, consisted of social statistics rather than mathematical papers. The first sophisticated application of statistics to social data for the purpose of influencing social policy was that of Yule in 1899. He used regression to study changes in the rate of pauperism in preceding decades; this was the first study to depart seriously from the tradition of using statistics to describe literacy, births, and deaths.

Death

When we turn to the lives and deaths of children prior to the second and third decades of the nineteenth century there is material scattered across the centuries. In the period 1250–1438, the life expectancy of Britons was no better than that of Roman Spain. Of those who survived the high rate of infant mortality, nearly a quarter, 22.4%, would be dead by age twenty-one (Russell 1937). In Cowgill's (1970) analysis of the population of York from the sixteenth century to the nineteenth century, only 2% were still alive at age forty in the sixteenth century. For

Colyton, in Devon, Wrigley's (1972) analyses show that life expectancy in the sixteenth century was higher than in the seventeenth or eighteenth century; the middle range estimates of life being, respectively, 43.2, 36.9, and 41.8 years. For children, the mortality rate for ages one to four years was highest between 1650 and 1699. Muller (1969) estimated that the average age of death in Normandy in 1730 was fifty-one; the average marriage lasted nine years, and the typical man or woman of fifty years had buried nine relatives and friends. In another part of France, Rumont, in the eighteenth century, over half the newborns were dead within a month, and three-quarters were dead by age five (Robert 1970).

In 1855, James Dawson McBurney ("Burn") published his Autobiography of a Beggar Boy. In his early fifties he reported, "During my wedded life I have had sixteen births, and twelve deaths to provide for." Vincent (1978) says that the deaths had risen to thirteen in the 1882 edition of the autobiography. For children in North Shropshire, Jones (1976) reported death rates of approximately sixty per one thousand births in the eighteenth century. This rate is about half of that in the preceding century, and represents deaths in the first month of life. Within the first year of life, the rate was about two hundred per thousand from the mid-sixteenth century to mid-eighteenth century, and it fell by about one-third towards the end of the eighteenth century. In the same last half-century, for England as a whole, Dr. Edmonds (1836) reported the following mortality rates for children under five years: 1730–1749, 74.5%; 1750–1769, 63.0%; 1770–1789, 51.5%. In Preston, mortality under five years between 1783 and 1791 ranged from 29.28% to 44.93%, or between one-quarter and one-half of all preschoolers (Clay 1844). For York, between 1770 and 1831 the average at death was 30.8 years, and the proportion dying under five years was 36.44%, according to Dr. Laycock, who gave evidence before the Health of Towns Commission in 1844 (Laycock 1844). Comparatively speaking, Liverpool in 1840 resembled Geneva in the seventeenth century, according to the great Chadwick (1842).

Families. In considering the death of little children before the nineteenth century, percentages and proportions are useful, but they do not transmit the carnage, the "slaughter of the innocents," which has been the sad and sorry tale throughout all of history. Until quite recently, a little before the span of people still alive, parents lost many children and bore a heavy burden of grief. In the eighteenth century, Hester Thrale and her husband, a brewer, saw only four of twelve children survive to adulthood (Quennell 1972). A little later, and closer to our period, Queen Anne endured eighteen pregnancies from which none of the children lived. Edward Gibbon was the only one of seven children to survive, a condition which Quennell says Gibbon considered "strictly a probable event," in the experience of parents. Robert Burns was one of nine survivors of eighteen births. It is pleasant to report the contrary, however. Jane Marshall, wife of a Leeds flax-spinning entrepreneur, bore eleven children and lost only one in infancy (Rimmer 1960).

In the instances just mentioned, relatively well-informed people saw death of children all around them. Far worse was the situation of abandoned children of the poor, the foundlings. One of the great movements of the eighteenth century was the establishment of places of asylum for abandoned children and orphans. Josiah Hanway and Thomas Coram were active in early philanthropy.

Foundlings. Unfortunately, any congregation of people, well or sick, old or young, was an occasion of risk, as it is today. For us, schools are the medium by which measles and other illnesses of childhood move through a community. For abandoned children, Foundling hospitals were a virtual sentence of death, however benign their establishment. Tanner (1981) reports that only 4000 of 14,934 admitted to the Foundling Hospital in Coram's Fields lived long enough to be apprenticed to a trade. In Dublin, the Foundling Hospital had a mortality rate of one-quarter in the period 1800–1808; only one child in five reached age ten (Robins 1980). For the three decades 1796–1826, virtually all of fifty-two thousand infants received died. In 1830, the Foundling Hospital was closed. In contrast, French policy and practice based on laws promulgated in 1801 and 1811 were comparatively benign and effective (Fuchs 1984).

In 1837, the French investigators Terme and Monfalcon reported eighteenth-century data on mortality from Foundling asylums. In 1788, mortality among foundlings in Florence and St. Petersburg was 40%; two years earlier, in Barcelona, it had been 60%; in Paris, the proportion in 1789 was 45%; and in Dublin in 1791 it was a phenomenal 88%. High mortality rates in foundling homes persisted well into the nineteenth century. The absence of breast feeding was considered the prime noninfectious cause of death by Dr. Routh in 1857, plus what he referred to as "abuse of the recumbent position of infants," a phrase which is later explained in *Lancet* as excessive swaddling. Dr. Routh reported mortality highest in spring among residents of foundling homes, and the low point was autumn, with a rate of mortality about one-half that of the spring.

Death Clubs. When Edmund Halley published his paper on the incidence of birth and death in Breslaw in 1693 he gave impetus to the practice of establishing Tontines. They were associations of people who jointly raised capital through their subscriptions. After a set period of years, or, at the extreme, on the death of the penultimate surviving member, the proceeds and profits were distributed. Halley's life tables became the basis for what is now the life insurance business, which during the nineteenth century often took the form of burial clubs. The existence of such groups needs to be understood in terms of Victorian psychology. Two elements will suffice; first, there was a theme, or perhaps undercurrent, of fear of being buried alive (proper attention to the end of life can be glimpsed in the writings of Poe); second, working-class respectability required a decent interment rather than the ignominy of being flung into the paupers' common grave.

In the early 1840s, William Cooke-Taylor undertook a tour of the manufacturing regions of Lancashire and noted that many workers belonged to burial clubs. For a relatively small investment, working people had the capital for a respectable burial. In the interim, they had an association to identify with in an age when fraternal groups were blooming in the North. A silk weaver told Cooke-Taylor (1842) that he belonged to an association of silk weavers called Noah's Ark; he paid eighteen pence a month and had received slightly less than four pounds in benefits. "All our children are in a burying club," he said, and he went on to say that "the payment is a penny a week." His foresight against the "strictly probably event" cited by Gibbon a century before was not unreasonable. The hazard arose when care-givers insured the lives of those they were paid by working mothers to protect. This practice compounded the risk posed by liberal use of opiates to keep children quiet.

We glimpse the problem of "Death Clubs" in the Reverend Clay's report from Preston to the Health of Towns Commissioners in 1844. In reply to a woman friend of the Reverend Clay who proposed to console a bereaved mother, she received the comment from the child's wet nurse, "Oh, never mind, ma'am, it's in two burial clubs." The "respectable secretary" of a burial society told the Reverend Clay of a child whose burial cost three pounds, and on whom three societies payed out nearly seventeen pounds. In the case of a child dying in Middlesborough, the parent's grief was in part compounded by the fact that "it would not have mattered so much in another week, as by then the insurance would have come in" (Hunt 1981). Returning to Preston, we find that the mortality rate among children under age five was generally 36%; among children insured with burial clubs, the rate was 68%. One child, according to Sauer (1978), was insured with nineteen clubs. To Dr. Ikin (1864), the situation was a public disgrace, and he said that his views of the unnecessarily high rate of infant mortality was shared by eleven of his medical brethren in Leeds. The Infant Life Protection Act of 1874 was proposed to reduce death due to disease. More concretely, the work of the Royal Commission on friendly societies reduced the death benefit on children under age five to six pounds, and to ten pounds on children under age ten. Under legislation passed in 1876, only parents or their direct, authorized representatives could be beneficiaries. By these progressions, the abuses which turned burial clubs into death clubs were reversed. However, as late as the 1890s the Reverend B. Waugh put the number of children killed in order to obtain insurance benefits at one thousand per year. As long as child mortality rates were high, the risk of detection was low. With improvements in survival rates generally came improvement in infants' probability of escaping murder for profit within the lower classes.

Mortality and Social Class

One of the realities of life and death in the nineteenth century was the marked discrepancy in life expectancy by social class among those who survived infancy. Edwin Chadwick told the Statistical Society of London in 1844 that the average age of dying in Manchester was eighteen years. He quoted Dr. Willis in Dublin who gave the mean age at death of the working class as 18.65 years. Among Bradford woolcombers, who were mostly Irish immigrants, the average age at death was sixteen years, with 70% of them under age fifteen (Thompson 1984). For the six years from 1837 to 1843, Reverend Clay (1844) calculated the rate of mortality of children by fathers' occupations. Mortality among children of Preston professional men and gentlemen was 17%. For tradesmen and operatives, it was 38% and 55%, respectively. From this we see that mortality risk doubled and tripled as the social level of fathers dropped.

Reverend Clay took his statistics one step further by calculating how many children would still be alive by social class at the end of the first, fifth, and fiftieth years of a birth cohort. At one year of age, the proportions of children born to the gentry, tradesmen, and operatives who were still alive would be 90.8%, 79.6%, and 68.2%, respectively. At the fifth birthday, survivors in the same parents' occupational groups would be 82.4%, 61.8%, and 44.6%. At age fifty, the respective proportions of survivors would be 56.0%, 28.1%, and 15.6%. In this regard, there is an interesting account of the ages of factory workers in Leeds presented by "Alfred" (S.H.G. Kydd) in 1857. He reported that among 1,079 male workers, only 22 were age forty or over, and only 9 were over age fifty. While not precisely an index of mortality, this age structure in the work force suggests that a relatively brief working life in factories was the rule.

In the same year, and testifying before the Health of Towns Commission to whom Chadwick spoke, John Johnson, the Registrar of Shoreditch, placed the life expectancy of the gentry at forty-seven years, that of trades people at twenty-three years, and that of labouring people at nineteen years. Of 1,300 laboring class deaths, the number under age ten was a phenomenal 802, or 61% of all the deaths. Another witness before the same Commissioners, but a year later, Mr. T. Shapter, brought information from Exeter on mortality by occupational level. The death rate among the well-to-do was 1.28%, and among the poor it was 2.69%. Commenting on a report to the National Association for the Promotion of Social Science by Mr. Robinson (1861), Dr. Gray reported that the life expectancy of the wealthiest class in Dublin was forty-eight years, and only twenty years among the "Artisan class." In 1894, Dublin's death rate was still high, especially among children, according to H.R. Jones. He reported mortality among children up to age five in four groups. The mortality rate among children of the upper class was 18.2 per thousand; among the middle class, 59.2; among the "artisans," 72; and among what Jones and other Victorians called the *residuum,* a startling 116.9. As late as 1930, infant mortality among children of low-paid English workers was still twice the rate prevalent among the middle and upper classes (125:53), according to Kuczynski (1946).

Today, we find gross differences in rates of child mortality offensive and intolerable. Only in the Third World, and in the pockets of distress we call the Fourth World, do gross discrepancies persist. The infant mortality rate for Western Africa is 146 per 1,000; the life expectancy is forty-six years, which is the allotted span of Dr. Gray's Dublin gentlemen (World's 1979). In Western Europe, it is 14 per 1,000, with a life expectancy of seventy-two years. We have come a long way in the developed countries, while other countries are, figuratively, still in the dark days of the last century, with childrens' death an everyday event.

Interment

In some respects, death was a theme of childhood and children's experiences in Victorian Britain. While the lives of children themselves were always at risk, and at a rate many times higher than today, death was also around them. Routinely, they encountered the complex of events which surrounded death, and after elaborate ritual, interment with witnesses. This last element ensured interment. Mearns (1883) reported that the bodies of nine infants were found in a box on an undertaker's premises in Long Lane, Bermondsey. Children were not shielded from death, because it usually occurred within the rooms occupied by the living, and they witnessed the loss of brothers, sisters, parents, and relatives. In any case, death forced itself into children's lives as epidemics spread and communicable diseases, the "zymotic disease" of Victorian pathologists, spread rapidly. Death had familiarity for children, and popular culture of the period provided an appropriate degree of response.

The nineteenth century was a religious age in Britain. While the pattern of church-going did not conform to the ascendency of the established church, people were fundamentally religious; that is, they believed in an afterlife and saw no alternative to Christianity in its permutations as the code to guide one's ethical and moral choices. These convictions were imparted to children early in life, so that they brought to the shock of sudden death a set of background values which a particular death served to reinforce. In practice, these inculcations were rather heavy-handed by our standards. Walvin (1982) has presented examples of poems for children.

Remember Kate Morris—poor, dear little girl So merry, so active and bright; So happy and full of gay spirits one morn A scorched blackened corpse the same night.

There is an explicitness here which oversteps the boundary of discretion when dealing with young minds, but death itself was not discreet; it was sudden, vile, and brutal, as friends, brothers, and sisters, and parents were taken. The culture sought to prepare children in a fashion as abrupt as the sight of ill-clothed, ill-fed people on city streets. As the poem had it,

. . . there is no armour against fate, Death lays his icy hands on Kings. . . .

When death laid his icy hand on the individual, he also put another hand into the purse. At all levels of society, a decent funeral was the tidy end to whatever style of life had preceded it. Two themes may be discerned, propriety and the obligation to put on a display of respectability. This was managed through care of the deceased, a process of visitation and interment. Within this process are the elements which sustain people in a period of grief. When one does not quite know what is called for, the support of precedent and a network of kin is highly beneficial. Grief at the loss of a child, or a second or third child, is something we rarely experience; but our forebears were always going to funerals, those of kith if not of kin. The propriety and convention of funerals provided roles for individuals to assume. After the interment, people wore black for extended periods of time, a phenomenon within living memory, which defined the bereaving in a public, conventional way.

Little children were not exempt from this practice, and they were expected to appear in decorous garments for prescribed periods contingent on who had died. Given the familiarity of death, people spent unbroken periods in black as first a parent, and then a brother or a child was claimed by sickness.

There was a circularity to sickness, death, and interment in the nineteenth century. To become ill was to experience a brush with death, because medicine provided little more than palliatives, and the body had to rely on its own mechanisms for the most part. When death ensued, interment became the second stage in the circular process. Until the reforms of Edwin Chadwick in the 1840s, cemeteries were a source of disease and illness to those attending funerals. Engels (1845) described the pauper burial ground of St. Brides as "a bare morass . . . filled with heaps of bones. Every Wednesday the paupers are thrown into a ditch . . . loosely covered . . . to be reopened the next Wednesday . . . as long as one more can be forced in."

Mr. Helsdan, a Dissenting lay minister who was probably a Baptist, reported to the Select Committee of 1842 on the health of towns that bodies were buried as close to the surface as two feet (Helsdan 1842). In one exchange in 1842, a Commissioner put a sharp question to John Eyles, bricklayer and part-time grave digger.

Q. "What was the depth of the coffin of Thomas Beale, a child?"
A. ". . . it was about two feet six inches from the surface. . . ."

The men who dug graves were, according to the Reverend Mr. Helsdan "a low, depraved, drunken class of men." The grave diggers themselves viewed drinking as medicinal in view of the stench that emanated from the graves. Contemporary accounts speak of summer smells and clouds of black flies surrounding graves opened to receive one more coffin. The density of interment was phenomenal; the graveyard of St. Martin-in-the-fields, a space about two hundred yards square, was alleged to have received sixty to seventy thousand coffins over the years. Enon Chapel was probably the worst, however.

We note, in passing, a second fear of the Victorians, which was that they would be buried alive, In fact, they had greater reason to dread being plucked from hallowed ground, for only by that mechanism could the great numbers of interments be managed. Testimony on the subject is graphic; to the question, "Can you not go so deep as three feet without finding a coffin?" A grave digger replied,

> No, you cannot, without moving children, or something; the children have been taken out and placed in a grave that is not above a foot and a half deep. Three bodies have been buried on the Sunday before and then there has been a grave ordered, and those children have been taken out . . ."

(Report 1842).

The consequences of graves so close to the surface was compounded by the number of coffins underneath. One witness before the Select Committee of 1840, "Walker of the Graveyards," said he knew of a grave twenty-three feet deep. The gases generated by its deteriorated contents were so noxious that a candle went out when only halfway to the bottom (Walker 1840). It was generally thought by physicians that malaria and typhus were vaporous products of ancient graveyards. The problems had been known for many years; one could smell them from a distance. One problem had an economic side, for grave diggers would sell children's coffin deal boards to the poor for fire wood (Walker 1846), and sell the lead from coffins for still more money. In 1817, an advertisement in *The Morning Chronicle* asserted that

> it is a well-known fact, that many hundred graves and vaults are constantly disturbed. . . the PATENT COFFIN. . . secures the mortal remains, but prevents the lead from being stolen. The additional price is three guineas and a half, and may be had at a few hours notice, of T. Jarvis and Son. . . .

The labors of Chadwick and Walker spurred reform. Parishes were enabled to combine in order to purchase jointly plots of land for new cemeteries. These tended to conform to well-established continental practices and were placed at a distance from the old sites. Eventually, cremation was introduced.

Another problem associated with a death in the family was the practice of delaying interment for several days. Respectability—but also custom lost in the midst of antiquity—required that the deceased be laid out, displayed, and made the occasion for a degree of hospitality. A full-scale wake required that the body not be left unattended and that quantities of drink as well as food be consumed. Friends and neighbors visited the house. In the case of a young blind boy, Toynbee (1844) reported that he was laid out in the neighbor's rooms. Unfortunately, the children of neighbor Hildebrand still needed a place to play, and a sick Hildebrand child needed a place to rest. The room assigned for the dead blind boy was fully used by the Hildebrand children, sick and well.

A complication invariably arose because interments were customary on Sundays, because a working day could not be spared. The consequence was that the family lived with the corpse until Sunday, and the risk of contracting infectious diseases was high. Thus, families not only lived with the deceased but ran the risk of joining him or her in saecula saeculorum. An instance was reported to the Health of Town Commissions of a body unburied for several weeks; the family was too poor to pay for a funeral and the deceased had to wait until there was enough cash at hand to pay the bill. In, How the Poor Live, Sims (1889) reported the case of a family with two daughters living in a room in Spitalfields. One child had died fifteen days before and remained unburied for lack of money. The appeal of the burial societies to those who recognized the inevitability of funeral expenses was high. Families would go to great lengths to avoid a pauper's grave. As late as 1854, despite the efforts of Southwood-Smith, Chadwick, and Walker, an Inspector of Burial Grounds in Bradford came away with a grisly memento, a jaw bone which had worked its way to the surface (Elliott 1982).

Such sites for interment in cities were a source of contamination of the water table. In such instances, poisoned water infiltrated wells and led to another cycle of illness and deaths. Sewers were also susceptible to damage, as grave diggers shoved coffins into whatever opening presented itself (Lewis 1952). At the Bayswater Road cemetery, coffins were known to explode (Meller 1981). Some of the drinking uniformly ascribed to grave diggers was an attempt to resist infection from graves and to restore their spirits after earning a little money by obliging the Sexton (Walker 1839).

It is clear that death and dying among a family's children has been the heritage of mankind, and a few of today's parents struggle with the syndrome of sudden infant death—SIDS. Although the nineteenth century saw eventual improvement, there was enough familiarity with death to make it a pessimistic theme of daily life. Even so, inquiry reveals things worse than the universality of children's suffering infantile diarrhea and infectious diseases—zymotic diseases as they were termed.

Within these phenomena we glimpse through the centuries the sinister theme of calculated death. It arises in the first recorded way in Captain John Graunt's (1662) essay on the Bills of Mortality. In his *Natural and Political Observations Made Upon the Bills of Mortality,* Graunt makes brief reference to "overlaying" as a cause of infants' deaths. The term refers to a situation in which a mother takes her infant into her bed and the infant is smothered as the mother overlays it—presumably by the normal process of turning in her sleep. The resulting death of the child was recorded as an accidental death. One response to overlaying was to develop ways to protect vulnerable infants from smothering by accident. Versions of a sort of woven basket were developed to cover the sleeping infant. The "arcutio" was one version (Caulfield 1930), while the Swedish version was called, by a Dr. Berg, the "Wattje" (Farr 1866). Sometimes the question of life or death was open to bidding. Greaves (1863) reported that "birth attendants" named two prices, one for delivery of a live child and a second figure for a more sinister outcome.

Returning to overlaying, we see that this convenient term recorded in tidy fashion a broad range of events. In Graunt's time, overlaying was recognized, but it was not an acute problem. By the end of the eighteenth century, the problem had grown, and it strained credulity that so many mothers had rolled over their infants in bed. Friedrich Engels, in a letter written in 1844 (Engels 1975) recorded an instance from Winchester in 1827 in which a woman was found guilty of infanticide. Two decades after Engels, Dr. Lankester asserted persistently that there must have been twelve thousand instances of "women in London who have murdered their children" (Miscellanea 1865), referring to mothers of illegitimate children in particular. Other particular sources to which the death of infants were traced by the Victorians were excessive drinking on Saturday nights, resulting in a day-specific and cyclic rise in recorded deaths (Jones 1894), and the use of Godfrey's Cordial (Hunter 1864; Jordan, 1987). Euthanasia has been speculated on by McLaughlin (1974) as an explanation concerning another group of children. Murder for profit in the form of the "death clubs" in which children were heavily insured was still another form of infanticide, but one that differed in the broader age range of children involved. The big drop in instances of overlaying was classified by Smith (1934) within the general decline in infant mortality evident as late as 1906. A decline in abuse of alcohol was the mechanism rather than passage of laws improving health and education in the middle third of the nineteenth century.

Closely grouped with overlaying was "starved at Nurse," meaning that wet-nursing had killed the child (Illick 1974). Both terms reflect a sense of inevitability which is only understandable when we recall

Graunt's dictum that "about one third of all that were ever quick die under five years old, and about thirty six per Centum under six".

However, to later generations it seemed reasonable to take a less accepting attitude and to be more scrupulous when considering infant deaths. In the late eighteenth century, Jonas Hanway (renowned among students for two things: not having invented the umbrella and for pioneering the care of children) began to ask sharp questions. Hanway found that Mary Poole, a children's nurse (or baby-sitter, as we term care-givers who take children into their homes), had an incredible stretch of bad luck—or worse—in one year. During that period, twenty-three children in the parish of St. Clement Dane's were placed in her care; by the end of the year, only five were still alive. At the same time, Hanway's inquiries revealed that none of the fifty-three children placed on the charity of a parish—the form of local government—survived after five years. Dependent children (orphans and foundlings) simply did not survive unless taken in by generous families, as with Fieldings' Tom Jones, adopted by Squire Allworthy.

"Baby-farming" was the practice of putting children away by paying someone to be a foster-parent. Advertisements in newspapers euphemistically conveyed the message that children could be boarded, and in a style which meant the patron need never hear of the infant again. In an age when the appearance of propriety, as opposed to the reality, was the key to respectability, there was a steady demand for ways to dispatch children from households. Healthy fees, as much as the prospective client seemed willing to part with for an anonymous and discrete service, kept the machinery operating. As one neighbor observed on the occasion of a public outcry over a case of infanticide, pregnant women and babies entered an establishment, but no babies seemed to leave. The baby-farmers offered a range of services which began with abortion. Beyond that there was accouchement, which few infants survived very long in a process which was downright grizzly on occasions. For infants already delivered, care in a manner leading to early death, speeded by medication, was also tendered.

An instance of baby-farming arose in Brixton in the summer of 1870. Several dead infants were found in a small geographic area, and it seemed obvious that a thriving business in murdering infants was in operation. The police charged that Margaret Ellis Waters and her sister Sarah were receiving the substantial sum of five pounds for each child they undertook to take into their home. The trail of infant bodies convinced a jury; and with Victorian certainty and swiftness, the proprietor of the Brixton charnelhouse, Margaret Waters, was hanged. A worse case was that discovered in 1895–96. During the winter, the bodies of forty strangled infants were discovered and traced to Mrs. Dyer of Reading who was, in due course, hanged for her known crimes (Hoffer and Hull 1981).

This degree of swift infanticide was the outer edge of a complex which for older but encumbering children began with boarding schools. Dotheboy's Hall in Yorkshire was not an exception in its abuse of youngsters, and Dickens's pen expressed reality in an unexaggerated and well-told way. Baby-farming was a social institution which persisted because it had lots of clients. It was the ultimate form of abuse of children, a phenomenon which ran through the Victorian society. At best, it was mouthed as "spare the rod and spoil the child." At worst, it was a savage delight in calculated cruelty which lead, in the end, to degradation of children and their death. The abusing foreman in the factory and the alcoholic farmer in the home were other expressions of a violent society whose ethos was as much private assault as it was public propriety and conventional morality. However, not every birth was associated with propriety and morality, to the detriment of the children in question.

Illegitimacy Rates

Undoubtedly, illegitimate children were at considerable risk of neglect. Our grasp of this set of youngsters is not very good. As with today, the occasional child from the wrong side of the blanket could be incorporated quite easily into a family with older children. Elsewhere (Jordan and Spaner 1981) we have reported current data on children born from juvenile pregnancies (mothers aged thirteen to fifteen). In those instances, the child became the youngest child of the grandmother in terms of nurture. This is a traditional, subcultural mode of solving the problem; the role of the child is that of youngest member of the household, and it undoubtedly occurred in nineteenth-century Britain. An additional item is the occasional regional-cultural expectation that marriage need not occur until pregnancy is established. In that style, premarital conception is the more precise formulation. The world is quite used to the alleged premature-by-month delivery of seven-pound babies to happy families.

Our attention to illegitimacy in the nineteenth century is not a concern for the wedding of the parents but for the presence of a bread-winning spouse to support the child. Data gathered by Hollingsworth (1981) suggest that there were regional differences in rates of illegitimacy. Norwich had the highest illegitimacy rate per thousand births in 1834 amongst towns in England and Wales, followed by Yarmouth and

Bolton. The lowest rates were in Swansea, London, and Plymouth. In the following twelve years, the rate per thousand live births dropped in the three towns with high rates, and rose in the three lowest-rate towns. It is in the nature of the statistics of the time that we cannot immediately conclude that these two trends were secular over the next decade (i.e., were getting better or worse as social trends). Equally tenable is the view that the six towns were extremes of a statistical distribution. In that construction, research workers expect regression towards the average when anything at the end of a continuum is measured for a second or third time. Lest this seem too conservative a view, consider that illegitimacy rates generally fell across the nineteenth century. For the years 1861 to 1901, rates generally dropped in England and Wales from 18.5 cases per thousand live births to 9.2. In 1861, the rate in Radnorshire had been 39.2 per thousand live births, and it fell to 14.4 by 1901. In Surrey it fell in the same forty years from 11.3 to 5.9. With this trend came a decrease in the number of children vulnerable to neglect and the attendant risk of disease and death due to faulty habits of nutrition and care. Among them were medicines and administration of harmful drugs.

Godfrey's Cordial

To a generation which sees the use of narcotic and hypnotic drugs as a new problem, there may be a slight relief in learning that the abuse of drugs is not new. Today's problems of drug-taking as a recreation of the bored or alienated has antecedents. Historically, the role of drugs has been for benign ends rather than to escape the tedium of life in the late twentieth century. A second difference is that previous periods of drug abuse were less conducive to crime; the reason is that there were few laws controlling the retailing of drugs. However, common to both the earlier and current phases of drug-taking is the element of danger to health and the virtual certainty of physiological dependence. The prime example in the nineteenth century was Thomas deQuincy, whose addiction began with a toothache (Jordan 1987).

To understand the origin of drug abuse, we must return to the earliest days of man, when foraging led to identification of roots which relieved sickness or which led to stages of religious awareness. The distinctions we now draw between medicine, religion, and magic were not evident to our earliest ancestors. By the sixteenth century, the place of extracts of plants in medical practice was central. Only with the advent of anesthesia in the middle of the nineteenth century did surgery become something more than another form of putting one's life at risk. Prior to the reduction of shock by anesthesia, pharmacy was about all the sick could turn to. Even today, digitalis, originally derived from the Foxglove, has a place in medicine, although many new, synthetic drugs have appeared to treat heart disease.

In the nineteenth century, a parent seeking help for a sick child had little to choose from beyond sedation. Street vendors sold "Walker's Chinese Pills," and the columns of *The Times* in 1839 advertised *Succedaneum* for decayed teeth. This product was developed by the "surgeon-dentist," Mr. Thomas, and could be purchased from several apothecaries in London. It seems likely that relief would be only temporary and that the pain would return. Much the same outcome followed administration of "Parr's Life Pills" (c. 1842) and "Pritchard's Teething and Fever Powders" twenty years later.

Perhaps the longest record of service lies with the juice of the poppy. Extracted by means of an incision in the head, the secretion yields the opium family of derivatives. When taken under the name "poppy tea," the drug seemed only benign; as "Dalbey's Carminative," its effects were more serious. The standard guides to medical practice in the late eighteenth century advised that children be given laudanum, or opium suspended in wine, to help them sleep. The drug, according to Berridge (1979), was frequently described in the middle of the nineteenth century as conducive to long life. So widespread was the use of Godfrey's Cordial that Dr. H. J. Hunter reported to the Privy Council in 1864 "the horrid statement made by almost every surgeon in the marshland, that there was not a labourer's house in which the bottle of opiate was not to be seen, and not a child but got it in some form." Twenty years before, the Health of Towns Commission was told that in Preston sixteen hundred families were giving "Godfrey" to their infants (Clay 1844). The salutary effects extended to include veterinary practice, and animals took poppy extract to fatten them up.

In some parts of the United Kingdom, endemic diseases under the generalized name of the ague, probably fevers and rheumatism for the most part, were tolerable only when treated with poppy tea. This was especially true in the Fens, where low lands adjacent to the Wash were always damp, and where susceptibility to aches and fevers was high (Report 1859).

The author of the anonymous Surgical Lectures in the *Lancet* in 1824, was Dr. Astley Cooper; he reported that he

> knew a woman in tolerable circumstances, in a village in Norfolk who was in the habit of taking large quantities of opium; she would buy a pint of laudanum at a time, at the chemist's shop . . . (Cooper 1824).

A few years after, in 1832, Christison reported to the *London Medical Gazette* the case of "a young lady of five and twenty (who) has taken it for fifteen years." When she was ten, her nurse secretly gave her opium, and "the unhappy lady was subsequently compelled to keep up the practice for her comfort" (Christison 1832). In an age when discretion was highly prized, the widespread notion that opium and tobacco were equally benign aids to coping with stresses of life was discredited quite slowly by general experience. In 1840, Sir Bernard Brodie observed to a group of colleagues that opium-eating "could never demoralize the habits and shorten life as gin-drinking did." It was easy to resist the idea that a substance readily at hand, which gave obvious relief to people with a variety of disorders of body and mind in an age with few specific treatments, was dangerous. Indeed, the great Sydenham was reported by Jeffries (1840) to have said of opium that "if it were expunged from the pharmacopeia, he would give up the practice of medicine." A victim of the prescription of opium was Jane Welsh Carlyle. In a letter to Mrs. Russel written at Cheyne Row in 1863, Jane spoke of her physician, Dr. Quain, sending her "an embrocation of opium, aconite, camphur, and chloroform" (Simpson and Simpson 1977).

Clearly, opium and its derivatives had more than folk wisdom to support them. The absence of alternatives is most striking, but there was scientific respectability too. In the 1660s, the great Chemist Robert Boyle visited Germany and made the acquaintance of the scientist-apothecary Ambroise Hackwitz. Returning to London with Boyle, Hackwitz did two things. First, he opened a shop in Southampton Row. There, according to Thompson (1929), he prepared Royal English Drops, essences for care of the hair, and medications. The second thing he did, allegedly, was change his name to Godfrey. His cordial for soothing fussy babies was most effective, and Godfrey's Cordial entered the scene. A more recent explanation by Berridge and Edwards (1981) traces the preparation to Thomas Godfrey of Hunsdon, in Hertfordshire. It was still in use under the name "Mother's Friend" in Salford in the first quarter of the twentieth century, according to Roberts (1973). The widespread usage in the mid-nineteenth century was said to have begun one hundred years before, according to a Manchester druggist conversing with Angus Reach of the *Morning Chronicle* in 1850 (Razzell and Wainwright 1973). Berridge (1978) cites de Quincy's account of opium consumption in Manchester in the early 1800s. Dr. William Buchan had warned of the danger to infants posed by opiates and alcohol in the eighteenth century. In Dr. Samuel P. Griffitts's 1797 edition of Buchan, physicians were warned that, "by errors of this kind I will venture to say that one half of the children who die annually in London, lose their lives" (Buchan 1797).

The economics of opium as a soporific for teething infants and adults with cramps were appealing. On the one hand, poppies grew wild in the fields, and there were efforts to grow them commercially near Enfield and in Norfolk during our period. On the other hand, opium became obtainable in commercial quantities from the East. Speaking to the Royal Medical and Chirurgical Society in 1840, Dr. Jeffreys reported to the meeting on 24 November statistics on the import of opium. He stated that the amount of opium brought into the country in 1820 had been 16,169 pounds. In the next twenty years, it rose nearly ten times to 131,204 pounds. According to Berridge (1978), consumption per thousand of the population rose from 2 pounds in 1830 to 3 pounds in the late 1850s. Some of the 50% increase was in the form of patent medicines such as cough remedies. A.B., a "chemist and druggist" in Nottingham, told Parliamentary Commissioners in 1841 that he knew a pharmacist who sold a gallon of laudanum per week (Report 1843). The fact is that opium-taking in the early and mid-nineteenth century was cheaper than alcohol. Testifying before the Select Committee on Drunkenness in 1834, the Rev. Robert Ousby said that opium was widely used by "agriculturists and small shopkeepers," primarily because they could become intoxicated less expensively (Report 1834). The volume of business can be gauged from testimony provided by the Nottingham Coroner. In 1841, he informed the Parliamentary Commission on children (Report 1843) that a local druggist mixed thirteen hundred weight of treacle with dissolved opium, annually. Two decades later, in a letter to the *Lancet* from the village of Rolvenden, in Norfolk, Dr. Thomas Joyce reported that about three ounces of opium were sold weekly in the district (Joyce 1869).

In Ely in 1850, the cost of laudanum per ounce had dropped in recent years from sixpence to threepence. Opium had declined in price from two-thirds of a penny to one-quarter of a penny per ounce. While the *Morning Chronicle's* reporter was questioning a retailer, a woman purchased one ounce of laudanum for a penny and followed it with a chaser of liquor also bought for a penny. Not every purchaser was so indelicate; farmers would buy it allegedly for their pigs, and some people made many small purchases at several shops in order to be discreet. The *Morning Chronicle's* reporter, probably Charles Brooks, said that a pennyworth of opium was as effective as a shilling's worth of "spirituous liquors" (Razzell and Wainwright 1973).

As late as 1894, a member of the Royal Statistical Society reported that a village in North Wales consumed three quarts of laudanum per week (Jones 1894). In Nottingham, a druggist, who was a member of the Town Council, said that he personally sold about four hundred gallons of laudanum annually. He estimated that half of it was taken by children (Opiates 1862). Clearly, sales were brisk and uncontrolled. Cheap to sell means cheap to make; in the *Morning Chronicle* of January 4, 1840, the public learned from an old woman that

> we took a penn'orth of aniseed, a quarter of a pound of treacle, and a penn'orth of laudanum ($1/4$ oz.); then we stewed down the aniseed with water and mixed up the whole in a quart bottle.

Hewitt (1958) stated that Godfrey's Cordial contained 1.5 ounces per quart. Of course, the strength depended on the whim of the preparer. In 1841, A.B. also reported that the Godfrey's Cordial sold to Nottingham lacemakers had more laudanum than that sold in London. Sometimes Sassafras was added (Horter 1864) and also "saccharine substances. . . to make the opium palatable to children" (Coulhart 1844).

When the physiological dependence created by opiates was recognized by the victim or by worried relatives and friends, the problem of treatment arose. Arthur Conan Doyle allowed his Sherlock Holmes to take drugs, an element introduced from Dr. Doyle's clinical observations. When the opiate was stopped suddenly, the sequelae, according to Dr. Joyce of Rolvendon (1869), were "overwhelming sickness, complete prostration of body and mind, severe rigors, great loathing of food, an utter inability to sleep, constant purging. . . woebegone expression." Treatment prescribed by Dr. Joyce in 1869 was that which he ascribed to Dr. Christison, "a liberal supply of brandy, the use of suppositories of morphia, and the cautious exhibit of India hemp." The effects of brandy, morphia, and hashish might well have made the cure worse than the illness. Failure to do anything in cases of extreme addiction lead by stages to grave illness and to attempted suicide, according to a report by Dr. Palmer from the Lincolnshire Asylum (Report 1859).

In the case of children, especially infants, the picture was clouded by their inevitably high rate of mortality, and by the apparently benign effects of medication on fussy children. Clever advertising also masked the risks by use of labels which were comforting. Mothers could ask the druggist for opium and for laudanum, suggesting a self-conscious purchase of materials. However, the retailer of pharmaceuticals—today a figure whose counsel is sought for minor ailments by even the sophisticated—might suggest a handsome bottle with an appealing and authoritative label. In that case, a conscientious mother would purchase Godfrey's Cordial, or she might receive opiates under the names *Infant's Preservative, Mother's Blessing, Batley's Syrup, Infant's Quietness, Dalbey's Carminative, Anodyne Cordial, Mrs. Wilkinson's Soothing Syrup, Daffy's Elixir,* and *Adkinson's Royal Infant Preservative,* the latter intended to convey that it was used in the nursery at Windsor, which may have been the case. In the earliest days of the twentieth century in Salford, Roberts (1973) recalled Infants Preservative was also known by the more direct name of "knock-out-drops," for the care of children. In North Wales, laudanum plus sugar was sold as *Punch* for children (Jones, 1894). Curiously, a name from the period which still exists, although not as a lethal substance, is that of J. Collis Brown's Elixir.

The use of Godfrey's Cordial to ease a cough or soothe a child in the throes of teething is understandable. We do approximately the same thing today, but with greater care, remaining aware of the dangers of abuse. Recalling Sydenham's words cited earlier, Godfrey, as it was often called, must have appeared to be sovereign remedy, a panacea. If useful as a restorative, it might also be a preventive medication. On that note Godfrey's Cordial was frequently at hand. Indeed, one of the activities of confinement in some homes was preparation of a dose of Godfrey's Cordial under the rubric described by the *Lancet* as "solicitous domestic doctoring" (Dosing 1882). The medication was administered routinely to the newborn and was continued. In this regard there is an interesting parallel to recent times. Administering tranquilizing, soporific drugs to the mentally ill and to prisoners had been attacked in recent years as use of chemical straitjackets. That act of restraint has a parallel in swaddling infants. Speaking to the Royal Statistical Society, an Austrian physician, Dr. Herz, pointed out that in his country alcohol was used to sedate babies; Dr. Farr pointed out that sedating was the equivalent of swaddling, or restraining (Farr 1866).

In considering the impact of Godfrey's Cordial, we need to keep in mind that some babies were, by current standards, small-for-date. Chemicals are prescribed in proportion to body mass or weight. Given an infant of, say, five pounds, the margin for error was small even when drugs were administered by a physician. In 1838, the *London Medical Gazette* published a brief and curious "note bearing the signature of J. R." on the hazard of "five minims of laudanum in the course of a day", even under urgent circumstances (J. R. 1828). Dr. Farr (1866) repeated the warning, observing that "a few drops of laudanum are fatal" to newborns.

For all infants, including those of the privileged, the risk of death was always high in the nineteenth century. Friedrich Engels in "The Con-

ditions of the Working Class" (1845) wrote of workers' infants that after
a regimen of Godfrey's Cordial they grow "pale, feeble, wilted, and usually die before completing the second year." Thirty-four years later, in
1879, children receiving opium derivatives presented, "heavy death-like
sleep, accompanied by convulsive twitchings, the scorched swollen eye-
lids, the bluish pallor of countenance, and growing heaviness of expressions." (Outside, 1879) No one knows how many children's deaths were
caused by Godfrey's Cordial; however, Berridge (1978) reports that almost three hundred deaths below age five were officially reported to the
Registrar General in 1861. Smith's (1864) Practical Dietary reports the
practice of feeding infants Godfrey's Cordial to supplement "a sop made
with crumbs of bread, warm water with sugar, and in some cases a little
milk," according to Burnett (1979). Much the same diet was reported to
the Privy Council in 1861 by Dr. Greenhow, and the resulting susceptibility to infection undoubtedly contributed to deaths ascribed to other
causes.

The most pernicious use of Godfrey's Cordial was its employment
by women and children hired to care for infants and young children.
Opiates became the obvious way to keep several children quiet until
mothers returned from work (Jones 1894). The "composing bottle" of
water plus tincture of opium was routinely administered to infants received by the Dublin Foundling Hospital (Robins 1980), a practice which
probably accounts for the nearly total mortality rate at the institution in
the early decades of the nineteenth century. For those, such as Little
Buttercup in *H.M.S. Pinafore,* who, when "young and charming," engaged in "babyfarming" (Jordan 1982), Godfrey's Cordial must have reduced infants and toddlers to stupefaction by the score. Avery (1970)
quotes a conversation between two professional beggar women discus-
sing technical aspects of renting children from their parents or custodi-
ans.

> A shilling a-piece! Vy then you've been done, or babies is riz; one or
> t'other—I only give sixpence for mine, and they feeds 'em and Godfrey's
> Cordials 'em and all, afore I takes 'em, into the bargain!

From these materials we see that the hazards of growing up in rural and
industrialized regions were compounded by extensive use of opium derivatives to combat illness, but also as a quick and convenient way to prevent infants from being a bother. Of course, alcohol was also used, but
Godfrey's Cordial had the advantages of volume and convenience of
preparation. With syrup of white poppies available at threepence an
ounce, cost was not a problem (Parsinnen 1983). As the nineteenth cen-

tury passed, the suspicion grew that the evil consequences of sedating—if not actually anesthetizing—children were persistent. Dr. J. H. Langdon-Down, for whom the form of mental retardation is named, asked in 1866, "Has the Nurse dosed the child with opium? Can it be that when away from the family attendant the calomel powders were judiciously prescribed" (Jordan 1966)?

Eventually, legislation imposed controls on the manufacture and sale of dangerous drugs. The Pharmacy Act of 1868 was a typical piece of mid-nineteenth century legislation. It considered dangerous drugs but did not convey a thorough exploration of the problems, and so provided only a partial remedy. The times were not yet conducive to thorough analyses in the formation of public policy. It was not until a half century later that war, that great engine of social change, generated a 1916 law that controlled opiates. In addition, new medications appeared, and people placed less emphasis on home remedies such as Godfrey's Cordial. Retailers were restrained by laws whose licensing functions effectively supervised over-the-counter transactions which threatened children's lives.

Causes of Death

To this generation, the search for causes of death is motivated in part by the unfamiliarity of that inevitable visitor in our lives and also by the fact that the quest is a reasonable one. When death of a child occurs, our sensibilities dispose us to expect a rational, causative agent, and contemporary pathology invariably provides an answer. Wasting away turns out to be Leukemia, and fever turns out to be a specific virus. Our grief is contained by the sequential nature of events, a cycle of infection or disease which diagnosis generally interdicts in the form of specific and successful treatment. Parents are spared the burden of believing that death is caused by sin or divine disapproval in the case of epidemics.

At the outset of our period, and indeed through much of it, both medicine and popular opinion took an ill-formed view of sickness and death. As late as 1879, the Royal Statistical Society published a paper entitled, "On a Probable Connection between the Yearly Death-rate and the Position of the Planet Jupiter. . . ." Overinterpreting correlation as causation, Mr. B. G. Jenkins compared the aphelion of Jupiter with the death rate over a period of thirty-nine years. The two profiles are indeed similar, but not as convincing to us as to the Victorians.

In the centuries before the nineteenth, Britain had known the Black Death and the regular cycle of epidemics. In such periods, children and adults died quickly, without respect for age or status. At what was later called the Black Assizes, three hundred people died in forty hours at Oxford in 1577, and typhus killed all those who had sat on one side of a courtroom at the Old Bailey in 1750, according to Duncan (1844). Plague died out by 1728, when, according to Mills (1978), the black rat was chased out by the brown rat whose fleas had no great taste for human blood. This fortuitous event gave some respite before the appearance of Asiatic cholera in the next century. However, a variety of fevers persisted through the eighteenth century and into the nineteenth; and only in recent years has smallpox been eliminated. Diarrhea was the great slaughterer of infants, and it remains a grave public health problem in the Third World today. In many such diseases, dehydration is a secondary effect of infection and proves fatal to infants. Correct treatment is often successful because attention is paid to conserving bodily fluids and to maintaining the balance of electrolytes. What was called "summer fever" had been a frequent killer of children, and beneath the generic name for a variety of specific infectious agents was the problem of bad drains and contamination of drinking water. As late as 1906, an article in the *Times* called for establishment of a "Sanitary Corps" within the army, on the basis that the army could expect to have twelve men incapacitated by disease for everyone disabled by direct military action. The date in question is within living memory of a few people and shows how fortunate we are to be protected from lethal neglect of elementary sanitation.

One aspect of disease as a cause of children's death is its cyclic nature. In some respects, this was known because Bills of Mortality had permitted calculation of the regularity of epidemics. However, appreciations of these events were gross, and they were not translated into preventive programs. In the nineteenth century, physicians and others had seen the phenomena clearly. In France, Villermé and Milne-Edwards showed in 1829 that mortality of infants was highest in cold weather. Belgian data from the 1840's (Vilquin, 1978), and Italian data from 1863 to 1882 incorporating more social data (Breschi and Bacci, 1986), confirm the role of month of birth in child mortality. Benoiton de Chateauneuf (1830) showed that the mortality rate of children of the poor was twice that of the rich. Guy showed in 1881, nearly half a century later, that over the preceding decades children under age five had experienced the greatest mortality rate in January, February, and March; however, the lowest rate had followed shortly after, in the trimester June to August. Of course, there was little appreciation at the time of longer cycles; for example, of rubella, with its six to seven-year cycles in which young fetuses were killed and the survivors left gravely handicapped. In part, the diseases were not necessarily recognized as separate entities. To illustrate that point we need merely to step back briefly to consider the family of scurvies, all of which were merely variations in the expression of a deficiency in vitamin C.

This point is relevant to children because diet as a cause of death of children had been documented by Cadogan in 1756, which is very close to the year in which Lind published his treatise on the scurvy (1751). Cadogan made it clear that the diet of infants contributed to their deaths once they left the protection of breast feeding. There are two aspects to this matter. One is that ignorant people fed babies wholly inappropriate sops of bread soaked in all manner of liquids ("pobbies"). Second, children later received insufficient quantities of essential nutrients so that rickets became a common problem and resistance to infection declined. In a report to the Privy Council, Dr. Greenhow (1861) stated that children left by mothers working in factories were fed "pap, made of bread and water, and sweetened with sugar or treacle . . . lumps of bread floating in sweetened water . . . the mother being able to nurse them only at night. . . ."

Northern and Scottish children in the Nineteenth century tended to consume better diets than children to the south, for the most part. Writers of the period spoke of the good diets of children in Cumberland, and of the nutrition value of oatmeal. In his diary, John Ward of Clitheroe noted as important the day around 1860 when "I got a good Cumberland breakfast of ham and eggs, which I cannot afford to get above once a year" (France 1959). Lamenting the decline of the physique of people in previous decades, John Beddoe (1871) recalled the ethnology of Berwickshire as "pretty nearly that of the county of Northumberland" and ascribed decline in physique, in part, to giving up oatmeal and milk. Matossian (1985) asserted that rye was susceptible to ergot and, when infected, was liable to produce convulsions. Accordingly, decline in consumption of rye bread would reduce mortality. In 1867, Liebeg introduced his perfect infant food, at sixpence per quart. It was composed of wheat flour, cow's milk, malt flour, and potassium bicarbonate (Barr and Mettler 1983).

Irish children, like their parents, ate a disproportionate amount of potatoes, a vegetable which is, otherwise, an excellent element in a varied diet. Of course, fish was available to adults and children near the Irish coasts, and Daniel O'Connell recorded consumption of potatoes and fish in the diet of Irish families in 1825. In 1842, Cooke-Taylor wrote of many meals of Irish families consisting of "Potatoes and Point," meaning "a Herring in the middle of the table which no one must cut, but at which each may point and enjoy its ideal flavour." This seems comparable to the Northern convention of "Shadow Broth" in which a piece of meat was, allegedly, hung so that its shadow fell on a bowl of warm water. In fact, that diet came close to reality in the case of apprentices in Wolverhampton. Speaking to the Children's Employment Commission in 1843, the owner of the Star and Garter at Wolverhampton, Mr. Paul Law, said that he knew

> a lock manufacturer who had from 30–40 apprentices. The master used to boil the beef and veal together in a broth, which was so poor that the boys frequently complained to him; upon which he merely told his wife to take the meat and bones and, 'Broth 'em over again" (Jordan 1982)!

These anecdotes are from the years after the Napoleonic Wars, and from decades when the lives of children were threatened by malnourishment traceable to economic and political trends. In the decades of the Napoleonic threat, the problem of feeding children was part of the larger problem of food for the population. Napoleon's continental system and prohibition of exporting grain to Britain from the Baltic ports affected domestic consumption of grain, so much at the center of the typical diet. Ragsdale (1980) estimated that the United Kingdom needed to import 16 million bushels of grain. By 1801, 3.5 millions, or one-fifth of the need, came in the form of imports from North America. In that year of need, the birth rate fell by 8.4% and the death rate rose by 11.5%; implicitly, the death rate of children rose. The connection between war and food is demonstrated in the cost of wheat. Gregson (1817) put the average cost of wheat in Lancashire in the 1790s at fifty-four shillings per quarter; by 1800, he recalled, the price had doubled to one hundred and ten shillings per quarter. In a letter to Patrick Colquhoun in 1800, William Hale reported that more than one hundred children in Spitalfields had died from want of food. Three years before, in 1797, Eden, writing "on the State of the Poor" said that "before the present war" people had eaten meat twice a week with their bread and cheese. In 1797, they were currently eating barley bread, no meat, and making great use of potatoes.

In summary, the causes of death and the predisposing conditions of life were in the very nature of the ways in which people lived in the face of economic and political hazards ill-grasped at the time. When understood, they were not seen as the basis for rational reconstruction of the ills of society. Such a concept presumes a sense of polity, of public affairs, in which the governors have an obligation to the governed. Such a collective sense was built slowly by nineteenth-century reformers whose social and clinical innovations protected the lives of Victorian children.

Causes of Reduced Child Mortality

The transition from life and death in the eighteenth century to the twentieth is a process in which many of our ancestors died and many more lived. There were periods in which births and deaths were almost equal, leading to a static and a generally younger population than today. Slowly, the balance shifted, so that child mortality fell and those who reached adulthood had a steadily lengthening life expectancy ahead of them.

In some instances progress was fortuitous. Mitchison (1970) attributed the decline in scarlet fever deaths in children to "a change in the nature of the micro-organism." As with the brown rat chasing out the black rat in the days of the first George (Mayhew 1851), the process went largely unmarked, and only the epidemiologists' retrospective survey discerned the trend away from death. But change begets change, and we should not be too sure of our situation even at the end of the twentieth century. We recall that the migration of plague-bearing rats to the cities is held by some to have followed reduction of forests to supply wood, leaving rats with nowhere to live. The wily rat is as adaptable as ever, and several of the world's large cities have a silent, little reported population of super-rats who scorn dogs and chase cats. The rat has a relation to man via disease which consists of parallel lines that have a nasty habit of intersecting from time to time, usually to our detriment.

When we turn to the study of the ways in which child mortality declined, the pattern of social advance appears quite different from our recent record of control of disease. In the case of poliomyelitis, basic research created ways to improve the body's resistance. In many parts of the world, children do not face the risk of polio, and the reason is a clearly demonstrable progression from the laboratory to mass inoculation of children. At the beginning of our period and just before, only inoculation against smallpox can be cited, although this single instance is an excellent prototype. Beyond that example, a review of the elements of progress is rather baffling. McKeown and Brown (1955) examined the matter quite thoroughly and reported that while eighteenth-century surgical techniques improved, the survival rate did not. In such matters vision is all, and we cite the ideas for surgical treatment of hydrocephalus by Dr. Conquest who, in early Victorian times, foresaw successful treatment by surgery. McKeown and Brown believed that improvements in obstetrics halved obstetric mortality; hospitals, especially for childbirth, remained places to stay away from until Semmelweiss's ideas were disseminated well into the nineteenth century. In Mulhouse, M. Jean Dollfus reduced perinatal mortality among the children of his workers from 40% to 25% by giving the new mothers six weeks of leave with pay. This was an improvement of 37% in the neonatal mortality rate (Redgrave 1865).

There is a good case to be made for a decline in child mortality and an improvement in health generally by indirect means. That is, as the standard of living rose, better self-care and general health education progressed. Of all the improvements, perhaps those with the most widespread effects were the improvements in general sanitation. The author of "Gatherings from Graveyards" (1839), Dr. Walker, had much to say to society about the threat posed by ancient burial graveyards. "Walker of the Graveyards" assembled information showing how badly managed ancient cemeteries had become, and how continental practices, if adopted, would lead to reduced risk for those who attended burials.

In considering sources of the decline in mortality there is an obvious, traditional contribution in the form of breast-feeding. Before the time when investigators began to relate child mortality to social factors, shrewd observers noted that mortality seemed lower among groups of people who practiced breast-feeding. For physiological reasons, not every mother could breast-feed, and there were several alternatives. One was cow's milk, but as Drummond and Wilbraham (1939) pointed out, cow's milk can cause stress because it forms a larger clot in the infant's stomach than human milk. Also, it carried disease in the period before dairy herds were closely checked for health. An additional complication was that milk was incorporated into pap with a consistency appropriate for hanging wallpaper. Another alternative was the wet nurse. Among the complications were the cost and the matter of choosing the right person, because it was widely believed that her moral traits were transmitted in her milk. In fact, a more concrete risk was transmission of physical disease, a mechanism thought to explain Samuel Johnson's eye trouble as a boy. From the time the factory system was established, working mothers simply had no opportunity to breast-feed until evening, leaving no choice but to choose the least evil alternative among those evident.

The value of breast-feeding as a way to keep children alive was evident to Villermé and Milne-Edwards who, in 1829, cited Italian sta-

TABLE 3.1
LIFE EXPECTANCIES, ENGLAND AND WALES, 1841–1901*

	Child Age	1841– 1851	1851– 1861	1861– 1871	1871– 1881	1881– 1891	1891– 1901
Male	0	38.50	40.46	37.81	38.96	42.67	42.96
Female	0	40.80	41.43	40.98	41.25	43.68	46.40
Male	5	48.16	49.25	48.04	49.67	52.99	52.70
Female	5	49.57	51.06	50.89	51.88	54.10	55.93
Male	10	45.14	46.68	45.22	46.65	49.91	49.38
Female	10	47.36	48.81	48.50	49.08	51.30	52.79
Male	15	41.69	43.11	41.30	42.81	45.46	45.37
Female	15	43.62	45.38	44.89	45.46	47.17	49.09

*Lentzner (1985).

tistics from Padua and Verona about thirty years earlier. It had been recorded that mortality among babies of Jewish mothers was half that of Christian babies who were at the breast a shorter time. The lower mortality among children of Jewish mothers, traceable to their breast-feeding, was evident all through the nineteenth century. As late as 1905, the phenomena was reported among Jewish mothers in the East End and in Manchester (Rosenbaum 1905). Two years later, Newman reported the same lessened child mortality among Italian women in north London. The difference was twenty-seven fewer deaths per thousand children among the children of immigrant Italian mothers, who always fed their children at the breast. The same phenomenon was evident in Bavarian villages in the middle of the nineteenth century. The mortality rate in Mommlinger was at least one-half of that in Schonberg and Anhausen, where breast-feeding was not the norm (Knodel 1968). In the same period, the survival of infants was improved when alternatives to breast milk were too expensive or scarce. The death rate fell among infants in two quite different places, but due in both instances to war. Child mortality fell during the siege of Paris in 1870–1871, when food was scarce and the breast was the obvious source of food. It also fell in Manchester, a few years before, when the Civil War in the United States cut off the flow of cotton to Lancashire mills (Newman 1907). The problem was virtually universal; in nineteenth-century Finland and Sweden, summer rates of infant mortality were polarized. In the warm months, mortality reached its lowest rate, but only among infants at the breast. At the same time, mortality reached its highest rate, but only among those not fed at the breast (Lithell 1981). Bad drinking water resulting from contamination of the local pump was a major problem.

Despite the negative aspects of children's health in the nineteenth century, life expectancy increased. In Table 3.1 are the life expectancies calculated by Lentzner (1985) for boys and girls at various ages over six decades. Between 1841 and 1901, a newborn added five to six years to the expectation of life despite the stresses and explicit risks to life. For five-year-olds, a group who had survived the major period of risk for death, living to their late forties was probable. Girls who reached ten years in the 1840s could expect to live ten years longer than newborns in the same period. To be a fifteen-year-old girl in the 1840s was to enjoy the probability of a further twenty-eight years of life; by the 1890s, it had risen an additional six years. While not a large expectancy by today's standards, the increases in Table 3.1 were evidence of progress. Further evidence on this question, in a highly privileged group, may be recalled from Table 2.5. The cause of improvement cannot be found in medical breakthroughs but in a rising standard of living and, more particularly, improvements in sewage, sanitation, and provision of clean water.

Chadwick's Work

By 1840, public health had declined as the factory system wrought its effects in the form of increased populations in towns, overburdened water supplies, and the crowded unsanitary conditions of congested slums. The window tax, which had led people to board up windows, had existed within recent memory, and the air was polluted both by industry and by airborne vectors of disease. The eminent man of Victorian public affairs, Lyon Playfair, recalled that his account of the drains at Buckingham Palace was so bad that his report was suppressed, the fear of scandal exceeding the fear of bad drainage—the phenomenon which probably led to Prince Albert's death at Windsor in 1861. Lewis (1952) placed the annual number of deaths from one disease alone, typhus, as larger than the deaths inflicted by Napoleon at Waterloo.

Chadwick's *Sanitary Reports* of 1842 showed that the death industry—the gaggle of undertakers, sextons, coffin makers, burial societies, drunken grave diggers, and clergymen—all maintained a system of burial in which the public at large suffered. The explicit cost to the public was in the form of contagion when visiting graveyards and illness from the "mephitic vapours" (Walker 1839) which infiltrated adjacent neighborhoods. The invisible harm was the damage to the water table and so to the water drawn from wells for household used by children and adults. A prickly man, whose knighthood was delayed until an advanced age by his many enemies in the public forum, Chadwick went on to tackle the problem of sewage and drinking water. The *Health of Towns* report is fascinating, dynamic reading, as the Commissioners, who included Lyon Playfair and Dr. T. Southwood-Smith, pursued their inquiries. Chadwick tackled the problem of sewers and saw that traditional brick construction was ineffective. Under Chadwick's leadership, sewers made of tile rather than brick were proposed, plus the revolutionary idea that ordinary people's houses should receive water to run the sewage system and also to provide uncontaminated drinking water. Eventually Chadwick prevailed and the metropolis and provincial cities developed reliable and safe public water and sewage services. This provided the basis for the subsequent decline of waterborne diseases, and the decline of fatal diarrhea in children may be traced to the indefatigable efforts of Edwin Chadwick.

To put Chadwick's great contribution in perspective, it is necessary to add the names of two other sanitary investigators whose contributions in their own countries, while substantial, did not have quite the impact of Chadwick's. Apart from the nature of their contributions, they were probably more tactful than Chadwick, for they could not have been less so, and thus lacked the great man's zeal. In the 1830s, Dr. L.R. Villermé was commissioned by the Academie des Sciences Morales et Politiques to establish the physical and moral circumstances of the working class in France. In 1840, Villermé published his two-volume report and gave details of nutrition, wages, illegitimacy rates, and the welfare of children in various towns. A decade later, in Massachusetts, Lemuel Shattuck and two associates published their "Report of a General Plan for the Promotion of Public and Personal Health. . . ."

In considering Chadwick's work as a cause in the decline of children's mortality, it is prudent to reflect on the relatively thin line which separates our low mortality rates from those of the mid-nineteenth century. The barrier is the social infrastructure of good sewage systems and unpolluted water. Medical "breakthroughs" do not protect us and our children from infections, waterborne disease, or epidemics as much as we think. The safety and communal health provided by inoculation are not magic, and people sometimes neglect that elementary precaution. Cholera is gone, and people need not fear a repeat of the 1831 epidemic which started in India and spread around the world. The disease which destroyed the Irish potato crop had been seen on the Continent and in Canada in the early 1840s. Society need not fear a return of either of these nineteenth-century evils, but poliomyelitis still exists and common infectious diseases such as influenza mutate with regularity. To preserve low rates of child mortality, we must remember the heritage of Edwin Chadwick and preserve it.

4.

WORK

The central reality of life for young and old in the nineteenth century was work. To the youngest, it could be the thief who stole childhood, while to the old—in experience and not necessarily years—it was the means to survive in an age before pensions and health insurance. Of course, our emphasis is on the former, but it does not hurt to glimpse the end of a stressful process which caught up children early and carried them through all their days of remaining health and strength. However, work was more than the reality of life, it was the motif. To the apostle of self-improvement, Dr. Samuel Smiles, work was the moral furnace in which other virtues would be forged—thrift, self-help, courage, and fidelity. From the practical necessity of contributing to the domestic budget, work reached its apotheosis as a moral virtue from which the other virtues devolved in the nineteenth century.

Work, in the form of a routine of reporting on time to a work station away from the place of residence, provided a new form of socialization. With the coming of the factory, the worker started on time and stopped work when the factory whistle blew. The worker, child and adult, became part of a complex whole and, in some respects, became one more resource moving into the maw of the "manufactory." Raw materials went in one door and workers entered another. Shift work, the process by which physical plant and machines do not stand idle at night, altered the life of the worker still more. The rhythm of eating and sleeping which had followed the cycle of sunrise and sunset, roughly speaking, evolved so that the workers' wakefulness and concentration no longer followed the circadian rhythms of nature. In the case of children, the stress was greater because they had to be awakened, and the discipline of the factory floor ignored their need for rest and food. The early reports of the Factory Commissioners, around 1840, are replete with testimony in which children worked long hours with no breaks for refreshment or rest. The stress of this regimen was impressed on children's minds and is reported frequently in the subsequent reminiscences of old men and women recalling their early experiences. In 1833, William Cooper reported his routine at age nine. He had begun work in Leeds at five o'clock in the morning and worked until nine o'clock at night. "We had no time for breakfast, forty minutes for dinner, and no time for drinking" (Factory Inquiries 1833).

Early socialization had three particularly relevant experiences. First, it stripped children of their childhood and their health. They began work before dawn and ended work after dusk in all but the days of high summer. Not for them the essential and regenerating moments of play, but only precocious entry into the world of adults' expectations and the physical hazards of the workplace. Second, there was the explicit denial of the sensitive period in which literacy and knowledge—schooling—are acquired. There were exceptions, in the form of benign owners who organized their work force in order to integrate schooling into the routines of the workday; an example is Robert Owen and his model factory at New Lanark in Scotland. However, there were no such opportunities for children working in brickyards and on farms, that is, in the majority of workplaces where cheap child labor was available to use and discard. Third, there was the implicit process of socializing the child into a compliant, sullen, adult who would conform to the needs of the machine and to the requirements of the foreman. In this sense, the nineteenth century was a gigantic school for life, in which an unschooled proletariat responded to a curriculum of occupational experiences and use of machinery. In the case of tasks which became "de-skilled" (Knox 1986) it was evident that factories could substitute children for adults as workers, thereby reducing the cost of the raw material known as labor. In the case of machinery, its impersonal demands overran the needs of people, since workers served the machine, and not vice versa. What makes the nineteenth century important is that these processes were not only implacable but inefficient. Insight consisted of commentaries on what had happened or what was happening. There were few people able to extrapolate beyond the balance sheet, and the "Condition of England" question of the 1830s exemplifies the level at which reflection occurred. In that formulation, it was evident that there were positive and negative aspects to industrialization. The discourse was at the level of propaganda, for the most part, with reformers and industrial apologists citing the extremes of child deprivation and abuse on the one hand, and the greater good, on the other.

The great commentators of the age were Frederick Engels and Karl Marx. We read Engels for a comprehensive if ideological view of the age. *The Condition of the Working Class in England,* published in 1845, looks like Dr. James Kay's 1832 report on life in Manchester. Facts are organized more skillfully and constitute illustrations of the theme of social and economic bankruptcy. For the purposes of this volume, it is important to point out that Engels made frequent reference to children. He records use of Godfrey's Cordial for infants, and also shows in detail how eyes, reproductive functions, and spine were all damaged by work at the lace factories near Hinckley. Describing bobbin lacework, Engels reported that

> the children work in small, ill-ventilated, damp rooms, sitting always bent over the lace cushion. To support the body in this wearying position, the girls wear stays with a wooden busk, which, at the tender age of most of them, when the bones are still very soft, wholly displaces the ribs and makes narrow chests universal. They usually die of consumption after suffering the severest forms of digestive disorders, brought on by sedentary work in a bad atmosphere. They are almost wholly without education, last of all do they receive moral training.

In the case of Karl Marx, we see contemporary facts bent to an overarching view of history, within which economic determinism, a monistic, implacable first cause, moves society towards a particular kind of transfiguration. Marx's view was a secular Millenianism whose apocalyptic vision was paralleled in the drawings of Gustave Doré. In them we see the gloom and despair of urban life in the early nineteenth century. Doré's drawings and the illustrations of women and children working in mines are the classic acts of witness to an epoch. In the case of Doré's drawings, their dark tones and harsh scenes evoke anxiety in the viewer. In the case of children working in the mines, simpler illustrations were very effective and stung the consciences of Victorian readers as superb propaganda for reform. These sets of drawings rank with Dickens's novels as illustrations that the sleeping conscience of the middle class, frequently predisposed by Evangelism, could be aroused. It had been evident to Alexis de Tocqueville (1833) that "the English have only a very slight capacity for appreciating general ideas." He was correct, and the English conscience was less moved by ideology than by specific instances of need. Unfortunately, the corollary is that reform of child labor and other abuses was couched in equally specific but limiting terms. Early legislation, that of 1803, for example, to "protect the health and morals" was directed to apprentices. They were a small group in the work force, working under conditions enforced by law for centuries. Not surprisingly, Josiah Wedgwood later recalled that the legislation of 1803 "never had the slightest effect upon our manufactory" (Report 1816). In the same vein, protection of children and women in subsequent legislation was tied to the industry, not to the status of children. Cotton mills were regulated, but not comparable manufactories. Workplaces employing fifty people or more were supervised, but not every place where a child might work. This inability to grasp on behalf of children de Tocqueville's "general ideas" aborted much reform. The prime example is the Ten-Hour Act of 1847, whose protection for children was stolen by the legal device of the split shift. The vision for reform of child labor was evident, but the ideas tended to be pushed no further than the minimum in the face of entrenched opposition and vested interests. Reformation of children working in agricultural groups under conditions of stress and abuse, for example, was not brought about until 1881.

In this propensity for the particular there is seen the ethos of an age. The role of law as a means of reform could not possibly protect children unless the public philosophy set the stage for a vigorous and central role for government and its arm, a bureaucracy. The reforms of 1832 attended to what existed and did not produce new structures. Strong local governments for the new towns had to wait for more development of the concept of polity and the common good. In turn, they had to wait until the earlier fear of Jacobinism, which was not ill-founded, had subsided; reform would seem neither capitulation nor encouragement to the turbulent lower orders. In this light, the Chartist movement demonstrated that ordinary people would stop short of upheaval.

The age structure of the working population in the nineteenth century was quite different from our own. Today, we expect a child to enter schooling at age four or five and to remain there until the middle or, increasingly, the late teens. The young person then enters the work force and can expect to remain there for fifty years. When retirement comes, in the twenty-first century, it will last about five years. Throughout the post-teen years the person will expect to undergo further training or

TABLE 4.1
ASPECTS OF THE BRITISH ECONOMY IN THE NINETEENTH CENTURY

YEAR	PERIODS OF INFLATION AND DEFLATION	MAJOR CYCLES TO 1850	BUSINESS ACTIVITY BY YEAR	PEAK PERIOD	PEAK YEARS	YEAR
1781	—					1781
1791	I N F L A T I O N					1791
1801			Depression	1802–1815 Peak years for enclosure (740k acres)[5]		1801
1811	—		Deep Depression	1811–1821 Peak decade of population growth (+16%)[5]	1810 Peak years <1860 for money wages[5]	1811
			Slow revival		1811 Peak year for agricultural contribution to GNP (35.7%)[5]	1812 Peak year for price of a quarter loaf of bread (4d. per lb.)[4]
1821	D E F L A T I O N		Depression	1820–1830 Peak years for hand-loom weavers (240k)		1821
1831	—		Depression			1831
			Depression			
1841			Prosperity	1840–1860 Peak period for importing raw and unfinished materials[3]	1847 Peak year railway track	1841
	—					

TABLE 4.1 (Continued)

Year		Inflation/Deflation			
1851	Uneven prosperity	INFLATION	laying (6.4k miles)[5]		Lowest Rousseaux price index[4] (1851)
1854			First year railway passengers >100 millions[4]		
1860					>5,000 tons of U.S. wheat imported[4]
1861			1861–1891 Peak period of real national income[5]		
1866	Prosperity		UK Coal output >100 million tons[4] (1866)		1868 Coal to London rail>ships
1871		DEFLATION	1871 N agricultural workers <50% of 1801 (15.1%)[5]		1871 Peak year of iron's contributions to GNP (11.5%)
1874	Mild prosperity		1874 Peak year employment < CA 14 years in cotton mfr. (13.9%)[5]		1875 Peak year of ship bldg. (£17.9 millions)[5]
1881	Recession		1881 Peak year for housing's contribution to GNP[3]		
1891					1891 Peak year for mfr. contribution to GNP[3]
1893	Depression	INFLATION	1893 Lowest retail price index[4]		
1901					
1911					

[1]Hohenberg, 1968 [2]Gayer, Rostow, and Schwarz, 1975 [3]Dean and Cole, 1975 [4]Dean and Cole, 1962 [5]Dean and Cole, 1967

education in a cycle of lifelong learning. For the nineteenth century child, the situation was quite different. For most of the period, schooling was irregular and might consist of sporadic attendance at a Sunday school, at best. Formal schooling on weekdays would end quickly and the work phase of life would begin. What would follow would be a relatively brief and stressful work career, terminated at an age we consider a period of vitality. Miners thought a man had insufficient strength for the coal-face by age forty. Dr. Thackrah of Leeds, according to Samuel H.G. Kydd, who wrote as "Alfred" (1857), found few men over age forty in the mills where flax was spun.

> We found that of 1079 persons employed, there are only nine who had attained the age of fifty; and besides these, only twenty two who had reached forty.

Of course, some men entered occupations which made fewer physical demands.

For those who led the life of itinerant worker with pick and shovel, the navvies who dug cuttings and built embankments for the railway lines, life was equally short. The railway laborer was cheap and expendable, and the toll of accidents was high. In fiction, Patrick MacGill of Donegal (1914) gave a vivid account of his life as a young digger in Scotland, sometimes soaked, frequently hungry, and often without shelter. Coleman (1968) says that few Navvies lived beyond age forty, and those who were age sixty looked seventy. One who survived cave-ins and living rough for years on end was James (Daddy) Hayes, who died in 1882 at the age of eighty-six. The risk was high that a boy navvy, one who led horses and their carts to tip excavated soil, for example, would be hurt in an accident or become chronically ill from poor food, excessive drink, and exposure to bad weather with insufficient shelter. The fact was that navvies, boys and men, were an invisible work force, working at a distance from the centers of population. They were known, disappointingly, to such Evangelical missionaries as chose to till human soil more rocky and unresponsive than that worked by the navvies on the Great Western and other lines.

When we look at the age structure of the population in the mid-nineteenth century, we see that the prospects for a boy entering the work force were not encouraging. In Table 4.2 there is information originally developed by censuses and taken from Charles Booth's (1886) research on occupations from 1801 to 1881. In any given year, the proportion of men in the forty working years from age twenty-five to age sixty-five is

TABLE 4.2
AGE STRUCTURE OF THE POPULATION OF
ENGLAND AND WALES
1851–1881 IN PERCENTAGES*

GROUP		YEAR			
		1851	1861	1871	1881
Males	25–65 years	19.8	19.7	19.5	19.2
Males	15–20 years	4.9	4.8	4.8	4.9
Children	<15 years	35.4	35.6	36.1	36.5
Males	20–25 years	4.4	4.5	4.4	4.5
Males	>65 years	2.1	2.1	2.1	2.1
Females	>15 years	33.4	33.5	33.3	33.0

Booth (1886, 319)

19%. The population of children under age fifteen is nearly twice as large. Males age fifteen to age sixty-five drop as a percentage of the population, while the proportion of males age fifteen to age twenty remains constant. Males age sixty-five and older are only 2.1% of the population, and do not expand. There is growth in the child proportion of the population.

In general, the young person entering the work force at that time to undertake anything but clerical and professional work faced a relatively brief work life. Thompson (1984) identified Irish wool combers in Bradford as a group likely to be dead by age sixteen. In Stockport, according to "Alfred," the average life expectancy was twenty-two years. Of course, this number was based on infants, but those who survived the 50% mortality of the early years could not anticipate the biblical three-score-years-and-ten. The working years pretty well defined natural life for all but the privileged, whose life expectancy tended to be double that of the poor.

Not everyone who needed to work did work; Charles Booth of Liverpool, who combined Evangelical zeal with a social worker's feel for the human predicament, was not loath to use the word "loafer" in his classic summary of occupations in London (Booth 1887). In his analysis of causes of "great poverty," he assigns mechanisms neatly. There is casual work, and there is irregular work at low pay. Booth recognizes "small profits," but he also recognized "loafers"—about 4% of his sample of sixteen hundred heads of families—who "will not work." The

problems of nonworkers he assigned to "questions of employment,"—
55%; "questions of habit," 14%; and "questions of circumstance," 27%.
In the case of the loafer, Booth points out that "such men live on their
wives." In the previous year, in a paper he presented to the Royal Statistical Society on May 18, 1886, Booth aggregated census data from 1861
to 1881 on paupers, prisoners, and the insane, labelling them "the useless classes."

When children entered the world of work in the earliest decades of
the nineteenth century, the range of occupations was not large. With the
victory at Waterloo in 1815, discharged soldiers attempted to enter the
work force at a time of economic depression. Throughout the nineteenth
century, the army contained a disproportionately large number of Irish
soldiers. Agriculture was a large sector of the economy, but it needed
fewer workers than in earlier times; enclosure produced economies of
scale and made the marginal, tenuous existence of farm laborers intolerable. They left for the factories of the towns, competing with others for
jobs. The fundamental trend of the century was in the direction of power
rather than people for factory work. First water power, then coal and its
derivative from water, steam, led to less reliance on human muscle. Jobs
became standardized and simplified so that children could do them, at
much lower wages. Building techniques remained unaffected and continue to do so in some respects to this day. Coal mining defied mechani-
zation owing to the thin seams or strata commonly encountered. There,
child labor was at a premium for, as one commentator in the 1840s
pointed out, it was only by starting to hew coal no later than at age
twelve that a boy could acquire the "peculiar" but necessary muscular
development of arms, shoulder, and back essential to hewing coal in a
two-foot seam while lying on the ground.

One of the hazards for children entering the world of work was
joining occupations which would become obsolete. The classic dead end
was weaving, whose history from the end of the eighteenth century is
that of a declining cottage industry in unsuccessful competition with
power. People could rent hand looms and set them up virtually any-
where, so to be a skilled hand-loom weaver was to compete with anyone
who had the capital to hire a loom when laid off from another occupation. To be a weaver's child was to be a useful child-worker in a cottage
industry, preparing materials for the loom and carrying them to sell to a
contractor. As an apprenticeship to an occupation, it was a passport to
ignominy and redundance; E.H. Hunt (1981) pointed out that, by 1826,
a fifteen-year-old monitoring two looms driven by mechanical rather
than hand power wove as much fabric as six hand-weavers.

Like the weaver's child, the country child had a role as a worker. Following the cycle of nature, with short winter days and long summer evenings, rural child-workers foraged, gathered crops, and weeded the fields. With only the sky over their heads, such children were cold and wet in winter. Schooling could not compete with the cycle of the fields, and education was scanty when the chance to earn a little money arose. Gibbs (1903) reported that a cheerful carter named Trinder in Gloucestershire had twenty-one children and an income of about twelve shillings per week. Not surprisingly, the boys were put to work in the fields by the age of ten. Compulsory schooling based on laws passed in Westminster meant little in the country when a family had mouths to feed.

A great abuse of children was their work in agricultural gangs where they were frequently overworked. Two laws, one in 1867 and the other in 1873, suppressed the practice. In actual fact, the abuses, like those of climbing boys earlier in the century, continued long after their status was corrected by law. The explanation is that any abuse in the country is less accessible than in the town, and passing laws in the metropolis meant little in the absence of a bureaucracy to enforce them. In 1851, according to Yeats (1855), only 1.32% of men were "engaged in Government," a proportion so low as to explain why government had limited impact, initially, as a means of reform. When country child-workers became adolescents, they had the option of working as casual hired labor or of working on a contract basis. Walvin (1982) reports that girls were employed annually as domestic servants on farms for a year which began at Martinmas. Of course, there was always the option of a factory job when times were good, and there were many to whom anything but the routines of country life was attractive.

In the last half of the nineteenth century, the trend of the previous fifty years of shrinking agricultural employment continued. Booth (1886) and Eversley (1907) demonstrated with statistics how strong this trend had been. In the fifty years beginning with 1851, the number of people employed in agricultural occupations diminished. The change involved more than laborers. The number of farmers dropped in the forty years after 1861 by twenty-four thousand in England (Eversley 1907), and laborers declined by nearly one-half. Curiously, the number of shepherds increased from twenty to twenty two thousand. In Scotland in the same period, Eversley's reconstruction from census data showed that in the years 1861–1901 the number of farm laborers dropped by 38%, and the proportion of farmers by about 20%. In Scotland also, the number of shepherds rose by about one-third, to nearly nine thousand, as the new century began. Among the nine thousand were many children, for tending sheep has been a traditional form of child labor since time immemorial.

Child Labor

Apprentices. Today, the general public views employment in a fairly sophisticated way, consciously exchanging services for wages and fringe benefits. Generally speaking, the idea of a quid pro quo is recognized by all. We have arrived at that formulation fairly late in the history of workers and employers. Traditionally, the balance has been in favor of the employer with whom the authority or law and government has been allied. Exceptions have been rare, as when the Black Death wiped out populations, and agricultural laborers were in great demand. For the most part, workers have complied with the demands of employers, and in the case of boys, did so in the form of legally bound apprenticeships. Reading thirteenth-century documents of apprenticeship, one is struck by the familiarity of the language. There is the "party of the first part," and there is the fixed obligation of the young person to serve for a long period of time. Closer to our period of interest, the continuity is evident. We digress to point out that apprenticeship does not apply to all childworkers but only to those who are to learn a "mystery" or craft. Once admitted to such study, the apprentice is to be clothed, fed, and housed reasonably. He must conduct himself obediently as a member of the household. When, in 1708, young Richard Selman was apprenticed to Thomas Stokes, Broadweaver of Corsham, Wilts; he was required to keep his master's secrets. He was also to stay away from taverns, dice, cards, and fornication, and "shall not absent himselfe or plong himselfe by Night or by day without his master's leave": we trust he didn't becasue he was to receive "meate, drinke, Apparrell, Washing (and) Lodging and all other things whatsoev fitting" (Dunlop 1912) in return. The probability is that an apprentice weaver in Wiltshire was fairly compliant, in contrast to city apprentices who had a bad reputation. The Merchant Adventurers of Newcastle, at one time, had trouble with their apprentices who had "become hawtie minded, high stomoked and wanton condycyoned . . ." (Dunlop 1912). The Industrial Revolution eliminated many apprenticeships as a form of child labor because there was no master from whom the apprentice could learn the "mystery." In addition, the masters had lost much of their zeal for propriety, as they were caught up in the spirit of manufactory. In such a climate, apprentices were merely cheap labor, and pauper apprentices in London were shipped off to northern cotton mills (Report 1815). In 1832, John Brown published "A Memoir of Robert Blincoe," the story of a boy placed in the St. Pancras workhouse and subsequently sent to work at Litton Mill. There, he was physically abused and in his later years showed scars on his head, face, and ears caused by pincers. When Blincoe became a supervisor in a mill as an adult, he treated child-workers well and shared his food with them. A curious aspect of child labor is that factory owners accepting parish orphans as workers were required to accept one mentally retarded child for every twenty orphans.

The more flagrant abuses of child-workers were prevalent in the earlier decades of the nineteenth century, before reforming laws slowly improved conditions through piecemeal legislation. The 1802 act to protect the "Health and Morals of Apprentices," applied to cotton and wool factories. The act prescribed that clothing be supplied, that the day be no more than twelve hours, that the sexes were to sleep apart, that an hour of religious instruction should occur on Sundays, and that there should be some education. The Justices of the Peace were to appoint visitors, and fines of two to five pounds could be assessed (Health 1959). As Josiah Wedgwood pointed in later years, the legislation of the time was ineffective; and the elder Robert Peel, when debating the Factory Bill of 1818, recalled that fifteen-hour workdays were common in 1803, when he personally had employed one thousand children (Peel 1818). The Act of 1816 raised the age for working twelve-hour days to sixteen years, and continued the earlier attention to lime-washing walls each year (Factory Act 1819). The 1831 Act continued to require annual lime-washing, raised the age for twelve-hour days to eighteen years and prohibited employment of children under nine years. These ameliorations were restricted to cotton factories, however. For comparative purposes, it is useful to contrast the early decades with progress in Massachusetts. There, the key provision of the laws was that a child under age fifteen must have spent three of the preceding twelve months in school in order to work in any factory (schools, 1839). In this regard, it is helpful to recall that Massachusetts had put everything in perspective as early as 1647 with the "Old Deluder Satan" act, which required that a school master be hired and paid from public taxes for every fifty children in a community.

Entry into the workplace is a matter of some significance. We have considered apprentices who were formally consigned to the world of work. Weavers' children worked when quite small because the loom was in one of the family's rooms or in an adjoining shed. Generally speaking, parents put children to work, and an old man in Lancashire told Cooke-

Taylor (1842) that parents working at home could be the hardest task masters. Another man called on Cooke-Taylor for "t'liberation o' t'white bairn slaves."

From the young person's point of view, going out to work could be a horrible experience, replete with Dickensian realities. However, there is another side of the picture which occasionally relieves the gloom. Several commentators in quite different decades of the nineteenth century had noticed the degree of emancipation from parental control which going to work, then as now, precipitated. In the 1830s parents would allow children to keep money earned for overtime (Factory 1833). Child-workers put in long days, but they would also ask the foreman for two or three hours of extra work; they were allowed to keep the two or three pence they earned. On January 4, 1850, the Special Correspondent of the *Morning Chronicle* noted that factory children in Manchester enjoyed a "precocious independence," something he recorded with alarm because it implied a weakening of parental control. In contrast, Ross (1986) has described the satisfaction of Will Crooks, in the 1860s, running home to present his first wage, a half-sovereign, to his mother at age thirteen. About the same time Henry Mayhew (1851) was reporting that costermongers' sons in London were leaving home at sixteen and setting up housekeeping with their girlfriends, a relationship rarely legalized. In 1868, Mr. R.S. Baker pointed out some of the perils of factory life for girls to the National Association for the Promotion of Social Science. He noted with alarm that factory life "leads girls to a spirit of independence of parental control," adding that "wages have become a power greater than natural affection."

The factory socialized children into the role of compliant worker, a being whose life was structured by the demands of the workbench. One element began a change in the sensibilities of children and adults which was repeated in the last quarter of the twentieth century. The factory whistle defined the beginning and the end of the working day, and so defined the time for waking and rising. In many northern mill towns the "knocker-upper" tapped on the upstairs bedroom window in order to rouse the workers in time to comply with the factory whistle. Out of those rituals came insinuation of a sensitivity to time in small units. Dawn was irrelevant to the factory, as was dusk, since both changed significantly with the seasons, but the mill and its machine endured. The hour was relevant, but the minute defined being punctual, and the work force acquired a sensitivity to minutes as useful divisions of time. Correspondingly, the use of trains to commute to work required cultivation of a feel for the minute; the traveller knew the train would depart for the suburbs on the appointed moment. A scientific curiosity is that the right time in Falmouth and in Dover in the 1840s differed by twenty-five minutes and twenty-eight seconds. With the advent of railways this east-west problem had to be faced, and so British time, as it was styled, was introduced. Time between Dover and Falmouth stood still, and all cities observed the time recorded at any moment at Greenwich. Today's plane traveller has an easier style, because airlines frequently define "on time" as plus or minus twenty minutes. The Victorian worker dependent on the train, like today's commuter, knew that the minute was not negotiable. The age of the railway and the factory inevitably changed our time-consciousness. Today, we make increasingly precise statements of time. Half-past yields to thirty-one minutes, as our digital watches and clocks erode the hour and its quarters and halfs. And so the process by which the young Victorian worker oriented to the factory whistle continues.

Occupations of Young People 1841–1881

Scholars acknowledge a debt of thanks to Charles Booth of Liverpool, not to be confused with "General" William Booth who founded the Salvation Army, because study of the place of young people in the work force depends largely on access to data through his work. Booth's 1886 paper, "Occupations of the People of the United Kingdom 1801–1881," is the aperture through which we see the structure of the work force. The title is a little misleading, because the bulk of the paper is almost a hundred pages of tables drawn largely from the censuses of 1841–1881. There is some information from the earlier period, but it is fragmentary and expresses an unsophisticated approach to gathering occupational and demographic data. Information on females tends to be no more refined than over or under age fifteen, for example. Decennial information is not always comparable, and Scottish and Irish inquiries tended to be unlike those conducted in England and Wales. Booth's contribution is the compilation and reduction of the data on occupations, but he also rationalized it and made it useable.

Table 4.3 has taken the process one step further, selecting from Booth's voluminous and detailed tables information on the occupations of both sexes under age fifteen. The table uses three time references, 1841, 1861, and 1881, and so covers nearly half a century composed of decades of vigorous economic change from the onset of the "Hungry Forties." The table uses seven occupational groupings, with one, manufacturing, broken down into four subgroups, for a total of ten occupational complexes. In addition, we have chosen to deal with three political

TABLE 4.3

EMPLOYMENT OF BOYS AND GIRLS UNDER FIFTEEN YEARS OF AGE IN ENGLAND AND WALES, SCOTLAND, AND IRELAND 1841, 1861, 1881 (IN THOUSANDS)[1]

Occupation	Sex	1841 England & Wales N (000)	1841 Scotland N (000)	1841 Ireland N (000)	1861 England & Wales N (000)	1861 Scotland N (000)	1861 Ireland N (000)	1881 England & Wales N (000)	1881 Scotland N (000)	1881 Ireland N (000)
Agriculture[2]	M	<159.6	<40.2	92.4	>119.0	10.7	35.4	68.2	5.8	17.5
	F	<56.8	>3.7		>6.1	>2.2	>5.8	>2.1	>2.2	>2.6
Mining	M	<42.7	<5.5	0.1	39.9	5.1	0.1	25.7	4.6	0.1
	F	<5.2			0.5			0.5		
Manufacture										
Fuel, gas, chemicals	M	<0.5			0.9			0.5		
	F	<0.3			0.2		.1	0.1	0.1	
Wood (Furniture, etc)	M	<18.2	>3.2	0.4	6.4	1.0	0.6	4.3	0.7	0.2
	F	<4.9			0.8	0.1		0.7	0.1	

TABLE 4.3 (Continued)

Textiles, dyeing	M	<83.2	<25.4	65.6	8.4	6.7	50.5	5.0	3.4
	F	<257.6		83.4	14.6	17.7	66.0	10.2	6.4
Dress	M	<46.7	<8.7	18.2	2.7	2.6	8.8	1.2	0.8
	F	<177.2		26.4	1.4	8.4	20.3	1.6	3.8
Navigation and docks	M	<12.1	<2.0	32.8	3.4	1.7	47.3	6.6	1.7
	F	<1.1		1.1	0.5		1.1	1.8	0.1
Railways	M	<0.1		1.1	0.1	0.2	1.8	0.3	0.1
	F								
Army and Navy	M	<6.9	<0.8	1.1		0.2	.5		
	F								
Domestic service (Indoor only)	M	<82.1	<6.9	8.0	0.7	4.5	6.2	0.2	1.8
	F			86.7	8.6	17.8	98.9	6.7	12.9

[1] Adapted from Booth (1886)
[2] Farmers and relatives, laborers and shepherds.

and geographical entities in order to show the differences and similarities in trends for Ireland, for Scotland, and for England and Wales. The data for girls are not extant, especially in 1841, but better techniques for conducting censuses remedied the defect by 1851.

England and Wales. In the England and Wales of 1841, many juvenile-workers were still on the land, and the Industrial Revolution, though a half-century old, had not yet altered the population of England and Wales into the prevalent pattern of urban life we know today. There were horses to tend and crops to gather. In the ensuring two decades, the number of child-workers dropped to about 126,000 in 1861, and then fell by about one-half to 70,000 by 1881. Mining enrolled nearly 50,000 children, mostly boys, in 1841, which is just before the great reforms which established children and women as protected classes. By 1861, girl mine employees were practically gone, and the number of boys had begun to decline. By 1881, largely owing to the Education Act of 1870, the number of boys under age fifteen was down to about 26,000. We surmise that most of them were close to age fifteen, and that the little children of earlier years had grown into adult mine workers and were not replaced by other little children.

In the manufacturing sector, textiles and the associated industry of dyeing was a substantial employer of young girls by 1841. For every boy there were three girls, a proportion in greater balance, but in a much smaller child work force by 1861. Girls still predominated by 1881, but the work force of young people was only about one-third what it had been forty years before. The school room rather than the mill floor was where the children were to be found by that date.

There were a few boys in the army in 1841, but they disappeared quickly. By 1861, there were only eleven hundred boys in the army and navy, and they were gone, with the probable exception of Midshipmen, by 1881.

The most interesting category of work in England and Wales is domestic service. This occupation enrolled somewhat less than 100,000 young persons in 1841. By 1861, it had grown, but not at an unusual rate. However, by 1881 it was about half again as large, with about 160,000 young domestics, the majority of whom were young girls. At Lark Rise, Laura (Thompson 1945) reported a stranger would have looked in vain for a simple country girl with a rustic air to her. It was the custom at Lark Rise, near Oxford, to send girls off to a domestic posi-tion at the age of eleven, adding that there were no girls of thirteen simply living at home. The process began by sharp remarks intended to leave a girl with the feeling that she was useless, an extra mouth to feed. There were standards, so that a girl's first job, or petty place, would not be as a farm servant, and at no time would she be placed in a public house. Occasionally, domestic service in a family could be a lifelong experience. In the home of young John Ruskin in Edinburgh, Anne was the *Meinie* (servant) who looked after him. In *Praeterita* (1886), he reported that Anne had "nearly starved to death when she was a girl, and had literally picked the bones out of cast-out dust-heaps to gnaw." In her years of service, from age fifteen to age seventy-two, she accumulated over two hundred pounds, and she left that not trivial sum to her relations. Towards the end of the century, the colloquial term for a young, overworked servant girl was "slavey."

The adult population that was engaged in domestic work nearly doubled in the forty years between 1841 and 1881, growing from 1 million to over 1.8 million. The growth of work opportunities as domestic indoor servants was fueled by migration from agriculture and by increasing affluence after 1850. Higgs (1983) placed the peak of domestic service in 1871. This occupation remained large for a few decades and then began to decline as taxation and evolving sensibilities put domestic service in a new light. Like weaving, it became an entry occupation for many which did not lead to later employment as an adult in a career line. This trend was more evident for males than for females, and it was in the southeast quadrant of Great Britain that the service component of the work force expanded most in the last half of the nineteenth century (Lee 1984).

In Victorian days there were occupations which do not now exist and whose names are meaningless today. They were vocations to which a Victorian youngster might be called with every expectation of a lengthy and useful career. Lee (1979) listed several obsolete job titles from the censuses of the nineteenth century. He gave the "Blabber," the "Bull-Dog," the "Burner," the "Crutter," the "Glan-Rider," and the "Ponty Sticker." Exactly what was done by the "tingle-maker," "Sparable Cutter," and the "Whim-Driver," beyond deductions from the verb elements—which are probably misleading—is lost in the Victorian mists.

Scotland. The view of Scottish working youngsters in 1841 is far from clear, despite Booth's labors. As with England and Wales, the Commissioners were not especially sensitive to females, and their questions are not ours of a century and a half later. Agriculture was the major employer of children, followed in our selective picture in Table 4.3 by textiles, dress-making, and domestic service. With omission of textiles, this order conforms to the pattern for adults. By 1861, there were about eleven thousand young females and an undetermined number of young males working in agriculture. Twenty years later, the number of young workers was pretty well known to be eight thousand, a quarter of whom were girls. For other occupations in 1841, 1861, and 1881, the numbers are small and relatively stable over the forty years. The number of young males in domestic service dropped from .7 thousand to .2 thousand between 1861 and 1881. The proportion of females dropped from 8.6 thousand to 6.7 thousand—a much smaller drop. At the same time, the number of females over age fifteen remained virtually stable.

Ireland. A third and different pattern of juvenile employment was evident through the period 1841–1881 in Ireland. The absolute number of young males in agriculture in 1841 was 92.4 thousand, and the number of females is unknown. By 1861, the participation of males in agriculture had dropped by nearly two-thirds, to 35.4 thousand, a phenomenon to be understood in terms of the catastrophe which struck Irish life in the form of the Famine. The effect of the potato blight of 1845 on the demographic structure of Ireland was one of the great population migrations of history. From 1841 to 1881, the number of boys in agricultural occupations declined from 92.4 thousand to 17.5 thousand, with the number of girls dropping in the same proportion. The other occupations listed in Table 4.3 did not employ many Irish young people in 1841. Textiles and domestic service jointly employed about 14 thousand young males in 1841, the former being manufacture of linen and other fabrics around Belfast. The 1861 census data are clearer, showing 24 thousand young people, mostly girls, engaged in manufacture of textiles, and almost as many, also girls for the most part, in domestic service. In 1881, agriculture was still the major occupation, although on a smaller scale. Domestic employment of young males and females had fallen over twenty years by nearly one-half, to about 14 thousand employees, with the proportion of females having risen from four to one in 1861, to six to one in 1881.

The fundamental picture we portray is that childhood employment meant different things in Scotland, in Ireland, and in England and Wales. The economies and peoples were different, and so the work history of youngsters in the years 1841–1881 was different. The base year of 1841 saw England and Wales facing the "Hungry Forties," which would be followed by vigorous economic growth. In contrast, Ireland stood on the threshold of disaster, in the form of the years of famine, from which the population never recovered and for whom work meant emigration. In Scotland, the highlands remained depopulated and poor, but the development of heavy engineering on the Clydeside brought prosperity and jobs for the young whenever shipbuilding was encouraged by trade and permitted by world-wide cycles of expansion and depression. Scotland in the nineteenth century may be contrasted with London, which lost a good deal of heavy manufacturing in the same period. Shipbuilding, for example, was largely extinguished, so that young East-Enders sought their livelihoods, increasingly, on the streets.

Mayhew's Children

To describe the occupations entered by young people in the terms of nineteenth-century censuses is accurate, but it misses the idiosyncracies of life, the richness and poverty of the ways people tried to make a living. Dickens's descriptions are wonderful, and we learn of the relation of master and servant as Sam Weller assists Mr. Pickwick. A contemporary of Dickens, who also worked as a reporter but established his reputation by investigative work, was Henry Mayhew. Unlike Dickens, Mayhew loved facts and would have been labelled a "Statist," to use the mid-nineteenth-century term. Like Dickens, Mayhew had an ear for the richness of language and an appreciation of the culture of the street. Mayhew contributed to the *Morning Chronicle's* series of reports from anonymous correspondents on the life of the working poor in 1850. As one reads the reports from various parts of England, there is a discriminable style in which the language of the worker is presented verbatim. Only one reporter does not correct the grammar and tidy up the syntax; this is Mayhew, whose ear and pen bring us 1850 in its own language.

In 1851, Henry Mayhew, then in his thirty-ninth year, published *London Labour and the London Poor,* in two volumes. The study is a series of brief passages consisting of several paragraphs, occasionally running to several pages, on a long list of occupations in six groupings. Mayhew gives a picture of occupations long gone—Jack Black, "Her Majesty's *Rat-Catcher*"; the Fantoccini Man who put on puppet shows; "the bird-catchers who are street-sellers"; the "pure"-finders who followed dogs, of whom Mayhew learned that there were two or three hundred in the metropolis supplying tanners' yards; and the street reciter who earned about ten shillings per week orating Shakespeare near theatres and public houses.

In addition, there were the children. There was the Jewish boy who thought he was twelve, and who sold cooked food on the streets. ("No, I wouldn't like to go to school, nor to be in a shop, nor be anybody's servant but my own. O, I don't know what I shall be when I'm grown up. I shall take my chance like others.")

There was the boy crossing-sweeper (see the jacket of Walvin's (1982) *A Child's World* for a painting of a boy street-sweeper), "a remarkably intelligent lad," according to Mayhew, who encountered him in the Strand. His reply to Mayhew's first exchange was "give a half-penny to poor little Jack," offered with an "expression of supplication" to the reporter. "After mother died, sister still kept on making nets, and I lived with her for some time . . . one day they went out, and came back and said they'd been and got married. It was him as got rid of me." Reporting how he and his fellow street-sweepers worked, he said "A broom doesn't last us more than a week in wet weather and they costs us twopence halfpenny each. . . . We go into the Haymarket where all the women are who walk the streets. They don't give us no money but they tell the gentlemen to. . . . Each policeman we give a regular name—there's Bull's Head, Bandy Shanks, and Old Cherry Legs."

Another boy street-sweeper was Mike; the old woman who kept the lodging house cried to him, "You ought to be ashamed of yourself—and that's the God's truth—not to go and sluice yourself after spaking to the jintlemin." Mayhew adds that, "Mike wore no shoes, but his feet were as black as if cased in gloves, with short fingers."

Margaret R. "used to go singing songs in the streets. At last the songs grew so stale people wouldn't listen to them, and, as I carn't read, I couldn't learn anymore, sir. Since Mother's been dead, I've had to mind my little brother and sister, so that I haven't been to school."

Ellen was one of the few girl sweepers, and fourteen-years-old. She was born in Liquorpond Street, Gray's Inn-lane, and her dead father had been an Irish bricklayer. She lived with her widowed mother.

> About a twelve-month after father's death mother was taken bad with the cholera, and died . . . I got a place as a servant of all work. I was only turned, just turned, eleven then. I worked along with a French lady and a gentleman in Hatton Garden, who used to give me a shilling-a-week and my tea. I left them because they was going to a place called Italy—perhaps you may have heard tell of it?

What we see in these anecdotes from Mayhew's *London Labour and the London Poor* is the social and personal context within which job titles and occupational groupings come alive. Mayhew's children live by their wits on the London streets. Some refer to families but others made no mention of relations at all in their conversations with Mayhew. Mayhew went out of his way to visit the rooms rented by a gang of street-sweepers and reported to his readers the circumstances to which the boys returned after their working day. Street-sweeping seems to have been a juvenile occupation for the most part, although there were adults who swept crossings for ladies and gentlemen. Beyond childhood, the young crossing-sweepers probably entered more profitable occupations, but they remained in the public life of the streets of the metropolis. To this day, all major cities have street merchants who seem to delight in the ebb and flow of pedestrians apart from the profit of their sales.

Mayhew had a soft spot for the costermongers and their children, although the link between these street-wise entrepreneurs and their children was frequently tenuous. These proletarians spoke to each other in their own patois of reversed words—"eslop" for Police—and some of their culture still gives vitality to street language today. In the 1830s and 1840s, this floating, seething population of indigenous London poor were Chartists, according to Mayhew, conscious of their identity and of the walls of privilege and respectability with which their enterprise collided. He learned of their hatred of the police and that "in case of a political riot every 'coster' would seize his policeman." Only about one-tenth were married to their women, and the legitimacy of their children was rare. Mayhew reported that the incidence of marriage was highest, "about a fifth of the whole," in Clerkenwell. In general, the children were not, in the words of Eliza Doolittle's father, Alfred, "victims of middle-class morality," preferring to observe their own folkways. About one in ten of these men and women could read. As children, a few attended "Ragged Schools," of the type initiated by John Pounds in Portsmouth and by Mary Carpenter for children of the streets. While rarely literate or numerate, coster children grew up in a verbally rich culture, learning the cognitive code which lead to grasping traditional rhyming slang— "apples and pears" for stairs, but only "apples" actually used. Mayhew cites an informed observer who concluded that the coster's love of tales, that is, of language as a medium, "augured well for the improvability of the class." Of course, the Education Act of 1870 caught up many of them and education was impressed on the minds of these nimble children of the streets. After compulsory schooling, these nineteenth-century entrepreneurs undoubtedly had more tales to exchange as they went about the business of the world, selling fruit in season, working as baked potato men, or buying and selling donkeys. Traditionally, a boy aged ten to fifteen accompanied a coster with his barrow of merchandise, and then went off with his own barrow at about age sixteen. Shortly after that he would set up the traditional coster household with a girl of the same age. As apprentices, they received twopence or threepence a day plus food, "and as much fruit as they think fit to eat, as by that they soon get sick of it." The youngest boys were taken along by their fathers as young as age seven, or when old enough "to shout well and loudly." One coster told Mayhew that, "a governor in our line leaves the knowledge of all his dodges to his son, jist as the rich coves do their tin." In that respect, the coster was parent-cum-master to his offspring until the adolescent chose to work for another master, himself.

The Master

The fate of a child-worker depended on conditions at the worksite. Country children were exposed to heat and cold, but they enjoyed fresh air and the occasional charms of country living. For town children there was the presence of the mill and the lock-step of the work cycle, offset a little by protection from wind and rain, although sometimes exposed to the enervating effects of high temperatures and noise. Beyond these accidents of environment, there was the reality of the boss. In weaving, this was a parent, who might be no less demanding than the factory overseer who, at least, had to abide by the hours prescribed by law. Out of the home, the boss might be a worker to whom a boy was apprenticed, the two constituting a small workshop. At the other extreme, the owner might be a financier able to hire a superintendent to control several hundred children and adults. In the last analysis, the character of the master determined the experience of the children working for him.

In considering masters in the nineteenth century, the tendency is to impute the worst motives to employers as a class, based on the enormity of abuses when they occurred. Lest that correct but stereotyped view go unchecked, we start by considering kindly masters, within the context of the times and Victorian sensibilities. Although the worst abuses of working children occurred early in the nineteenth century, so did some of the more benign acts of industrial organization. The prime example is Robert Owen, who began in humble circumstances, married well, and, in the factory he bought at New Lanark, safeguarded the lives of the five hundred working children he found there. Owen had a Utopian streak and attempted to build a model community at New Harmony, a Rappite colony on the banks of the Wabash in Indiana. In that enterprise, which was probably foredoomed, he failed, but his zeal was unabated. He returned to Great Britain and plunged into unionism and cooperative movement designed to help workers. However benign the saintly Owen's intentions, his efforts sometimes went beyond the tolerance of lesser mortals. Ward (1962) records that a woman quit her work at Owen's factory because "there were drills and exercises and they were dancing together till they were more fatigued than if they were working." Similarly, one observer was driven to complain about "Robert Owen's interminable lectures."

Mr. S. Greg (Two Letters 1840) explained his sense of responsibility to working children in two letters written in 1835 to Leonard Horner. Shortly after building his mill, in 1834, he

> thought it time to establish a Sunday-school for our children. The girls' school now contains about one hundred and sixty children. As soon as the Sunday-school was fairly established, and no longer required my immediate attention, I began to think of establishing games and gymnastic exercises among the people. In the autumn of last year I established some warm baths in our colony, which have been brought into very general use, and have contributed materially to the health, comfort, and cleanliness, of the people. The men and women bathe on alternate days. When anyone wishes to bathe he comes to the counting house for a ticket, for which he pays a penny.

About the same time, near Bolton, Henry Ashworth was developing his factory. In Ashworth there is a blend of caring and distance for, according to Boyson (1970), he strongly opposed "co-partnership" with his workers because he thought it divided responsibility; however, he also wished to see his workers improve themselves. Boyson says that Ashworth was proud of the fact that thirty to forty of his employees went on to become successful owners or managers themselves. Ashworth was solicitous for children and opened a school at his New Eagley mill in 1825, and new structures were built in 1831 and 1833. Speaking to the House of Commons in 1844 (Boyson 1970), John Bright used Ashworth's philanthropy as an example of what could be done. Later in the same decade, the Akroyd family of Yorkshire established the Copley Factory School (Brown 1986), a practice widely emulated in the northern factory towns.

For a century, much of what we know about Samuel Oldknow was based on Robert Owen's memoirs. In 1921, a cache of Oldknow's accounts and letters was discovered in an abandoned building near his former cotton mill (Unwin 1924). born in 1756, Oldknow was one of the great entrepreneurs of the early Industrial Revolution. A portrait made in his prime shows a benign aspect, a generous and warm nature. A bachelor intent on his business, Samuel Oldknow courted two ladies—being turned down by Miss Drinkwater and never quite getting to the altar with the second, the frail Miss Shaw. His interests were broad and he liked music and the empirical aspects of science, especially the technology of weaving.

It is for his kindness to his employees that this former weaver is best known, and for his attempts to make life comfortable outside his mills in the villages of Mellor and Marple. An account of the time, around 1790, describes neat houses, well-clothed families, and tidy garden plots. Dependent children in the parish of Clerkenwell were sent from London to Stockport to work for Oldknow. From Ashford, in Kent, he received four boys aged nine and ten as apprentices until age twenty-one. Perhaps the strongest endorsement of Oldknow's magnanimity is the testimony of Robert Dodd, a kind of professional ex-factory child, whose pen was deadly. He had worked for Oldknow, recalling his fellow child-workers as happy and comfortable, enjoying shorter than usual working hours; a six A.M. to seven P.M. working day was two to three hours less than the average around 1800. Food was excellent, with meat every day and fruit in season. A former apprentice responded to stories of child abuse in Oldknow's cotton mills by stating firmly, "No one ever had owt to complain of at Mellor" (Unwin 1924).

Another benign master in the early days of the Industrial Revolution when child abuse was at its worst was John Smalley of Preston, who built a mill at Holywell in Flintshire which Samuel Oldknow visited in 1787. Most of the workers, numbering close to three hundred, were village apprentices. They were separated by sex and live in whitewashed dormitories fumigated three times a week. The children slept three to a bed, two when older, and there was an attending doctor.

And yet one should not view the benign employer as one who necessarily shared our current views on opportunity for the lower orders. Today, many people expect the person entering the world of work to rise on the occupational-managerial ladder. We view jobs as a vehicle for the development of human capacities as an end in itself, parallel to benefit to the organization as a value. In some occupations, it is very hard to resist promotion; nurses, for example, find themselves engaged in supervisory work, rather than direct patient care, early in their careers. People who understand and operate sophisticated word processors-cum-computers were in leadership roles among office workers at one time. In contrast, nineteenth-century occupations in general had a static quality. In part, this was due to work being "de-skilled" (Knox 1986) and simplified so that children might do it. In addition, there was the harsh sense of social class which led Henry Ashworth to be ambivalent about his workers and paternal to them. It led Sedgwick at the Manchester meeting of the British Association in 1842 to express with clarity the attitude of the times.

> In talking to men whose brows were smeared with dirt, and whose hands were black with soot, I found upon them the marks of intellectual minds, and the proofs of high character; and I conversed with men who, in their own way, and in many ways bearing upon the purposes of life, were far my superiors. I would wish the members of the British Associa-

tion to mingle themselves with these artisans, and in these perhaps over-looked corners of our great cities; for, as I talked with them, the feeling prevailing in my mind was that of the intellectual capacity in the humbler orders of population in Manchester. This is a great truth, which I wish all the members of this Association to bear away with them, that while the institutions and customs of man set up a barrier, and draw a great and harsh line between man and man, the hand of the Almighty stamps His finest impress upon the soul of many a man who never rises beyond the ranks of comparative poverty and obscurity. Do not suppose for a moment that I am holding any levelling doctrines. Far from it. I seek but to consolidate the best institutions of society. But I do not wish that the barriers between man and man, between rank and rank, should not be harsh, and high, and thorny; but rather that they should be a kind of sunk fence, sufficient to draw lines of demarcation between one and another, and yet such that the smile of gladness and the voice of cheerfulness might pass over, and be felt and heard on the other side.

There were some boys who overcame the adversity of working as children. Such a self-made man was John Buddle, who became manager of Lord Londonderry's coal mines and an opponent of reform. Another was George Smith, who addressed the National Association for the Promotion of Social Science in 1870. Thomas Dixon of Sunderland worked all his life as a cork-cutter. Self-educated, he was a keen student of letters and corresponded with the literary figures of the age. Dixon is credited with introducing Whitman's Leaves of Grass to William Rossetti. Another was the abused workhouse apprentice, Robert Blincoe. After great privation necessary to accumulate capital, he launched a successful career as a businessman and dealt in raw cotton. Despite ups and downs, he prospered and saw one of his sons ordained a minister in the Church of England. However, serious review of the origins of successful businessmen by Crouzet (1985) reveals that very few of them had proletarian origins. It appears that most successful entrepreneurs were well-positioned by the previous generation through access to capital and to patrons.

There were employers who out of pietism or a sense of amelioration sought to make the workplace the core of social improvement. Addressing the National Association for the Promotion of Social Science in 1868, Mr. R. Smith Baker gave the example of the Nottingham owner, Mr. Adams, whose great object in life he estimated as, "to promote harmony and well-being among his people," who amounted to just over four hundred employees. Mr. Adams put a chapel in the basement of his new warehouse, in which a paid chaplain conducted a daily service of twenty minutes. He provided a schoolroom, a library, a savings club, and a cricket club. Punctuality at work was rewarded with cash, on an annual basis.

A benign view of the working day was not incompatible with self-interest. Robert Gardner of Preston wrote to Leonard Horner in 1845 about the relationship between hours of work and the quantity and quality of the product. One year before, Gardner had reduced the workday from twelve hours to eleven hours, and he planned to reduce it by a further half-hour. His manager, Mr. Heaton, told him that the workers paced themselves, and Gardner observed that more bad work was done in the last two hours than in the first nine hours. Gardner's willingness to introduce shorter hours was rational as a manager interested in a quality product. Of course, he maintained quality and quantity without paying for the extra hour while also reducing the working day to a humane length. In this regard, we note that human welfare was good business. In Germany, the house of Krupp raised paternalism to new heights by providing housing. The noncompliant Kruppianer put his house as well as his income on the line. In Yorkshire, Titus Salt constructed Saltaire, to be followed in later decades by the philanthropy of the Cadbury's and by the development of Port Sunlight and the Lever complex near Liverpool. As a final example, we note one more instance of art imitating nature; Dicken's Cheeryble Brothers were based in part on the Grant's of Lancashire, doing their best to treat their fellow beings in a benign and considerate way. This aspect of life must have been highly attractive to children who otherwise faced a life of toil in the fields. The factory presented concrete benefits, and it also provided a sense of *gesellschaft,* or community based on formal status, in Tonnies' idiom (Bacon 1964), as towns grew around mills and factories. The owner who closed his plant for maintenance but announced a week's vacation without pay might be perceived benignly by his workers, because it is an ill wind that does not blow somebody good.

When we turn to the privileged who abused workers, we distinguish several styles of abuse. There was ideological abuse, in which an apologist for child labor saw benefits in the factory system. The Hammonds (1923) cited a Mr. Wortley, who addressed the House of Commons in 1811. He asserted that the public good was served by sending children into apprenticeship, and that work took children of the lower orders of society from their miserable and depraved parents. In 1816, the Manchester millowner, G.A. Lee, told the Parliamentary committee which also heard from Robert Owen and Josiah Wedgwood that his workers, adult and child, worked from six A.M. to eight P.M., for a total of seventy-six hours per week. For the Committee, the Chair conducted the following interrogation:

Is the Committee then to understand that the evidence which you have heard in this room has made no such impression upon your mind as to induce you to ameliorate the condition of the children employed by you, by diminishing the hours of labour?

I have no intention to make any alteration whatever, not thinking it would improve the condition of the people, all circumstances considered.

The Committee is then to understand that unless any legislative provision takes place to compel you to diminish the hours of labour, you have no intention, voluntarily, to do so? I have no intention to alter the average hours of labour; if I could make them more regular I would, and will.

Do you mean by making them more regular, that it is your intention to refrain from causing the children to work additional hours in consequence of the occasional holidays that take place? I don not; I mean in that case that they should take less holidays, and not diminish the time of work.

You mean to say the, that you will diminish the number of holidays, but that those holidays which you do give you will still repay yourself for by the extra labour? Precisely so.

Then the Committee is to understand that the evidence which has appeared relative to children working extra hours in order to repay the proprietors for holidays, has made no impression on your mind so as to alter your plans? None whatever.

The great apologist was Dr. Andrew Ure, who wrote "the Philosophy of Manufactures" (1835). In his book, Ure points out that "all the hard work is done by the steam-engine, which leaves for the attendant no labour at all, and literally nothing to do in general." With regard to children in particular Ure pointed out that, in spinning, "if a child remains at this business twelve hours daily, he has nine hours of inaction." In riposte to Michael Sadler's description of some workers who were fearful amidst machinery, Ure said that they "may be observed in cotton factories idle for *four* minutes at a time, or moving about in a sportive mood. . . ." He goes on to say that "in power-loom weaving . . . the muscular effort is trifling . . . it is reckoned a very healthy occupation . . . I have never seen, among a like number of young women of the lower ranks in any country, so many pleasing countenances and handsome figures." In Bradford, at a later date, an opponent of factory reform set forth the view that the pall of factory smoke constituted a protection from infections, and so was no harm to workers, but a benefit to their health (Elliott 1982).

Another abuse was reported in the *Morning Chronicle* of January 3, 1850, by the Special Correspondent covering Staffordshire. He reported that miners were required to engage in clearing rubble out of mine tunnels at no pay, because they were paid to mine coal not rubble. This exploitative requirement was a relic of the days when a monastery was constructed at Builtass in Shropshire by the forced labor of the peasantry. The historical incident was retained in the culture by use of the term "Builtass work" to describe compulsory but unpaid labor. A related abuse, in the sense that it occurred in mines also, is reported in the same article. It is that there was not a single engineer employed by the owners of the Staffordshire mines. The Special Correspondent believed that the conditions of work were so poor that to see the technology and circumstances in the mines was "like going back a century." The procedures for raising loads made no distinction between people and coal, and an old blind horse supervised by a child frequently raised both. As another example of the historical conditions of work enforced by owners, Lasker and Roberts (1982) report that Tyneside miners in the eighteenth century had to give six months notice of intent to quit their jobs.

In appraising the role of masters, we need to recall the times and set aside our current notions of management as a humane science. Today, many expect reciprocity in human relations between people of high and low status. That was not a nineteenth-century expectation, and the role of the master was always strong. Children are a powerless class today, and they were even more so in the last century. As cheap, replaceable labor, they represented a blend of low wages and docility. It took the general raising of society's sense of its own nature, through political self-consciousness, for the working children of working parents to even glimpse an alternative world of childhood. Until that evolution occurred, poor children were targets of physical abuse, stress and economic exploitation within the din of noisy factories and noisome environs.

The Environment

Work in manufacturing towns was dangerous to workers in another way, that is, in the form of damage to the environment. Within living memory, clouds of black smoke hung like a pall over many towns. When combined with mist in a static weather pattern, dense fogs were precipitated. The content of chimney emissions was noxious and toxic, and it deposited soot on the cleanest lace curtains which no domestic vigilance could prevent. Many a town appeared to its inhabitants to be built of black stone; sandblasting in the mid-twentieth century revealed pale limestone which gave town halls and railway stations a novel and attractive aspect. Of course, the particles which darkened buildings darkened bronchi and lungs. The result was that children outside factories were affected, if to a lesser extent, as well as those actually at work. The quantity of smoke was an index of waste, in the form of materials not oxidized or materials unintentionally lost. Hilton (1967) reported that the copper works in Swansea put ninety-two tons of sulphuric acid into the atmosphere in 1848. Seventeen years later, sulphur worth two hundred thousand pounds was lost in the atmosphere. When this degree of loss was identified, steps were taken to recover the materials, on economic rather than health or environmental grounds; however, children benefitted and probably experienced less lung disease as adults.

In the case of rivers and streams, the effect of effluvia from factories was worse. Historically, the Aire above Leeds was a place to catch fish, and Kirkstall Abbey was built there by the Cistercians in the twelfth century for that reason. With the coming of the Industrial Revolution, the river became fouled, and a misplaced step probably would have lead to death by poisoning before drowning. Of course, it was the flow of water down both sides of the Pennines which lead to the establishment of fabric mills in Yorkshire and Lancashire. Dyes and chemical effluvia killed the fish and made the water undrinkable. Polluted rivers reached their peak in 1858, when the Thames, overburdened with sewage to a degree that the tidal flow could not flush, created what was labelled at the time "The Great Stink." Whitehall was oppressed by the odor, and the seat of government was overcome by the waters flowing by. Chadwick's admonitions of earlier years were heeded, and a degree of clean-up ensued. Recalling that the presence of horses was enough to make streets odorous even in cool weather, the addition of fragrance from the Thames elevated the problem beyond tolerance.

In referring to these examples of how work and its processes affected the environment in which adults lived and children grew, it would be wrong to infer that the destruction wrought on nature by the factory system and the rise of towns was uniquely an offense of the nineteenth century. It is true that the slag heaps and coal tips rose higher in our period, and that the fouling of streams and denuding of hills accelerated. However, it is also true that the process had begun long before. In the area around Swansea, the assault had been under way for two centuries before the expansion of scale we call the Industrial Revolution. Hilton (1967) records that trees were cut down for iron-making in South Wales at a rate of two hundred thousand per year in the seventeenth century. The steam engine meant that mines already stripped of coal were made deeper and newly productive because pumping was available. The scale of extracting iron ore had depleted reserves early in the nineteenth century, and ore was imported from South America by 1827 (Hilton 1967). Erosion was induced by the early abuses which stripped hills of trees and created hills of shale and overburden, and this in turn led to reduction of crops and elimination of cattle. But these were the extensions of the previous short-sighted views of factories and the primacy of work. Today, young Britons seek jobs in places where nature and obsolete equipment have displaced workers permanently; there are sites where two centuries of inhabitation and manufacture have left people and nature exhausted. The jobs have gone but the people remain, persisting in their search for work and a living wage.

Income

The condition of people in the nineteenth century was an expression of the degree of development of the technological innovations we call the Industrial Revolution, which began around 1780. Estimates, especially that of Harley (1982), suggest that the economy was more developed at the close of the eighteenth century than has been generally supposed. Early output may have been twice our estimates, indicating that manufacturing and its need for workers was intense, a picture complicated by the Napoleonic War and its impact on the structure of national life and the economy. In the post-Waterloo period it was apparent to people that the pace of social change, of urbanization and the rise of manufactories, for example, was accelerating. Many viewed the changes with alarm; the writer of "Plain Sense and Reason" ("Author," 1831) was suspicious of concentrated wealth and frightened by industrialization, saying, "unrestrained machinery demoralizes society . . . it has pauperized the peasant, pauperized the citizen. . . ." He was, of course, correct in several respects, but the "Mighty Moloch of Steam" was not to be denied. At the time that "Author" was railing, Messrs. Gott and Son in Leeds were competing for women workers by paying a two-shilling premium above the typical weekly wage of nine shillings to operate power looms (Collett 1891). Competent men were reluctant to leave their hand looms. Part of the problem was displacement and the inability to match would-be workers with jobs and to train them. "Messrs. Taylors, St. George's Fields, London, have invented machines to complete pins without manual labour . . . will displace ten thousand hands . . . to what can they change?" cried "Author". Given the surplus of labor in one place and the jobs in another, the use of children was practical. Two decades later, in 1850, the *Morning Chronicle's* Special Correspondent noted that "the tendency of every improvement in machinery is to dismiss adult labor, and it seems to be possible that factories may one day be worked almost entirely by children."

To the family, childrens' wages were a vital element in the domestic budget, until adolescence and its inevitable cry for independence led the child away. In the cotton mills at Stockport, at the beginning and the middle of the nineteenth century, there would be several members of the same family, including children, reconstituting the generations of the household on the factory floor (Litchfield 1978). This was evident at the turn of the century when eight members of a family named Derbyshire all worked in Samuel Oldknow's mill not far from Stockport at Marple (Unwin 1924). Seeing children go to work was hard for mothers. A Welsh mother told Seymour Tremenheere in 1839 that her boys had gone into the mine at age eight; "after they once went there, they turned stupid and blind-like, and would not learn anything," she said. But work they must, and Cooke-Taylor (1842) defended "infant labour" on the pragmatic grounds that it was "a mere question of meat, drink, and clothing."

Apart from availability, children were cheap to employ, and they were submissive. In his 1841 "Narrative of Experiences and Sufferings," Dodd reported his stressful experiences from 1810 to 1824, and those of his three sisters, near Kendal. At age six or seven, he began work for the weekly wage of one shilling and sixpence. Ten years later, in 1820, he was making five shillings, and he was up to twelve shillings in 1827, when he was about twenty-three years old. He would not have been alone as a child-worker. At the time, Carlisle, to the north of Kendal, had two thousand looms, of which just over a third were worked by children, according to Armstrong (1981). The work was hard and stressful; Dr. Roberts, in 1876, reported that flat feet were five times more common in factory children than in country children, and the hours were long. Money wages were not always assured, because some people were paid in "truck," the system by which goods were exchanged for payment of services. Even more exploitive was the situation in which children were employed at no wages. In the late 1880s, Mrs. Stuart-Wortley (1887) reported that some employers in the East End paid youngsters nothing at all in their first jobs. The justification was that they were being given an opportunity and were learning how to make a living. As beginners, they were of little use to the employer, he reasoned, and so the opportunity to work was payment in itself.

Wages in cash or kind eventually recompensed the worker, although the rates of pay varied considerably by occupation, place, and decade. The modern reader is struck by the lengthy lists of occupations engaged in a single industry, for example, the manufacture of yard goods from cotton or wool. Each step in the process had its own set of hand-workers and some had their own pay scale. Across the occupations the rate of pay could be strikingly different. DeMotte (1977) provides several examples from Manchester. Bobbin winders might earn eight or nine shillings per week. A tailor might labor seventy-two hours at his skilled trade to earn twenty-one shillings. At the same time, a skilled soapmaker might earn thirty shillings for working fifty-eight hours. In the case of the skilled trade of bootmaking, the Irish *Crispin* in London, John O'Neill (1869), recounted fifty years of reasonably well-paid work. Bootmakers appear to have worked at home and also in small workshops where they got a "seat" or place. Frequently, O'Neill picked up extra work, and his narrative lists frequent changes of employer. Unfortu-nately, he appears to have had a lifelong habit of making ill-advised loans and undertaking doubtful ventures at the expense of an otherwise fairly steady employment and income.

In the case of the place where one worked, all depended on the boss and how he ran his business. To work for a man who purchased cotton from Egypt in the early 1860s presented opportunities quite dif-ferent from those created by purchasers of American cotton soon to disappear for several years. For the little-known weaver of Clitheroe, John Ward, in the same period, the volatile price of cotton, which fell by a penny a pound per hour in one period, determined whether the master had work for him to do.

In 1860, David Chadwick of Salford could show improvement in pay over the decades in Manchester as well as in his own city, where he was Treasurer. Over twenty years, wages in the building trades had risen from 11% to 32%. In the mechanical trades, the increase was 45%. At the same time, there had been a wage decline for those engaged in mak-ing beaver hats, calico printers, and block-cutters and printers. In addi-tion, prices had dropped with repeal of the Corn Laws and reduction of excise taxes. The result for a representative workman cited by Chadwick was a net increase in purchasing power of 14% over the preceding twenty years.

Much of our grasp of wages is due to the various studies reported by A. L. Bowley around the end of the nineteenth century, and to David Chadwick (1860) for the period 1839–1859. For the woollen industry, wages were steady between 1830 and 1850. They rose by 1860 and soared until 1874, when they began to decline but remained above the rates for 1830–1850 (Clark 1981). Table 4.4 shows the growth of wages in eight occupational groupings from 1850 indexed to the rates of pay in 1891 (=100), according to Bowley (1898). In addition, Bowley allows us a glimpse into comparative conditions in the United States and in

TABLE 4.4
COURSE OF AVERAGE MONEY WAGES IN SELECTED TRADES IN UNITED KINGDOM.
WAGES IN EACH TRADE EXPRESSED AS PERCENTAGES OF THEIR VALUE IN 1891.*

YEAR	1840	1850	1860	1866	1870	1874	1877	1880	1883	1886	1891
Cotton	50	54	64	74	74	90	90	85	90	93	100
Wool	74	79	87	92	97	105	114	110	105	100	100
Building	66	69	78	90	90	98	100	98	98	98	100
Mining	61	59	68	74	72	100	75	70	75	71	100
Iron	77	76	80	87	90	103	97	94	100	96	100
Sailors	61	59	70	79	72	90	86	71	82	77	100
Compositors	79	80	83	86	94	95	96	96	97	97	100
Agriculture (England)	75	71	87	90	92	110	112	104	100	94	100

*Bowley (1898).

France. Both started out at lower levels, with the United States well behind the United Kingdom. By 1893, American wages had achieved a higher rate of increase than those in France or the United Kingdom. This was presaged by rates of increase in the third-quarter of the nineteenth century as follows; United Kingdom, 60%; United States, 61%; France, 54%.

For girls in sweat shops producing "slops," or ready-made clothing, earning a living was corrosive. When busy, they worked six days of sixteen hours, according to the *Morning Chronicle's* Special Correspondent for London. Wages had declined sharply in the needle trades between 1820 and 1850, and there were two substantial periods of unemployment: December to March and August to October—which amounts to nearly one-half of the working year. In those periods, many girls turned to the streets, creating the phenomenon of large-scale prostitution in an age many people think of in terms of propriety and evangelism. Of course, it was an age of burgeoning middle-class morality and convention, but it was a period in which the range of human conditions was much wider than our own. In 1888, Charles Booth found it necessary to scale *Poverty,* in descending order to *Want,* of which the further degree is *Distress,* as representing the worst condition. To the Victorians, in an age without social benefits, the loss of work was terrifying, because people could drop precipitately, with the transition from Booth's Poverty, through Want, to Distress being all too swift. A haunting image is evoked by Nathaniel Hawthorne's encounter while United States Consul in Liverpool. On one occasion, he heard someone singing in the street for a living. Apparently, it was a woman with a trained voice. She moved on, and we surmise from the beauty of her voice that her circumstances were straitened and her modes of accommodation not diverse. The number of people, including children with parents, who slept rough in the large cities was a frightening lesson to the man who had a job. To be unemployed in an era before national insurance schemes, "out of collar," as Thomas Wright (Journey man Engineer 1868) recorded the slang term, was a terrible prospect.

With economic growth and a rise in the standard of living after the Hungry Forties, working-class people began to sort themselves out, and there emerged status differentials. Hobsbawm (1964) ascribed the term "labour aristocracy" to one who had good and regular earnings and security, who enjoyed good relations with managers and the social groups adjacent to his own, and who enjoyed good living conditions plus prospects of advancement. The earnings aspect, amount and regularity, were the most important. To R. Giffen, President of the Royal Statistical Society in 1883, the progress of the working classes in the last half century had been excellent. Life span had increased by two years for men and by three to four years for women. The currency was sound, prices were low, and Giffen could say with confidence and with pride that "the sovereign goes as far as it did forty or fifty years ago." The worker could report much the same from time to time, when work was steady and prices declined as a result of mass production. In such a climate, John Ward took an entrepreneural fling by taking a five pound share "in a cooperative weaving and spinning factory" near Clitheroe (France 1953). Ward did not prosper, but he generally had enough to eat, and he enjoyed the marriage of his daughter Jane to Bernard Knowles. Presumably, his grandchildren also entered the cotton mills, but at a later age, after receiving some education. They certainly were protected to a greater extent than John Ward was as a child. Legislation and its agent, a bureaucracy, brought into the lives of the young what Lord Ashley in 1840 called "mercy by statute" (Infant 1840). Such mercy came selectively, for children were a valuable component of the economic machine in an era of vigorous competition.

Children in the Economy

The condition of children in nineteenth-century Britain is inseparable from economic history, and the degrees of abuse and reform are the consequence of the ways in which economic forces interacted with political trends and technological events. Our purpose here is to discuss childhood in the economic context of society. We hazard a portrait of the century whose earliest cohorts recalled the loss of the North American colonies. The last cohorts of the nineteenth century are linked to our generation in the form of a few survivors, and by our reconstruction of an era which appears to many, in retrospect, to have been a simpler and happier age.

In the most general terms, the nineteenth century was a period of alternating phases of roughly twenty-five years in which inflation and deflation followed each other, in a process beginning with the years of the Napoleonic Wars. Within the first half of the century, Gayer, Rostow, and Schwarz (1975) distinguish five major cycles. The last of them, 1842–1847, came in what later generations called "the Hungry Forties," but which set the stage for the succeeding period of prosperity; it marked the high-water mark of Victorian economic growth, especially in the key component of manufacturing.

By 1811, agriculture made its peak contribution as a proportion of the national economy, and jobs for children and adults in manufacturing opened up. It is important to point out that 1811 came approximately thirty years after the nominal and arbitrary start of the Industrial Revolution. This was also the period when the quartern loaf (4.25 lb.) reached its highest price (1812) of 4d. per pound. A decade later, saw the peak year for employment of hand-weavers, the prime example of a declining occupation, who amounted to almost a quarter of a million people in 1821 (Deane and Cole 1967).

TABLE 4.5
CHILDREN UNDER FIFTEEN IN
THE TEXTILE INDUSTRY 1851–1901*

| | | % of Total Work Force | |
Year	Males	Females	Total
1851	14.2	17.10	15.60
1861	14.3	15.70	15.00
1871	14.5	15.90	15.20
1881	11.9	11.50	11.70
1891	17.7	13.40	13.50
1901	9.8	10.10	10.00

*Census 1911 (1917).

The 1840s were years of recession and hard times, although Peel's repeal of the Corn Laws in 1846 opened the grain market to free trade. Childhood in that decade was recalled for Unwin (1906) by a number of elderly people of humble origins as a period of grimness and hunger. By the 1850s, prosperity arrived and this was the peak period for expansion of manufacturing and the concomitant importation of raw materials. In 1866, the output of coal exceeded one hundred million tons annually, and real income reached its peak for the century (Deane and Cole 1967). A good deal of the coal went into the production of iron, which made its maximum proportional contribution to the GNP, 11.5%, in 1871. This period also saw the peak year for employment of children under age fourteen in cotton mills (1874), and they constituted 13.5% of the work force (Deane and Cole 1967). The peak year for the number of blast furnaces (N = 629) was 1875, and for building ships worth 17.9 million pounds (Deane and Cole 1967). The year 1893 was significant for ordinary people because it saw the lowest retail price index in decades (Deane and Cole 1967).

Overall, the picture was one of increasing prosperity, with money and jobs growing by fits and starts. The sweep of the century takes us from an agricultural country embroiled in war and suffering "the Great Immiseration" from the effects of loss of trade with the Continent and North America to the age of steel, Victoria's Jubilee, and the rising hegemony of Kaiser Wilhelm and the industrialists of the Ruhr. For children, the cycles of prosperity and unemployment of the head of the household were primary influences. Children in Manchester were affected when the supply of raw cotton from the states of the Confederacy was cut-off in the early 1860s. Paradoxically, infant mortality dropped, as mothers were able to breast-feed their infants, having no work to leave home for. The role of children in the economy was slowly extinguished as piecemeal legislation defined children as a protected class, reducing their hours of employment and raising the minimum age for beginning work.

For a minority of children, those of the economically favored, the nineteenth century economy of the United Kingdom sustained a sophisticated way of life. Such children were denied only immunity from disease, although vaccination for smallpox was available. The life expectancy and mortality rates for children of affluent parents were higher than that of poor children, but less than ours. Money could provide education in the form of home tutors for boys and girls, or a boarding school experience. The latter was abominable in the early decades, but it evolved into the public school system of higher, if less than impeccable, repute.

5.

LEARNING

A Little Learning

Looking back on his schooling at the Manchester Free Grammar School in the early 1800s, the radical weaver and poet, Samuel Bamford, recalled his first day as a pupil.

> The old gentleman . . . took me to a confectioners shop in Smithy Door where having purchased a pound of the best ginger-bread, he toddled, and I after him, across the churchyard, and down Long Mill-gate . . . my conductor, depositing the ginger-bread in a penel on the table bowed and withdrew. . . . On a sign from the master, a boy approached, and taking me with one hand, and the parcel of ginger-bread with the other, he led me to his class, which was that of the spellers, into which I was joyfully received. The boy who led me thither and who was the head one of his class now went round and delivered to each boy of the class, sitting in his place, a cake of the ginger-bread . . . in five minutes I had a score or two of new acquaintances, asking questions, giving me information, and ready to lend me a helping hand . . . (Bamford 1849).

The days which followed were less pleasant, frequently boring, always long, and interrupted by physical assault in the name of discipline. Another pupil was Frederick B. Calvert, who left a detailed account of the Manchester Grammar School (Glen 1979). The essential elements in the curriculum were the classics and the Bible, but other subjects were available for a fee, something Calvert's circumstances did not permit. Schoolboys of the time, said Calvert, wore a jacket cut close to the body, with trousers rising up to the arm pits. The course of instruction was equally constrained, and was pressed home "by the powerful inculcation of the cane," a process which "depended entirely on the humour our master happened to be in." In the case of the Reverend Mr. Gaskill, Calvert reports one eccentricity remarkable in the putative relationship of boys and master—they were not allowed to speak to him. When the inevitable need to leave the room arose, "we used to circle round his desk at a respectful distance, keeping constantly in motion and bobbing our heads in an unbroken succession of nods in order to catch his eye . . . 'till at length he gave the long looked for sanction."

In some respects, Manchester was above average in the quantity if not quality of schools. A Blue-Coat school to educate eighty poor boys between the ages of six and fourteen was founded in 1653. The Grammar School was founded in 1520, with the building attended by Samuel Bamford and Frederick Calvert erected in 1776. The school developed a substantial endowment, and its 1825 income of four thousand pounds funded twelve Exhibitions or scholarships at Oxford and Cambridge. In 1823, a school for the deaf and dumb was opened, and a school for the blind occupied a portion of its space. Forty girls were trained for domestic service at the Jubilee School established on the fiftieth anniversary of the accession of George III. Finally, in this summary of schools for young Mancunians from the anonymous, *Manchester As It Is* (1839), there is the Royal Lancasterian School in which just over one thousand children were instructed by the monitorial or multiplier system; the teacher instructed pupil monitors who then taught other pupils.

Of course, there were other schools, but these are the ones of which Manchester was most proud. In addition, there were private academies and Dames schools for which parents paid fees. What was conspicuous in Manchester in the 1830s and in other towns was the enormous development of factories and populations of workers without the social services that modern people take for granted. Schools were the obvious example, especially because the continental countries and North American had already embraced the concept of State-supported education for the masses.

In Britain, the problem of social lag, the differing rates of social change, was acute. Consensus held that voluntarism and private initiative was the way to take care of social needs; schooling had been provided, traditionally, by the charitable endowments and private, local enterprise. This system had been effective in previous centuries and appeared to be sufficient. Protection of the nation from Bonaparte had hushed the voices which found Tom Paine's observations increasingly persuasive. Society remained stratified but without the obvious excesses of the ancient regime. Things Gallic and continental, such as Rousseau, could be set aside as inherently un-British, and vested interests had everything to gain by delaying change. In that context, the Reform Act of 1832 was effective conservatism; it eliminated rotten boroughs, such as Old Sarum near Salisbury, but did nothing for the municipal government of growing cities such as Manchester and Birmingham; the older cathedral cities slumbered on. Untouched was the social agenda, so that the window tax and the Corn Laws were reminders to all but the rich of changes yet to be rung on the bell of liberty. The outstanding item after 1832 was the set of laws supporting the price of grains, and they had their protectors. Young J. Passmore Edwards, born in 1823, recalled that in 1842 the Mayor of Penzance was hostile to Edwards's attempts to educate the poor on behalf of the Anti-Corn Law League. The Mayor, Mr. Samuel Bidwell, threatened to imprison him, he said,

> because you have given my son, and distributed in the neighborhood, seditious tracts on the Corn Laws, and if you do so again to him or anyone else in this town I will have you arrested and sent to prison. Be off now, and don't let me see your face or hear of you again, or it will be the worse for you (Edwards 1906).

And yet all was not calm even in Penzance despite its Mayor and its renowned constabulary. Since 1780, it had been apparent that large-scale industrialism was changing the face of the nation. In Turner's painting the *Fighting Temeraire* was towed away to serve as a prison hulk, probably, by a steam-driven paddle boat. On land, factories' whistles rather than the rising sun called workers to their labors. Only the insensitive could fail to see the pale faces of children returning home from the unyielding discipline of the manufactories. Towns acquired a new class of resident, a lumpen-proletariat in whom traditional values had been swept away. Adaptation to the demands of life in slums consisted of unprecedented crowding and filth for which cheap drink was one solace. The other traditional adjustment, that of seeing God's plan as explained by a church which combined spiritual and patriotic elements, was not available. Working people no longer listened to Anglican churchmen, except as represented by Parson Bull of Bierley, Yorkshire.

Rather, it was John Wesley and his dissenters who brought God's ways into the life of men. Parallel to that stream of spirituality was the increasing surge of Irish people whose rural ways were even less adapted to factory towns that the local country folk. With their distinctive speech and names, the Irish, after 1820, brought their Romanism, little modified since St. Patrick's day and uncompromised by the expediencies of Tudor politics. Their schools suppressed in Ireland, and the tradition of "Hedge-Schools" a fragment of their rich, ancient legacy, the Irish were unlettered and unwelcome. No school system existed at state expense to teach their children the ways of the big cities across the water. A majority of the population, by the end of the first quarter of the nineteenth century, was alienated from the elements of society which civilize, which teach the ways of coping, and which transmit the social heritage that binds society into a whole.

To be sure, not everyone was poor, urban, and desperate. To those for whom life offered a modicum of comfort, schooling and cultivation were available. In the *Morning Chronicle* of September 4, 1817, a parent could read the following:

> TO PARENTS AND GUARDIANS.—A LADY who has been accustomed to the Education of Children, and who now keeps a Day School in an airy situation in town, is desirous of receiving under her care three of four YOUNG LADIES as Boarders. It is her determination not to exceed that number. They will be treated with the tenderest attention, be constantly under her immediate inspection, and form in every respect part of her family; they will be instructed in the French and English languages, History, Geography, Writing, Arithmetic and Needle Works. . . . Terms 30 guineas per annum.

The patrons of this genteel establishment probably received good value for their fees. Their daughters associated with young ladies of an appropriate station in life while acquiring the decorative skills of needlework and French, plus a smattering of utilitarian arithmetic and writing. For young gentlemen, Mr. Hughes of Petersfield advertised that his school was

> conducted on the principles so strongly recommended by the Messrs. Chambers. Latin, Greek, Hebrew, Mathematics, French, and German are included in the educational course. The treatment is liberal and gentlemanly, and the terms will not exceed Forty Guineas per annum, including all extras. The situation is delightful, and there are two coaches daily from the White House Cellar, Piccadilly to the School.—References in London are permitted to be made to George Harlen, Esq. merchant,

Arthur Street (West), London Bridge, City, and Seneca Hughes, Esq. 15, Bedford-Street, Covent Garden.
The number of pupils is limited to twenty five.

Schools such as these exist today, allowing for inevitable adjustments in size, cost, and curriculum. In the early decades of the nineteenth century money was the guarantee of education, and only if parents were attentive. If they were of adequate means and were inattentive, there were always boarding schools to which children could be consigned, then as now, on the basis of a higher need transcending the value of home life and family bonds. Of course, it is Dotheboys Hall run by Mr. Wackford Squeers which we think of in this regard. What is generally not appreciated about this element in *Nicholas Nickleby* is that there was a perfectly respectable boarding school in Yorkshire whose proprietor was driven into bankruptcy by the public's perception of Dickens's account as a roman á clef (West 1975).

Below the level of middle-class families the range of resources included the free Grammar School attended by Samuel Bamford, who appears to have been hungry for books; Frederick Calvert, for whom straitened circumstances attendant to his father's death were compounded by fraudulent deprivation of a family inheritance, needed the same Manchester free Grammar School to maintain a semblance of bourgeois respectability. Beyond this scant provision, there were few options. The most fortunate of the poor were the very bright children whose intelligence penetrated the social miasma of their early lives. Young Thomas Cooper of Exeter recalled the following:

> At three years old I used to be set on a stool in Dame Brown's school, to teach one Master Bodley, who was seven years old, his letters. At the same age I could repeat by heart several of the fables of Aesop—as they were called—contained in a little volume purchased by my father. I possess the dear relic, though tattered and torn, and minus the title page . . . (Cooper 1872).

In his memoirs, originally intended solely for private circulation, the successful Cornish entrepreneur J. Passmore Edwards (1906) recalled his hunger to read.

> On winter evenings the room in which the family mostly lived, was lighted by a single candle. . . . I, however, by the aid of such a light, managed to read while others were talking or moving about; and hundred and hundreds of times I pressed my thumbs firmly on my ears until they ached, in order to read with as little distraction as possible.

Samuel Bamford was equally blessed with talent and with motivation, but the window to learning which opened for him with a flash of illumination also closed.

> I first discovered that I had made some progress in learning one Sunday morning, at home . . . I found that I could read slowly verse after verse, almost without spelling a word. This was a joyful event to me; I read to my father when he came into the room; I read to the old Apothecary, and the latter, patting me on the head, gave me a silver sixpence.
>   . . . the day had come around when . . . a general promotion took place. . . . I being the first boy in the first English class . . . my father did not wish me to go into the Latin class. . . . My master . . . looked at me incredulously; studied,—questioned me again,—and with an expression of disappointment, motioned that I should return to my place. . . . Had the threshold of the Classics been once crossed by me . . . I should not have stopped short of this side of the university I think (Bamford 1849).

Later in the century, Laura of Lark Rise was put on the road to reading by her father, who used Mavor's First Reader. He taught Laura the alphabet and some phonetic syllables before his work took him away until weekends. One day, after several weeks in which letters in words baffled her, she found she could extract meaning from sentences by skipping the undecipherable words, and she realized she was reading (Thompson 1939).

Ann Yearsley of Bristol was less successful in achieving full fluency as an adult but capable enough to impress Hannah More. She became a poet, and Miss More observed

> If her epithets are now and then bold and vehement, they are striking and original; and I should be sorry to see the wild vigour of her rustic muse polished into elegance, or laboured into correctness (Vincent 1982).

In the case of Richard Gammage, a hunger for learning came well after he left school at age eleven. He became a voracious reader and is best known for his history of Chartism, a movement largely written about by people external to it. Despite his limited schooling, he was able to produce a coherent document at age thirty-four (Gammage 1854).

In his *Autobiography of a Working Man* (Behan 1967), Alexander Somerville recalled a man named Robert Wallace who worked with his father in 1817. Living all his life near Dunbar, near the Forth, Wallace was an autodidact, a self-taught expert on astronomy. Styled a "lost genius" by Somerville in 1848, Robert Wallace spent his old age scraping mud from the surface of a turnpike road for a pitiable wage.

Literacy and writing stories and songs led two Irish boys to a better quality of life in London. Early in the nineteenth century, John O'Neil left Carrick to work at a boot-maker,—a Crispin, as they were known. In his "Fifty Years Experience of an Irish Shoe-Maker," John O'Neil (1869) recounted his success at writing poems which became popular songs when set to music. At the end of the century, Patrick MacGill wrote two autobiographical novels, "Children of the Dead End," and "The Rat Pit." Patrick MacGill recalled running away to work as a navvy and to live as a tramp in Scotland. One day, he found a scrap of verse which struck a responsive chord, leading him to discover novels and, eventually, a successful career as a journalist in Fleet Street. In both instances, literacy and considerable native intelligence opened new horizons and led to personal fulfillment. For the Crispin, John O'Neil, it did not alter his life course as a frequently distressed journeyman with mouths to feed. However, he reported that the occasional two guineas for a poem frequently came at an opportune time. At the end of the century, Patrick MacGill's words were the passport for a better life as a man of letters. For both poor boys, the ability to read lead to voracious consumption of books and to an active mental life of composition. In addition to a sense of personal recognition, both men enjoyed a sense of recognition and approval from family and friends.

More typical of the literacy of the poor is the following extract from a letter written to Stubs and Wood, pinmakers of Warrington.

> We write to inform you, that we three write to now wether you wants any Jourmans or not, Thomas Wittington and John Cowles and James Hill. Thomas Wittington have left the Warehous ever since the strik, but he gone to Marsh and Gooden Mills to work but cant find im half him ploy, and is wife is dead and he is determined to leave Glocester, and James Hill have left is Father ever since the strike he works for George Martin, Leather Bottle Lane, im doing all heads and small shafes. And so no more at Present from your Humbly Servants Thos. Wittington, John Cowles, James Hill, and send we Answer by return of Post (Ashton 1925).

The mantle of reading and writing lay lightly on the shoulders of these three men willing to walk from Gloucester to Warrington in search of work. Their schooling was probably acquired at a Dames school within a few years. For boys such as Thomas, John, and James in the first half of the nineteenth century, education was a hit and miss affair, designed, at best, to yield a better workman who knew his place; for girls the opportunities were still fewer.

The Welsh child, Robert Roberts, born in 1834, remembered when he "was a little urchin about three years old,"

> the tall figure of my grandfather . . . as he sat in the carved oak arm-chair by the wide fire-side with the large family Bible . . . and myself . . . sprawling on the table close by and commencing to learn the letters from the large capitals at the beginnings of the chapters. Then comes a recollection of being found one day . . . my mother's scolding me for meddling with grandfather's books, of my pertly replying, "I can read it mother", of the astonishment of the family when I read out without hesitation the first chapter of St. John, and the prodigy I was accounted in consequence (Burnett 1982).

Home Instruction. In the case of the Scottish boy, Alexander Somerville (Behan 1967), instruction in reading began at home. He entered the local school at Birnyknows at age eight only when there was money to replace the patched and re-patched garments he regularly wore. A pattern of education available to the well-to-do was to educate children at home by retaining a tutor or governess. Horace Mann, author of the education report on the 1851 Census (1854) estimated the number of middle-class children being educated at home at fifty thousand. He concluded that the process of schooling usually lasted no more than six years even under the comparatively benign influence of a home with money to spend on the education of children. The hazards in home schooling were, and remain, several. Successful education at home requires that parents have a clear grasp of the ends and means of tutoring and that they have, as well, a certain method to measure outcomes at regular intervals. In addition, use of the home denies children the company of others, so that instruction lacks a socializing dimension beyond the presence of brothers and sisters. A high degree of responsibility is concentrated on one person, the tutor or governess.

Selecting a governess in the nineteenth century was a casual affair. A governess or tutor was not, in the culture of the period, a trained teacher; rather, he or she would probably be middle-class and well-educated but the victim of circumstances such as bankruptcy of a previously well-off father. Under these conditions, and especially if not gifted with charm and appeal likely to lead to marriage, the governess would accept employment from Jane Eyre's Mr. Rochester; under less Gothic domestic arrangements, the governess would probably dine with the family and accompany them on tours, with the explicit duty to familiarize the young barbarians with the uplifting local sights and to keep them away from vulgar amusements. As members of the entourage, tutors and governesses would be introduced to visitors and would be expected to keep up the conversation and create a positive image. The single great instance of the effective role of the tutor is that played by the man who directed the formation of the young Prince Albert of Coburg. Baron Stockmar guided the development of the young Albert, and some of the credit for Albert's amiability, sense of duty, and overall quality must go to him. Of course, he appears to have had an ideal pupil, but the Baron guided Albert to the realization of his potentials, and he remained an advisor to the Prince Consort in his later years. A more traditional Maecenas was Joseph Price of Shropshire, who recognized the talent of his apprentice, the son of a farm laborer. With Price's help, William Farr became one of the great Victorian reformers in public health.

Among the nineteenth-century figures of note who were educated at home were John Stuart Mill, Anthony Trollope, and F.E. Smith (who became Lord Birkenhead). In Mill's case, it is hard to think of a realistic alternative to home education, because his intellectual maturity would have been impossible to cope with in a classroom; such precocity remains, even today, beyond the responsiveness of conventional education. In the case of the much-loved Arthur Hallam, death at age twenty-two extinguished the talent which enabled him to read Latin at age seven. A little-known instance of intellectual power was John Thompson who, it is alleged, even just before his death at age eighty-six, could read a newspaper and pronounce it verbatim the next day (John O'London 1912).

For parents considering education at home, the domestic guides of the time listed the size of household appropriate to an income. Burnett (1974) cites the 1825 domestic guide by Adams; in it, a Butler is to be hired at fifty pounds, a French male cook at eighty pounds, and a female teacher at thirty pounds per annum. A figure also given by Neff (1929). Such would have been the salary of Mary Carpenter, who spent the period 1827–1829 working as a governess before returning to Bristol to open a girls' school. The clash between salary and educational attainment indicates the ambiguity in role which governesses endured. While admitted to the parlour, she was effectively consigned to the children's quarters. Servants were cruel in realizing the incongruities of the person, as well as the role. Mrs. Gaskell, in her life of Charlotte Bronte, recorded that Charlotte, in 1839, had written of her services as governess to the children of Mr. and Mrs. Sidgwick of Stonegappe, Lancashire, as follows:

> The children are constantly with me and more riotous, perverse, unmanageable cubs never grew . . . a set of pampered, spoilt, turbulent children. . . .

With regard to Mrs. Sidgwick, Charlotte wrote:

> [I] had done my best, strained every nerve to please her . . . I have never had five minutes conversation with her since I came, except while she was scolding me.

In the case of Mr. Sidgwick, she reported:

> [He] spoke freely and unaffectedly to the people he met, . . . and I had orders to follow a little behind (Gaskell 1863).

It is interesting to note that Anne Bronte's novel *Agnes Grey* was about a governess. Mrs. Gaskell reported that Charlotte Bronte had confirmed to her that the novel described Anne's personal experiences. Anne spent two years as governess to the children of Mr. and Mrs. Robinson of Thorp Green. Our picture is extended still further by the fact that Branwell Bronte joined Anne as tutor to the Robinson's boy for a time. In passing, we note that Mrs. Gaskell met Charlotte Bronte when both were guests of Dr. and Mrs. Kay-Shuttleworth in the Lake District. The Shuttleworth seat in Lancashire was only about twelve miles, as the crow flies, across the moors from the Bronte's at Haworth.

With regard to the children educated by a governess, children who did not leave home to learn had no sense of the unique role which children in classrooms acquire. Schooling on premises other than the home teaches the role of pupil and also induces deference and compliance to teachers. Given the ambiguous role of the governess, children saw her as half-servant, half-teacher, and obviously took advantage of it in some households. The children's own role did not necessarily evolve into the complex of behaviors appropriate to learning and contingent, in part, on being in a special place with appropriate models of behavior. The influence of the mistress of the household would obviously help or hinder the effectiveness of the governess. Were the mistress of the house to add noninstructional duties, the teacher's role would be weakened still further; and, of course, there is the inherent tension between parent and teacher over understanding and appreciating children in any age.

The ambiguities of the governess's situation can be illustrated by the case of Miss Harriett Wilson in the family of the Countess of Sandwich. Sir Henry Wilson represented himself affronted that his young kinswoman, to whom he wrote affectionately, was a governess. He proposed to provide a pension for her if she would resign her position. She did so, but Wilson did not provide the stipend. Harriett sued at King's Bench. The Lord Chief Justice found for Miss Wilson and Sir Henry had to pay up.

Victorian benevolence eventually saw the broad nature of the problems faced by governesses. The result, in 1843, was formation of the Governesses' Benevolent Association. It helped governesses between jobs (for the children they cared for eventually grew up) and after they were too old to work. Queens College to train governesses was opened in Harley Street in 1847. Twenty years later, Miss E. Davies reported to the Schools Inquiry Commission that the Home and Colonial School Society were preparing to educate a group of prospective governesses and "give them either six months or a year . . . chiefly in the art of teaching." An interesting note on the word governess lies in the Society's plan "to test governing power as well as teaching power . . . they do it by observation." The Society would also certify governesses in a range of subjects, "English grammar, reading, spelling, Religious knowledge, history, geography, domestic economy, natural history, teaching power and governing power" (Schools Inquiry Commission 1868). With the availability of new occupations for women as the nineteenth century came to an end, alternatives to the sometimes stultifying role of governess evolved, and educated women had a little more opportunity. They could use their talents in a noneducational way or in a wider range of types of schools mandated by law and by parents' growing sophistication in educational matters.

Voluntary Schools

Factory Schools. The prime mover among industrialists was Robert Owen of New Lanark. Purchasing a mill from the man to be his father-in-law, David Dale, Owen discovered several hundred child-workers who had been well-treated under Dale's administration. Owen proceeded to set up an elaborate system of schooling which appears to express the themes of the eighteenth century set forth by Rousseau. It stood in contrast to the mechanistic, monitorial system advocated by Bell and Lancaster, who demonstrated that a few teachers with student monitors in a pyramid-like social arrangement could school children by the hundred, simultaneously, at low cost. Owen introduced play and a child-centered view of methodology which emphasized individuality in the process of forming character. The school was a benign microcosm of society, a view which was to fall short of implementation in an adult form on the pleasant banks of the tree-lined Wabash river at New Harmony.

When we recall the abominable state of life in city and country slums, and the enormity of the destruction of poor infants by neglect of the public order in an age of *laisser passer, laisser faire,* it is easy to overlook that there were caring people who tried to help children. In 1819, there were 145,952 children receiving an education free in endowed schools, while 168,064 received a free education in unendowed schools; a total of over 300,000 (Aspinall and Smith 1959). Within these apparently large numbers, dwarfed only by the larger numbers of those quite un-schooled, there were a few dedicated people trying to help the children of the poor. Typical is Mr. John Wood, a friend of Michael Oastler and the Rev. George Stringer Bull, who opened a school in Bradford in 1830. In addition to feeding intellects, John Wood also established a diningroom where, Samuel Kydd tells us, there was "in Mr. Wood's face an expression of satisfaction and enjoyment which 'stores of gold' could not have awarded" (Alfred 1857). John Wood, Henry Ashworth, and Samuel Oldknow were not reformers in the organized or ideological sense, but men of the workaday world with payrolls to meet each week. Their sense of proportion allowed them to discern the essential merit of their child workers and the prudence of raising the educational and social level of those who looked to them for a livelihood. Equally enlightened and benign was the outlook of Mr. Samuel Greg, who wrote to Leonard Horner on the quality of his factory school in 1835.

> As long as it is thought that the summum bonum of plebeian education consists in a knowledge of reading, writing, and arithmetic, and that when these have been learned at a village school before the age of twelve or thirteen, the education of the working man is complete, or that when education is carried on to a later period, the communication of positive knowledge (frequently merely scientific) constitutes the only means of civilisation, and the production of a few clever men who have risen above their fellows, is pointed to as a proof of the success and efficacy of a system or institution, I think the *best* and indeed the only *real* ends of education are entirely lost sight of, and the exertions that are made for the improvement of the lower orders can be expected to produce only a scanty harvest (Greg 1840).

Such an outlook was not widespread in the early days of the nineteenth century, when times were hard and human values of the preindustrial age had not survived the rise of the factory. The Education Act of

1802 began the process by requiring that apprentices be schooled in a portion of every working day. In 1833, the new act required schooling but put the onus on parents and guardians. As one reads the testimony of factory owners responding to Parliamentary commissioners decade by decade, a sense of proportion reappears. It takes the form of a utilitarian conclusion that a literate worker, child or adult, is a better bet than an illiterate one. By the 1860s, even farmers began to see that they were better served by someone who could think, count, and follow general directions. Such a person trained since childhood to the conformity of the classroom had learned how to learn, how to run complex and expensive machinery, and how to maintain it in a rational, linear style of reasoning. Thus, the schoolroom with its discipline for rational learning became the antechamber to the discipline of the factory floor. Morality too had its place; a morally developed worker was less likely to steal and more likely to see the essential right-mindedness of a world where hierarchy was a law of nature. Obedience to authority was a virtue, whether the principle was secular or religious. As early as 1839, Leonard Horner could identify factory schools in Lancashire which he thought superior. The Grants of Bury were on Horner's list, as were Messrs. McConnel of Manchester.

In 1840, Lord Ashley questioned Horner, who was responsible for monitoring about eighteen hundred factories large and small. To the surprise of the Select Committee, Horner reported that there was a factory school he rated highly although it did not offer instruction in religion. It was sponsored by Messrs. McConnel, and Horner drew on a letter from Mr. McConnel in which he stated that

> formation of the school took place in June, 1837; that the children were found for the most part to be utterly ignorant even of their A B C; that they thought it desirable for some time after the opening of the school to direct the attention of the master as much as possible to the simple elements of education, reading, writing, and arithmetic; that it had been their wish and intention, in the summer of 1838, to introduce religious education into the school, but that they had been delayed in the execution of their purpose partly by the circumstance of the parents of the children being very much averse to the introduction of anything touching upon doctrine, and partly from the uninstructed state of the children in the elements of reading, as, by an attendance of two hours a day, great progress could not be made in a short time by children of nine to thirteen years of age; that in conformity with their preconcerted design of giving religious instruction when the children were sufficiently advanced in reading, they commenced, on the 1st of January, 1839, with the Irish Extracts, &c. which they had previously shown to the parents, which had been circulated among them, and which they ultimately approved

of; that since that period these works have been constantly read, the children have been regularly questioned on religious subjects, and the master takes every opportunity of inculcating moral and religious sentiments; that the books now used in the school are the following: The Irish National School Books, Part 1, 2, 3, and 4; the Scripture Lessons, Nos. 1 and 2, comprising St. Luke's gospel and the Acts; Sacred Poetry; English Grammar; the First Book of Arithmetic, and the Treatise on Mensuration; the Scotch Sessional Collection; Reed's Rudiments of Modern Geography, containing an outline of sacred geography; the Intellectual Calculator; Hickson's Tune Books; and the Irish National School Maps of the World, Europe, Asia, Africa, America, England, Scotland, Ireland, and Palestine, and that they are pursuing their plan of teaching singing (First Report 1840).

However, even the philanthropy of McConnel's was not boundless. In 1847, Leonard Horner had heard

that a very large number of children were about to be sent from the factory of Messrs. M'Connell, hitherto taught in a school on their premises . . . (Report of Leonard Horner 1847).

With the assistance of "some generous friends of the education of the humbler classes," Horner and his assistant, Mr. J. Nicholls, were able to set up a school at the Manchester Lyceum, and Horner received a grant of twenty-five pounds from Sir James Graham of the Privy Council. Sanderson (1967) calculated the connection between the size of the childwork force in Horner's best schools and found an average of sixty-three children at work. This suggests that good schooling was a matter of organization, in part, so that complex organizations could organize superior instruction as an expression of their overall efficiency. Of course, that presumed that the factory owner was free to apply his own convictions of how to organize and run a scheme of education. Inevitably, tensions rose as the factory inspectors used their extensive powers to summons and to discredit. The tension between workplace and education seems inherent, whether we discuss the implicit vocationalism of the farmer's son learning to handle the horses or the apprentice in the works. Short-term needs invariably prevail over the inherent needs of the full life-cycle, and they prevail over the patterns of employment which evolve inexorably, then as now, over the decades from childhood to retirement.

Sunday School. In a world from which religion had not yet slipped away it was taken for granted that acquisition of Christian doctrine was a part of growing up. And yet there were only seven days in the week, which meant education and religion, could not be allowed to interfere with the workaday world of lay-teacher and student. Accordingly, the devotional and practicing portion of religion grew to include formal instruction in religion through schooling on Sundays. The father of the English Sunday School system was the printer-publisher of Gloucester, Robert Raikes. He was not the first teacher, nor the first to see the role of instruction on Sunday. Rather, he was the first organizer of instruction, a step he took in 1781. On walking through a part of town where poor pin-makers lived, he recorded his thoughts as follows:

> I was struck with concern at seeing a group of children wretched ragged, at play in the street . . . I then inquired . . . if there were any decent, well-disposed women in the neighborhood, who kept school for teaching to read. I presently was directed to four: to those I applied, and made an agreement with them, to receive as many children as I should send upon the Sunday, whom they were to instruct in reading and in the Church catechism. For this I engaged to pay them each a shilling for their day's employment (Lacqueur 1976).

Recalling the letter written by the Gloucester pin-makers seeking work in Warrington, it is interesting to speculate whether their minimal literacy, enough to help them seek work in a distant region, was due to Raikes's efforts in previous years. Raikes's works were popularized, to some extent, through his newspaper, but his good works became known nationally, and eventually he was invited to meet George III and Queen Charlotte. By 1785, there were enough Sunday Schools to form the interdenominational Sunday School Society. It was followed in the years of the nineteenth century by other organizations attuned, for example, to the dissenting groups and their particular doctrines. Growth of Sunday Schools was phenomenal; Horace Mann, gave the following numbers for the decades prior to 1851:

As Table 5.1 indicates, there were 1,800 Sunday Schools at the opening of the nineteenth century, about one-half of which were run by the Established Church. The remainder were Methodists of various sorts, independents, Baptists, and Catholics. The process of addition over the first half-century was little more than competition between Methodists in several sects and Anglicans. In the first decade, about twenty years after Raikes sponsored his first 4 schools in Gloucester, the two major religious groups opened as many Sunday Schools as had appeared betwen 1784 and the end of the eighteenth century. By 1821, the numbers expanded to 1,325 Anglican Sunday Schools and 1,059 Methodist Sunday Schools. In the next decade the numbers increased, and

TABLE 5.1
SUNDAY SCHOOLS OPENED, 1801–1851*

Denomination	1801 to 1811	1811 to 1821	1821 to 1831	1831 to 1841	1841 to 1851
Church of England	843	1325	2291	2459	1071
Independents	378	471	403	452	514
Baptists	210	329	307	358	396
Wesleyan: original connection	415	810	783	903	924
Methodist: new connection	16	35	45	72	38
Primitive Methodists	4	14	139	361	542
Bible Christians	1	3	16	85	115
Wesleyan Association	8	13	25	152	86
Calvinistic Methodists	214	173	130	135	121
Roman Catholics	7	21	22	55	106
Other Denominations	74	124	125	167	439

*Adapted from, 1851 Census Great Britain. Reports and Tables on Education England and Wales and on Religious Worship and Education Scotland. *Parliamentary Papers*. 1854, *11*, Table 25.

they jumped still higher in the 1830s. In the decade ending with the census, the Anglicans opened nearly 2,500 Sunday Schools and the Methodists over 2,000 schools. Those numbers mean over 200 new Sunday Schools each year, which is about 20 new Sunday Schools each month. The Catholic Sunday Schools grew from 6 to 106 in the same period.

The weight of numbers conceals the selective nature of growth in various places. In Manchester, for example, in 1839 there were 86 Sunday Schools, of which 9 were Catholic, a proportion well above the national average conveying the size of the Irish population. Independent Nonconformists abounded in Manchester, so that New Jerusalem church and the Arminian Methodists—to be distinguished from the Welsh Methodists and Independent Methodists—also had a Sunday School. There were 25 Anglican Sunday Schools and 18 Wesleyan Methodist Sunday Schools, the two totalling about one-half of the entire number (Manchester 1839). By 1864, the *Manchester Guardian* could report 58 Anglican, 40 Methodist, and 7 Catholic Sunday Schools in Manchester (Statistics 1864). In terms of numbers attending Sunday Schools, nationally, the proportion of the age group between five and fifteen years reached 56.5% by the 1851 census. When the population is further

TABLE 5.2
DAY SCHOOLS, SUNDAY SCHOOLS AND PUPILS 1818, 1833, AND 1851*

	N Day Schools	N Day Scholars	N Sunday Schools	N Sunday Scholars	Proportion of Day Schools/Population	Proportion of Sunday Scholars/Population
1818	19,230	674,883	5,463	477,225	1:17.25	1:24.40
1833	38,971	1,276,947	16,828	1,548,580	1:11.27	1:9.28
1851	46,042	2,144,378	23,514	2,407,560	1:8.36	1:7.45

*Adapted from, 1851 Census Great Britain. Reports and Tables on England and Wales, and on Religious Worship and Education Scotland. *Parliamentary Papers.* 1854, 11.

specified by social class, the number in attendance of working-class background in the age range five to fifteen years reached 75% by 1851.

Lacqueur (1976) compiled enrollment data by county for three years: 1818, 1833, and 1851. The first year, 1818, provided the lowest percentage of the population at Sunday School; the North Riding of Yorkshire had the lowest rate at 1.3%, while Northamptonshire had the highest at 7.6%. In 1833, Derbyshire had the highest rate at 18.2%, and Middlesex had the lowest at 3.7%. In 1851, the year of the great religious and educational census, Bedfordshire had the highest attendance rate at 19.7%, and Middlesex was again the lowest at 5.9%. Middlesex and metropolitan London were not effectively evangelized until the last decades of the nineteenth century. In 1851, however, Bethnal Green and St. Luke's parishes were tied for the highest enrollment of youngsters aged five to fifteen, at 33.5%, with west London having the lowest rate of enrollment at 3.7%. Sunday Schools continued to enroll students and reached their peak in 1881, according to Lacqueur (1976), with 5.7 million enrolled in schools of all denominations. After 1881, the percentage declined but stabilized at 15.16% until 1911. In Table 5.2, we present data from Horace Mann's educational report of 1851; there we see how greatly education expanded in three decades ending at mid-century.

To the child attending Sunday School these statistics summarizing the scope of this important vehicle for education would have been meaningless. To a child in a Lancashire town, Sunday School was a matter of attending lessons in the neighborhood with local children. The teacher probably lived close by and knew the child's parents. There is a picture of what Sunday School looked like from Mr. J. Fletcher, who described St. Peter's Sunday School in Oldham. Mr. Fletcher was testifying before the Commissioners looking into the employment of children, and he provided the abstract in Table 5.3 of a day at Sunday School in 1842.

> The space in the church being limited, only half the children of the upstairs school go to chapel at once, and none of those in the infant-school. The classes of the upper school form two divisions for the purpose of attendance at public worship. While one division is absent the other pursues the plan above stated; forming graduated classes throughout the rooms, on the national-school system. Owing to the great deficiency of teachers, these classes are too large; but in the girls' school especially, valuable assistance has been afforded by the members of families of the richer classes. The numbers assembled, the earnestness of their labours, their purpose, and the time and manner of its pursuit, were all remarkable; and not the least impressive when all these young people united their voices in song with the tones of a harmonicon, the work and gift of a former scholar (*First Report 1842*).

TABLE 5.3
ST. PETER'S SUNDAY-SCHOOL PLAN

MORNING.	ORDER.	TIME ALLOWED	TIME OF CEASING
1/2 past 9.	Call Registers.	5 min.	20 m. past 9.
20 m. past 9.	Singing and Prayer.	15 min.	25 m. to 10.
25 m. to 10.	The appointed Lesson, which has been perfectly committed to memory; and also, if time permit, some additional reading.	30 min.	5 m. past 10.
5 m. past 10.	Call Registers. Classes prepare for Chapel.	15 min.	20 m. past 10.
20 m. past 10.	Singing; and Reading Lesson, with questions and explanations: if time permit, Catechism or a Spelling Lesson to be introduced.	60 min.	20 m. past 11.
20 m. past 11.	Singing; and a short Address from the Superintendent.	25. min.	15 m. to 12.
15 m. to 12.	Singing and Prayer.	15 min.	12 o'clock
2 o'clock	Call Registers.	5 min.	5 m. past 2.
5 m. past 2.	Singing and Prayer.	10 min.	15 m. past 2.
15 m. past 2.	Call Registers. Classes prepare for Chapel.	15 min.	30 m. past 2.
30 m. past 2.	Reading Lesson, with questions and explanations; and, if time permit, a little Catechism.	45 min.	15 m. past 3.
15 m. past 3.	Singing. Spelling, or an interesting Story—at the Teacher's discretion.	30 min.	15 m. to 4.
15 m. to 4.	Singing and Prayer.	15 min.	4 o'clock.

It was on days such as this that many children received their only schooling. The curriculum was the Bible, supplemented in enlightened places by the "interesting story" scheduled here for "15 m. past 3." Missing is writing, for one of two possible reasons. First, because writing was considered unnecessary; that certainly was the case in earlier days when Hannah More avoided writing because poor children should not be elevated above their station. Second, and more probable in this instance, was the lack of time for much beyond religious training except singing and spelling.

However liberal the curriculum, it could influence children only as long as they chose to attend. In such matters local norms are important because young people wish to put away childish things when peer group pressure dictates, not when schooling has run its course. In the early years of the century, children were sent to school at age two or three, and that was understandable when the function was day-care and instruction, and the teacher more qualified to give care rather than instruction. The informality was evident, in the case of Thomas Cooper, whose teacher, "Old Gatty" was renowned as a teacher of knitting in Gainsborough. Leaving such a school was hardly dropping out, and children tended to spend only a few years at school even when sponsored by the local church or chapel. Lacqueur (1976) calculated that from 1800 to 1860 the mean length of attendance at the Stockport Sunday School grew from under two years to almost four years. At the same time, the age of entry rose from 9.75 years in 1800 to 13 years in 1860. For Leek, the mean age of entry rose from 6.2 years in 1803–1812 to 11.2 years in 1838–1840. The years of Sunday schooling increasingly conformed to the elementary school years. In those optimal, critical years children were introduced to the Bible and reading and, for those who stayed beyond the normative four years, to a wide range of subjects from music to science. Not the least benefit was the moral training which conveyed a set of values which were the core of character development for the great mass of ordinary folk. In this regard, we set aside whether the sponsor was church or chapel, although to the churches the matter was fundamental. Throughout the nineteenth century, the Dissenters fought the Established Church, often at the price of education as a whole. From 1839 on, administrations stranded themselves on the rocks of partisan Christianity in an atmosphere of contention paralleled in the secular sphere in later years by the Irish question. The tactical victory went to Dissent in 1843 and in the long term, Dissent's triumph postponed any major overhaul of British elementary education for a quarter of a century. The triumph lay in postponing the inevitable national system of public education which the 1870 and 1902 bills finally organized. Even after 1870, the Sunday School movement had much to contribute; half-time pupils found instruction on Sunday more palatable than schooling which competed unsuccessfully for childrens' attention and energy with the workshop and the factory floor.

Ragged Schools. To the man with skills acquired by diligence and capable of providing him with a livelihood few things are as practical as training the young. A brief movement in the nineteenth century which should be evaluated less in terms of its numbers than in terms of altruism is the Ragged School movement. All ideologies have their nominal founders—although in this case the informality at its core makes exclusivity unlikely—and it has been customary to cite the cobbler, John Pounds, as the first Ragged School master. Pounds added some of his nephew's friends as students while working in his little shop in Portsmouth. Over the years, not more than forty boys were schooled by Pounds, but they would probably have gone totally unlettered otherwise; to have touched the lives of forty children to the good was no little accomplishment early in the nineteenth century.

When we turn to the Ragged Schools as an educational movement, we shift from Portsmouth to London and the organized effects of the City Mission Society to evangelize the poor. In 1840, five schools opened "for children raggedly clothed," mostly in the East End, and they were attended by 570 children. By 1845 another thirty-five schools were added and, subsequently, Ragged Schools opened in several provincial towns. The next innovation was the strategy of seeking out children with the help of recruiting agents, a ploy which added nine thousand children to the rolls of the Ragged Schools fairly quickly. Setting aside the quality and quantity of teaching and learning, Ragged Schools provided an alternative to life on the streets and gave shelter and protection for a little while. In some places schools met in the evening, and they convened on Sundays in other places; at all times, they were held in humble places.

The essence of Ragged Schools as a social response to a need of children was personal philanthropy. People from John Pounds to Lord Ashley gave aid to children of the poor in order to bring them Christianity. Of course, there was an inherent difference in growth of the number of ragged children and the expansion of Ragged Schools. The private, voluntary system was essentially a village model in an age when towns and their populations expanded enormously. Unlike Adventure and Dames schools, which required a fee from parents, Ragged Schools went to the hard core of the problem of child welfare, seeking out street arabs and abandoned children. Schupf (1975) reported a survey of 260 ragged pupils conducted in 1846. Forty-two had no parents at all, twenty-one had only a stepmother, twenty-seven had been in prison, and forty-one begged for their living on the streets. Seventeen were barefoot, and twenty-nine had no bed to sleep in. All were probably malnourished and destined for vagrancy and lives of crime. In the sense that Ragged Schools addressed a class below the poor (children of the perishing classes, in Mary Carpenter's ringing phrase), they were an inspired example of voluntarism. What the informality of the system could not cope with was the extent and severity of the perishing class of children. In London, the Ragged School Union aspired to organize the boys who swept street crossings. Beyond that occupation, they began in the 1850s to organize "the London Shoe Blacks" (1855) so that forty boys began to earn a livelihood with the approval of the police. The Union thought that being a shoe-black in an official red coat could be the occupation of as many as four hundred boys. The overriding religious tension of the mid-century, the struggle of the Established Church and the Nonconformists to control education, overarched the period. In some respects, Ragged Schools existed on Tom Tiddler's Ground, as the churches cancelled out large-scale development of education. The contrast is sharp, because the Ragged Schools probably aided several tens of thousands of perishing children; in the same period, Dissent and Establishment reduced popular education to a scale by which they kept each other from controlling expansion of education. Once that question was settled by Forster's Act of 1870 and its generic form of Christianity acceptable to most, but not to the growing number of Catholics, Ragged Schools disappeared under the economies of scale and the rising quality of elementary schools. With the requirement that all young children attend school at least half-time, voluntarism had run its course. The scale was always at the neighborhood level, and the Ragged School Union was a federation rather than a monolith. Its publications were informative and practical, and they attracted Mary Carpenter, Lord Ashley, and other prominent people as authors and sponsors.

By its little way, the Ragged School movement showed the shallowness and self-serving nature of the churches at the expense of children over several decades. In a more constructive vein, the Ragged School Union paved the way for a series of private initiatives such as homes opened by Dr. Thomas Barnardo of Dublin and the Royal Society for the Prevention of Cruelty to Children. Today, we have the Spastics Society and the National Association for the Mentally Handicapped. While their target audiences are unique, they share with the Ragged Schools the conviction that individuals can serve the public good in unique and profitable ways which State initiatives cannot quite match. Ragged Schools dealt with local children, and local patrons provided support.

Proprietary Schools. The Rev. Patrick Bronte cut into shreds a silk dress of his wife's, even though she had known better than to wear it because it was too fancy. This odd man was credited by Mrs. Gaskell (1863) with burning his children's shoes because they were too colorful. His judgments were no less clouded when, in 1824, he sent Maria and Elizabeth, followed by Charlotte and Emily a few months later, to a boarding school. Situated at Cowan Bridge, on the road to Keighley, it was intended for clergymen's children. The headmaster was Mr. Wilson, whose bad judgment combined with nosiness appears to have been a major source of trouble. The cook was incompetent, so that the little Bronte girls, delicate at best, would rather avoid meals than eat them. One teacher, Miss Scatchard, was especially hard on little Maria, soon to die from tuberculosis. The school at Cowan Bridge was also unhealthy. At one point, forty girls came down with fever, one of whom died at home, subsequently. Eight-year-old Charlotte took it all in, and gave the world Lowood School in Jane Eyre many years later. The school was closed at Cowan Bridge and subsequently opened at Casterton on more hygienic lines.

At a second boarding school, Charlotte Bronte met Miss Wooler. The combination of far more rational management, better sanitation, and a good deal of freedom was a boon to the girls in residence. Charlotte Bronte and Miss Wooler established a friendship which was to last many years after Charlotte left the boarding school. At one point, Charlotte and her sisters planned to open a boarding school in the Howarth parsonage. It was with a certain amount of relief that the Bronte sisters had no takers. Considering the site, it is not surprising that parents seeking boarding schools looked elsewhere, the air around Howarth being chilly even on the warmer days; annual flowers, for example, could not be grown in the summer.

Organizing a boarding school was not a simple matter. The basic requirement was space for sleeping and for schooling, and so a building of some size was called for. Then as now, large residences with many bedrooms and substantial grounds have much to offer. There were teachers to hire and there appears to have been no shortage of well-educated young persons who turned to teaching in an era when the list of job titles, especially respectable ones, rarely extended beyond the law, the church, and the army. Accordingly, teachers could be had cheaply, much like young Nicholas Nickleby, although generally they found more salubrious premises.

Food in boarding schools is always a ticklish matter, especially to boys. In the case of George Sala, it appears that it was food, one dish in particular, which drove him to sea, or a stab in that direction. He recalled his days at Mr. Bogryne's boarding school at Ealing. The cause of young George's nautical excursion was The Pie.

> There was a dreadful pie for dinner every Monday; a meat pie with a stony crust that did not break, but split into scaly layers, with horrible lumps of gristle inside, and such strings of sinew (alternated by layers of fleshy fat) as a ghoule might use for a rosary. We called it kitten pie—resurrection pie—rag pie—dead man's pie. Old Bogryne kept Giggleswick the monitor seven hours on a form with the pie before him, but Giggleswick held out bravely and would not taste the accursed food (Sala 1853).

At Hurstpierpoint School in 1868, daily meals were as follows:

> Breakfast, 8 a.m. Thick bread and butter, as much as can be eatin in half-an-hour, with a half a pint of new milk and hot water.
>
> Dinner 1 p.m. Meat, bread, vegetables, and half-pint of beer daily; puddings also four days a week.
>
> Tea 6 p.m. Same as Breakfast.
>
> Supper, 9:30 p.m. for prefects and captains. Bread and cheese and beer. (Schools Inquiry Commission 1868).

Recalling our consideration of the quality of food as a part of the general problem of ill health among nineteenth-century children, it can be seen that each meal could well be an adventure. Beer was frequently available to boys, and it presented the lesser of evils when compared with the water used at the Cowan Bridge school attended by the Bronte girls.

In 1866, the annual cost of food for a boy ranged from £7.57 at Christ's Hospital, London, to £19.94 at Haileybury, with the total cost ranging from £11.2 at Christ's Hospital to £33.2 at Marlborough. For that amount, amenities provided beyond food were washing, fuel and lights, medical services, and furniture repair—amounting to £2.36 at Marlborough. Instruction was highest at Marlborough, at £18.1 (with a discount for the sons of clergymen), and lowest at Christ's Hospital. In a set of nine schools analyzed by the Schools Inquiry Commission, Marlborough was consistently the most expensive.

In the case of girls, the North London Collegiate School in Camden Town provided board for thirty-three guineas and tuition for nine to twelve guineas, for a total of forty-two or forty-five guineas. Subjects offered in the 1860s were French, drawing, music, and "English subjects"; about thirty girls took Latin and German, and Italian and singing were available at extra cost. This school is interesting because it opened in 1850, suggesting a reasonable market for the education of young ladies. The curriculum is ornamental and excludes utilitarian matters such as mathematics and science, or physical training; such subjects did not become important until the end of the century for girls, and scarcely earlier for boys.

The Public Schools. While numerically never large, the revival and subsequent preeminence of the Public Schools is one of the distinctive elements of childhood in the nineteenth century. Public in the sense of not being run for a private proprietor, the schools we know today as efficient and probably happy institutions had sunk into disorder in the early nineteenth century. Teachers supervised boys in the classics, frequently in one large hall for all ages, and then left the young gentlemen to themselves, for the most part. In consequence, something approaching civil war was common, and the authorities resorted to troops in a few instances to suppress riots. Hippolyte Taine's inquiries led a gentleman to inform him that English boys had Viking blood in their veins and were naturally ferocious and untameable. As an example, there is the experience of Lord Pauncefoot who entered the first class at Marlborough in 1843. At that time, according to Mowat (1929),

> on cold winter nights small boys were sometimes dangled by their elder comrades by ropes from high window ledges.

At Marlborough, the last disorder came in 1851, although our earlier listing of a charge for broken furniture suggests all was not yet calm in 1866. Among the depredations was the exploitation of smaller boys as servants, a system ritualized as fagging and thought beneficial, then as now, by participants. The great reformer was Thomas Arnold at Rugby from 1828 to 1842. In those fourteen years, Dr. Arnold gave vigorous leadership and institutionalized religion, athleticism, discipline, and the Classics in a form others sought to emulate. The school days of Tom Brown, recounted by Thomas Hughes, were fictional, but they accurately refracted the values of the school for a wide audience who thereby grasped the vital principles expounded by Winchester, Eton, Shrewsbury, Westminster, Rugby, Harrow, and Charterhouse. Muscular christianity, being well-rounded, and adherence to principle were not bad elements on which to prepare leaders of a growing nation and expanding empire. To be sure, for every Tom Brown there were some like Flashman, but the norm was clear. A lad was to become idealistic, well-rounded, and athletic. To reach that stage, Harrovians were led by C.J. Vaughan, and H.H. Almond led Loretto in prayer and cricket. Almond has been de-

TABLE 5.4
DAILY SCHEDULE AT CHELTENHAM COLLEGE, 1862*

Lessons and Compositions, August to December, 1862

	Lessons	Compositions
Sunday		
	Voluntary attendance at the Principal's communicant class, $9^1/_2$ to $10^1/_2$ a.m.	
Monday		
9 to 10.	Lecture on Prayer Book.	Latin Prose (original and
10 to 11.	Thucydides, Vi, VII.	translation).
11 to 12.	Mathematics (in three divisions)	Latin verse (hexameters, elegiacs, and lyrics) gener-
2 to 3.	Preparation of Juvenal or Persius.	ally translations.
3 to 4.	Juvenal or Persius.	
4 to 5.	Mathematics or French or extra subjects.	
Tuesday		
9 to 10.	Greek Testament, Act.	Greek iambics, Greek prose
10 to 11.	Thucydides.	translation.
11 to 12.	Mathematics.	
2 to 3.	Modern history lecture.	
3 to 4.	Horace's Epistles (without preparation).	
4 to 5.	German or extra subjects.	
Wednesday		
9 to 10.	Composition at desk without dictionary (generally Latin or Greek prose).	
10 to 11.	Juvenal.	
11 to 12.	Mathematics.	
	Half Holiday.	

TABLE 5.4 (Continued)

Thursday

9 to 10.	Church History.	Three exercises shown up
10 to 11.	Aristophanes.	each week, on Tuesday,
11 to 12.	Mathematics.	Thursday, and Saturday,
2 to 3.	Preparation of Tacitus'	which are corrected, and
	Histories, V.	then re-written for the
3 to 4.	Tacitus.	second correction.
4 to 5.	French, Mathematics,	
	or extra subjects.	

Friday

9 to 10.	Greek Testament.	An English essay occasion-
10 to 11.	Aristophanes.	ally substituted for one
11 to 12.	Mathematics.	such exercise; and an accu-
2 to 3.	English Literature	rate analysis of the Prayer
	lecture.	Book lecture required each
3 to 4.	Horace's epistles	week.
4 to 5.	German or extra	
	subjects.	

Saturday

9 to 10.	Composition at desk.
10 to 11.	Tacitus.
11 to 12.	Mathematics.
	Half Holiday.

SUMMARY OF LESSONS.
HOURS

Religious (including Greek Testament).	4
Greek (including Greek Testament)	6
Latin	6
Mathematics	6 or 8
History	2
French and German	2 or 4
Composition in school	2
Preparation	2
Extra subjects	2 or 4

Total (in any case) 30

*Report (1864)

scribed by Mangan (1981), and we see in his photograph a vigorous man with a slightly eccentric view of dress for his time, a functionalism in which academic and physical development were related in the curriculum. Almond's emphasis on health apparently was too successful, because he began to attract feeble boys in need of remediation, which is not quite the same as promoting *mens sana in corpore sano*. In retrospect, we hope that the traditional high rate of bronchial distress among Britons, comparatively speaking, was not compounded by Almond's influence on young Scots. At the least, Almond's influence was a health-seeking contrast to the raging tuberculosis of earlier generations in the nineteenth century. We recall the Bronte children, for example, and the diseased state of young Maria at the Cowan Bridge boarding school. Loretto emphasized cold baths, open windows, open-necked shirts, and "sensible" living styles. This stands in contrast to the traditional Public School, which emphasized the Classics and thought sports inherently character-building.

In Table 5.4, we present the timetable at Cheltenham, which was the first of the schools founded in the revival of the Public Schools. Of course, the obvious elements are mathematics and the classics; history, for example, got two of the thirty hours, and science got none. This is a curriculum intended to convey external, classical values, not to open the mind to questions of contemporary society or to the challenges posed by nature to Mr. Charles Darwin.

Mangan has provided the daily routines at Uppingham in 1857 and at Stonyhurst in 1866, in Table 5.5. For its time, the reformed, revived Public School was an irresistible model, and so the process of imitation began under a series of bright, self-confident men, frequently clerics, all of whom had a gift for leadership and aspired to join the Headmasters' Conference organized in 1869. Lansing, Loretto, and Beaumont are examples drawn from three quite different milieux, with all three helping to put forth an ideology for the sons of the middle-class, for Scots and Catholics. Wellington became, eponymously, a base from which to prepare for Sandhurst, and Haileybury led to India. Not the least of the benefits gained as the century progressed was the sense of identity with a class and an ideal. The process of socialization accounted for all the hours of a boy's day and much of his year. He conformed or perished, so that many a sense of identity was forged in the hearth of bitter tears. Eventually, values became internal and personal, and the unhappy boy accepted his place and role in what we call today a *total institution*. (Goffman 1962).

As the nineteenth century advanced, the assured place of the Public School boy eroded in a world of commerce where technical competence as an engineer was more important than the ability to read Greek. Forced to seek wider opportunities, the Old Boy could call on the Public School Emigration League to find an opening in Canada, and also in Australia, South Africa, and New Zealand. Dunae (1983) reports that an extensive network of social and employment contacts extended across Canada from Halifax to Victoria. There, the ideology of the public schools was applied successfully; pluck became persistence at removing stumps, and grit was a virtue in the long Canadian winter. In time, schools resembling the originals in England appeared in North America, as in the Upper Canada College in Toronto, and in the boarding schools of New England, *mutatis mutandis*. Among the changes were the emergence of high academic standards in a world where merit, achievement, and technical qualification increasingly counted. The social elite of the Public Schools became a social and academic elite.

Considering the size of the British population from a distance, the amount of energy expended on preparation of the elite was inordinate; but that is how elites manage affairs. The ethic of service and of honesty prepared men who could face the social crises their parents' generation turned away from. In the last half of the century, leaders tended to come

TABLE 5.5
DAILY SCHEDULE AT UPPINGHAM AND STONYHURST*

Uppingham 1857		Stonyhurst 1866			
6:30a	Rise	5:30	Rise	4:50	Bread and Butter
7:00	First School	6:00	Mass	5:10	Chapel visit
8:30	Breakfast	6:45	Studies	5:30	Night studies
10:00	Second School	7:45	Breakfast	7:00	Supper and recreation
12:05p	Free Time	8:00	Schools	8:30	Prayers and bed
1:30	Dinner	12:30	Dinner		
2:30-4	Mathematics (three days)	1:00	Recreation		
7:00	Preparation	2:30	Studies		
9:00	Supper, prayers and bed	3:00	Schools		

*Mangan (1981).

from the middle classes as well as the upper classes, and it was their sense of service which made eventual reform an honest enterprise, not merely humbug. The pity is that it took so long for the elite to see beyond immediate self-interest to the broader self-interest of reform, itself a theme of the early nineteenth-century Benthamites. Robert Lowe, who insisted on "payment for results" in the education of the poor, was honest in expressing his aversion to the popular vote; but in 1863, his office did not flinch from doctoring reports submitted by Inspectors in the field (Danford 1977). The success of the Public Schools in socializing the young was offset by the majority of the population for whom education, and even literacy, was delayed by decades. The contrived but rigid relationship between caste and education was perpetuated by the revival of the public schools. To this day, British education is caught up in distinctions which are fundamentally social rather than pedagogic, questions which have been resolved in many parts of the world in favor of the common man. Yet, we cannot set aside the legacy of rigor and high academic standards which the nineteenth century public school has transmitted well into this century.

Going to School

The Schoolroom. Through the first two-thirds of the nineteenth century, many children received their schooling in the neighborhood from teachers with little or no schooling, in quarters which were really designed for other purposes. For working parents, there was relief that while they worked, their children were not roaming the streets and they gladly paid a penny or two to Samuel Wilderspin at the school he conducted in Spitalfields. For him and others, opening a school pursued the purpose of instruction, but it was little more than care-taking in many cases. Gatherings for instruction were called Dames' schools when led by a semiliterate old woman; they were called Adventure schools and Hedge schools when run for profit by self-styled teachers and autodidacts such as Wilderspin. For him, a now legendary discovery that play was a teaching medium for young children led to a lifelong career advocating early education with an overlay of Swedenborgism and phrenology. Presumably, the "Adventure" lay in the urge to survive amidst similar-minded competitors. Both Dames and Adventurers employed nonspecialized space, a kitchen or a former bedroom, and provided a service unschooled parents thought value for their money. Gardner (1984) recorded Christopher Thomson's account of opening a school at Tickhill, Yorkshire, in 1827, which failed. He acquired a reputation for not beating boys and for teaching poetry, a combination which put him out of business and back into the theatre. Early in the century, the noted Phre-nologist, George Combe, who was to associate with the Prince Consort in later years, attended a school in Edinburgh at Portsburgh. He recalled in his autobiography that

> the School was up a stair; it consisted of two rooms, having the partition wall removed at the end next to the windows, and there was placed the teacher's desk, from which he look into both apartments. The rooms were small, low in the ceiling, and without means of ventilation except by opening the windows. . . . In the course of the summer the heat and oppression of bad air completely overcame me (Gibbon 1878).

In Blackwater, near Truro, an injured tin-miner named James Blackney opened a school in a room nine feet square and charged twopence a week. When the children were about ten years old, the rate went up a penny, and J. Passmore Edwards (1906) remembered the day around 1833 when Mr. Blackney came to claim the extra penny, and he also recalled the exchange between the two adults. Eventually, Blackney moved to larger quarters, but, apparently, did not raise the fee. About seven years later, Passmore Edwards himself, and his friend John Sy-mons, opened a school to teach reading and writing to men on weekday evenings and Sunday mornings. When surveying schools in Carmarthen-shire in 1846, Mr. J.W. Pugh visited the Llandovery Academy at Llan-dingat.

> I visited this school on the 20th of October. It is held in the back prem-ises of the master's house. I followed him up a yard, and up a staircase, into a small room, wherein were gathered 12 girls and 45 boys. Those who have been accustomed to visit manufactories, climbing up a dilapi-dated staircase into a room clearly crowded with children, will have an adequate notion of the school-room and its approach.

On the same day he visited Mr. Thomas Price's school.

> It is held at his house in an upper room, at the entrance of the town, near the top of High-street. The staircase may be said to lead through a bed-room. There was a bed placed on a kind of side-landing, past which the stairs led, and which was open towards them. The School-room itself resembled a neglected lumber-place, of uncouth, irregular shapes; 17 children were present.

(Second Report 1862)

Slowly, schoolrooms began to appear as space designed for a purpose, but schools cost money. Only when the nineteenth century was one-third gone did money begin to trickle from Westminster via the National Society for Promoting the Education of the Poor in the Principles of the Established Church and the British and Foreign School Society; the first allocation was £20,000 in 1833. With creation of the committee on education of the Privy Council and the decade of James Kay-Shuttleworth's great influence, money became a little more available. National Society schools got much of the money in the early days, and expanded school construction was authorized in the 1840s. Some of the Board Schools of late decades of the nineteenth century still stand. We see two-story buildings with small play grounds whose narrow halls and staircases required close discipline and model comportment, for space determines behavior and predisposes buildings and children to tension or relaxation.

A brief sketch of the context in which children learned in the nineteenth century, which is a partial explanation for how little they learned, would be as follows:

Space. Room was undifferentiated for activity, but teachers' space was considered sacred.

The school day. It was a long day, either spent in the classroom or at work, with much boring time. Time was organized in blocks little related to the attention span of children at particular ages.

Activity. Children worked in groups at tasks providing little exercise for big muscles. Individuality of speed and learning style was ignored or suppressed. Repetition rather than insight was the mode of learning.

Thinking. The goal was for all children to acquire the same content. Today, we call it convergent thinking, and encourage divergent, idiosyncratic thinking; e.g., nineteenth-century children learned that there was a correct answer to the question "What are bricks used for?" Today, we want to hear as many novel answers as possible.

Personnel. Teachers were high status people to whom deference was to be evident and public.

Procedures. Uniformity of procedures and conformity to written rules made the classroom a microcosm of Victorian life. The ritual

of taking attendance is a handy example of clerical tasks elevated
to the level of a sacred ritual in British classrooms.

Of course, some of these elements are recognizable today, but the excesses have disappeared in all but the least progressive backwaters.
Attendance. For many children in the nineteenth century, school was
not the central element we think of today. Even when schools were available to the poor, parents tended to think of it as an irrelevance. Hannah
More's philanthropic zeal to educate poor children in Cheddar was met
with the attitude that she should pay parents if she wanted their children
in her school. The entire notion of schooling was wrapped up in social
strata so that the bourgeois who did not see the point of much schooling
for the poor found that the poor tended to agree with them. Acceptance
of schooling as an element in children's lives came slowly, and patterns of
attendance showed the pace of internalizing the radical notion that every
child belonged in school. Madoc-Jones (1977) reported that attendance
at the Mitcham National School in the late 1830s was hit and miss;
about one-third of the children on the rolls were likely to be in attendance in a given week. The other two-thirds were in and out, especially
when the weather was fine and there was a chance to earn a little money.
In the 1851 census of education, the author of the report to Parliament,
Horace Mann (1854), describe an alarming situation within a national
sample of a quarter of a million children by calculating the proportion of
"scholars, employed and undescribed." Those proportions were applied
to the three million children in England and Wales, and produced the
numbers in Table 5.6. Among boys of all ages, the ratio of those in
school to those not is about two-fifths. At age twelve, the proportion of
boys in school almost equals the number working, but the combination
of those two groups is less than the number who are "undescribed." By
age thirteen, the number in school was half the number working and
only one-fourth of the total. For girls, the number in school never
equalled the number working, and at age thirteen was about one-fourth
of the total. For Boys and girls, the interesting column is the relative
stability of the "undescribed" from age seven to age thirteen. In contrast,
the columns marked "scholars" and "employed" have numbers which rise
and fall reciprocally; the "undescribed" tend to be stable, a population of
which we know virtually nothing as late as 1851, which amounted to
almost five million. The census tells us, also, that the average years of
schooling between age five and age fifteen was 4.4 years.

In contrast, the reports from Northumbria described an Arcadian
peasantry who were sober and industrious, and who valued education

TABLE 5.6
ESTIMATE OF CHILDREN IN SCHOOL AND NOT IN SCHOOL, ENGLAND AND WALES, 1851*

AGE	MALES — Number of children who are				MALES — Proportion per cent at each age who are			FEMALES — Number of children who are				FEMALES — Proportion per cent at each age who are		
	Scholars	Employed	Undescribed	Total	Scholars	Employed	Undescribed	Scholars	Employed	Undescribed	Total	Scholars	Employed	Undescribed
3	49,168		179,681	228,849	21		79	50,621		177,478	228,099	22		78
4	92,167		131,242	223,409	41		59	86,661		135,962	222,623	39		61
5	111,229	425	106,779	218,433	51		49	89,544	780	127,153	217,477	41		59
6	123,030	1,030	89,817	213,877	57		43	101,099	1,213	110,341	212,653	47		53
7	134,492	2,128	73,084	209,704	64	1	35	107,216	2,570	98,646	208,432	51	1	48
8	125,919	7,032	72,919	205,870	61	3	36	102,488	5,400	96,548	204,436	50	2	48
9	122,085	14,287	65,972	202,344	60	7	33	101,235	9,674	88,224	199,133	50	5	45
10	110,126	27,508	60,690	198,324	55	14	31	89,401	14,787	89,995	194,183	45	7	48
11	89,918	43,173	62,229	195,320	46	22	32	75,298	21,110	95,342	191,570	39	11	50
12	71,639	69,275	51,609	192,523	37	36	27	65,547	35,586	88,420	189,553	34	19	47
13	47,116	88,485	54,502	190,103	25	46	29	43,050	52,066	92,661	187,777	23	28	49
14	29,639	128,431	29,655	187,725	16	68	16	28,160	74,869	83,070	186,099	15	40	45
3 to 15	1,106,528	381,744	978,179	2,466,481	45	16	39	940,320	218,055	1,283,840	2,442,215	38	9	53

*1851 Census (1954).

highly. Mr. J. J. Henley reported the evaluation of the Rev. John Young, Presbyterian Minister of Bellingham for thirty-eight years as follows:

> A few shepherds on the hills keep a school master among them and they lately commissioned me to procure for them Virgil, Horace and Caesar. . . .

J.J. Henley also reported the statement of Mr. Duncan, the Schoolmaster, at Wooler.

> At this time there are four boys in his school learning Latin: one the son of a groundskeeper, another the son of a shepherd, the third the son of a skinner of sheep, and the fourth son of the widow of a railway porter. Four others learn French and Euclid; one of those is a sheperd's son, the other a hind's. This shows the anxiety of the preparation for education.

Mr. Henley concluded with the following personal statement:

> I cannot too often repeat that in this district the pressure for education comes from the people themselves, through the higher motives which dictate it may have been instilled into them by their spiritual pastors (Second Report 1869).

Speaking to the National Association for the Promotion of Social Science twelve years later, J.A. Bremner (1866) reported that less than half of ninety-four thousand Manchester children of school age were in attendance. In the case of rural children, investigators frequently reported throughout the century that schools emptied when there were pennies to be made in the fields by gleaning, picking fruit, and "tenting" (an all-purpose verb which covered weeding and scaring-off birds). There was year-round employment to keep children out of school as the following calendar from the Fens in 1868 shows:

January.	
February	dibbling beans, for boys and girls over 7 or 8.
March.	"
April	Twitching and weeding corn. Women, boys, and
May	girls over 8, in private gangs. In public gangs
June	rather older children go.
July	Singling mangolds. (Osier peeling.)
August.	"
September	Harvest, making bands, and tying-gleaning.
October	Twitching, taking up mangolds, and (in small

November. quantities) potatoes.
December   Treading wheat, for boys and girls in some soils.

(First Report 1868).

In East Anglia the problem was acute because of children's work gangs. Given the state of the agricultural poor, perhaps better described as those who lived in rural rather than urban slums, schooling ran a poor second to contract labor as a priority. Parliamentary inquiry on town children had begun in the 1830s, but study of rural children came three decades later. The letter of Francis C. Beets, "43 years a village schoolmaster at Grimstow, near King's Lynn, Norfolk," explained the situation to the *Norfolk Chronicle* in 1848.

> Within the last 30 years the light and knowledge of scriptural instruction has spread through every village of this land; but there is a system which has begun the last six years . . . that of forming young children into gangs . . . (of) those young children so employed a very few of them ever attend the Sunday Schools . . . If the rising generations are to be entirely deprived of instruction in youth, to what a state of ignorance must that class of persons arrive . . . in this county moral feeling appeared to be in a very degraded state (Sixth Report 1867).

The contrast with children who attended day schools was like night and day to Mr. J.E. White, who reported to the Commissioners on children's employment from Norfolk.

> [Schooling increases] order decency, morality and religion . . . it pervades the parish, and year by year a great and beneficial improvement is effected . . . I am glad to say that there is a marked difference in the conduct of those who have been properly educated in our schools (Sixth Report 1867).

The problem of educating country children was pressing in North Lancashire. At Poulton-le-Fylde, Mr. G.H. Porter stated:

> I have 80 scholars on my books, but the average attendance does not exceed 40, and half of the school are away for five or six months. None stay longer than 12, and many leave before 11. There is no payment, the education being given gratuitously, and my opinion is that on that account it is not appreciated. People think that what costs nothing is worth nothing. Quite one-third of the children in this parish do not go to school; the parents are so indifferent about it, and those who do attend

school leave so early and are absent for large a portion of the year that
they do not derive any benefit from it.

The Rev. G.W. Osborne of Fleetwood added the following:

> The only way in which children are employed in this place to the neglect
> of their education is in "cockling". There are from 30 to 40 children
> thus occupied for a considerable portion of the year. They are chiefly the
> children of Irish who here engage in this business. Their children are
> taken on the sands at about 7 or 8 years of age, and as they have re-
> ceived no education before that age, they certainly get none afterwards.
> None of them attend Sunday schools, and they grow up heathens. The
> language habitually used by these children proves them to be in a very
> degraded condition. As the sands are not resorted to in bad weather or
> regularly in winter, there is time enough left for some education (Second
> Report 1869).

In the report on women and children working in agriculture (First
Report 1868), the educational level of the boys working on the one
thousand-acre farm of Mr. Howell near Cirencester was described as
shown in Table 5.7 by the Rev. James Fraser.

The table shows that three boys began to work by age six, four by
age eight, and three by age nine. The three who started to work at an age
when others begin to learn to read remained illiterate. One of four who
began work at age eight could write, and only three of the total of
thirteen could write.

Learning. Until the passage of the 1870 Education Act, schooling was
irregular and many children received little or no systematic instruction
within the brief years, if any, of attendance at a school of any variety.
After the enormity of the problem penetrated the consciousness of
thoughtful men, Parliament directed inquiry into the literacy and knowledge of children. One Inspector was J.E. White, who addressed several
questions to Annie Holt, aged twelve, of Hales Owen. She did her best
to answer the dignified gentleman's questions, but she had not heard of
France or *London,* and said that the Queen's name was Mary. In his
report to the Commissioners on Children's Employment in 1864, Mr.
White reported the following about James Price, aged thirteen, also of
Hales Owen, near Birmingham:

> Didn't go to school long. (Can scarcely spell). Heard about Jesus Christ,
> at the Church school, but it's so long since that I've forgot about Him.
> Do not know whether He did miracles or wonderful things, or how He

TABLE 5.7
EDUCATIONAL HISTORY OF BOY FARM WORKERS NEAR CIRENCESTER*

NAMES	AGE	AGE ON COMMENCING WORK	AMOUNT OF EDUCATION READ OR WRITE.	DAY SCHOOL	SUNDAY SCHOOL	NIGHT SCHOOL
William Smith	16	10	Read	2 years	—	—
John James	15	8	Read	1 year	1 year	—
Edwin Long	13	8	Read & write	2 years	4 years	—
Thomas Clappen	13	10	Read & write	3 years	4 years	—
George Walker	13	12	Weak mind	—	—	—
Edwin Butlin	12	9	Read	3 years	4 years	two winters
William Long	12	6	—	—	6 months	—
George Welavin	12	9	Read & write	2 years	2 years	—
William Messenger	11	9	Read	6 months	1 year	—
William Long	10	8	Read	2 years	3 years	—
John Long	9	6	—	—	—	—
William Kilbey	9	8	Read	1 yr. 6 mos.	1 year	—
Henry Long	7	6	—	—	—	—

*First Report (1868).

was killed, and have not heard of Noah and the flood. Jesus made the world in six days. The Queen has a name; it is "Prince."

Mr. White added in his observations ʾhat

as many as 32 persons, averaging over 12 years each, and including a young man of 20 and three girls or young women, one of 18 and two of 17, could not tell the Queen's name. Q. "Is it Victoria?" A. "Oh no, I don't know it when I hears it so." "Can't understand them things". Some did not know of her existence; others showed a dark and lately got glimmering by such answers as that she "is the Prince Alexandra," "is the Prince of Wales," "him and her got married" "she belongs to all the world" and so on. Indeed, a question about her when put was scarcely ever answered. These 32 persons were in a variety of work places and occupations; 28 of them in Birmingham, one at West Bromwich, and three girls, the eldest of them 16, near Stourbridge, very few indeed of them were under 11 (Second Report 1864).

Another Inspector, Mr. J.W. Pugh, reporting to the Parliamentary Commissioners on the same general question of how much children had learned stated:

Of the commonest and simplest objects of nature, flowers, birds, fishes, rivers, mountains, sea, or of places such as London &c., in England, or other countries out of it, or how to get there, many knew little or nothing. London, however, "is a county" but also "is in the Exhibition". Ireland "is a little town". A violet "is a pretty bird"; lilac "is a bird"; "believe I would know a primrose, it's a red rose like"; "don't know if a robin redbreast is a bird, or if it flies." A boy of 11 could not tell how many pennies there were in a shilling, or, till after much explanation, how many in six-pence; I counted 80 before a girl of 14 could tell what 3 and 2 made (Second Report 1864).

The significance of children's answers to questions depends very much on the times and the circumstances. In our day, such a lack of common information would be viewed suspiciously and might lead to an individual intelligence test. In the 1860s, conclusions were reached differently. Mr. J.E. White commented on the poor response to his questions.

I may here remark that the amount of ignorance in portions of the manufacturing classes disclosed in your First Report, which appeared during the period of my stay in Birmingham, caused general astonishment, and formed the subject of public comment. It was indeed thought here almost incredible, so much so that opinions have been intimated to me that the fault must have been more in the modes used for testing it than in the persons assumed to show it. This gives me occasion to explain as regards the evidence following, what in any case it would perhaps be desirable to do, that here ignorance of very simple facts has been professed, I have never assumed it till a repetition of the question in various words and shapes, and leading to or almost suggesting the answer, failed to show any further acquaintance with the matter, or reasonable hopes of drawing it out. In such cases the fact may of course still have remained in the mind of the person questioned though the method failed to bring it out. But as there is a limit to the time which the necessity for passing to other inquiries allows to be spent on individual instances, and as the want of power to take in the meaning of simple words and questions, or to supply the answer if known, is in itself one of the strongest marks of the want of any training of the mind, at least of such a kind as to be of any real use in the common affairs of life, I have thought it better in such cases, at the risk of a possible injustice to the individual, to assume the apparent ignorance to be real. Again, in several cases where a knowledge of the fact asked is shown in the answers it had been at first denied, and only drawn out in the manner referred to (Second Report 1864).

The locus of the children's deficiencies was the scope and nature of their schooling. The monitorial method proposed that learning was a passive activity in which memory was paramount. A teacher could teach an infinitely expandable number of children by using child monitors to relay instructions. The teacher instructed the monitors, who then instructed the pupils. The system depended on tight discipline and inflexible transmission of instructions. That messages became garbled, and the fact that discipline was more evident than learning took some time to sink in. The enterprise of teaching by the Lancasterian and Bell monitorial systems confused means with ends, so that the economies of the means outweighed the achievement of the ends.

Apart from the process of instructing, there was always the question of what to teach in the schools attended by the children of ordinary people. Hopkins (1969) has presented the course of study followed by children at the Old Swinford Hospital School at several dates in the nineteenth century. In Table 5.8, we see how thirty to thirty-two hours of classroom time was used in 1838 and 1876 by the third and fourth classes. The curriculum is lean and utilitarian, but not without Spartan virtues. Such a course of study would fit a child for the Victorian world of a county town. By that criterion the school at Old Swinford would be judged a success.

Of course, failure to choose the right criterion is a common mistake, even today. British education, historically, has favored examinations, although they have been routinely subverted and discredited over

the years. With refreshing simplicity, teachers around the world will always teach the criterion series once society decides what it is. The sub-
version lies in the assumption that the examination takes a sample from
a universe of accomplishments. Once nineteenth-century inspectors were
told by Robert Lowe to examine for results before local boards would
receive grants, a step which took place in 1862, teachers knew what to
do; memorization, frequently without understanding, became the preeminent methodology. "Our father wichart" and "bringing in the cheese"
(sheaves) are two examples of Sunday School learning in which meaning

TABLE 5.8
THE CURRICULUM OF A CHARITY SCHOOL 1838 AND 1876*

1838 3rd and 4th Classes		1876 4th Class		1876 3rd Class	
Writing	6	Writing on Slates and Paper	4	Writing and dictation	6
Reading	4	Reading and Dictation	4	Reading	6
Spelling	4	Sums	4	Arithmetic	6
Arithmetic	8	Reading, Spelling and Sums	6	Arithmetic and Grammar or Geography	4
Reading and Tables	4	Geography, Spelling, Scripture	4	Reading and Sums	2
Catechism and Bible Reading	4	Arithmetic and Geography or Scripture	4	Grammar	2
Hours	30	Catechism and Geography	2	Geography	2
		Scripture	2	Catechism and Geography	2
		Hours	30	Scripture	2
				Hours	32

*Hopkins (1969).

is absent. Young Charlotte Bronte was assigned the task of memorizing entire essays after she outstripped other pupils in class.

Slowly, there appeared formulations of achievement at acceptable levels. An example is the work of Assistant Commissioner Winder, reporting to the Parliamentary Commission on the State of Popular Education. Winder saw the following functional skills as the good for the ordinary man's children:

> Fluent and intelligent reading in any book or newspaper; the power of writing from dictation ordinary sentences, such as would naturally occur in a letter, almost faultlessly as far as spelling is concerned, and in a very tolerable hand; a knowledge of all the practically important rules, and probably, of the whole range of arithmetic, integral and fractional; a sound general notion of the map of the world, with an accurate knowledge of British geography; a connected, though slight, outline of the course of events in English History; and an ability to parse, and probably to analyse, any ordinary sentence.
>
> A child, in fact, who has spent some time in the upper division of the first class in this school, has received a sound education, abundantly sufficient for awakening his mind, enabling him to go on with self-instruction, and fitting him for any situation in life which he is likely to be called on to fulfil (Reports of the Assistant Commissioners 1861).

Children's performance began to improve with slow acceptance of the model lesson plan of Johann Friedrich Herbart, a technique which is found around the world and which, with a few reservations, is still unmatched in its efficacy. The Herbartian lesson plan was structured as a series of stages in which the initiative of the teacher was stressed as preparation, presentation, comparison, generalization, and application. The other great German educator, Froebel, saw in the spontaneous play of the very young the processes of an inquiring creative mind in a garden of children. James Kay-Shuttleworth particularly liked the ideas of Pestalozzi, who emphasized experiences for children such as demonstrations and touching objects.

For the preparation of teachers, Dr. Kay-Shuttleworth's brother, Joseph Kay, especially favored the ideas of Vehrli at Kreuitzlingen on Lake Constance. Unfortunately, Vehrli's ideas emphasized selecting the best rural youth and maintaining their Swiss rural values through study and farming before sending them off to the cantons to educate more rural youth. Part of the emphasis on farm work while studying was to keep the young men in their station and so avoid having them use their education as a vehicle to other positions. However, the history of educating teachers around the world has shown the impossibility of educating people without raising their aspirations in all areas. Indeed, one of Kay-Shuttleworth's ideas, that of pupil-teachers introduced in 1846, intended to improve preparation of teachers, and it became a vehicle for social ascent of the poor but bright child. In return for assisting with teaching in a quasi-apprenticeship, the pupil was given further schooling. A pupil could aspire to still more education as a Queen's Scholar. A youngster installed on the ladder of improvement by ability and drive could rise still further from humble origins. The problem in terms of moving to a higher status was that the child had to be so outstanding in an age when little beyond rote memorization was recognized. The waste of talent was enormous, and the loss to the nation in an era of increasing economic competition was deplorable. Science was a gentleman's occupation until the twentieth century, and much of what we recognize as nineteenth-century science was the work of talented amateurs. The nation paid a high price for a pace of educational change that was at best three decades behind other modern states.

Ireland. On John Bull's other island, the welfare and education of children expressed the history of that sad place. Riven by sectarian religious problems and governed from Westminster after dissolution of the assembly in Dublin, education did not fare well. In 1806, there were two hundred thousand children in school, and the number rose to just over five hundred thousand in 1824; four-fifths of those in school in 1824 paid a fee to learn from the teacher of an informal Hedge School (Daly 1979). With the establishment of the national school system in 1831, education improved. It added educational opportunity to become literate to that available through parish schools run by Catholic clergy and religious orders. Among the latter, the Christian Brothers had an established tradition of teaching boys, one which still exists today. For girls, especially those beginning factory work, the Sisters of Mercy ran evening schools. In Belfast, the average attendance was 425, three-quarters of whom were between age twelve and age twenty-one, averaging age eighteen. A report of the time speaks of knowledge as "a shield of sweet protection" for "moral danger" (Adult 1856). Because practically all the girls were working in the mills, the danger was substantial. At the time of the report, Ireland had 1.5 million illiterate families. Accordingly, the Sisters' goal of educating to the fourth level of elementary schooling was practical. In the essential matter of materials for learning and teaching, Ireland had contributed an innovative series of reading and spelling books through the Kildare Place Society. It became active in the second decade of the nineteenth century, and its publications were received well in England in the following decade. The successor to the Kildare Place

TABLE 5.9
EDUCATION IN IRELAND 1841–1901*

Year	Illiterates >5 years (%)	At School 5–16 years (5)	>200 days of School per annum (%)	Irish-Speaking by decade of birth	Irish-Speaking —all ages
1841	52.70	20.00			
1851	46.80	25.00		19.20	
1861	38.70	30.00	8.90		
1871	33.40	42.10	6.20		
1881	25.20	46.50	6.80	13.80	18.20
1891	18.40	54.10	5.80	10.80	14.50
1901	13.70	60.20	7.20	4.90	14.40

*Thompson, W. J. (1913).

Society was the Commission on National Education; this body also produced attractive reading materials for children.

Much of our knowledge of the educational level of the Irish population as a whole is derived from census data, especially that in the 1911 report. Sir William Thompson's report to the Royal Statistical Society in 1913 incorporated data from the nineteenth century. Table 5.9 combines several sets of data selectively in order to give a picture across several decades. In 1840, half the population over age five was illiterate. The decrease in the subsequent decades can be understood as a decline in the older portion of the population and an infusion of children who received more education. Of course, emigration was an element in the picture, but it is not apparent whether the least educated emigrated or could not afford to do so. In either case, the level of illiteracy fell and the proportion of children at school rose threefold over the last six decades. Schooling needs to be qualified, however; we see that the number attending extensive schooling in any year was not large, and fell slightly. The proportion of Irish speakers was not large and fell drastically in the remaining years of the century. Of course, the numbers reversed with the Gaelic revival of the late nineteenth and early twentieth centuries. Eventually, Irish became an element in the school curriculum, restoring the language of scholars and saints.

For all elements in the curriculum, the level of education in Ireland rose slowly but steadily. In 1853, for example, the number of convicted criminals in Dublin who were illiterate and innumerate was 410; by 1859 it was down to 167, a decline of 40% (O'Shaugnessy 1861). In the forty years after 1841, the number of children attending school, a wholly voluntary act at the time, rose from 475,559 to 675,036. In the same four decades, the number of persons able to read and to write rose from 1.96 million to 2.72 million. The number able to read but not write dropped from 1.41 million to .71 million. The number capable of neither reading nor writing dropped from 3.76 million in 1841 to 1.16 million in 1881. Of course, not all of the change in the literacy rate over four decades should be traced to education. Decade by decade, schooling added to the proportion of the literate and numerate children, and death progressively drained off the elderly, among whom illiteracy was proportionately greater.

6.

SOCIAL LIFE

T he reality of life for the Victorians was work, but even the most
overworked of people enjoy a network of friends and family; and society
provides a framework within which even work, life, and death take their
place. In this chapter, we consider the elements of life in the broadest
sense which children and their families experienced in the nineteenth
century. We shall examine several institutions, including holidays from
work and the social movements of the age. Many of these elements are
not really divorced from work; in the case of vacations, their essential
nature is that they are nonwork periods. My intention is to balance the
role of work with the elements of life children experienced outside the
demands of the master or the factory whistle. In so doing, I hope to
convey the richness of the nineteenth century with its preindustrial origins and, toward the end of our period, the rise of organized, professional sports. The latter is a culture complex still evolving, one which
absorbs an inordinate amount of energy in our century (as, perhaps,
religion once did amid the Evangelicals of the nineteenth century, although with a less benign outcome).

For children, induction into the culture of one's social class and place occurred through the unselfconscious processes of growing up in a particular home in a given town. Parents, relatives, and companions introduced the relevant version of religion, of sport, and of use of alcohol and tobacco. Identification with parents and neighbors produced a sense of self and a sense of location in the Victorian world. Social institutions reinforced the sense of place through patterns of language, modes of education, and through the clear messages of social class membership and place. The homogeneity of people in niches of place and the social order was important to the Victorians. Best (1971) records the view of Captain O'Brien, who, addressing a Select Committee of the House of Commons in 1852, said

> with us the distinction of classes, is a national characteristic. There may be considerable kindness between classes, but there is no cordiality.

Accordingly, a knowledge of the appropriate version of social institutions, acquisition of accents and outlook, and a keen sense of "them" and "us" gave the Victorian child an automatic mastery of the skills for living amid social conventions and for making the choices appropriate to one's circumstances.

The Victorian child acquired sensibilities, a perception of the world mediated powerfully by the processes of socialization. Those masters of irony, Gilbert and Sullivan, hinged many of their plots—for example, that of "that infernal nonsense, Pinafore"—on the accident of birth into a stratum of society. In that typical plot, the British sailor is any man's equal, except that of the speaker, Sir Joseph Porter, K.C.B., ruler of the Queen's Navee. Beyond the rigidity of class and culture lay accident of birth, so that when babies were misplaced, the imbalance could only be redressed by having characters abandon their acquired roles in order to live out the original roles prescribed by the social class of their parents. From the accident of parentage and subsequent misrearing, Gilbert and Sullivan told their audiences where pirates came from, and how a sailor might aspire to love a captain's daughter, and how a maiden saw the world "in my simple Japanese way." Sensibilities were inculcated, and there was a proper way to behave according to one's station. One was born to be a "Liberal or a Conservative," and that was that. Respectability was the password for the rising lower middle class.

For the upper-class child, a sense of assured superiority and eventual membership into a vast network of the privileged were expressions of that sensibility. The network itself expanded substantially over the course of the nineteenth century, consolidated by marriages and other connections. By and large, the children of privilege fell into three groups in the first several decades. The most established group of families had their wealth based in land. As the century progressed, manufacturers in provincial cities amassed fortunes providing material comfort for their generally evangelical families. The second group were financiers in the City; they were Anglican and residents of the home counties rather than the North. The gravity of finance and climate inevitably drew privileged families to the southeast. Within that region, the privileged worked out the matrimonial and social connections of their young, with propinquity lubricating the process. Rubinstein (1977) points out that the City men and landed aristocracy were both Anglican, a bond not shared, for the most part, by the Northern manufacturers. For children of all social classes, there was a unique culture to assimilate. For some, it included work rather than education at an early age. For girls, all social classes deemed education a minor matter, and all class cultures placed a higher valuation on boys. Within each social stratum there were elements such as games which were transmitted from older to younger children.

The Culture of Childhood

For young children, the business of life is play, the process by which children's imperfect grasp of reality allows them to reconstruct the elements of daily living into forms and meanings adults do not share. The old philosophical chestnut about what is real has validity when we look into the world of childhood. Piaget has taught us that maturing includes an evolving formulation of reality. Objects are not static to children, and causality is as different in their minds as in the minds of Amazonian forest dwellers. Accordingly, games are not "adult recreation engaged in by short adults"—that is, by children. Rather, they refer to thinking about the world in a magical, changeling way, so that the contents of the joint world of adults and children are formulated differently by children. It is a little like seeing things in stereo rather than in two dimensions, or like adding color in the world of black, gray, and white. Of these alternative realities, we adults have given up the richer and experience the poorer, for the prize of objects' stability and a degree of predictability. Games are how reality seems to those whose reality is evanescent, mutating, and transient. Games are perceptual manipulations of things, of people, or words and meanings within reality that is wholly subjective and evolving.

In the context of nineteenth-century Britain, it seems likely that children's play changed with the appearance of mass education, so that the play life of children was altered by schooling, and the adults they became were also altered. With regard to the former, schooling does two things for the mental life of children. First, it introduces the structure of language into thought to a degree which inhibits other modes of thought—intuition and the informal. Language through its syntax is logical and structural, so children who are literate are probably more adept at the use of abstractions caught in a formal way. Second, schooling also introduces content, stories, and facts; they are raw materials beyond the encounters of the neighborhood which expand the themes and content of phantasy. With regard to the evolution of children into literate adults, the consequence of education is to form a less manipulable person. The early nineteenth century establishment was aware of this fact. Early resistance to education, especially to reading, was based on the accurate perception that literate children would evolve into less tractable adults. One read of worries that literacy will lead to a loss of religious feeling and contribute to nascent republicanism. The mental life of children was changed by education, and the mechanisms of play were probably modified and enriched by schooling. Equally, the form and content of play shifted as toys evolved. Early in the century toys were simple and allowed a fluid reality to change them in marvellous ways. With metal fabrication, toys became less ambiguous and more representational, which was probably a loss for creativity and imagination. Toy trains looked only like trains, for example; although dolls probably resisted conformity to a greater degree. In this century, thoughtful toy makers have restored much of the imagination of the youngest children by giving more imaginative plasticity to play materials.

On the other hand, games survived the century in fairly unchanged ways. That is, rules for running and throwing became more formal, as in tennis for girls and soccer for boys; but games not needing equipment, such as hide-and-seek, probably are the same as they were centuries ago. The equipment-dependent games of the late period of the nineteenth century evolved to a degree we might formulate as ritualistic; for example, only eleven on a cricket team, only fifteen on a rugby team, and so forth. In those games, formality rather than phantasy predominates, which is rather a shame.

Balance requires that we address the continuity of children's games. Considering this topic leads to discovery of the lost Tribe of Children.

That is, games are elements in the culture of childhood, a phenomenon as unique as the culture of the Stone-Age. If we adopt the attitude of anthropologists, we find that childhood is a tribe whose members transmit the lore of the group to the newest, youngest members. It is not adults who teach hide-and-seek or tag but children. The fidelity of this transmission is remarkable, and variations tend to be localisms, that is, horizontal evolutions rather than progressive and cumulative changes. Early Victorian society lost much of its preindustrial, agrarian culture (e.g., the loss of traditional holidays) to the factory calendar. However, the culture of childhood continued to transmit traditional rules of games. Many games have an oral component, a good example of which is the song which accompanies skipping a rope or bouncing a ball. The fidelity of what a child would sing a century or more ago, and today, is remarkable. The Opies (1959) record the rhyme

> Queen, Queen Caroline
> Dipped her head in Turpentine
> Why did she look so fine?
> Because she wore a crinoline

which they trace to the early nineteenth century and the coronation of George IV. Riddles, puns, and jokes persist in the same way. The question

> Q. "Why did the cow look over the wall?"
>
> A. "To see what was on the other side."

is at least 150 years old. Not going to school on May 29, Oak Apple Day, is another aspect of the culture of childhood. In the Cotswolds, memoirs of the Stuarts persisted; Laura of Lark Rise recalled a game she labelled "grim." In the game of "Daddy," one player circled the ring of children and struck one on the neck who, beheaded, then fell down. Similarly, J. Arthur Gibbs (1903) recorded the ballad of "George Ridler's Oven," passed down from generation to generation in Gloucestershire. The ballad says nothing about an oven, and Ridley is held to be Charles I. The East London tradition of the Grotto is an old element in the culture of childhood. Children put together a collection of attractive objects such as sea shells, flowers, and rocks, and they ask passersby for a coin. One explanation traces back this element of the culture of childhood to Crusaders exhibiting the wonders of the Holy Land on their return (with a probable opportunity to purchase a nail from the true Cross for the credulous, or a thorn from the crown made on the first Good Friday). The point is that grottos were not made by adults, nor were children taught to make them except by other children. In the case of games, the process is the same; for the culture of childhood is transmitted by children who teach their younger chums the rituals of the age group and of the locality. That "tig" or "tag" is the name for the running-touching game is a minor matter. What counts is that children mark the event, and they, rather than adults, note the season for marbles and sanction the cycle of games. The consequence is that we can look for continuity between our day and the nineteenth century in children's games; we do not find the discontinuities which bedevilled the adult world and changed it in the nineteenth century. As in the nineteenth century, children celebrate Halloween and Guy Fawkes night, the latter with, perhaps, less overt anti-Popery than when Catholicism was, numerically, a cult, or the religion of an immigrant minority.

Of course, with Christmas children participate in the broader age-range, but with special status as recipients of gifts. The nineteenth century saw the introduction of Boxing Day, the twenty-sixth of December, on which presents in boxes were distributed. With his marriage to Victoria, Prince Albert introduced the charm of the Christmas tree and its decorations to delight young and old.

In the case of the Christmas tree, as with similar matters, the experiences of children with games and celebrations were largely determined by social class. In the years before the 1870s and the educational reforms begun then with greater vigor, childhood as a subculture ended when children went to work. For those entering the straw-plaiting industry in Bedfordshire, and other cottage industries, childhood barely started, because there were little jobs which children of four could manage. The 1851 Census reported 1,282 girl straw-plaiters under age nine in Bedfordshire, according to Horn (1974). Education in local schools was little more than training in the craft. Burnett (1982) records that Mrs. Burrows joined an agricultural gang at age eight and worked fourteen hours a day in the Fens; there was little time for play in her childhood around 1850. Walvin (1982) cites a report from Birmingham in 1905 of three children, aged eleven, nine, and five, assembling hooks and eyes, "working as fast as their little fingers could work." To children, factory work was sometimes lighter than work at home, and the discipline was less harsh. Poor children who did not work had restricted space for play in the first half of the century; parks were a creation of the era after the Hungry Forties and a few playgrounds came with schools. For country children, work scaring crows and gathering stones started at an early age.

Recreation for poor children in the form of games acquired importance as the last decades of the nineteenth century appeared. The context was the news that while further "degeneration of the race" seemed no longer inevitable, there was much to be done in order to restore a dissipated stock to vigor and maturity. There was truth to the observation about Britain's cities as places where wealth accumulated and men decayed. Vigorous exercise for children was a national agenda item, an aspect of the public philosophy of leadership, in the face of declining stature, unacceptable recruits for the army, and the lessons to be drawn from the rise of Prussian hegemony and the defeat of France. Children's health and recreation became important as a means to a national, military, economic, and social survival. German children played at physical exercise in the school and in the Turnverein. Swedish children engaged in graceful exercises and grew strong.

Adults introduced organized recreation into the subculture of childhood with success. Churches organized Boys Brigades, and the lads marched and drummed their way to fitness. Walking on one's own had always been Hobson's choice in the face of a lack of transportation. Children and adults took walks on the Sabbath, apart from walking to Chapel. Behan (1967) reported that the young Scottish boy, Alexander Somerville, would walk six miles just to handle a book, hoping that, in years to come, he might buy it. Young Charles West Cope frequently arose at five in the morning to walk nine miles to Harewood Bridge to fish. John Baldwin Buckstone, a popular comedian, walked seventy-two miles to London in search of work as a young man and spent fourpence halfpenny while on the tramp (John O'London 1912). Earlier, John Ward recorded in his diary of 1860 instances of walking several miles to view a new mill, to attend a weaver's meeting, and to visit his daughter and son-in-law. Clearly, the line between walking for business or for pleasure was a fine one, when Shanks' Mare was the only mode of travel.

For the children of the bourgeois, recreation differed throughout the century in several ways. Toys were available because there was discretionary income in the family and there was the time to play with them. Access to class-oriented sports introduced children to spectator sports such as horse racing, and also to participate by learning to ride. A frequent gift to children from their wealthy parents in the middle third of the century was a cart pulled by a pony or, occasionally, by a large dog. For boys enrolled in public schools, after they were civilized by Dr. Thomas Arnold and his emissaries, there was introduction to specialized games such as rugby football, fives, the wall-game, and badminton. As Gentlemen, some met Players on the cricket pitch from about 1840 on. In some respects, cricket is anomalous; it is essentially a bat and a ball, and thus analogous to soccer in its simplicity; but it had both class and regional characteristics. Only natives of Yorkshire may play for the County, and this populism is anomalous in the face of other middle-class attributes, notably the de-emphasis of winning in favor of the process of the game. The values of a leisure class are evident in that one can "declare" and retire from further competition. In this principle, we see an illustration of the steps by which the exuberance of Georgian cricket was subdued. Sandiford (1983) points out that the Victorians froze cricket into a preindustrial mold and eliminated occasions for excessive emotionality in favor of stoicism. Of course, there is a little magic in all games, and the leisurely course of cricket is evocative of quiet summer evenings on the village green. Tennis came late in the century, and with it an opportunity for girls, because the sport was something like badminton. Field hockey eventually appeared as a vigorous sport for girls—as did swimming, as opposed to sea bathing and paddling. Skating was traditional for young and old when the seasons permitted the local pond to freeze. Also late in the century was bicycling, but its initial role was transportation for the breadwinner; the sporting side was a parallel activity in which girls as well as boys could participate when the seasons and weather permitted.

Fresh Air and Fun

One of the pleasures which nineteenth-century children were the first to experience was a visit to the seaside, usually to a nearby town which had grown from a well-situated fishing village into a busy and prosperous resort. The phenomenon of resorts had its origins in visits to spas to take the healing waters. With the rise of Bath, drinking the water which Dickens likened to drinking flat-irons acquired social connotations. Prinny's visits under the tutelage of Brummell made Bath a place for the healthy and socially ambitious to visit. In all resorts, the clink of sovereigns made the case in the minds of local entrepreneurs, and the love-hate relationship between locals and visitors was on.

At the beginning of the nineteenth century, travel was difficult. Walvin (1978) tells us that it took William Hutton and family three days to get from Birmingham to Blackpool. From the metropolis, Brighton could be reached in the earliest decades by coaches which ran on regular schedules. The trip was lengthy and fairly expensive. For those who felt that money was no object, there continued to be trips to the continent, an adventure in the years after Waterloo when travel abroad was resumed. Baden-Baden and the spas were the usual targets, because moving with ease from place to place awaited speedier modes of travel than the coach. The places visited at home or abroad, with the exception of the long-established spas and major cities, tended to be villages that had been established in order to facilitate shipping and which therefore had harbors or were strategically situated for cargo and passenger ships. Others were fishing villages with picturesque sites and prospects such as Brighthelmstone; still others, for example, Eastbourne to the east and Bournemouth to the west, were creations of the approaching railway age. In the early decades, the emphasis was on health more than pleasure, nominally, and the therapeutic value of sea-bathing was emphasized. In his printed lectures (Surgical 1824), which probably are amongst the earliest versions of in-service education, Dr. Astley Cooper reported the advice he had given to a man from Charleston, South Carolina, who had an enlarged organ. "I advised him to go to Margate . . . his general health was improved by seabathing." Margate had become a favorite seaside resort for Londoners in the late eighteenth century and was accessible by coach or, for the nautical, by the hoy which had brought corn to London (Whyman 1973).

Of course, the general case that a change is good for the family followed quickly, and taking the waters at Harrogate competed with more frequent trips to Southport for Lancashire manufacturers. Walton (1974) says that well-to-do Lancastrians went to Blackpool in the years until the trains arrived, and that sea-bathing had been the custom there in the eighteenth century.

Sir George Head, a gentleman of epistolary bent who had written *Forest Scenes and Incidents in the Wilds of North America,* undertook a tour of Northern manufacturing districts in 1835. In his book *A Home Tour* . . . (Head 1836), he described the sports enjoyed on the sands at Southport: they included the familiar donkey-races, sack-races, blindfold wheel-barrow races, a greasy pole, and a greased pig. An interesting contest for young men was dipping for "drowned money" in a bowl of treacle syrup. Ten silver shillings were dropped into a large bowl of treacle and lads took turns ducking for the prize money.

The Resorts

The rise of popular resorts was dependent on the railways which brought day-trippers to coastal villages, which in turn underwent swift and explosive changes leading to annual invasions by the bucket-and-spade crowd and their parents. To adolescents, the opportunity to see and be seen were caught in the following poem:

> . . . But strange! I relate what has happened of late,
> 'Tis true though I heard on't but now tete a tete,
> Still lest you mistake me, I'll fully explain,
> Young Cupid, 'tis said, lies hid in yon main,
> And philters each wave that role to the shore
> A draught daily drunk by the rich and the poor,
> The ladies well pleased by a potion so sweet,
> Come here in groups their fond lovers to meet,
> And gentlemen too, who are friends to the fair,
> Come under pretense to enjoy the fresh air.

This pattern of the young seeking out the young established itself quite early, anonymity of flirtations being assured to the day-tripper and brief visitor alike. The pattern exists today from Brighton to Fort Lauderdale and the Black Sea, as the young in each generation go through their tribal rites. The young mill-hand from Heckmondwike in Wakes Week visiting "Slowcombe by the Sea," as the poem quoted above puts it, would recognize the ritualized passing of groups of young people today, their spirits buoyed by salty air and escape from the routines of life at home and school. Resorts had something for everyone, simply because they were a change from familiar surroundings. Our nineteenth-century forebears recognized this, and the annual trip was a treat for young and old.

In time, some of the seaside towns proved more accessible and others more attractive. With that sorting out, some towns began to grow at an unprecedented rate. Climate and propinquity to centers of population were probably the chief stimuli to growth once the railway network was established. In the case of Southport, Liddle (1982) has shown that the actions of two families controlling 97% of the land led to relatively well-planned development.

Brighton. Around the middle of the eighteenth century, about three hundred fishermen and their families lived at Brighthelmstone, a village in a dip of the Downs overlooking the Channel and providing access to Boulogne and Dieppe across nature's moat via the Chain Pier. The same nature provided a Chalybeate spring at St. Ann's Well and at Wick. In the eighteenth century, the novelty of the waves and the alleged therapy of the mineral waters attracted visitors. Generating the increase were the baths of Mahomet, the German Spa opened by Dr. Struve of Dresden, and the interest shown by the Prince of Wales, whose residence, the Marine Pavilion, is still one of the perennial sights of the town. The two thousand people in 1760 were forty thousand by 1840 and one hundred thousand by 1881 (Gilbert 1949). The height of Brighton's cachet as a watering place was in the three middle decades of the nineteenth century. After that it became progressively more demotic; the locals moved to Hove to avoid the crowds, and Eastbourne to the east attracted the gentry shortly after the railway reached Brighton in 1841. Brighton became the place for children to paddle in the water, to hurl pebbles from the shingle beach, and to explore the wonders of the pier. In time, the pattern of day-trippers was paralleled by residents travelling to work in London by fast trains. The town, apart from vacationers, acquired more stable aspects. By 1870, there were 165 boarding schools (Gilbert 1949). Just to the northwest of Brighton and Shoreham was, and is, Lancing, the Public School. Brighton acquired a niche as the window to the sea for London's boys and girls, and generations have enjoyed its pier, esplanade, and invigorating climate.

Blackpool. It was only logical that young Albert's parents, in search of fresh air and fun, should take their lad to see "t'tower" and the proverbial lion. To the workers of west Yorkshire and Lancashire in the nineteenth century, Blackpool became the place to spend "Wakes Week," the traditional, preindustrial holidays of the North. Walton (1974) dates Blackpool's role as a resort back to 1780, with families bringing their children from Manchester and Birmingham since the early nineteenth century. As early as 1790, Blackpool was hailed in verse as the best place in the Fylde valley to recuperate.

> *Of all the gay places of public resort, At Chatham, or Scarbro',*
> *at Bath, or at Court There's none like sweet Blackpool, of which*
> *I can boast, So charming the sands so healthful the coast*

Around 1840, Dr. A.B. Granville (1841) visited Blackpool and approved particularly of the inexpensive lodgings, "in which the highest charge . . . is only five shillings a day, and in some cases as low as three shillings." Dickens visited Blackpool, and its bourgeois respectability lasted until the 1840s, when the middle class moved on to what Granville called Winander Meer, and to Morecambe, both a little to the north and at a greater distance from the mill towns. Some of the Northern well-to-do had always used resorts other than Blackpool. Scarborough, on the coast of what was then called the German Ocean, had a spring, and Harrogate, between the coasts, had equally fresh air but without the tang of the sea. Still other families preferred Southport and Brighton to Blackpool. Even so, "Muckpool" had great appeal, and the coming of the railway established the town's character in a form which has been clear for over a hundred years. Children played on the sand beaches, paddled in the water, and rode on the backs of patient donkeys. Children also got lost, ate too much, and became tired. There was "fratching" between irritable brothers and sisters, and parents coped with the strange ritual of sleeping-in, if only briefly, as a respite from the rhythms of factory life. Each mill town had its own Wakes Week, and so the capacity to absorb weekly visitors was stretched but not broken as Rochdale folk came and Preston folk went.

Blackpool acquired several piers as the years went by. Large-scale buildings of hotels did not occur, and boarding houses absorbed visitors who stayed overnight, frequently receiving the same families year after year. The town grew, spreading along the coast line to the north and south. With electricity, the season was extended to include the autumn display of illuminations, consisting of designs using colored lights. The opportunity for a trip to the seaside was buttressed by the view of G.J. Symons (1880), who observed the following to the Sanitary Institute of Great Britain:

> It has been said, and I think with truth, that whereas in past years the Autumn holiday was a *Luxury*, it has, through increasing exhaustion due to modern high pressure, become a *necessity*.

Of course, the weather was critical and children did not play on wet, cold beaches. Inside entertainments flourished, and companies of singers, comedians, and minstrels entertained every day. Victorian Blackpool provided an unmatched degree of excitement for the hordes of working-class people who arrived for day trips on Bank Holidays. By the mid-century, people could leave Manchester at seven A.M. for Blackpool and return in the evening for half a crown; children cost one shilling and sixpence. The Tower opened in 1894 and dazzled Northern children with its height when seen from the ground, and by the view from the top which was spectacular on clear days. To the north, the viewer could also see Morecambe which had arisen near Poulton-le-Sands. Perkin (1976) says that Poulton could accommodate only a few of its visitors in simple cottage accommodations in 1824. At one point, it became known as

"Bradford-by-the-Sea," because of its many Yorkshire visitors. Perkin quoted a 1891 newspaper description of Morecambe as "rough honest-hearted . . . a little primitive . . . slightly tinged with vulgarity. But never dull" (1976). By the end of the century, it was established as an alternative to Blackpool, although perhaps a little less noisy.

Granville on Spas

As Brummell was to fashion and style in clothing, so Granville was to spas. His two-volume work, *The Spas of England and Principal Sea-Bathing Places,* was published in 1841 and became the Baedecker of health-giving resorts. The man himself is interesting; born to the Post-master of Lombardy, Carlo Bozzi, in Milan, 1783, he took the name of his English mother, Granville, styling himself A.B. Granville. With the help of the hapless William Hamilton, British Minister in Naples, he embarked on a series of appointments as surgeon on British warships, establishing himself in England in 1812 with his English wife. Well-respected in his career as a physician, he died in 1872.

Granville's first literary efforts were not well-received. His 1832 *Catechism of Health* provides the following exchange:

> Question. Is it proper to sit opposite to an open door or window, or between both, in other words in a draft or current of air?
>
> Answer. This is particularly injurious after sun-set (Review 1832)

Granville had much more success with his 1841 *Spas of England,* which he dedicated to Queen Victoria in terms suggesting a degree of acquaintance on her part. The work is chatty, but it is also well-based, presenting the mineral content of thirty-six spas in two "Chemico-Pneumatic and Thermometrical" summaries of chemical investigations. Granville's observations are close and acute, addressing the question of prices—Brighton's food being one-third more than the cost elsewhere—the medicinal value of the springs in various places, and the ease of access. We shall have more to say about access shortly, for Granville's views on the new railways were amusing and informative, to us, if not to his audience in the 1840s. Granville records the biography of Sake Deen Mahomet, who arrived in Brighthelmstone around 1800, after service in the Indian army, and who struck Granville as a vigorous figure at age ninety-two. While suspending judgment on the application of Maho-met's baths to children, Mahomet appears to have been living testimony that his regimen had benefited at least one person. He showed Granville his display of "crutches, spine-stretchers, leg-irons, head-strainers, bump-dressers, and clubfoot reformers. . . ." It was, however, the German Spa that struck Granville as the reason to seek better health at Brighton.

The impact of Granville's *Spas of England* lay in the combination of a little chemical fact, albeit derivative, plus the physician's advice on where to go. In the case of Brighton, he warned off the bilious, the febrile, those with "organic derangement of the head," and circulatory disorders. Brighton, said Granville, "is a place for convalescents, not for patients." Within this authoritative sweep the reader could select a resort with confidence. Adding to this chirurgical note was Granville's aside to the wary traveller by rail in the 1840s. In relation to visiting spas, the reader is assured that all will be civil and smooth on the South Western railway, but beware of the management of the London and Birmingham line! Thus armed, the traveller wishing to protect little ones and spouse on their trip to a resort could make arrangements with confidence. Thousands did so, and Dr. Augustus Bozzi Granville became their *vade mecum*. Of course, there were other patterns for travel, and Bradshaw replaced Granville. Still another style was a collective outing in which someone organized travel for a group of people.

Factory Outings

Factory life was grim, but the high spirits of young people prevail in all but the most wretched of circumstances. People living together and working on a daily basis learned to get along and occasionally engaged in recreation, under sponsorship of the works, in the form of what were called at the time "gipsy parties." An example of the structure of a works outing was recorded in the letter from a correspondent to the *Morning Chronicle* in 1851. The Chronicle sent Henry Mayhew, Angus Reach, and others around the country, and they sent long and detailed reports on working people to the newspaper. In reporting Birmingham factory life, one of the correspondents gave a list of the rules handed out before the trip to Hagley and the Clent Hills. The rules were drawn up by a joint committee of workers and managers at Messrs. Hinches, Welles and Co.

The holder of this ticket must ride there and back in this conveyance.

Time of Starting. Half past six o'clock precisely; anyone being late will be left behind, and their money forfeited.

The Road.—In getting out of the cars, to walk up the hills (on the road); you are requested not to mix with other parties; but to keep pace with your own conveyance.

The Park.—In passing through the park the same order to be observed as in riding; to walk four abreast, and under no pretense to move out of the line; anyone seen injuring or destroying trees, hedges or plans, will be discharged.

Clent Hills.—On the hills, dancing and other amusements. You are requested not to roam in small or detached parties, otherwise you will incur the severe displeasure of your employers; at the sound of the trumpet, the whole to return to dinner in the same order as in first passing through the park.

Time of Returning Home.—Eight o'clock precisely. The same order must be observed in returning as in going. You are requested not to sing, or otherwise make a noise in passing through the streets; and it is hoped that the greatest order and propriety will be observed throughout the day.

The tone conveys the discipline of work in Birmingham at mid-century. The *Morning Chronicle*'s correspondent recorded that no embarrassing incidents of drunkenness or misbehavior occurred on the 13 July outing of several hundred people, young and old.

St. Monday

Our lives are attuned to the minutes of the hour as meetings being on time, trains—and, on occasion, planes—depart punctiliously, and the wheels of society mesh in fine detail. Children accept the need to be at school before the bell rings and workers clock in and out in order that production be without interruption. This sensitivity to time and to the nonnegotiable demands of the workbench is a product of the nineteenth century and so arrived fairly late in industrial history. Well into the last century, apprentices acquired the conviction of their master's that Monday was a holiday, a festival observed scrupulously and perhaps devoutly as befits a Saint's day.

The origin of St. Monday is ancient, and its meanings several; Benjamin Franklin recorded in his biography that he did not observe St. Monday. To piece workers, it was the day to show up to collect materials to be worked on at home. The raw materials could be picked up late as easily as early in the day. The only contingency was that the pace of work must compensate in the subsequent days in order to assure a living wage. To others, the people Thomas Wright ("Journeyman Engineer") discussed in 1867, St. Monday presented the morning after the night before, and was also known as Blue Monday to John O'Neill, the Irish shoemaker. Those who had drunk incautiously on Sunday evening were immobilized less by convictions than by paralysis. There is an echo of this version of St. Monday in the contemporary folk wisdom to avoid buying cars assembled on Mondays, although we have forgotten the colorful terminology of the nineteenth century and earlier.

St. Monday had its origins in a leisurely sense of pace in the working week. It reflected an era in which working people were entitled to several holidays and expressed a less than compulsive sense of time among workers. In contrast, farm workers, then and now, know that cows have to be milked every day and animals must be fed whatever the calendar may say. When men began to mold the calendar to their advantage, the apprentice saw St. Monday start to slip. To factory owners, idle equipment was profit unmade, and their opposition came early. Brown (1982) cites Josiah Wedgwood's complaint that "our men have been at play four days this week . . . I have roughed and smoothed them over but it is all in vain." In some respects, St. Monday was a relic of preindustrial life in towns and died when that simpler but not idyllic period came to an end. Wright, in 1867, wrote of the "almost universal belief that Jack should have a share of play as well as work." Reid (1976) placed emphasis on the impact of the Saturday half-day closing on the opportunity for recreation. With Saturday afternoon came Saturday evening and the opportunity for a block of nonwork time. That set the stage in 1850 for the rise of popular entertainment, and a raucous, or at least late, Saturday night was followed by a sleep-in on Sunday. The pressure was removed from Monday for Wright's inebriates, and Monday seemed less necessary as a safety valve or day of relief. However, St. Monday was perceived as a prerogative by some skilled workers, and we may assume that their apprentices absorbed the day as a prerogative of the working-class elite. This latter group emerged as wages rose faster than prices and stability, based on life becoming a little more predictable for the skilled worker and his family, spread through various occupations after the Hungry Forties. Hobsbawm (1964) placed emphasis on the stability of earnings as a key element in the self-respect of working men.

In the same period popular values were evolving and the ethic or work as a virtue for the lower orders of society began to take shape. Samuel Smiles found a needy audience for his lectures in Leeds in the 1840s to young mechanics bent on self-improvement. The bench began to generate more than the price of food, and the long working day more than a hope for respite. For Dr. Smiles, it begat Thrift, Self-Control and

Opportunity, virtues which the young worker need only cultivate to achieve Success—but within one's station in life. Under the circumstances, St. Monday could not resist the work ethic, and it disappeared amid the clamor of the forge and the pace of life as a traditional if informal holiday.

Traditional Holidays

The first Bank Holiday, in August 1871, was known for a time as "St Luddington's Day," after the sponsor of the Act which expanded the number of days for recreation. When Church opposition to licentious use of the Sabbath, which meant practically everything except churchgoing, was championed by Cardinal Manning in the 1860s, Sabbatarianism fell back. Henceforth, Sunday excursions would be encouraged as a form of constructive recreation for families. Sunday of each week could be added to the three great working men's holidays listed by Thomas Wright, the Journeyman Engineer, (1867) who pointed out in "Some Habits and Customs of the Working Class" that "on each of the three great occasions, Christmas, Easter, and Whitsuntide, the bulk of the working classes secure from three days to a week's holiday. . . ." In addition, the convention of Wakes or celebrations went back into the 1600s. By the nineteenth century, they had lost their association with the anniversary of founding local churches and assumed the apparent form of mass vacations in factory towns. Another casualty was Plough Monday, whose demise was not due solely to increasing urbanization but due in part to a deliberate effort to extinguish its excesses, especially drunkenness and threats of violence. Malcolmson (1973) says that Plough Monday celebrations recorded the start of agricultural work after Christmas on the first Monday after Twelfth Day. Shrove Tuesday was also a traditional day for football games, which vanished in the routines of factories and their impersonal schedules. The Derby game between St. Peter's and All Saints' parishes drew five hundred to a thousand on each side in the early nineteenth century (Malcolmson 1973). To a child observing the game, the line between sport and civil disorder would have seemed fine, indeed. However, as a part of the process of socializing children, its violence probably fitted expectations for young males. That is, it would appear manly to engage in the pandemonium, and boys would look forward to the time when they would be permitted to participate. Contemporary accounts made it clear that play became quite rowdy and posed a threat to public order. Given the discipline of life in the nineteenth century, a safety valve was necessary. Sanctioned violence on a

public holiday probably reinforced the status of the Shrove Tuesday cele-
bration. However, it did not survive the onset of industrialization and the
need to maintain factory production and schedules on weekdays.

Sundays and Weekends

To all but the most pious children, or those inured to the routines
of a devout household, Sunday was an interminable day. The routines of
the community halted, to be replaced by churchgoing, keeping a wary
eye on parents' drinking, or the occasional outing. At the beginning of
our period, the Established Church was out of step with the population,
and large sections of the population either ignored the religious aspects
of the day or observed it in the evangelical fervor of the chapel. The
proletariat of South Wales and the industrial North and Midlands pursued Methodical enthusiasms, John Wesley's labors being a living tradition. For children, Sunday sometimes presented an opportunity for
schooling, and Sunday School provided the only education for factory
children in the early decades of the century. In 1834–35, Manchester
had 117 Sunday Schools "affording sabbath instruction to 42,950
scholars," according to a publication of the time, *Manchester As It Is*
(1839). The Established Church educated 10,284 boys and girls, and
mainstream Wesleyan Methodists educated 9,066 children. In that period, more than a decade before the Famine, there were 3,880 Catholic
children being educated in Sunday Schools, and the total number of
children receiving Sunday-School education was 33,196. In Salford there
were another 9,754 children, so that on Queen Victoria's coronation
forty thousand Sunday Scholars could assemble on Ardwick Green,
"who sung in one vast chorus, the national anthem" (Manchester 1839).

In this anecdote we glimpse the central, unifying theme in the lives
of churchgoers which the Church presented. Accordingly, Sunday began
as a dedicated day for the godly, and Sabbatarianism as a movement
calling for abandonment of secular themes was a vigorous and popular
movement. Within the all-embracing theme of the Evangelicals there was
little that was appropriate for children beyond the religious. Toys were
put away and some families restricted reading to religious materials. In
the 1880s, Young Arthur Goffin, Burnett (1982) tells us, went to chapel
twice and also attended Sunday School on Sundays. Of course, this en-
tailed much walking to and fro, and so the hours of a long Sunday were
filled. Eventually, Sunday walks included the recently established public
parks, and devotions were augmented by secular education in the form
of exposure to fresh air and refined company. The concept evolved to

include the idea that Sunday was also a family day, and the stage was set for use of the day for family outings and excursions. Perhaps contributing to this was the establishment of the Saturday half-day which broadened the nonwork period to include a night preceded and followed by periods of rest. The stage was set for the weekend which, if combined with a Bank Holiday, produced a useful period for leisure and holidays. Of course, some families held to a pious observation of the Lord's Day, and many still do today. However, the secularization of Sunday occurred, and children found it one more day of relief from school or work. In the latter instance, the process of laicizing Sunday reduced the probability of attending Sunday School. Fortunately, the decline of Sunday came about when tax-supported schools had become more common, and so the instructional potential of Sunday was complemented by the reality of schooling five days per week.

Sport

Within the general context of children's recreation lies the more particular form of sport, meaning, today, a culture complex of adoring boys and girls watching their idols play tennis—immensely skillful young men and women earning large salaries when professional, and a sea of spectators who model their clothing and ambitions on these athletes. It was not always so, although there have always been strong, skillful young people who could run, throw, and wrestle. Their semipeaceable use of strength is something people have always admired. The urchin kicking a cracked tennis ball in the gutter dreamed of growing up to play for West Ham. The Hampton roar of nonparticipants gave adolescent Glaswegians a sense of identity ready-made. Effortless performance, to the casual observer, added balance to the academic achievement of young men rowing to Putney Bridge. All of these aspects of sport took on their recognizable form in the nineteenth century.

Before that time there were elements which persisted well into our period. Cock-fighting and bull-baiting endured until Victorian sensitivities were exceeded. Dog fights and rat-killing by dogs centered on beer houses, and many publicans had a side business of selling rats for threepence (Shimmim 1856). The Clitheroe weaver, John Ward, recorded in his diary in 1860 that he had followed avidly the bare-knuckle fight between Frank Heenan, The Benicca Boy, and Tom Sawyer. Curiously, it was also recorded by Miss Emily Hall in her diary (Sherrard 1966). She recorded that it was a draw, had three thousand spectators, and was finally stopped by the police. One of the few pugilists to emerge unscathed was William Thompson, who fought under the name Bendigo, a name he adopted from the unscathed Shadrach and Meshach (Greenwood 1881). The element of violence in life was quite evident to children, as parents engaged in casual brutality under the rubric of discipline or under the influence of drink, two modes of expressing hostility all too common even today.

Children in the early years of the century saw traditional games akin to soccer on Shrove Tuesday. Horse racing was common, having established itself firmly in the eighteenth century. Its change in the nineteenth century was less an internal matter than a reaction to the spread of transportation. Children at York saw people from other parts of the country and heard the Baroque vowels of the South East and Home counties. The culture of sport spread as society in general became more mobile. Slowly, the traditional group sports of young men became standardized, and a pattern of uniformity embraced all parts of the country. The euphemism of "body-contact" sports was not yet coined, but the prospect of a good kick and a swift jab excited the new mass audience. Intercity rivalries emerged and continue to this day, with youthful spectators sometimes more violence-prone than the actual participants on the playing field.

Soccer is the best example of a sport encountered by the poorest boys, a game whose appeal is rediscovered when parents wince at the price of equipment for other sports. It is a long way from the abandoned tin can nimbly dribbled, then and now, by a poor lad, to the expensive equipment of the tack room and the ice hockey rink. Like basketball in the twentieth century, the sport provided an opportunity to organize and control the impulses of young men. To the churches, organized sport combined sponsorship, religion, and a sense of identity. To those appalled by what we have called in an earlier chapter, the Degeneracy Problem, the lack of expense and the physical exercise seemed an excellent way to increase the strength and vigor of young boys. In some instances, these virtues were combined in an ethic of muscular piety to which was attributed the power to build character. For a few skillful lads towards the end of the century, soccer provided a way to become a celebrity. Korr (1978, 1986) has described the emergence and evolution of the West Ham Football Club among the employees of the Thames Iron Works in Canning Town. Arnold F. Hills, the owner, was a vegetarian and reformer, and he thought that providing a variety of clubs for his workers was both a civic obligation and industrial safety valve. Through clubs such as the Hammers, a few talented boys found acclaim and local recognition. The pay was not great, but love of the game and the status and recognition accorded the young professional soccer player were rewards of a different but no less welcome kind.

However, before soccer reached that stage of public recognition, it existed as the prerogative of schoolboy descendants of the apprentices who for centuries had played an unrestrained game with much physical assault on Sundays and on public holidays. There tended to be local versions of the game which had unique rules for the number who formed a team, the size of the ball and of the pitch, and the length of time for which a game lasted. A violent game, soccer was well-suited to the sub-culture of boyhood in the public schools. Rugby, Harrow, Eton, and others were wild places in the early nineteenth century. What happened outside the classroom was generally left to the boys, and they enjoyed soccer as one of the violent sports of the young. Decorum was to come later, with Dr. Arnold, and in the early years soccer was an excuse for a blood sport without the need for horses, grooms, and foxes. Ariès (1962) records the many instances of violence and states of civil insurrection in the public schools. The last year of great unrest at Eton was 1832, and Marlborough's last outbreak was in 1851. Former pupils returned to their home communities and encouraged formation of teams and competition in leagues. Walvin (1975) says that Crewe Alexandra was formed in 1863 by workmen of the North Staffordshire Railway and became, eventually, Stoke City. Young men had the energy to play after work and also came to use Saturday afternoons for playing or watching the game. Boys became men who taught their sons, and a working-class cultural element was established.

There were variants beyond normalizing the size of the team, the length of the game, and other procedural aspects which boys soon knew by heart even when they couldn't quite grasp the pence table. The love of rules which is a stage in the psychological developmental of morality in children was well-served by the nineteenth century urge to tidy up, to rationalize, and to order. Soon, uniforms appeared, and small boys were captivated by that aspect, followed by awards for skill and prizes for winning.

A different evolution, one shrouded in superstition, occurred in the by-now civilized public schools. Dunning and Sheard (1979) have little regard for Bloxton's story that William Webb Ellis picked up the ball at Rugby School and ran with it. They believe that the oval ball became customary in the second quarter of the nineteenth century. The act of tackling the runner is a physical assault continuous with the pre-nineteenth-century violence of the towns and their apprentices. With its separate rules for the size of the field, an oval ball, and a larger pitch,

Rugby football could not be continuous with soccer, and it evolved into League and Union varieties played in different regions of the country. Rugby League became professional, and a tradition of playing that fearsome game developed in Northern working-class families. For some adolescents, to play, if only briefly, was a rite of passage to manhood.

Eventually, Rugby became associated with the middle class, and soccer with the working class. Ambitious secondary schools and universities fielded rugby teams; the poor and working classes played soccer, and later watched with passionate enthusiasms the professional soccer teams. The boy athlete could evolve into the soccer player for the 'Spurs, whose name was spoken reverently by the young and whose dribbling was critically evaluated at White Hart Lane on Saturday afternoons. Arnold F. Hills's Hammers created local pride in the East End and eventually assumed the form of a well-run middle-class business, an aspect scarcely glimpsed by small boys intent on viewing their heroes.

The formalizing of the informal and literally popular began with establishment of the Football Association in 1863. The first F.A. cup was won in 1872, and the Cup Final became a central, apotheosis-like element in the game. Relevant was the availability of leisure time produced by shorter working hours. Not the least element in the remarkable story of growth of the sport perhaps most widely played in the world was the development of the network of passenger railway lines. Saturday afternoons and Bank Holidays provided the time for spectator sports. Easy transportation allowed teams and supporters to move from town to town. The small boy who kicked the ball could play for his school team, or church team, and evolve into a lifelong fan who followed the future of the team at home and away.

Trains

Boys and girls love trains; they represent travel, novelty, and a sense of great energy controlled. In the nineteenth century, these qualities were heavily accentuated. Steam trains are only a memory now, but in their day they made much more of an impression on the juvenile mind than today's diesel-electric locomotives. To travel by steam train was to see in smoke and vapor evidence of power harnessed—but poised to break away down the rails to an unknown destination. Our juvenile travellers heard whistles blow and doors slam as dignitaries with watches, flags, and whistles dispatched Leviathan and his contents on their way. For children born after 1840, the age of the railway had come, and the ensuing decades connected hitherto isolated cities by swift and reliable transportation.

For children, the railway brought the first contact with resorts and the brisk breezes of the Channel, the Irish Sea, and the German Ocean. Pleasure-filled days on the sands were rounded off with the excitement of train travel from the coast. For the day-tripper, an early rise and a busy day eating heaven-knows-what were followed by a dreamless sleep on a crowded train returning to London, Birmingham, or Manchester. The rhythmic clatter of the wheels spelling out L-N-E-R, L-N-E-R, for youngsters returning from Bridlington or Scarborough to Horsforth on the London and North Eastern Railway brought sleep quickly after a wonderful day at the seaside.

We speak here of trains in a context of recreation, but the rail system was more than that. It merits attention as a phenomenon in its own right, an expression of the age of iron and steam which radically altered the face of Britain. The steam railway was the index of the age expediting travel, undergirding the manufactory system with rapid distribution of goods. Railways started when private and public corporations were enabled by acts of Parliament to purchase ground, survey it, and to lay down a rail system. The result was an overbuilt, nonrational system of connections with parallel and redundant facilities. Initially, the pace of railway construction was slow. Deane and Cole (1967) estimated the total mileage in 1825 at between three and four hundred miles, composed of quite short sets of track usually no more than twenty-five miles long. Such small enterprises served coal mines and so were familiar to only the portion of the population, child or adult, engaged in related work. The newspaper *The Scotsman* foresaw the impact of a network of railways on the towns and villages isolated by poor roads in 1825.

> Were a foreign enemy, for instance, to invade England, 500 steam-wagons could convey 50,000 armed men in one day to the point assailed . . . it would be rash to say that even a higher velocity than 20 miles an hour may not be found applicable . . . Such a new power of locomotion cannot be introduced without working a vast change in the state of society.
>
> *(Harvie, Martin, and Scharf 1970)*

In 1825, a boom in railway speculation began and Parliament passed acts to enable construction of lines longer than twenty-five miles. With construction of the Darlington to Stockton line in the North East, passengers as well as goods were transported. The peak year for starting to lay iron rail track came in 1847 and consisted of just under sixty-five hundred miles of rails. About half that many miles were under construction in the following year, and the mileage begun annually until 1870 was generally seven hundred to a thousand miles. Of course, it was a good business, and the scope of the enterprise at intervals of a decade in the last half of the century grew rapidly, if chaotically. An interesting item is the number of miles of track actually opened. The decade of the forties and a few years at the end of the fifties were the peak of railway activity. The result was that the increased prosperity after the Hungry Forties had an outlet, among others, in use of the railways to spend discretionary income on recreational visits to resorts and to visit, for example, the Great Exhibition of 1851. Railways were profitable in the nineteenth century, and those whose capital was in horses and wagons, or barges, saw their investments shrink. Of course, there were selected waterways which were successful, and we cite construction of the Manchester Ship Canal. However, the railway swept across the countryside, so that between 1844 and 1900 the lines opened grew from twenty two-hundred to almost nineteen-thousand miles.

One of the more remarkable inventions in the history of technology is something boys and girls living either near Dublin, Paris, Exeter, or Croydon could have seen in the late 1840s. The Atmospheric Railway was the technological alternative to steam locomotives and consisted of an iron pipe from which air was evacuated by a pumping engine. Carriages on rails were connected to a piston in the evacuated pipe and were pulled along as the atmosphere rushed into the pipe and so propelled the piston. The line between Kingstown and Dalkey was opened in 1843. There, Frank, the son of the Regius Professor at Dublin, Dr. Ebrington, achieved an unsought fame by travelling at eighty-four miles an hour. This hypervelocity was inevitable when the engine accidentally started before the carriages were connected to it. Rolt (1970) records that young Frank went from Dunleary to Dalkey in one and a quarter minutes. In the case of young railway watchers in Devon, Mr. Brunel's version ran with some regularity in 1848, reaching nearly seventy miles per hour for four miles with a load of twenty-eight tons. In these days of magnetic trains, it is salutary to recall the imagination of George Medhurst, who proposed the idea in 1810; of the Samuda brothers, who patented the idea; and of Isambard Kingdom Brunel, who did his best with the materials of the time, iron pipe and leather, in the face of extremities of weather which froze lubricants in winter and evaporated them in summer. The Irish line did not close down until 1885, and the short line near Paris lasted until 1860. In the period, adults and children experienced silent, swift, propulsion which would have astonished Dr. Granville, bearing in mind the anxieties he had expressed about more conventional propulsion in 1841.

In recent decades of this century, the presence of buses and cars has required many spurs and branch lines to close, and many a Victorian station with its prize-winning bed of flowers has passed out of memory. Forgotten with equal celerity is the role that railways played in child labor. Those who dug cuttings and levelled hills were originally called "navigators," later shorted to navvies and extended to include any one using a pick and shovel. Boys worked as navvies, sometimes leading horses and carts full of excavated soil and rock. In time, they progressed to using shovels and the paraphernalia of the trade. A colorful band, they worked hard, played hard, and were a source of consternation to respectable locals as they worked their way through a district.

The hazards presented by railways in their earliest years went beyond inconvenience, the impertinence of clerks, and attacks of the vapors. Railways were also expressions of brute power and of dead weight capable of terrible accidents. In Manchester in 1830, young J. T. Slugg and some chums placed themselves to watch the progression from Liverpool to Manchester of the first train, among whose important passengers on the maiden voyage was the reformer of the Corn Laws, William Huskisson. In 1881, Slugg recalled the vivid impact of that day, September 15.

> [We] waited as patiently as we could till nearly one o'clock, but still no procession came in sight. It seemed strange for the procession . . . started from Liverpool at half past ten o'clock . . . and reached Parkside. Mr. Huskisson . . . hastened to the carriage of the Duke (of Wellington) . . . and was shaking hands with him when a cry was raised that the other train was approaching on the opposite rails . . . Mr. Huskisson . . . stepped back on the other line, and was knocked down by the engine, the wheels of which passing over his thigh fractured it in a fearful manner. . . . He expired at nine o'clock the same evening.

In 1868, at Abergele in North Wales, seven-year-old George Grundy saw two trains collide at a combined speed of 120 miles an hour (Burnett 1982). Young George and a friend were sitting on an embankment a mere fifty yards away when the accident happened. Attending the funeral service, the youthful George burst into tears, recognizing the enormity of the event he had witnessed. Thirty-nine people died in carnage requiring only small coffins which were interred in one grave.

Railways remained dangerous places for workers if not for travellers, and the mechanics of coupling and uncoupling carriages still places workers at risk in even the most technically advanced marshalling yards. Reviewing records of accidents at the end of the century, Cunygnhame (1902) reported the mortality rate of shunters, men engaged in moving carriages around, at 5.08 per thousand, an incidence far above the rate for miners of 1.37. Their injury rate was also the highest among a group of manual workers.

The model figures of the early railway age are George Hudson of York, who made and lost a fortune in his chequered career; Isambard Kingdom Brunel, whose engineering genius was paramount; and Thomas Brassey, who built railways in Great Britain and abroad. Brunel is the most interesting of the three, being surveyor, designer, and engineer, best-known for the rail-bed for Bristol. At the time, it was known as "Brunel's Billiard Table," owing to the flatness of the trail selected and the low gradients it presented. Here was a figure for boys to admire, one of the heroic engineers of the nineteenth century whom Dr. Samuel Smiles wished the young to emulate for their Thrift, Honesty, and Application. With his tall hat and ever-present cigar, he dug the Millwall Tunnel under the Thames, built the Great Western Railway memorialized in friezes recognizable as today's trains pass through Reading, and went on to build the first iron ships driven by propellors. His *Great Britain* may be found in Bristol, restored after abandonment in the south Atlantic decades ago. Paddington Station, which he designed, is a monument in Romantic Iron to Brunel and his genius, and his statue points to the West by means of his toe polished by many admirers.

Once the rails were laid and resorts became accessible, there arose the worry that it was harmful to children and ladies to move at speeds in excess of thirty miles an hour. Dr. Augustus B. Granville reviewed the hazards of travel for the delicate, and he concluded, in the 1841 *Spas of England,* that

> there is not much of truth in the alleged medical grievances . . . that being wafted through the air at the rate of twenty or thirty miles an hour must affect delicate lungs and asthmatic people . . . that the movement of rail-trains will cause apoplexy; that the sudden plunging into the darkness of a tunnel . . . make work for the oculist . . . that the air in such tunnels is vitiated . . . the bottom of deep cuttings or excavations, being necessarily damp, will occasion catarrhs, and multiply agues!

Granville also records the hazards of travel on the London and Birmingham Railway and the treatment he received from the officials as he started his journey.

> The railroad from London to Birmingham is in fact an ill-managed concern. Present yourself in any garb you please to the counter of their offices, assume the most affable or beseeching tone of inquiry you can, still you will either get no answer at all, or one which you would hardly give to your own menial servant. . . . The rapacity of the persons managing the concern has no end . . . not only was *safety* and *expedition* promised, but *economy* also . . . They have raised the principal carriage fare by an additional half-a-crown. . . . Their behavior with regard to the charge for luggage is even more reprehensible.

Eventually, railway personnel standardized procedures, and passengers' expectations paralleled reality. The prospective traveller could consult Bradshaw's guide and travel with wife and children with a reasonable expectation of arriving in good spirits.

In this example, the role of the railway is passive in conducting the traveller to his destination. However, the railway system was also generative; that is, it facilitated urban development by making a resort or population center more accessible. Rarely was there a deliberate attempt to create business at a place with resort potentials. One of the few instances was the effort of the Carlisle and Silloth Bay Railway company in the 1850s. As documented by Walton (1979) a group of Carlisle businessmen attempted to create a resort and a clientele for their railway service. The plan did not fare well for fundamental business reasons, but there were some short-term steps which illustrate the lack of vision of the planners. Two examples in Walton's account are the construction of a fertilizer plant on the windward side of town, and erection of a vitriol plant which compounded the assault on Victorian noses. Obviously, the benefits of bracing air could be carried too far in the case of Silloth. No invalid needing rejuvenation or parent seeking a holiday for the family would require the degree and form presented at Silloth.

Victorian railways were usually a means seized on by shrewd businessmen. Thomas Cook began by organizing transportation to a temperance meeting at Loughborough as Secretary of the Association at Leicester in 1841. The excursion trains were a great success and Marchant (1954) reports that a great excursion train left London for Brighton in 1844. Hordes of children and their parents delayed the train's departure from London Bridge station by half an hour. Eventually, four engines pulled forty-five carriages out of the station, but only to be joined by six more carriages and an engine at New Cross, plus an extra engine at Croydon. The Great Exhibition of 1851 expanded the popularity of excursion trains, and the economies of scale dropped the round-trip fare from Leeds to London to five shillings.

The Great Exhibition

Of the wide range of experiences available to the Victorian child, few approached the excitement of the Great Exhibition of 1851, housed in what was to be known as the Crystal Palace. Under one roof—a structure of glass, like the walls—a distinguished committee chaired by Prince Albert presented objects and natural wonders from around the world. The chemist Lyon Playfair organized the exhibits into four groups. There were machines, objects from the fine arts, raw materials from which goods were manufactured, and a variety of manufactured goods ranging from the preposterous to the familiar. In one sense, Playfair's grouping ranges from the inert to the sublime, via the useful and the foolish. In the latter category, children and their parents could see the world's largest folding knife, which had three hundred blades, and a patent fumigator which burned tobacco. In the aery realm of aesthetics were numerous statues of female Greek slaves in degrees of nudity and drooping against broken columns. Not everything could be exhibited, but little was left out by thirteen thousand sponsors of displays from around the world. One item proposed by the mathematician Charles Babbage was a railway to move visitors through the Exhibition with dispatch. In a curious book with the misleading title *The Exhibition of 1851,* Babbage proposed an elevated railway, with wooden tracks and rubber-bound wheels eight feet above ground, between "six or more intermediate stations." Babbage's railway was not built, but, even so, six million children and adults passed through the Great Exhibition in Hyde Park between May 1 and October 15, 1851. Hobhouse (1937) states that attendance was brisk on Shilling Days, and that daily attendance was high in the last six weeks.

However, the building itself was worth a visit, and the tawdriness of some exhibits did not diminish the value of the journey for people who came considerable distance by train. What the visitor saw was not the Crystal Palace which stood at Sydenham from 1855 until it burned on November 30, 1936. That structure was a taller, wider building whose surface of glass was nearly twice that of the original, which had a simple aesthetic clarity to it.

The 1851 building was an inspired improvisation developed in about nine days by Joseph Paxton, a protégé of the Duke of Devonshire. The Prince Consort's committee included many luminaries, among whom were Isambard Brunel, Henry Cole, and Joseph Paxton. The committee rejected all of more than two hundred designs submitted, and almost adopted a design by Brunel which looked a little like Paddington Station surmounted by a wholly disproportionate dome. Eventually, the committee adopted Paxton's elegant, simple design, whose original sketch on blotting paper is in the museum at South Kensington. The design combined prefabricated structural iron with glass which was a novel material for sheathing at the time. Iron and glass evolved into a three-tiered airy building with horizontal lines uninterrupted by decoration and capped by an arch.

Young visitors saw a palace of crystal, a structure not of brick but of shimmering transparency, a magic building to celebrate the accomplishments of the age. Necessarily, such acclamations are ad hoc, and represented the sensibilities of the current and the preceding time. Only John Ruskin objected, observing that the building looked like a cucumber. And yet the building showed the young mind a vision of what became preeminent in twentieth-century architecture, the idea that walls are a skin, not necessarily a load-bearing element. In this regard, the building was more important than the contents it protected, an amalgam of crude, powerful machines in the age of steam, vulgar Victorian antimacassars, and plush furniture orotund and rococco in extremis.

Finally, the native population—replete with prejudices—saw foreigners and their works and pomps, especially the French and the Germans. The destruction of the insular society solemnly forecast by Colonel Charles Sibthorp did not come about, even though women and children saw the remote French and even more exotic types from distant parts of an empire at its zenith. The Exhibition came and went, and the Nation endured, although perhaps now susceptible to *élan vital, cinq à sept, schadenfreud,* and other concepts which had crossed Nature's Moat.

7.

CITIES

Across the decades of the nineteenth century, the greatest phenomenon was the expansion of towns, a process wholly inimical to childhood
as a whole. Rural life had never been easy for any but the Squire and his
family, but it permitted children to grow in fresh air exposed to the
rhythms of nature. The explosion of growth in towns caused by the rise
of factories created a new set of hazards to child welfare, from swifter
transmission of disease to pollution of air and water. In the rise of cities
we see the greatest set of social discontinuities. Housing fell behind demand as families settled around factories, and the cities made worse the
overall decline in the health of town dwellers. London was no exception,
its green-brown fogs being labelled "London Particulars"; its great river
became a noisome sewer from which drinking water was pumped. With
each decade, London's population grew, and the city spread inexorably
into surrounding areas. Amid this steady expansion, children were born
and died quickly and early in the rookeries of St. Giles and Saffron Hill.
Only those living on the outskirts were spared the immediate effects of
urbanization. One such lad was young George Augustus Sala, and he
was fed up; his boarding school was unpleasant, so he decided to go to

sea. Armed with his pocket knife and supported by a half-crown and his small accordion, he set forth into the clear Ealing night for Portsmouth and a life on the rolling wave. Youthful geography being what it is, he fetched up next day at Hyde Park Corner. A "wild debauch on raspberry tarts and ginger beer," followed by a second day of bread, cheese, and beer, and a night under the stars. Subsequently, he made rather unsteady progress through Wandsworth Common, Roehampton, and Putney to Kingston-upon-Thames and reached Guilford. That was as far as young George went and the world of letters was the better for it, eventually (Sala 1872). An hegira across metropolitan London as early as the 1830s and 1840s was a substantial undertaking. The metropolis had spread through the interstices of Middlesex, Surrey, and Kent, so that freestanding towns and villages were now continuous, and useable space was disappearing rapidly.

London was not alone in this regard; the early nineteenth century saw an enormous growth of major cities, as well as the comparative bypassing of other, ancient boroughs. The expansion of cities was not uniform because the mechanisms were different in each case. Edinburgh's population grew most steadily after 1840, and the population growth of other towns, as Figure 7.1 shows, was steep throughout the nineteenth century. In the case of London, the Infernal Great Wen, as William Cobbett styled it early in the century, the mechanisms were unique, because London declined as a manufacturing center but burgeoned as a commercial and government center. In the City the paradox was greater, because the permanent residents declined and were replaced by an army of clerks from Camberwell (Dyos 1961), office boys, and other diurnal visitors. By night the City still loses its population only to materialize the next morning, with the aid of bus and tube.

The loss of population was a permanent rather than cyclic event for some areas. The number of children and adults in many counties declined as agriculture and natural resources, such as Cornish tin mines, lost their centrality in people's lives. For counties essentially rural, the growth in the nation's population applied for only the first several decades. After that, they lost population despite the increase in life expectancy. Longstaff's (1893) data show that the rural population in 1851 amounted to 49.92% but fell to 27.95% by 1891.

Still other places, the cathedral cities for example, experienced little change and survived the age of iron and steam to enter the age of high technology in the late twentieth century in a form not unrecognizable to their eighteenth century residents. To James Dawson Burn (1855), who had tramped over all of the United Kingdom except Wales several times, the cathedral cities "set the laws of progress at defiance. . . . In my mind

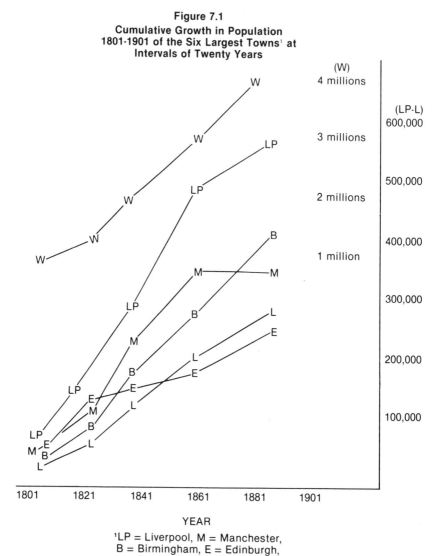

Figure 7.1
Cumulative Growth in Population
1801-1901 of the Six Largest Towns[1] at
Intervals of Twenty Years

YEAR

[1]LP = Liverpool, M = Manchester,
B = Birmingham, E = Edinburgh,
L = Leeds, W = London

they are invested with a melancholy grandeur . . . exercise a species of tranquil contentment over the minds of the inhabitants." Beyond tranquility, there is resistance to change; Wakefield could have grown vigorously, but the better-off residents of the district would not permit it. Titus Salt, for example, wished to build his mill in Wakefield, but, according to the *Wakefield Express* (1861) quoted by Cowlard (1979), he was not encouraged to do so by "the obstinate short-sightedness and impulsive conduct of certain of the aristocracy of the time. . . ." Bristol too failed to progress and yielded to Liverpool the bulk of the atlantic trade.

Thus, towns rose or stagnated in the nineteenth century. Some, of which Crewe is the prime example, rose with the technology of the railways (Chaloner 1950). The late twentieth century has seen town economies based on repair and maintenance decline as railways have shrunk from their Victorian pre-eminence and from the effusion of branch lines into connections between the largest cities. Victorian childhood prospered or failed to thrive as Victorian city economies moved and pulsed to the rhythm of the mercantile world.

The growth of towns was not at a uniform pace decade by decade or town by town. Mr. Price-Williams's (1880) data show that for the sixteen largest towns in 1801, excepting London, the average rate of growth until 1811 was 21.48%. It rose to 29.50% in the next decade, and peaked by 1831 at a rate of 37.77%. It then declined to 17.32% by 1871 (See Table 7.1).

In the first decade of the nineteenth century, Brighton was the most rapidly growing of the sixteen largest towns, with a 64.05% rate of increase. From a fishing village with 7,440 inhabitants, Brighton grew to 12,205 people in 1810. It then proceeded to double its size, and it had 24,741 people (102.21% increase) by 1821. The rates of growth in subsequent decades were 69.75%, 17.09%, 41.20%, 25.33%, and 18.83% for the decade 1861–71; in the latter year, the population at the popular seaside resort was 103,758. Of course, Brighton's population was large on any nice summery day, owing to the presence of day-trippers arriving by train. However, they tended to confine themselves to the shingle beach and the environs of the road to the railway station, so that even on the busiest days the larger community, then and now, remained largely unchanged.

In contrast, there is Newcastle, whose rate of increase, after a decline of 1.44% in the first decade of the nineteenth century, was generally between 20% and 30% in the period 1811–1871. The peak rate of population growth was in the period 1831–1841, at 32.69%. Rates of 20% to 23% describe the three decades 1841–1871. In the first decade covered by Price-Williams's report to the Statistical Society in 1880, the three highest rates of population growth for 1861–1871 were the Yorkshire cities of Bradford, Sheffield, and Leeds. Their neighbor, Manchester, grew by only 5.97% in that decade, having had its peak rate of 44.93% in 1831–1841.

TABLE 7.1
POPULATION GROWTH OF TEN TOWNS 1811–1871*

Town	Year 1811	% Decade Increase	Year 1831	% Decade Increase	Population at Two-Decade Increase (%) Year 1851	% Decade Increase	Year 1871	% Decade Increase
Liverpool	104,104	26.50	201,751	45.82	375,955	31.23	493,405	11.14
Manchester	91,130	18.68	187,202	44.93	316,213	30.14	379,374	5.97
Birmingham	82,753	17.10	143,968	41.55	232,841	27.29	343,787	16.11
Leeds	62,534	17.63	123,393	47.25	172,270	13.28	259,212	25.12
Sheffield	53,231	16.34	91,692	40.47	135,310	21.80	239,946	29.58
Bristol	61,153	16.81	104,408	22.68	137,328	9.73	182,552	18.57
Wolverhampton	43,190	41.22	67,514	27.36	119,748	28.42	156,978	6.30
Bradford	16,012	20.73	43,527	65.46	103,778	53.55	145,830	37.29
Newcastle	32,573	-1.44	53,613	28.29	87,784	24.81	128,443	17.72
Stoke-Upon-Trent	31,557	35.57	51,589	28.21	84,027	22.77	124,493	23.00

*Adapted from Price-Williams (1880).

In appraising these numbers by town and by decade, we point out that they represent net changes. For children, the object of our consideration, the picture is one of decreasing mortality as the standard of living slowly rose. More children survived the earliest years, and the base for a subsequent cohort of births was slowly augmented. However, we note in passing that menarche came later in those days, although a secular trend to earlier menarche began in the period in question. The girls born in 1821, who survived in childhood, were mothers by 1841 and grandmothers by 1861. The rate of increase was modulated by circumstances, however. As early as the 1839 report of the Leeds Town Council to the Statistical Society (Report 1839), it was evident that fecundity was related to social level. In the Leeds report, the mean number of children of textile workers was 2.53 children, and it declined with rising occupational level to a mean of 1.92 children for "Independent and Professional" people. Thus, the population of towns grew, but at a higher rate among the poor. Only slowly did the rise in family income offset their growing number of mouths to feed. Eventually, the rate of increase in the standard of living decreased mortality among children and raised their level of civilization and education. The populations of cities evolved into literate, responsible people. The social ills of the cities, especially alcoholism and the complex of child abuses associated with it, declined. The habitus of the population improved, but the nineteenth century had ended some time before the degeneracy problem which haunted urbanologists subsided.

Each great town had unique problems. To live in the southeast sector of York meant facing displacement when the Foss rose above its banks (Finnegan 1982). London had its rookeries, into which a Fagin could vanish, such as St. Giles and, to the east, Jacob's Island. Manchester had Angel Meadow and Edinburgh the Gorbals. For Leeds, the enclave known as Boot and Shoe yard was a perennial problem, and, in nearby York, Water Lane and Grape Lane were sites of crime and vice. For Merthy Tydfil, it was "China" to the northwest, Stafford had Caribee Island (Swift 1985), and Belfast had its Menagerie. Angel Meadow is not always recognizable even to Mancunians, but Deansgate is still known, for it contains the retail complex of the city center. People may walk safely by day and night, a far contrast from the "Devilsgate" of the nineteenth century. Smith (1979) records this as an area of ten acres, heavily overbuilt and overcrowded, and penetrated, for the most part in the nineteenth century, by alleyways ("ginnels" and "snickets") rather than streets. The average house had eight occupants, and there were 350 people to the acre, a stressful density which may be compared with the London levels in Table 7.4. Two households had fifteen members; the first included six children and seven lodgers, while the second had four children and nine lodgers. Three dwellings housed twenty-seven, twenty-eight, and thirty people, respectively, composing several households in each of the three dwellings. Deansgate was known to Engels as the haunt of thieves and prostitutes in the 1840s. A distressed group were 108 children under age fourteen, in 1851, cared for by forty-nine widows and the twenty children of nine unmarried mothers. We can only speculate on the life of these children in Deansgate. Their lives were probably briefer than those of other children, their health poorer—one thinks of chronic ear infections and chest colds—and their education close to nil. Smith reports that the area was largely rebuilt by the end of the century, having peaked as a center of crime in the 1870s.

In Dublin, conditions were equally bad. Dr. Mapother, who occupied several positions in public health simultaneously in the 1860s, reported that there were eight thousand houses each room of which was rented out as a separate dwelling (Mapother 1866). One room in Cuff Street, he reported, was occupied by six adults and two children. In Chapelizod, Leinster, eight factory girls plus the father of one girl all occupied a room "not quite twelve feet square." A few years before, in 1864, Dr. Mapother had given statistics on the density of the population. Mapother cited the inquiries of a Mr. Robinson, who studied an alley near Menth Street. In thirty-three houses, with a total of 171 rooms, 915 persons slept in 294 beds. There were 27.72 people to a house, 5.35 people to a room, and 3.11 people to a bed or mattress. In 1853, a model lodging house was opened in Marlborough Street. There, about thirty families dwelt at a weekly rent of one to three shillings (Urlin 1865).

Transportation

Had young George Sala, our Jack Tar manqué, wished he could have travelled by coach either through London or on to Portsmouth; for, by the early nineteenth century, coaches travelled from Gloucester to London in less than twelve hours. Leeds took thirty-one hours, and Norwich twelve hours. Such travel was not comfortable, but it was scheduled and predictable. Dickens had Mr. Samuel Pickwick and colleagues leave the George and Vulture for Dingley Dell in a fashion nothing less than routine. Equally routine was intra-city travel once Mr. George Shillibeer introduced travel "for all" (omnibus) by putting the Parisian coach onto London's streets. It was expensive, and it was dangerous. In July 1842, Mr. and Mrs. Reeve were living in Paddington with their five-year-old,

Charlotte Maria. The unfortunate child dashed into the street just as a horse-drawn onmibus named "the Dart" came by. Charlotte was struck and killed. The jury returned a verdict of "Accidental Death," which was accepted by the Coroner, the well-known Mr. Wakley (Coroner's 1842).

There were other vehicles on the street, of course; cabs of all kinds, wagons delivering beer, all of which were pulled by horses. Sometimes streets were clogged by herds of sheep and cows destined for someone's dinner table. The cumulative effect was smelly and, when combined with the polluted Thames in the middle years of the nineteenth century, gave streets a noisome odor.

An innovation was the introduction of rails on which coaches were pulled by horses. The coaches acquired an upstairs—the old "outside" of coach travel—and eventually they were electrified into the tramways which served many cities around the world well into the twentieth century. Introduction of the bicycle with pneumatic wheels did much to free the working man from the tyranny of his pedestrian pace, and it multiplied his radius for seeking work by at least two or three times. In this regard, the boy was made the equal of the man and also gained access to recreation over a much wider part of his hometown.

Railways. The earliest relationship between railways and towns was delicate and restrained; railways approached centers of population but then stopped. The result was that the boon of intercity travel did not immediately dismay city residents; as an example, the Liverpool and Manchester Railway picked up its passengers much as airlines do around the world today, in the city center, and transported them to the fringes to board the train. The Mancunian family wishing to visit relations in Liverpool went to the company office in Market Street and boarded the free horse-drawn omnibus for a ride to the train waiting at Liverpool Road. The routes were posted and train travellers were invited to hail omnibuses which followed three routes to the distant stations. In the accommodation of town and train, there was an obvious inconvenience to passengers, but only slowly did shareholders take up the idea of centrally placed stations. Indeed, the diversity of railway companies—476 of them in 1867, according to Bradshaw (1869)—and their competitiveness led them to duplicate each other's facilities. In most cities of the world there is one twentieth-century airport, but there may be several nineteenth-century railway stations. Eventually, the convenience of boarding trains in the city center prevailed and trains began to penetrate to the urban cores. The public welcomed the idea, and Francis Head (1849) described the railway as "the greatest blessing which science has ever parted to mankind." The hallmark of respectability came relatively soon after Dr. Granville's fulminations, for, in June 1842, Queen Victoria and Prince

Albert, accompanied by Mr. Isambard Kingdom Brunel, returned from Windsor to London via the Great Western Railway on a train of six coaches pulled by the locomotive *Phlegethon*. The royal party paused at Slough, left at noon, and pulled into Paddington twenty-five minutes later to the "most deafening demonstration of loyalty and affection . . ." (Her majesty's, 1942). We presume the royal children were fully informed of the details by their affectionate parents.

The ease of the trip from Slough to Paddington was not without cost, for railway stations and their approaching rails exacted a high price. This penalty was borne by displaced families and by discomfitted generations to follow. Railway Directors were ever people of influence and were identified in Parliament as "the Railway Interest." Only the "Cricket Interest," an evanescent coalition, could stop them. In 1888, they stopped the plan to allow the Great Central Railway to cross the pitch at Lord's (Sandiford 1983). Legislation authorizing right of way into city centers was generally approved, and no thought was given to the social consequences of those who were, literally, in the way. Kellett (1969) has described the impact of railways on cities most thoroughly. For our purposes, the important aspect is that the homes of children and their parents were erased in order for trains to enter cities. And yet, the locomotive did not always win. The station at York lies just outside the walls; and in London, trains stopped at Victoria, Euston, and Paddington, but did not reach into Mayfair.

The impact of the train on the lives of ordinary folk was extensive. Dyos's (1957) analysis lists sixty-one Acts authorizing railway extensions affecting the "Labouring Classes." Two undertakings around 1860 each affected almost five thousand people. As late as 1898, widening approaches to Waterloo Station displaced twenty-five hundred people. Such wholesale evictions were not without precedent for there had been large-scale dispossessions in order to build docks and to create new streets. Today, we require calculation of social as well as fiscal costs, but the nineteenth century saw only Progress, with virtually no regard for the lives of those who got in the way. This disregard existed at the time of railway expansion, but its consequences persist until this day.

More radical were the final approaches to some London stations. In the case of Kings Cross, a deep cutting was required so that street traffic from east to west was interdicted, except where tunnels were built. Small businesses which were physically untouched were greatly affected by the eviction of their customers, whose diaspora was final. For owners and employees of such businesses, and the service workers who provisioned and cleaned them, railway clearances were a disaster. It reached its peak, according to Dyos between 1859 and 1867, when thirty-seven thousand displacements of persons occurred.

In terms of families, less visible effects appeared as viaducts carried trains above ground. However, the viaducts proceeded without thought for their consequent disruption of streets. Neighborhoods were strangled by railways and deteriorated into slums as a consequence. Shopping patterns were destroyed, peremptorily, much as local access may be cut off today by a motorway. Neighborhoods and families were left to struggle with the unforeseen or neglected consequences of progress, such as streets which became dead-ends and courts cut off from fresh air and daylight.

In order to understand how trains affected children and their families in the nineteenth century, we need to take one further step. Its premise is that housing was scarce for the poor and expensive at the best of times. Railway expansion did three related things at the same time. First, it destroyed existing housing stock and so complicated the market by increasing competition for housing among the poor. Second, destruction of housing stock did not require parallel or prior construction of new housing, and so the demoralized poor spilled into adjacent areas, thereby creating new problems for those communities. At the very least families had to put a roof over their heads and to earn their bread; however, they had to do so in the face of a new base from which to get to work, plus the probability that the old job had disappeared with the old neighborhood. Third, destruction of houses for railway expansion forced the poor who were honest to share neighborhoods with the dishonest, and increased the risk of juvenile delinquency.

Balance requires the recognition that railways created jobs and therefore supported families of those who worked for them. From the earliest days, railways were expansive and aggressive, and a smart lad could grow with them. Young Mark Huish left the Indian Army as a Captain and became the Secretary of Glasgow, Paisley, and Greenock Railway (Gourvish 1972). Later, he became the driving force of the London and North Western Railway, and primus inter pares among the administrators of the numerous railways of the 1840s. The L. & N.W. expanded, and many jobs were created. They ranged from positions within the railway companies—such as working in the tearoom at the Wolverton station, described in amusing detail by Head (1851)—to the complex of business generated in cities by train travel. In Bradshaw's railway guide for 1869 there is an advertisement aimed at the family trade. Ashley's Hotel, Covent Garden, describes itself to "FAMILIES AND GENTLEMEN" as sited in an "airy and central part of London," with beds at 2/6d., and private sitting rooms at 3/-. Sharing in this secondary form of railway-generated business would be cab drivers and porters who delivered families and their baggage to their hotels. Regretfully, we cannot close the economic circle by speculating that the new jobs were filled by people displaced by new railway lines for homes and former jobs. The problem of unskilled labor in nineteenth-century London was always enormous; jobs as "boy wanted" which seemed attractive at age fourteen had a way of petering into nothing at age nineteen, leaving only the army as an alternate to an endless search for jobs requiring little or no skill at low pay. Those with soi-disant "skilled jobs" were loath to tolerate the unskilled, whose services would always be underbid by the next casual worker. The families and children of such men had modest prospects indeed, as housing shrank in the face of planned destruction without replacement.

The Tube. In the case of the railways intended to move people around the inner core of London, disruption was less intense. Existing railways above ground were absorbed, and new lines running through iron tubes were laid in trenches which were then filled, thereby restoring the surface to utility. The earliest line ran from Paddington to Farringdon Street and proved a success. Other lines were still less disruptive, because they were far underground and well below the conduits carrying sewage, electricity, gas, and telephone lines. Employment opportunities here were considerable, and the tradition of career lines with "the Tube" is taken for granted today. Tunneling has not ceased; and remodeling of stations, in the style of the Bond Street and Baker Street Tube stations, suggests that employment continues to be generated in secondary ways by the underground railways running under streets, offices, and homes.

Housing

To look at public buildings is to have a sense of experiences shared with the Victorians. When we turn to the dwellings in cities, the sense of continuity is justified, for Victorian housing stock covers the landscape. A survey in Leeds by Wilkinson and Sigsworth (1963) found that of 2,585 houses, 18% had been built in the period 1850–66. Of the remaining, 33% had been built before 1882. In Swansea, about the same time—1961—20% of fifty thousand houses had been erected before 1875 (Hilton 1967). A 1968 survey in Ulster cited by Hillyard et al (1972) estimated that 40% of all housing stock was more than eighty years old. As a consequence, our search for a sense of Victorian children and their houses requires no great ingenuity, for we see the housing in which they lived all around us. Indeed, it has antiquarian value, for an appreciation of Victorian aesthetics and workmanship has undergone its eventual and probably inevitable revival. Of course, much Victorian housing stock is the worse for wear a century or more later, but we can glimpse the child's ambience in the structures we encounter.

Country Housing. There are few valid generalities about how Victorian children lived, because circumstances varied by region and unique local circumstances. Country living was neither better nor worse than city living in its quality, although as the century progressed, more people lived in bad housing in cities because that was where the population was concentrated. Living in a Fylde valley cottage of "clat and clay" could be miserable in winter (Dickson 1959), but it was probably cheaper. In 1840, according to C. R. Weld's testimony before the Health of Towns Commission, three shillings a week would rent a room in Westminster—which was not the choicest neighborhood at the time—or an entire house in Manchester. In Hinckley, Leicestershire, John Brooks, a weaver, could house his children, his wife, and his loom for just over two shillings a week (Weld 1840). Of course, rural housing was crowded, and Mills (1978) reported two parents and six children living in three rooms at Melbourne in Cambridgeshire. In such crowding, Horn (1974) reports, people ate in shifts for lack of seating. Of course, even that was less stressful than using beds in shifts, which was the custom for some Lancashire mill workers, child and adult. The gentlemen of the Manchester Statistical Society who studied three parishes in Rutlandshire reported to their colleagues in the London Society that "instances of squalid misery so frequent in large towns were here extremely rare" (Statistical 1839).

The home life of the country child was not idyllic in the nineteenth century; drinking water drawn from butts or from wells liable to pollution was normal. The homes of country children frequently lacked privacy and warmth, contained pests and communicable diseases, and had structural deficiencies. Alexander Somerville's family frequently were assigned by farmers to live in windowless sheds. His parents, who were remarkable people according to his account of their actions (Behan 1967), made a small window with one pane of glass and moved it from shed to shed. The child of the agricultural worker was expected to leave the shed or cottage to work in the fields at an early age and in all kinds of weather. To do so, in Cornwall, was almost a necessity; the *Morning Chronicle*'s correspondent reported in 1851 that, "In all cases where there were two rooms, the family crowded into one, to leave the other room for the lodgers. . . . For two shillings a week they got their bed, their washing, their tea and breakfast, and ordinary vegetables at dinner." However, there was less risk of tuberculosis, even when crowding was evident. Although ventilation was poor, there was always fresh air to be had by stepping outside. When the good diet of Cumberland farms is added to the picture, the home of a country child could be beneficial. In contrast, living away from a town could be merely substituting a rural slum house for a city slum house. Welsh children in the Rhondda Valley knew industrial pollution and foul air as thoroughly as any Birmingham child. Stepping from the overcrowded company house into the open air merely substituted one foul atmosphere for another. Of course, not every country child was poor, nor every country town a slum situated in swampy ground. Accordingly, we acknowledge the existence of privileged ways of life for children of the well-to-do. But even here, the twentieth-century mind spots restrictions. Boys happy in prosperous houses eventually went to boarding schools. In the case of the Public Schools before Dr. Arnold, such a child left a comfortable home for induction into a culture of mannered barbarism leavened with occasional uprisings. The loss of home for a boy was no less immense when the process of acculturation led to membership in a privileged, well-connected caste. For girls, the pleasantries of privileged country living

TABLE 7.2
NUMBER AND CONDITION OF HOUSES
IN ENGLAND AND WALES 1801–1901*
(in thousands)

Year	Occupied (K)	Unoccupied (K)	Being Built (K)	Decennial Increase in Occupied Dwellings (K)	Population Increase (%)
1801	1575.92	57.42			
1811	1797.50	51.02	16.20	13.80	14.00
1821	2088.16	67.71	19.27	16.20	18.10
1831	2481.54	119.91	24.76	18.80	15.80
1841	2943.94	173.25	27.44	18.60	14.30
1851	3278.04	153.49	26.57	11.60	12.70
1861	3739.50	184.69	27.30	14.00	11.90
1871	4259.12	261.34	37.80	13.90	13.20
1881	4831.52	386.68	46.41	13.40	14.40
1891	5451.50	372.18	38.39	12.80	11.70
1901	6260.85	448.93	61.69	14.90	12.20

*Census 1911 (1917).

yielded to "the Season," the elaborate but stylized introduction to the marriage market via coming-out in London. In a minority of instances, children of the affluent, in the country as in the city, were tutored at home. In that style, the country house was the matrix for childhood and adolescence, providing psychological as well as material support.

In Ireland, housing had long been a problem. In 1841, about one-third of all parents and children lived in what were called by the Census fourth-class houses, which were built of mud and had only one room and one window (Pim 1876). Some children had been even worse off, such as the newborn twins of a woman in Cork who, "had no covering or shelter but the projection of a large rock" (Report 1822); to such a family, a mud cottage would have seemed ample. By 1901, the proportion of such terrible shelter had fallen to under 5%. In the same period, the proportion of families living in houses of the first class rose from 2% to 7% (Matheson 1903).

However, it is not enough to count houses, for we must also consider who lived in them. In Dublin at the end of the nineteenth century, one-third of all families, 36.70%, still lived in one room, 10% were so housed in Cork, 7% in Derry, while only 1% were so housed in Belfast. For purposes of comparison, the proportion had been 25% in Glasgow in 1881 (Dawson 1901). Dublin housing was the worst in Ireland; one-quarter of houses used as tenements were unfit for human habitation. Those twenty-three hundred buildings were occupied by thirty thousand people (Eason 1899). The quality of such accommodations is, perhaps, conveyed by a statement about housing in Belfast made by the Rev. W. M. O'Hanlon some decades before, in 1853. In his account of bad housing in Stewart's Court, off Carrick Hill, he reported that he could say little, "having been wholly unable to enter it, because of the effluvium which met us on the very threshold" (O'Hanlon 1853). Given the large numbers of children living in such conditions, it is no wonder that sickness prevailed amongst those who survived infancy. O'Hanlon added that "to compare their condition with that of the beasts of the field would be paying but an indifferent compliment to the lower animals."

Model Housing

Housing poor families has always been complicated by the pattern of their having more children than better-off people. Even so, there were proposals to house poor children and their parents from the earliest decades of the nineteenth century. In 1831, Thomas Postans, in a docu-

ment addressed to Sir Thomas Baring, presented a design for model
cottages to house agricultural workers. It was simple and would replace
decaying, ill-ventilated, damp dwellings with a more suitable, healthy
dwelling of modest proportions. Another innovation, one which
achieved considerable success for a brief time, was the model lodging
house for single men. By 1850, this innovation had proved itself. One
such organization in Drury Lane rented eighty-two beds at two shillings
a week (Report 1849) from 1847 until much later in the century. In the
following year, a down-market version in George Street offered 103 beds
at 4d per night. The latter offered a place for the destitute, of whom
there were many, who passed the night sitting on Waterloo Bridge
(Greenwood 1881), or sleeping rough under the arches of a railway via-
duct. Mann (1898) reported that a Model Lodging Association was active in Glasgow in the 1840s, and in Leeds Beckett Denison opened one
in 1851 (Roberts 1858). The Philanthropic Lodging House at 11 Union
Court, Holborn, charged three pence a night and provided heat for
cooking (Beames 1850). Most large towns had them, and they catered to
respectable working men.

Housing offering any sort of protection from the elements for a
mother and her children could be rented out by owners. Church (1966)
cites the case of a Nottingham resident who kept a pig in an abandoned
caravan. He evicted his pig and rented the caravan for 2/3d per week. In
Gaslight and Daylight (1872), Sala recorded his encounters in a model
lodging "House of Poverty" with a sickly young needlewoman and a man
who was dying of starvation. As the century progressed, such charitable
agencies increased.

By 1883, Sir Rawson Rawson could report to the Statistical Society
that many years before he had visited several model lodging houses situated behind Grosvenor Square, Bryanston Square, and Portland Square.
In such places young mechanics could live respectable if regulated lives;
for philanthropy in the nineteenth century was self-serving and ever
sought to inculcate proper values—deference, the Smilesian virtues,
etc.—in those assisted. An extreme example is the set of rules guiding
those accepted into the Almshouse at Ravensworth established by Lady
Ravensworth in 1836 (McCord 1972).

Persons admitted to the Ravensworth Almshouses are to consider themselves as Residents only upon sufferance, and that they may be dismissed
by the Lady Ravensworth, or any person deputed by Her Ladyship for
any offense, or reason, that Her Ladyship may deem sufficient: and it is
to be understood that drunkenness, dishonesty, want of cleanliness,

quarrelling, meddling with or slandering their neighbours will be considered sufficient reasons for dismissal.

Of course, such philanthropy served only a few people. By the middle of the century the scope of housing schemes had expanded. Near Halifax, Edward Akroyd built several housing complexes for his workers, the largest of which, begun in 1859, was called Akroydon (Burnett 1982). In nearby Bradford, Titus Salt established Saltaire, which aspired to nearly one thousand homes. In the same period, Alfred Krupp in Germany saw the value of company housing and created dwellings at low rents for his Kruppianers. The motives in these ambitious enterprises were a mixture of paternal benevolence, shrewd control of the work force, and utopianism. In Scotland, according to Melling (1981), many companies on the Clydeside built housing for their workers. Considering that the utopian Robert Owen had begun his rise at New Lanark with what he hoped was a model community, the Scottish ventures extended a regional precedent.

A related and decidedly philanthropic stream of housing developments existed in London. In 1841, the Rev. Henry Taylor had sponsored rented housing in Spitalfields through his Metropolitan Association. By 1875, Gatliff could report that 32,435 people lived in 6,838 "improved dwellings." In Pentonville's model houses, infant mortality dropped by nearly one-half (Finlayson 1981). London also saw the birth of a form of sponsored housing which can be seen today. The Massachusetts businessman, George Peabody, donated £150,000 to support housing for working people of moral character and good conduct. The first building went up in Spitalfields to the design of Henry Darbishire (Tann 1966) and was opened in 1864, under the supervision of one of the great builders, Thomas Cubitt. Most Peabody Trust apartments had two rooms, and rents were from 2/6 for one of the few one-room dwellings on the top floor for old women to 5/- for a three-room flat. Others followed, especially in the ten years starting in 1875, and there is a Peabody building in Drury Lane. Today, the close supervision of residents, who felt like prisoners in the nineteenth century, has eased. At that time, a rowdy child or a persistent lack of decorum led to prompt expulsion. "All of us children had to be vaccinated and you weren't allowed to play in the square outside after seven in the winter or after eight in the summer." (Weightman and Humphries 1983). Because eviction could mean a loss of access to employment, Peabody families toed the mark.

Another block approach to housing which exaggerated the high density of the Peabody system, but in a different configuration, was the back-to-back house of the northern cities. Row houses share common side walls, and back-to-back houses also share their back wall with another structure, so that three houses are contiguous. Such houses present problems of light and ventilation because those vectors of health can only come from one direction. Generations of children grew up in such houses, of which Leeds had the highest proportion. Indeed, the back-to-back was being erected there until well into the 1930s. This was model housing, but in the negative sense of what not to do.

The obvious disadvantage to children and their parents was the high density of population in small back-to-back houses and the associated health problems. The advantages were obvious to the builder, who could put many houses onto small plots with a proportionately high rate of return on the investment. Beresford (1971) points out that Leeds was predisposed by the earlier tradition of "folds," complexes in which garden space was used as a building site, which began in the eighteenth century. The infamous Boot and Shoe inn yard near Briggate was named in the report of 1839 to the Statistical Society as a site of overcrowding and filth. Construction of back-to-back houses persisted in Leeds despite the efforts of reformers. Their popularity was probably a combination of high return on capital—for housing was an excellent investment in the nineteenth century—and a comparatively attractive rent for the working classes. In the case of eastern Leeds, York Road and Harehills Lane met at the site ironically named Shaftesbury. Beyond that point development progressed after a sharp demarcation into semidetached and row housing much more suitable for families. Those residents, for the most part, previously occupied back-to-back houses and left them behind as promptly as their circumstances permitted. As late as 1899, Leeds children and parents had little beyond back-to-back housing to choose from. Beresford (1971) cites Corporation figures showing that as late as 1899, 72% of annual house construction in Leeds was back-to-back. It had been 72% fifteen years before and would not drop sharply until 1914.

In Glasgow, a special form of housing existed for the poor. In a report to the local Philosophical Society, John Mann (1898) described the process of "ticketing" a house. A place with no more than three rooms and a cubic capacity under three thousand cubic feet might be occupied at a rate of three hundred cubic feet per person over age ten; those younger were not counted apparently. Each ticketed house was visited at night, and the owner could be prosecuted for overcrowding. Mann reported that the number of such houses had dropped from twenty-three thousand to twenty-one thousand between 1887 and 1898. The chief advantage to the poor was that the rent of ticketed houses was half that of other dwellings available to them.

TABLE 7.3
TENEMENTS AND OCCUPANCY IN RURAL AND URBAN AREAS 1891 and 1901 AND LONDON 911*

Rooms per Tenement	Persons per Room						5 Counties with Highest Proportion of Tenements <4 Rooms 1911		5 Counties with Lowest Proportion of Tenements <4 Rooms 1911	
	1891			1901			County	% of Tenements	County	% of Tenements
	Urban	Rural	London	Urban	Rural	London				
1	2.24	2.16	2.24	2.03	1.77	2.04	Northumberland	55.90	Peterborough (Soke)	7.40
2	1.77	1.58	1.82	1.67	1.47	1.74	London	54.10	Bedfordshire	8.00
3	1.45	1.33	1.45	1.39	1.26	1.38	Durham	50.60	Isle of Wight	8.00
4	1.19	1.10	1.29	1.14	1.05	1.24	Yorks, W. Riding	30.00	Leicestershire	9.50
All Sizes	1.39	1.21		1.30	1.13		Shropshire	28.60	Derbyshire	9.50

*Abstracted from Census 1911 (1917).

At the bottom of the scale of housing, and scarcely meriting the term, were the inhabited cellars found in large towns. Greenwood (1881) reported troops of cellar-dwelling children, naked, climbing up and down ladders to enter cellars in St. Giles. Cellar-dwelling was common in Liverpool and Manchester, but not in Birmingham (Hopkins 1986). Commentators in the period reported that adults and children frequently cohabitated with a pig in dwellings occupied by the Irish. Such a situation was reported from Leeds, with the additional element that an Irish woman cellar-dweller was dying in the presence of a pig (Report 1839).

Liverpool is credited with a very high rate of occupancy of cellars in the mid-nineteenth century. About 10% of the total population lived in cellars (Treble 1971), out of a segment of 35% who were very badly housed. Manchester and other large cities also had cellar-dwellers. Obviously, children reared in such circumstances were at grave risk for perishing from the combination of damp walls, muddy floors frequently flooded, and the miasmic air to which the Victorians inaccurately traced infectious diseases. In north Liverpool in 1841, the Scotland and Vauxhall districts presented over one hundred occupied cellars out of a total of nearly two hundred (N = 197). In south Liverpool the situation was worse; out of a thousand occupied cellars (N = 1,055), 42% were in South Toxteth; Rodney Street and North Toxteth supplied two hundred apiece. Obviously, life was much harder for children in Liverpool's south areas. The typical cellar in West Derby housed just over four people, two of whom we may suppose to be children.

Towards the end of the nineteenth century, large-scale housing plans began to assume more comprehensive form. Glasgow had its Glasgow Improvement Trust, which improvidently built houses here and there on the strict principle that they make money rather than on the premise of a targeted clientele to be served. The undertaking, according to Mann (1898), failed on that score too. The Glasgow Corporation was more successful in its efforts, however. The Cadbury family's Bourneville was a community, not just a set of dwellings. The Rowntree settlement at New Earswich was a parallel development. Near Birkenhead, Lever built Port Sunlight, whose design was enlightened by imaginative use of ground and variation in houses. Using Old English and Flemish facades and curving streets, Port Sunlight pursued a high goal on 330 acres (Wilson 1968). By 1898, nearly three hundred houses had been built. With the Garden City paradigm, mass housing for families left the strictly poor behind and embraced the relatively well-to-do.

In appraising attempts to house the child of the poor in the nineteenth century, we do not apply a standard of satisfaction with twentieth century accomplishments. When successful, planned group housing for the poor invalidates itself. That is, the deserving are socialized into new expectations, which society is supposed to supply in the form of still higher-class housing. The young, ever restless, may still find outlets in destruction and defacement; in contrast, the nineteenth century child was quite successfully socialized into compliance with middle- and upper-class needs. However, there never was that much model housing in city cores. Suburbs coupled with the reduced train fares that Gatliff had called for in 1840 (at a rate of ten miles to the penny) partially filled the gap, especially in the metropolis.

London

Among the many travels of his youth, the ex-beggar boy, James Burn, remembered his first experience of London in the 1820s.

> . . . London was far too large for me. I was fairly lost in a wilderness of human beings; I was a mere atom in a mountain of humanity. No man can form the most distant idea of the misery and human suffering that wanders the streets of London . . .(Vincent 1978).

Of course, young James Burn viewed the largest city in the nineteenth-century world from a worm's-eye-view, having just worked his passage on a boat from Liverpool with little money and no prospects. His was the ambience of the poor, which existed cheek-by-jowl with other Londons. It was no great distance from the rookery of St. Giles to the West End. In fact, the smell of St. Giles was worthy of record in Flora Tristan's *Promenade dans Londre* in 1840 (Palmer and Pincetl 1980). The smell bothered middle-class residents of New Oxford Street in 1849 to the extent that they formed a party to visit that rookery, only to learn that the inhabitants shared their displeasure at the noisome offense. The visitors withdrew across the social, if not the olfactory, barrier. Another example of how close the poor were at times to the comfortable was given by Octavia Hill (1875) in her description of the houses she renovated for the "residuum," the desperately poor, with the help of John Ruskin. The court,

> is not far from Cavendish Square, and daily in the season, scores of carriages, with their gaily-dressed occupants pass the end of it . . . In many of the houses the dustbins were utterly unapproachable, and cabbage leaves, stale fish, and every sort of dirt were lying in the

passages . . . the kitchen stairs were many inches thick with dirt . . . so
hardened that a shovel had to be used to get it off . . . the rain was
coming through the roofs. It was truly appalling to think that there were
human beings who lived habitually in such an atmosphere. Truly a wild,
lawless desolate little kingdom to come to rule over (pp. 23–76).

The poorest found it necessary to stay close to central London.

A problem for workers in a period when transportation was unreli-
able and expensive was that they had to live near opportunities for casual
work. This economic fact of life meant that the social segregation common in many towns was not quite possible. The wealthy saw demolition
projects as ways to rid themselves of dangerous neighbors; for the threat
of violence existed for the first fifty years, only to evaporate with the
final Chartist fiasco and the improving standard of living which eventually trickled down to the poor and desperate.

Slums. In referring to London in the early nineteenth century as the
Infernal Wen, William Cobbett was expressing the country man's unease
at the prospect of cities, but he was also calling attention to the appalling
conditions in which a large mass of the nation's poor existed. Children
and adults competed for work in a town with a decreasing share of
manufacturing. Only those prepared by literacy and a respectable appearance could participate in the growing ranks of the clerical force in
the city. For those below that level, life was a battle to pay the high rents
and to scrounge for food. The poorest and most disorganized people
lived in the rookeries, slum areas of greatly concentrated population.
Such areas had accumulated over the centuries, so that by the middle of
the nineteenth century the city was a patchwork of highly differentiated
regions. To the north, west, and southwest of Trafalgar Square lay well-
established estates owned by the Crown and by wealthy individuals. To
the south, across the river, was another strip of desirable land. To the
east and southeast lay a few large tracts of land surrounded by larger
properties; the pattern is well described by Shepperd (1971). The consequence was that land development in the metropolis was subject to vagaries of management and development. A responsible and farsighted
owner might sell or lease land to a speculative builder such as Thomas
Cubitt and thus an Eaton Square appeared. On the other hand, a series
of leases and subleases was more common so that only short-term finan-
cial return guided property and land management. In this last context,
several rookeries emerged over a period of centuries. The most notorious
in the opinion of the Reverend Thomas Beames (1850) was St. Giles,
approximately southeast of Oxford Street and Charing Cross Road; Saf-

fron Hill a little further east and the home of Italian immigrants, and Jacob's Island in Bermondsey, were next in infamy.

The residents of St. Giles, formerly known as Cock and Pie Fields, were not wholly without initiative in seeking improvement in their way of life. In 1849, forty men and fourteen women, all residents of Church Lane and Carrier Street, wrote to *The Times,* which published their letter on Tuesday, July 3, 1849.

> Sur,
>
> May we beg and beseach your proteckshion and power, We are Sur, as it may be, livin in a Wilderniss, so far as the rest of London knows anything of us, or as the rich and great people care about. We live in muck and filthe. We aint got no priviz, no dust bins, no drains, no water splies, and no drain or suer in the whole place. The Suer Company, in Greek Street, Soho Square, all great, rich and powerful men, take no notice watsomedever of our complaints. The Stenche of a Gully-hole is disgustin. We al of us suffer, and numbers are ill, and if the Colera comes Lord help us.
>
> Some gentlemens comed yesterday, and we thought they was comishoners from the suer Company, but they was complaining of the noosance and stenche our lanes and corts was to them in New Oxforde Street. They was much surprized to see the seller in Number 12, Carrier Street, in our lane, where a child was dyin from fever, and would not beleave that Sixty persons sleep in it every night. This here seller you couldent swing a cat in, and the rent is five shilling a week; but theare are greate many sich deare sellers. Sur, we hope you will let us have our cumplaints put into your hinfluenshall paper, and make these landlords of our houses and these comishoners (the friends we spose of the landlords) make our houses decent for Christians to live in.
>
> Preaye Sir com and see us, for we are livin like piggs, and it aint faire we shoulde be so ill treted.
>
> We are your respeckfull servents in Church Lane, Carrier Street, and the other corts.

Presumably, the dying child died, and the "Suer" company continued in its ways until forced to change by people more powerful than John Scott and the other residents of Church Lane. Smells and filth surrounded babies and children, and only the rats and bed bugs flourished in St. Giles. The "Two Nations" alluded to by Benjamin Disraeli would touch briefly, and the visitors from New Oxford Street returned to their remote station in life. Only the physical destruction of St. Giles and the further disorganization of the lives of its residents would end the offense to the nostrils of the comfortable. Two days after the letter from the residents of Church Lane, *The Times* printed a letter demonstrating that Battersea had a ditch five hundred yards long which was a "cesspool of the most horrid kind." The author believed the "deadly vapours" would lead to an outbreak of cholera (J. 1849). The submerged population so clearly represented in Henry Mayhew's *London Labour and the London Poor* persisted in their misery. Dickens's Mr. Wilkins Micawber lived on the threshold of this stratum, an abyss into which his children could be dropped by the death of their breadwinner, or even a loss of employment. An event of some frequency—recorded, for example, in the memoirs of the Irish shoemaker John O'Neill (1869)—the consequences were swift and terrible. For children, the Reverend Mr. Beames thought the consequences were direct.

> You seem for a time to leave the day, and life, and habits of your fellow-creatures behind you—squalid children . . . women without shoes or stockings—a babe perhaps at the breast, with a single garment, confined to the waist by a piece of string . . . young boys gathered around . . . looking exhausted as though they had not been to bed (Beames 1850).

These circumstances persisted throughout the nineteenth century, but the middle and upper classes slowly acquired an appreciation of the extent of the seething mass of poor and destitute just beyond their immediate perception. One of the great cries on behalf of poor children and adults did not appear until 1883. In that year, the Reverend Mr. Andrew Mearns published, anonymously, "The Bitter Cry of Outcast London." This short work of twenty pages addresses the "poverty, misery, squalor and immorality . . . of the great dark region . . . toning down everything (lest readers be) insufferably outraged." In careful prose, Mearns documented

> courts reeking with poisonous and malodorous gases . . . accumulations of sewage and refuse . . . walks and ceilings black with accretions of filth. Here are seven people living in one underground kitchen and a little dead child lying in the same room . . . a poor widow with her three children, and a child who has been dead thirteen days. Her husband . . . committed suicide. Who can wonder that little children taken from these hovels to the hospital cry, when they are well, through dread of being sent back to their former misery? Here is a mother who has taken away whatever articles of clothing she can strip from her four little children without leaving them absolutely naked . . . for coals and food

So extreme were the health problems of children and adults residing in high Victorian London that they were thought to constitute a unique medical problem. Sir James Clark coined the term "Cachexia

Londinensis" to describe the unhealthiness endemic to the metropolis (Angus 1854). Of course, the conclusion was overdrawn, but the sheer size of the population magnified problems for a generation which had only just received Snow's findings. By mapping the spread of cholera, Snow was able to introduce determinism into the question of cause, even though the *vibrio* organism was not yet isolated. A generation unable to draw on epidemiological concepts much beyond a hypothesized Miasma as a cause of disease—a confused acceptance of communicability of some diseases—could easily conclude that London was a uniquely un-healthy place with its own diseases.

In some respects, the circumstances of the London poor were ac-centuated by the Victorians' habit of not thinking through the nature of social problems. In the 1820s and 1830s, factory legislation on behalf of children would address the manufactors of a given product or use of a raw material. The result was that a process differing merely in the name of the raw material could abuse children without breaking the law. As late as the 1870s, legislation remained ill-conceived; Cross's Artisan's Dwelling Act of 1875 envisaged rehousing poor families. Unfortunately, redevelopment of land after a Medical Officer had condemned housing reimbursed landlords for their property at a level which was rigged by last-minute "improvements." Jones (1971) cites an instance in which the St. Giles slumlord Thomas Flight received seven times the fair value of a condemned property. Some portion of that profit probably was used to increase the reimbursable value of other properties among the eighteen thousand houses owned by Flight at one time or another. At times, more profit was made out of evicting the poor than housing them. However, wringing the last copper out of the poor was a well-tuned art. Rents were high; they were generally collected weekly, but Greenwood (1881) re-ported from his soundings of the "Low-Life Deeps" that in many apart-ments the rent was collected nightly; expulsion could follow nonpayment before the sun went down. Such was the competition for housing that one woman rented the floor around her bed to a family as sleeping quarters. Adding to the misery of the compulsory clearances of slums was the nonappearance of an appropriate scale of housing for the dispos-sessed. When it did exist, the Reverend Mr. Mearns reported, the rents were beyond the resources of the dispossessed.

A parallel threat to families was built on Crown land in 1847, and it increased the site's value. New Oxford Street destroyed many slum dwellings, as did Queen Victoria Street when it sliced through slums in 1851. Today, the value of these street-improvement schemes is evident, although movement is still slowed by the sheer volume of traffic. What is not evident is the impact at the time on the poor families rudely evicted

TABLE 7.4
DENSITY OF PEOPLE AND HOUSES IN SELECTED DISTRICTS OF LONDON[1]

District	1841				1861				1881			
	N Houses	Houses per Acre	People per Acre	People per House	N Houses	Houses per Acre	People per Acre	People per House	N Houses	Houses per Acre	People per Acre	People per House
Kensington	7,277	2.13	15.32	7.15	19,168	5.61	42.68	7.61	33,402	9.77	79.10	8.19
Westminster	4,994	23.12	249.44	10.79	4,703	21.77	244.42	11.22	4,285	19.84	215.51	10.86
St. Pancras	14,776	5.57	48.91	8.79	21,852	8.24	74.93	9.10	24,701	9.31	89.05	9.56
St. Giles	4,959	20.24	221.60	10.95	4,690	19.14	220.72	11.53	3,962	16.17	185.23	11.45
City	4,477	21.22	157.44	7.42	3,367	15.96	120.15	7.53	1,360	6.45	47.32	7.34
Whitechapel	8,834	23.75	192.92	8.12	8,664	23.29	212.29	9.11	7,528	20.24	191.84	9.48
Wandsworth	6,459	.57	3.50	6.17	11,186	.98	6.18	6.29	30,748	2.70	18.47	6.84
Camberwell	6,843	1.54	8.96	5.83	12,098	2.72	16.06	5.19	27,316	6.14	41.93	6.83

[1]Adapted from Price-Williams (1880).

and forced into still harsher competition at higher rents for the remaining stock of housing.

When we turn to precisely where the loss of housing was greatest in London, we learn that there was considerable variation from district to district. Price-Williams's (1880) data list the changes in the number of houses in 141 subdistricts aggregated into twenty-nine registration districts. Table 7.4 shows that Kensington in 1841 had two houses per acre and several people per house in 7,277 houses. By 1861, there were 19,168 houses; and in 1881, there were 33,402 houses with 8.19 persons per house. In the forty years from 1841 to 1881, the density of people per acre rose from 15.32 (in 1841), to 42.68 (in 1861), and to 79.10 (in 1881). In the case of St. Giles, a steady drop of housing is evident. The number of houses fell from 4,959 in 1841, to 4,690 in 1861, to 3,962 in 1881. Camberwell, which has been extensively studied by Dyos (1961), had 6,843 houses in 1841; twenty years later, there were 12,098 houses, and by 1881 there were 27,316 houses. In the first twenty years, from 1841 to 1861, the number of persons per house dropped slightly, to 5.19 in 1861, but rose to 6.83 in 1881.

The notorious Saffron Hill had 1,454 houses in 1841, and a density of 240.69 people per acre; the average house had 9.93 inhabitants. By 1861, the stock of houses was down from 1,454 to 1,105, and people per acre dropped to 200.20; however, the density per house had risen to 10.87. Twenty years later, in 1881, there were only 731 houses, compared to the 1,454 of forty years before. People per acre was down to 108.88, and people per house was 8.92.

In 1841, the highest density of population in 149 subdistricts was Berwick Street in Westminster at 435.37 persons per acre; the average house held 13.03 people. Forty years later, in 1881 the highest density of population was 324.42 people per acre, in St. Andrew's, Holborn. Forty years had only dropped the density per acre a little from 382.21 persons per acre. In contrast, Berwick Street declined in people per acre over the forty years, to 169.75 people per acre from the 1841 figure of 435.37.

Whatever the background to life, nineteenth century London children had the sights and sounds of the metropolis to entertain them. Walter Besant encountered a group of girls on an outing at Hampstead.

> I may safely aver that language more vile and depraved, revealing thoughts more vile and depraved, I have never heard from any grown men or women in the worst part of the town (1886, 418).

The vilesness of their language, he reported, shocked some workmen who overheard their boisterous talk with disgust.

James Greenwood, George Sala, Henry Mayhew, and other authors functioned as journalist-cum-voyeur in reporting to the middle classes the "low-life" of London as a source of entertainment. Learning from one girl what her wages were, Greenwood pointed out that she could make twice as much as "nursemaid or kitchen maid in a respectable family." The answer she gave him forms a valuable anecdote for understanding the socialization of adolescents at the time. Replying to Greenwood's query as to why she did not take up such better-paid, higher status work she replied:

> "Because I'm above that poor scum that mustn't wear a feather or a ribbon, and because I likes my liberty."

She gave Greenwood a curtsey, he records, and she was on her way.

However, when viewed as a whole, London had unique problems. Greenwood (1869) listed *The Seven Curses of London*. They were: neglected children, thieves, beggars, fallen women, drunkenness, gambling, and the waste of charity. The first six of these we obviously accept, but the seventh requires explanation. Waste of charity meant that defects of character and morals accounted for much of life's problems, in the view of the middle and upper classes. Indiscriminate charity encouraged dependency and led to encouragement of cadging. Establishment of the Charity Organization Society was intended to coordinate philanthropy so that the undeserving poor could be set aside in favor of the deserving poor. Given the enormous number of unskilled workers and London's declining manufacturing economic component, plus a declining child mortality rate which put more young people into competition for jobs, the deserving had to be distinguished from the undeserving. We need to keep in mind, also, that the source of philanthropy was the privileged, not government. Neither local nor central government did very much for people and made few arrangements for children. However condescending their approach, the philanthropists, large and small, were meeting an obligation generated in the private virtues. Public virtue did not extend very far in the direction of charity or social reform. Accordingly, Greenwood's seven curses went largely unremedied. As late as 1888, Charles Booth reported that there were one hundred thousand people dependent on casual earnings in Hackney and Tower Hamlets, constituting 11% of the population. Below them were a further ten thousand people even worse off.

Within East London there were unique populations. The Irish gathered there in considerable numbers. Jewish immigrants who had fled

Czarist pogroms settled in what Fishman (1975) named "a Stetl called Whitechapel." They were memorialized in Zangwill's (1892) *Children of the Ghetto,* and had been touched on earlier, in 1872, by George Sala. In the following decade, Beatrice Potter (1888) gave an account of Jewish working men and women and children; she reported that, "the men remain sober, the women chaste, and men and women alike sacrifice personal comfort and ease to the welfare of their offspring." An avowedly criminal subculture was recorded in fiction also by Harding in 1886 in his account of life in the Jago, a nidus of six thousand people with Spitalfields to the south and Shoreditch High Street to the north. This last complex is recorded factually in Samuel's (1981) story of Arthur Harding.

London's population was augmented by other groups in the nineteenth century. We have mentioned Saffron Hill's Italian community, whose children George Sala (1872) thought indolent—probably confusing malnutrition with a moral defect. The Italian colony in Saffron Hill dated from at least as early as the 1830s. A committee of the London Statistical Society (Report 1843) identified

> eight lodging houses each with 30–40 Italian boys and each under the superintendence of a man and his wife who bring them over to this country as a speculation.

Of course, other cities had their ethnic minorities. As early as 1831, Glasgow's population was over one-sixth Irish (Cowan 1840), and Liverpool had a distinctive Welsh enclave (Pooley 1977). Continental disturbances brought German Liberals to London after 1848, and there was always a commercial presence. In this regard, London was like other cities. Bradford had a substantial German contingent; and Sir Jacob Behrens had settled there early in the century, raising his children with the town's prosperous middle class. Of course, the advent of Prince Albert of Saxe-Coburg in 1840 opened, however briefly, the sensibilities of John Bull to other influences.

Among London notables were some characters-around-town whom a child learned of, if only indirectly. Sala (1872) introduced his readers to the Ferry-man, "Powder Dick," who had lost both legs and an arm in an explosion, but still ran his service with the help of a strong wife who carried him on her back to the local pub after work. There was Madame Girardelli, earlier in the century, the "Fireproof Lady," who placed molten lead in her mouth and spat it out, ran a red-hot poker over her body, and put her hands into flames unscathed. In "Past and Present" (1843), Carlyle remarked on "that great hat seven feet high, which now perambulates London streets; which my friend Sauerteig regarded justly as one of our English notabilities." Richard Physic, known as "Brummy" (Greenwood 1881), apparently was an achondroplasic dwarf paid to fight bull dogs barehanded—and he won! There was the shambling young pituitary giant "Big Bill," who assisted at a pub in the East End, and Patrick O'Brien who was nine feet tall when he died of tuberculosis. In due time, there was Major Tom Thumb, and Chang and Eng, the Siamese Twins, appeared. Also, for a fee of one penny, Charles Taylor would allow people to see his wife billed as "The African Lion-Faced Lady" (Benson 1985). The kaleidoscope of the population constantly whirled, and the streets of the metropolis, if not its houses, were home, educator, and entertainment to the children of London.

Balance requires that we record that life could be pleasant for children in nineteenth-century London. There were enclaves which recalled an earlier time when districts were separate communities; one example was Palmer's Village in Westminster, whose site is now traversed by Victoria Street. As with country children, the range of living styles and standards was enormous. Molly Hughes (1977) was born in the 1870s and enjoyed a happy childhood in Canonbury in the 1870s. The house was large and comfortable and her parents were enlightened by anyone's standards. Molly and her brothers had a happy childhood and romped through their parents' large collection of books.

The City and the Land

In one respect, the Romantics of the nineteenth century were correct in their view that the present should be understood through the prism of the past; that is, the property which architects sought to design was usually private—e.g., Lord Bute's Cardiff Castle, decorated by William Burges. Most certainly the land underneath it had been privately owned for two centuries. Scott's (1982) appraisal of land ownership for 1872 revealed that four-fifths was owned by seven thousand people; in Scotland, one-fourth of the land was held by a mere twenty-five estates. The consequence was that the development of some towns was very much at the discretion of landed owners, who ranged from active and responsible in the management of their property to those who were absent and indifferent—which had long been the special problem of Irish property.

In Cardiff, the Bute estate took an active role in development of the area at the opening of the nineteenth century (Davies 1982). Especially under the third Marquess, there were good managers and Cardiff's development went well. Under the second Marquess, good housing had been built for tenants and their families. In 1947, the family gave Cardiff Castle and park to the city. In the case of Southport, two families—the Heskeths and Scarisbricks—had 97% of the land. In particular, Charles Scarisbrick planned a model community and laid down clear rules for developers (Liddle 1982). Bournemouth was rather late to develop, according to Roberts (1982), having only six hundred inhabitants at mid-century. With the arrival of the railway in the 1870s, the pace quickened. The land owners kept a low profile and generally saw the benefit to their holdings from careful development designed to attract the comparatively well-to-do. In some respects, Bournemouth appears to have benefitted from the lateness of its expansion, which occurred at a time when local government had acquired some sophistication. Eastbourne's development also came comparatively late. In this instance, tensions existed with the Devonshire estate which owned much of the land. Locals felt that they lacked control over their destiny for decades. Eventually, accommodation was reached, and the town continued its growth based on salubrious areas such as Meads and a population whose death rate in 1899 was only 10.8 per thousand (Cannadine 1980). Of course, one of the unique aspects of Eastbourne is the sharp difference in role from Brighton, its neighbor beyond Beachy Head. Eastbourne's children have been largely untroubled over the years by the lower-class visitors who, traditionally, day-tripped from London. The town has always insisted on a genteel atmosphere, and its beaches, pier, and hotels have remained quite distinct from its cousin to the west. Finally, we touch on the example of a small industrial town, Huddersfield, whose development has been described by Springett (1982). Generally speaking, development came early to the northern mill towns, as they provided the forge in which the Industrial Revolution was hammered out of the raw materials of people's lives, coal, and wool. In the case of Huddersfield at mid-century, land was held by three groups, with the Ramsdens holding most of the land in the town center. They followed a pattern of sixty-year leases until 1869 and then moved to ninety-nine-year leases. Small pieces of land were commonly leased, and so the return in the form of rents had to be proportionately intense from middle- rather than working-class residents. In general, Springett concluded that the Ramsdens failed to manage their land to advantage by discouraging speculative builders and developers. Interestingly, one of the discouragements was Ramsden's prohibition of back-to-back houses. That early and benign step in the absence of an area-wide policy to that effect simply meant that such houses were erected elsewhere, not on Ramsden's holdings.

Implicit in this last example of tensions involving expanding communities and prior patterns of land holding was the fortuitousness of housing in the nineteenth century. Money which could rent a house for a Huddersfield family would provide a room in London. In his moving cry, *How the Poor Live* (1889), George R. Sims reported that a coster he knew paid eight shillings a week for a single room. The large local property holder might be the factory. In that case, building might be philanthropic, as in the case of the Ashworth's in Hyde, Lancashire, where children and parents were assured of amenities since early in the nineteenth century (Collier 1964). In most towns, housing expanded in very small units, and lodgers were a convenient way to augment wages and help pay the rent. Only with the advent of mass transit—horse-drawn carriages, followed by electrified tramways much later—could distant and cheaper housing be combined with urban factory jobs. When that stage was reached, street was added to street and villages close to towns grew into suburbs with distinctive styles.

Building the Neighborhood

It is clear that appalling circumstances surrounded the urban child. On the small base of eighteenth-century towns, the following century created an explosion of industrialization and increasing social disorganization. The world of childhood was a dangerous place, and survival was a fifty-fifty proposition under age five. The physical habitat contested with life in the form of breeding grounds for disease. And yet children survived and even prospered. Slowly, the nineteenth-century town, a habitat still recognizable to us, emerged.

In some respects, the nineteenth-century town became a triumph of the will. We see around us buildings whose decorations are beginning to be appreciated by those who live in more sterile dwellings. We look again and see a triumph of intention over the material circumstances of the times. Northern cities might be grim, but those who prospered on the theme that "where there's muck there's money" began to aspire to better things. The world of their childhoods might have been grim, the ambience foreboding, but they sought a city more comfortable, more respectable, more inspiring. It would not necessarily be healthier, because progress was to be visible rather than functional, but when that could be accomplished economically, as in the case of piped water at threepence a week (Ashton 1844), it was certainly welcomed by all.

Looking at the world inherited by late Victorian children, people some of us have known in their mature years, we see civic improvements accumulated on a piecemeal basis. Here is no overarching theological glimpse of The City, as if it were to be the New Jerusalem, but a reality composed of the familiar approached in the spirit of amelioration. Material resources and the absence of national policy prescribed no Haussmann-like sweeping away of the winding streets, and traffic must learn to adjust to traditional roads and the bends of hills. To be sure, rivers were spanned, but improvements beyond sanitation and railway networks were very much on the pedestrian's side. Unlike late twentieth-century buildings, Victorian structures can be accommodated with a glance, given sufficient perspective.

Closest to the eye of the walker was the erection of dwellings for the people. The typical builder was a speculator who put up houses in rows. They were on two or three levels, sometimes with a basement or cellar half-below ground. Hopkins (1986) reported that a court off Bromsgrove Street in Birmingham, whose width was fifty-seven inches wide, was thirty-five inches wide at its entry. Some were Jerry-built while others have stood the test of time well into the twentieth century. By and large, new houses conformed to no larger glimpse of life than to have four walls and a roof. That is, housing did not incorporate a feel for how families live within a neighborhood, or to a vision of how they might live and raise their children through control of the environment. Play space for children was accidental within a set of row houses. Shopping and the provision of space for retailers was not thought through. For the most part, nineteenth-century households relied on traditional open-air markets and on street peddlers for purchase of food. Of course, there were shops, but they tended to specialize in meat, or wines, or cheese, especially early in the century. In the case of Manchester, with its explosion of population and roughly dependent increase in speculative building, there were few shopkeepers in 1830, but over a thousand by 1840 (Scola 1975). Over each of the following decades the number increased so that by 1872 there were 2,716 shopkeepers out of a total of 5,748 retail outlets. The majority of 3,032 outlets specialized even in 1972. Scola points out that manorial law imposed restrictions on sale of meat and fish in Manchester until 1846. Bradford operated under equally archaic restrictions on its commerce until laws relevant to previous centuries were repealed. The Municipal Corporations Act of 1835 started the process of modernization, but obsolete laws were a problem for several decades more.

The net effect was to put housing in one place and keep amenities—in the case of food necessities—in another place, all too frequently. While house-building and social planning have a long way to go, we recognize—as the Victorians did not, until late in the nineteenth century—that community or *gemeinschaft* is really the core concept when thoughtful builders operate on a reasonable scale. The rhythms of visiting the grocery with its smells and colors is a vital component of socializing children. The experience provides language stimulation and sensory training, but it also engenders a sense of shared experience and community. Bland, identical terraces of row-houses were economical to build, but they overlooked some elements of living we recognize as essential today. Balance requires that we acknowledge the poverty of thought which has given us high-rise, vertical slums in which children and old people experience isolation. For the Victorian child, a trip to the market was a colorful experience sometimes necessary because of neighborhood deficiencies.

A prime student of the nineteenth century housing was H. J. Dyos. His exposition of Camberwell (1961) has shown us the dynamics of working class housing in South London. In particular, he has presented the operations of the builder, Edward Yates, who emerged in 1867 as the builder of nine houses in Lambeth. Over the next three decades Yates built three large developments, usually on leased ground. His third and largest housing estate, known as the Waverly Estate, was built on nineteen acres of freehold ground at Nunhead, later supplemented by several other parcels of land some of which were leased, the whole amounting to over fifty acres.

In the context of the welfare of children and families, it is interesting to note that Yates controlled the development of shops. The "Waverly Arms" was opened, and then a school and a church. The area is characterized by the uniform, grid-like array of streets. The church site appears to be the otherwise unuseable apex of the broad triangular development. However, the site for the school is not ungenerous and appears to have been equally accessible for children living in all areas.

However, Yates's development and those like it proved to the Victorians that life was ever a series of trade-offs. At the time that good, cheap suburban housing was called for, so was open space readily accessible from the center of towns for recreation and fresh air. In 1887, Lewes saw the paradox clearly; "It is manifestly no longer to the interest of the public at large to encourage the covering with buildings of all land that can possibly be covered" (1887, 680). Where then to get the fresh air and open ground for recreation? Early in the century the idea of admitting ordinary folk to botanical gardens and zoos was approached gingerly. Children really should not use pubs as sites for recreation, but, surely, they would abuse such ornamental grounds as were opened to them, however gingerly. In fact, they did not, and opening recreation facilities in the 1840s produced no damage to Cardiff's Castle Park or to the

Edgbaston Horticultural Garden in Birmingham (Reid 1976). Children did not damage shrubs and plants. Edgbaston's visitors on Saint Monday took advantage of the opportunity to do something besides drinking and sitting around. Harrison (1971) records that Titus Salt gave Bradford one thousand pounds towards the cost of its first public park, and that Birmingham rejected Joseph Sturge's offer of a field rent-free for use as a park. The teetotalling M.P. for Halifax donated its first park. In contrast, Leeds residents had visited Woodhouse Moor traditionally, and its "Feast" was an annual event enjoyed by children and adults. In 1872, the Corporation of Leeds purchased Roundhay Park to the north. Briggs (1968) puts the purchase price at £139,000.

It is interesting to see how well-behaved the swarms of visitors were when admitted to the various Peel Parks and Victoria Parks. James Greenwood (1881) reported his pleasure at seeing millhands in Manchester enjoying fresh air at Ardwick Park. He thought that many of them appeared to have walked considerable distance to enjoy the fountain "and enjoy at their ease the beauties of nature." Slowly, speculative housing ventures turned into neighborhoods, and children began to acquire the culture of the district. Parks appeared as well as theatres, drinking establishments and schools. Towards the end of the century sports were encouraged, and with the rise of professional teams, town solidarity was strengthened across the traditional lines of class, religion, and culture.

The Ambience

The typical large town in the 1840s was a mess. On to a regional trading center, which also provided small enterprises in traditional trades, were dumped manufactories and houses for the people who worked in them. As Figure 7.1 showed, the population of the great towns was well into its steep growth by 1840. Considering Manchester, the *Illustrated London News* (1842) reported that

> the town is not distinguished for architectural beauty; its chief streets are occupied with warehouses and shops . . . Market Street, the chief mart for retail business, was not many years ago a mere lane . . . (August 20, 1842).

Juvenile Mancunians had much to learn from the sheer excitement of busy streets, but they were streets whose buildings their grandfathers would have recognized, as we would not. By mid-century, the beginning of a period we now call High Victorian, cities themselves became the object of attention for self-made men who knew the value of "brass" and had begun to look around at the world they had made. No longer could Bradford settle for its smoky atmosphere unrelieved by edifying sights, or Bristol settle for its central districts pierced by docks rapidly emptying but still a disruption. Little by little, cities' buildings were replaced with edifices more representative of the times, and which boys and girls would come to regard with awe.

Children were not the intended audience of Victorian architecture, but awe was a mood designers had in mind. Victorian art contained a symbolism implicit to designers, from the church in which a baby was baptized to the memorial covering its grave. Recessed windows conveyed mystery, and repeated arches represented order and continuity. In the case of tombstones, the symbols were commonly understood. For children, the Victorians used the lamb; an interrupted life was shown as a broken column; and an upturned torch was a life extinguished. The obelisk showed that life continues, the willow signified mourning, and the tree represented immortality and regeneration (Meller 1981). For buildings, Taylor (1973) has sketched the eighteenth-century origins of the code as the Beautiful, the Picturesque, and the Sublime. For aesthetes who hated the factory towns, public buildings could inspire a sense of higher things. Railway stations became the cathedrals of steam. Factories such as Adams's mill in Nottingham (Church 1966) could be decorated with symbols; public buildings from prisons to town halls could be objects for passive, tacit education of the viewer. The code can be read finely, so that a prison window at Reading is narrow for security reasons, but is surrounded by a broad band so that the narrowness of the window is exaggerated to the extent that it is, overtly, depressing to the spirit.

The most exuberant buildings were the town halls we see today. However, they can be more accurately glimpsed in the sketches their designers submitted, usually under noms de plume, in competition for the contract. There we see Gothic-gone-mad with effulgent dormers, turrets, and vistas. In William Burges and his design for Cardiff Castle (Crook 1981), we see elaborate motifs executed superbly. Burges designed down to the level of a washstand to be seen in the Victorian and Albert Museum. Others were content to deal with edifices and elevations, an attitude evident in the nonfunctionalism of expensive, empty space—since, in such instances, inspiring people was the function of a public building. In some respects, the new Houses of Parliament at Westminster, and the New Law Courts a few decades later, set the pace with their Gothic presence, and others followed.

Bradford built St. George's hall in the 1850s, a place for concerts in which the great organ could lead the massed choirs so greatly favored at the time. Leeds followed with its burst of civic pride in the form of its town hall built, according to Briggs (1968), at a cost of £122,000, which far exceeded the original planned cost of £40,000. The structure itself is a series of vertical lines in which a tall tower is somewhat gratuitously placed on a lower-level structure, the whole looking like a wedding cake. Four lions guard the south side, and small children still learn that at midnight the lions come to life in order to protect the Lord Mayor sleeping within. Birmingham and Manchester followed Leeds in the 1870s, Manchester's town hall being Gothic according to the design of Alfred Waterhouse (Archer 1982). All of the submissions in the competition for the contract were ornate, some looking like the sanctuary of Count Dracula, especially that of Thomas Worthington. In the comparison of Leeds and Manchester town halls, the differences are readily apparent. The Mancunian's pride sits in a nondescript, modest open space, forbidding and severe. Leeds's town hall, elevated on its site and inspiring in its classical verticals, gives eloquent testimony to the loftier vision of Loidensians.

However, we need to add a final example of public buildings in the form of Sir Charles Barry's design for the town hall at Halifax, the home of Akroydon, a model housing development for workers. Placed on an awkward site, the design overpowers the structure with its exuberant mixture of the Baroque and "the vaguely reminiscent," because just about every element was incorporated, from gloomy wells with deep windows—presumably to inspire the young with "terror" at the prospect of having their name and address taken—to obelisks and effulgence likely to topple onto someone passing by on a windy night.

However, it is the well-built, highly decorative architecture which surrounded and, one hopes, inspired the Victorian child which forms a link to the nineteenth century. Our eyes do not see what they saw, for sensibilities evolve, and we are not Victorians. However, we appreciate the stolidity which Victorians built into their public edifices in order to convey their sense of the world they were building amid the social rubble of their age.

An aspect of the urban milieux is the utopian city of Victoria proposed by James Silk Buckingham in 1849. In his model community of ten thousand souls, Buckingham drew on his observation of Rappite and Shaker communities in the United States. He thought Lowell, Massachusetts an estimable community, "the best conducted, and occupied by the happiest labouring population in the world." He set forth thirty-one propositions on which his model community would operate; they ranged from specifying ten thousand acres for raising food to specifying social segregation by occupational class. From his sketches, Victoria took the form of concentric squares at whose center stood a decorative tower.

Children entered into Buckingham's thinking in two ways. He proposed to limit the labor of children under ten years to four hours per day, and he called for free education. His scheme was singularly lacking in details of procedure, management, and political process. It presumed that human nature was without flaws and that people were capable of living in a highly dense community without the problems which arise in the best of environments.

Six years after Buckingham, Robert Pemberton proposed his "Happy Colony," to be established in New Zealand. As with Buckingham, the community is dependent on architecture to structure the routines of life. Unlike Buckingham, Pemberton's model community was a series of concentric circles; in both communities, schools in which the young would learn were important. Pemberton placed his education buildings and related structures at the center of the Happy Colony. In addition, his text devotes a good deal of attention to his theories on education of children by natural means.

8.

VIRTUES AND VICES

Violence

Children encountered stress inside and beyond the Victorian family. Abuse of spavined horses on the streets was a common sight, and it led to organized, voluntary effort to prevent cruelty to animals. Blood sports ranging from fox hunting to cock fighting were common events, and bare-knuckle boxing and the mass violence of some festival days were the milieux of growing children. In the days before juvenile delinquency had its special social services, it was not unknown for the police to chastise a delinquent boy on the spot. An old servant at Oxford recalled vividly the warmth he experienced when a policeman had administered stern, swift punishment for his rowdyism as a boy (Gillis 1975).

The violence that children encountered in the workplace took two forms; first, there was the probability of accidents as children tended ill-guarded machines; second, there was casual brutality in the form of chastisement of children for errors or slowness in work. The parliamentary reports of the early decades of the nineteenth century record many such events in the proceedings of Select Committees, such as that chaired by Michael Sadler in the early 1830s. After Waterloo, the early years of the factory system generated testimony on factory violence to children.

The occurrence was not new even then; George Harrison received a six-month sentence at the Chesterfield Quarter Sessions plus a fine of twenty pounds for having "kicked and otherwise abused (a child-worker) in a very unmerciful manner, and afterward drew it up by the Neck with a Cord" (Collier 1964).

Another form of violence was abuse between husband and wife in the home. The traditional view was that the husband stood in loco parentis to his wife as well as his children. She was held subject to his will and to his correction according to working-class conventions. Abuse of alcohol increased the likelihood of wife beating and, as today, battered wives and children sought shelter from abusive husbands whose hostility was compounded by drinking. Unemployment and money problems were common causes of assaults on wives. Tomes (1978) estimated that a London working-class neighborhood would average ten serious assaults per year, a figure probably understating the problem. She also ascertained that the number of aggravated assaults on London women dropped from eight hundred in 1852 to two hundred in 1889. These examples of violence within the home were witnessed by children who learned to scurry away when an ill-educated, tired father, who had dissolved his tensions in too much beer, returned home in an abusive mood.

Violence to children is traditional; sometimes the adage about sparing the rod and spoiling the child is invoked to justify physical assault, and sometimes violence is simply gratuitous, the predictable consequence of frustration among immature people who also happen to be parents. In the nineteenth century, child abuse was common, and even those who did not oppose corporal punishment in principle were taken aback at the hurt done to children. B. Waugh and Henry Cardinal Manning (1886) cited an abusing father as saying, "My father did it to me and nothing was done to him!" Child abusers tend to have been abused themselves, and the Victorians believed in punishment. In consequence, the stage was set for violence toward children in particular families, in the guise of firm discipline.

Abuse also took the form of chronic mistreatment of children. Manning and Waugh catalogued instances of child abuse, including a woman who

> put her little son into an empty orange box, and having corded it up thrust it under her bed, leaving it there until she turned the key in her door at night . . . she did this daily for weeks . . . Happily, sometimes he was drugged (1886).

Abuse of this type is pathetic rather than malicious, but the effect on the child was probably the same. The abuse was probably the well-meaning act of a friendless woman who, in this instance, sold oranges on the street and wished to protect her infant by hiding him.

One of the ironies of reform on behalf of children was that it turned child offenders into victims. That is, the processes intended to provide correction and care sometimes introduced further violence and abuse into children's lives. Because penal reform moved slowly, children were imprisoned to the end of the century and beyond. A uniquely qualified observer whose powers of description were beyond reproach was Oscar Wilde, who served a term of imprisonment at Reading. On the occasion of a newspaper report in 1897 of dismissal of a Warder for giving biscuits to a child prisoner, Wilde wrote a letter published in *The Times*. He gave a graphic account of the mindless, bureaucratic harm done to imprisoned children through the stress of confinement and diet.

> The terror of a child in prison is quite limitless. I remember once in Reading, as I was going out to exercise, seeing in the dimly lit cell right opposite my own a small boy. Two warders—not unkindly men— were talking to him, with some sterness apparently, or perhaps giving him some useful advice about his conduct. One was in the cell with him, the other was standing outside. The child's face was like a white wedge of sheer terror. There was in his eyes the terror of a hunted animal. The next morning I heard him at breakfast-time crying, and calling to be let out. His cry was for his parents. From time to time I could hear the deep voice of the warder on duty telling him to keep quiet. Yet he was not even convicted of whatever little offense he had been charged with. He was simply on remand.
>
> The second thing from which a child suffers in prison is hunger. The food that is given to it consists of a piece of usually badly-baked prison bread and a tin of water for breakfast at half-past seven. At twelve o'clock it gets dinner, composed of a tin of course Indian meal stirabout, and at half-past five it gets a piece of dry bread and a tin of water for its supper. This diet in the case of a strong man is always productive of illness of some kind, chiefly of course diarrhoea, with its attendant weakness. In fact in a big prison astringent medicines are served out regularly by the warders as a matter of course. In the case of a child, the child is, as a rule, incapable of eating the food at all. Anyone who knows anything about children knows how easily a child's digestion is upset by a fit of crying, or trouble and mental distress of any kind. A child who has been crying all day long, and perhaps half the night, in a lonely dimly-lit cell, and is preyed upon by terror, simply cannot eat food of this coarse, horrible kind. In the case of the little child to whom Warder Martin gave the biscuits, the child was crying with hunger on Tuesday morning, and utterly unable to eat the bread and water served to it for its breakfast. Martin went out after breakfasts had been served and

brought the few sweet biscuits for the child, who, utterly unconscious of the regulations of the Prison Board, told one of the senior warders how kind this junior warder had been to him. The result was, of course, a report and a dismissal (Hart-Davis 1962).

In understanding chronic abuse and stress, we need to appreciate that it is more than the body which is tyrannized. No less enduring is damage to the spirit. One looks at photographs of children rescued by the Victual Societies and philanthropists, and sees dull eyes and broken spirits. It is testimony to the resilience of the human spirit that abused children in any age can progress towards maturity and balance. In that regard, our expectations are probably less than those of the Victorian reformers; we know that there are degrees of abuse and neglect which damage children beyond full repair. In the Victorian age of violence there were many damaged children, and the moral resolve of reformers was the balm available to soothe their wounds.

Children of the Perishing and Dangerous Classes

While it is true that the "World We Have Lost," in Laslett's phrase, was something less than a glimpse of Arcady with happy children playing in a Constable landscape, our nineteenth-century ancestors could only look with unhappiness at the world around them. Things, surely, must have been better, children healthier and happier, in the years before the twin apparitions, Bonaparte and Steam. The former was dismissed to die in obscurity in the south Atlantic; the latter devoured children in factories and set parent against child as adult workers were displaced and massive social upheaval took place. From the point of view of child welfare, the prime victim of the Industrial Revolution was the working-class family. At the beginning of our period, the population was largely nonurban and the family had a sense of continuity with the rest of the small town or village. The social organization was what social scientists call *gemeinschaft*, meaning, in Tonnies's useful terminology, a gathering of people with a sense of identity and support. It became hierarchical, as in Elberfeld, where a paternalistic form of social welfare was effective; but there was a nexus of shared values below the squire-archy which wove very different families into the same social tapestry.

With urbanization and factories, the family of working people was subjected to great stresses. Income was uncertain, and work habits, beginning with St. Monday, were upset. Crowding together around factories increased the transmission of disease, and child mortality rose. Family life lost much of its stability as women worked outside the house, leaving children—and an occasional unemployed husband—to cope. Of course, children revelled in a lack of supervision in the early decades of the nineteenth century before Forster's Education Act rounded them up. The consequence in the form of juvenile delinquency was substantial, and it occurred at a time when there was a substantial cultural lag; that is, social institutions had not yet accommodated to the greatly accelerated rate of social change. In this respect, the Reform Act of 1832 has more than political significance, for it is evidence that reform was perceived as palpably easier to accommodate than revolution. The courts, however, remained rooted in the eighteenth century, and legal reform to cope with a changed and ever more changing society lagged behind the views of perceptive observers. In particular, the rise of juvenile crime and the increasing temptations to unsupervised children were evident.

In his testimony before the Select Committee on Criminal and Destitute Children on March 11, 1853, Captain W.J. Williams reported the circumstances of the following two families and their children, among others:

L_____, shoemaker. This man had had one boy transported, and another is undergoing 12 months' imprisonment in the Westminster Bridewell. A fact he was unacquainted with, until informed by the schoolmaster, who accompanied me. He had heard nothing of the boy for some months. Is a shoemaker, making shoes for export houses; earns about 18 s. a week. Ascribes the criminality of his sons to the lodging-houses which they used to frequent. "They first began stealing vegetables in the markets and selling them for a night's lodging to the keepers of these houses; then other and more valuable articles of provisions, which were disposed of in the same way. I have frequently taken them out of the lodging-houses in Kate-Street. The Boy A_____, who is now in Westminster, is incorrigible; he has been in prison at least nine times. When he has been at home, and thinking I was not looking at him I have seen him practising how to pick pockets. I have taught him my trade, but could never keep him at home. The other boy, that was transported, was just the same; he would not stop in. I stripped him naked one night and put him in the work-room, leaving my tools. He found some hemp there, and with the awl put it together, and made a sort of pinafore, let himself down from the window into the street, and was brought back by a policeman in that state at two o'clock in the morning. I say the lodging-houses are the ruin of boys; they not only encourage them to thieve, but purchase the stolen articles of them. My sons found through them that they could live without work, and would do nothing; they frequented the plays and gaffs. All the learning they have has been got in the prison schools. If my boys were to work with me, we could earn an excellent livelihood; but single-handed it is hard work, and sometimes no work at all. There never was a man, I believe so troubled with his children. Another child in the room—that boy there—will not go to school, if I send him; he goes somewhere else; and if I were to beat him, the chances are he would not come back." Has a family of three children besides these boys. Rents the whole house (a miserable, dirty tenement), at 4 s. a week, letting the lower part out to lodgers. This boy (the one now in Westminster Bridewell) was once sent to a reformatory school in Kentish Town, from which he ran away. He had an offer to go in a second time, but refused.

*   *   *

P_____ F_____. This man is a bricklayer's labourer, and has for some time been out of work. His daughter, the only one, was recently released from the Westminster Bridewell, and has been received into an asylum at White Lion-street, at the instance of the prison chaplain. She has been there five weeks, and her father reports favourably of her conduct in the institution. This girl is 15 years of age, and appears to have been entirely led away by the love of dancing at licensed public-houses. The father appears to be a very good sort of creature, and most devotedly attached to his daughter, even now thinking her to be better than she really is; he has given himself a world of pains to look after her, and once got himself locked up in the station-house for his overearnestness, or perhaps violence, in seeing her home from a dancing room. To go to these dances and the plays when he was at work, she used to take everything she could lay her hand upon to sell, and the father was obliged on three occasions to bring her before the magistrates. His words are, "Though a strict Catholic myself, I kept her always at school, giving her the entire liberty to be Catholic or Protestant as she liked, so that she were not a scandal to me; she was never in any situation; I earn 18 s. a week when in work, but have been out since Christmas; I have been receiving bread from the parish, but only four times; the parish deal very hardly with us poor people. Pays 1s. 6d. a week for his room; is a good way in arrear of his rent, but has a kind landlord, who has seven houses, and allows him to work out his rent in repairs; a kind honest creature, indeed, both wife and him are." Room exceedingly neat and clean.

Looking at penal reform for juveniles, one is struck by the incompleteness of vision and the partiality of selected reforms. For example, reformers were conscious of the work on the continent, especially at Mettrai where a good deal of vigorous outdoor work was emphasized. However, we should understand Mettrai on its own terms, not those of our century. Turner's and Paynter's 1846 report on Mettrai to the Philanthropic Society makes clear the prevailing themes. The boys were grouped as "families," but military discipline by bugle and drill prevailed. No physical punishment was permitted, but no offense went unpunished. Fatiguing work was a prime technique of control. Turner and Paynter reported that 88% of 521 boys were successfully placed in jobs

after a period of training at Mettrai. There appears to be little mention
of the pioneering House of Refuge established in New York in 1824.
This institution served a broad range of problem children, and it emphasized care for those most salvageable. In contrast, Parkhurst tried to be
progressive but aimed at the hard core of juvenile offenders, a process
which sowed the seed of later discontent when Point Puer boys later
turned recidivist.

A second anomaly was the recognition that bad families led to
delinquent children. Thomson of Banchory (1852) reported the instance
of an Aberdeen girl

> at present confined for the ninth time, whose grandfather, grandmother,
> mother, aunt and two uncles, were several times in prison, and whose
> step-father and two uncles were transported. . . .

Elementary logic suggests that there is a corollary, namely, that good
families reduce the possibility of all but minor escapades. On that premise, it is surprising how irregular was attention to re-creating family and
small group contexts for the experiences of children in care. To the modern mind, the importance of socializing and acculturating children
through family dynamics is an all-important aspect of habilitation. In
the nineteenth century, Miss Isabella Tod of Belfast pointed out the error
in the traditional institutional view that

> you had done all that was necessary . . . if you got for this poor little
> shivering body and frightened soul the one hundredth part of a matron's
> care, and the one hundredth part of a schoolmaster's, and the one hun-
> dredth part of a relieving officer's . . . (Tod 1878).

Actually, institutional care of children was more than psychological bru-
talizing, for it was also life-threatening. In Ireland at mid-century, pauper
children had a mortality rate twice the national average, and it rose to
more than four times that rate in the workhouses of Dublin and Cork
(Hancock 1862). Scotland was distinctive in the early adoption of
boarding out pauper children, and Ireland was the slowest, while also
the poorest. The differing laws of the three countries had much to do
with this, although the wrongness of educating children in workhouses
had been pointed out since the young Victoria became Queen. In Scotland, the Industrial Feeding Schools of Aberdeen combined excellent
teachers with boarding out, so that few children were reared in a workhouse. Progress in Ireland was slow, for even after the start of the twentieth century the number of pauper children boarded out was only 28%,

while it was 60% in England and 78% in Scotland (Millin 1909). What is especially anomalous is that the cost of boarding out a child averaged seven pounds per year, while workhouse care cost eighteen pounds. The absence of boarding out made no sense on fiscal or psychological grounds. Because frugality was perennially attractive to policymakers, delay in wide use of boarding and the constructive use of family dynamics may be viewed as one of the discontinuities we hypothesize in Victorian life and social policy.

An object lesson on the power of group dynamics lay in the evident social cohesion of agricultural gangs which exploited child-workers in the country. Despite the long hours and irregular food, it is likely that members of such gangs had a sense of group identity and purpose, suggesting that dynamics are much the same whether the intended aim is good or bad. In fact, Quaker ideology of the early nineteenth century, which heavily influenced penal practice, sought to isolate adult and juvenile prisoners. Sentences often began with a period in which the value of silence prevailed. Within the quietism that the Quakers found conducive to hearing a tiny voice within themselves, they sought the reform of all. Connected with this ideology of isolation was the provision of mindless, deliberately pointless turns at the treadmill or winding a functionless crank in a cell.

Of course, there are instances of family-style care. Mary Carpenter's house in Bristol was familial because of the historic form of the Red Lodge, but the dynamics of the process were group instruction in a nonpenal, schoollike context, with sleeping and eating arrangements. It was not until Dr. Thomas Barnardo began his work on behalf of abandoned children that reform self-consciously sought to create social units resembling families. Of course, the reason lay in the primacy of moral failure as the salient explanation, for the failure of delinquents' families were also moral shortcomings. It awaited Dr. Bernardo for quasi-family groups to appear as modalities of healing, therapy, and moral growth for children. As a consequence of addressing the worst cases in a manner ignoring the healing balm of the family unit and its growth-inducing powers, juvenile reformers set themselves a difficult task, but gradualism has ever seemed cowardice to the ideologically overcommitted. Such commitment may have proved a balm, for not every Victorian reformer was effective; in selected cases, incompetence proved fatal to children. Conley (1984) has recorded the sorry record of Laura Addiscott, the Deptford reformer, who took money from parents to care for seventeen children aged two and up. Two girls died, and the trial brought testimony about barely clothed children eating garbage. Laura Addiscott received a sentence of eighteen months, during which, presumably, she reassessed her commitment to child welfare, and the relationship between ends and means.

The twentieth century has had its share of ideology. The exact reverse of the Quaker's emphasis on inner failure as a source of evil acts is found in Behavior Modification's view of the empty organism. In that influential ideology, acts are merely what they seem; phenomenalism is all, and behavior can be shaped by the precise relating of actions to their consequences. One records carefully and then shapes desirable behaviors and discourages undesirable ones by loss of privileges, isolation, and other aversive consequences. Such manipulations, however, can be performed within a family setting, so that the therapeutic context is not neglected. Today, we approach moral development in a behavioral way. Kohlberg (1972) has described observable stages of moral development in a fashion permitting both assessment of childrens' attainment and specification of plans for moral advancement. While we possess excellent techniques of analysis, we have difficulty finding reformers with the zeal of Mary Carpenter and her nineteenth-century co-workers to safeguard children from the dangers around them.

Child Victims

Understanding crime in any age should begin with the observation that children are a handy class of victims. They can be bludgeoned with little risk of a return of violence and, once abused, can be cowed into silence by the threat of more violence. They can quite readily be taught the tricks of thievery under the penalty of abuse.

The earliest offense to which a child may be subjected is deprivation of life in the period of gestation. Aborting foetuses was a common practice in the nineteenth century, and Chadwick thought the number of deaths prenatally by abortion was higher than that for deaths after normal delivery. Cruickshank (1981) has described abortifacients in the form of pills made from lead plaster, doses of quinine, turpentine, and use of the knitting needle. In an age when death certificates for infants were an uncommon occurrence, dead infants who had been eased out of this world when entering it were not hard to cover up.

Once beyond delivery, children were exposed to the risk of murder—infanticide—by deliberate action or by neglect. Earlier, we discussed illegitimate children; it is helpful to recall that such children were at risk of extreme violence and their mortality rate exceeded that of legitimate children Behlmer (1982) reported that Mrs. Martin of 23 Dean Street, Soho, was hanged for the deaths of over five hundred foetuses and infants. By means ranging from aborting-drugs before delivery to excessive doses of Godfrey, illegitimate and other unwanted babies were bound to yield their slender grasp on life. Bott (1972) presented a sketch of five young women who were in prison for life at Woking in 1889. Each has two red stars on her person as insignia of infanticide. They appear to be quite ordinary women, for murder is usually a consequence of transient strain or impulse. The warden reported them to be "the best behaved of all female transgressors, many of them being truly penitent, thanks to the Chaplain." Not every woman who killed her child was imprisoned or, indeed, had committed a crime. In the case of self-induced abortion, mothers could not be charged with their own abortions for, in law, it was a crime committed upon another person. In 1844, Engels (1975) reported the 1827 case in which a woman accused of infanticide went free because of a technicality in the form of the oath. The jury's verdict was expressed "upon their oath," but their oaths at swearing in as jurors were individual, and the verdict should have been phrased "upon their oaths." By that technical error the verdict at Winchester was set aside and the woman went free. In this anecdote we see one more instance of a traditional legal system coping inadequately with greater sophistication by Counsel in the face of a crime not, historically, much detected or brought to trial. Dr. Edward Lankester, the Middlesex Coroner, concluded that the general state of the law dealing with the death of infants was not efficient. A woman might be tried for concealment of the birth of her child much more effectively than for its murder. The legal problem, according to Dr. George Greaves of Manchester (1863), was that a victim of murder had to be "a reasonable creature in being, and under the King's peace." Even the fact of the child's "having breathed is not a conclusive proof," stated Greaves, especially if the umbilicus had not been separated. "It might medically be a living child, but not legally." The consequence was that many infanticide mothers, unlike the five women in Woking prison, were prosecuted for concealment of birth, when justified, and served two years. Greaves went on to point out that there were midwives who stated that "their fee for the delivery of a living child is so much; for one still-born so much more." Mrs. Winsor, the wife of a Devonshire laborer, was reported in the Nation (England 1865) to have had a steady trade and "would make away with babies for a few shillings." Mrs. Winsor was hanged in 1865, but the crime against children continued actively until at least the end of the century.

One of the seamiest problems in all generations is sexual abuse of children. In Victorian times, public morality, as opposed to private behavior, was repressive; children and adolescents were denied safeguard

against the privations of debauching adults. In Hornchurch, Lincolnshire, a Mrs. Belton inducted both of her daughters into prostitution in
1840 (Davey 1983). One of Burnett's (1982) recollectors of youth, Edmund Punter, recalled that he had resisted seduction by a male member
of the gentry who offered him a shilling in a cowshed. As cited earlier in
this volume, Hannah Cullwick recorded in her diary how two gentlemen
gave her a ride home in their pony and trap. When she got down, the
driver went on; the other gentlemen made overtures to her which were
interrupted by two laborers walking round the bend of the country lane.
Closer to home was the problem of incest; very often it took the form of
a farm laborer expecting his oldest girl to assume the sexual role of her
pregnant mother. How many rural illegitimate babies were the result of
incest we shall never know, but the problem was substantial. In part,
there was the stress of overcrowding, so that brother-sister relations were
fostered by the lack of privacy and an unavoidable intimacy, with consequent sexual license.

Work provided no necessary relief from sexual exploitation for
girls. The early reports of the Factory Inspectors are filled with references to sexual exploitation of women, a workplace relationship which is
still open to abuse (Lambertz 1985). In the country, especially in the
agricultural gangs of East Anglia, the problem was persistent. The Rev.
J. Rumph of Huntingdonshire called attention to the ruin of girls at the
age of thirteen or fourteen (Horn 1974). The *Parliamentary Papers* of the
period are replete with witnesses citing the sexual license of agricultural
gangs, and the abuse and exploitation of adolescent girls. The testimony
of Mr. Fraser C. Beets of Suffolk in 1867 to the Commissioners on
Employment of Children and Young Persons is typical. At Downham
Market Sessions on August 6, 1866, the Magistrate sentenced "Mr. C."
to two months hard labor, after the testimony of A.B., a girl of thirteen.

[He] pulled me down and pulled up my clothes, pulled up my clothes
only to my waist. I think there were a dozen in the gang, it was in the
sight of the gang, we were sitting down to our dinners. The other boys
and girls in the gang were round me. I called out, the other laughed. He
said, 'Open your legs more.' He had a stick and I had not run away with
it. I told my mother, not directly I got home (at night). I told her half an
hour after. My mother spoke to me first. C_____ hurt my hand when
I tried to get up. He was on me and I could not get up, he was laying on
me flat, I was on my back on the ground. I don't know how long he was
on me. He did not say anything to any of the others, the others saw it.
C_____ has threatened to flog me, if we told any tales; this was before
the assault.

Two years before, in 1863, an offender received a combination of civil and informal punishment. The man in question, referred to as D.E. in the records, got six months "for an assault upon a young female in a field at Tyd St. Giles. Upon this occasion a man passing by gave him a sound thrashing, which made him ill for a week" (Beets 1867). At the Hillington Petty Sessions in Norfolk in September 1865, a group of boys in an agricultural gang assaulted a man with a reputation for exposing himself. They "dragged him into a field, tore open his trousers . . . applying a quantity of gas tar to his person, and stuffed his clothes with stinging nettles." The gang master admitted to having provided the tar. The magistrates dismissed the case brought by the victim, cautioning both the plaintiff and the defendants, "as to their conduct in the future."

In the large towns, sexual promiscuity was rampant, and in York one half of the prostitutes were under age eighteen over several decades (Finnegan 1979). Public opinion on the matter was confused, for, apart from the devout, the rest of the population took a very casual attitude towards licence. That is, the upper classes had a freewheeling morality which countenanced practically anything which did not frighten the horses. In loveless marriages, partners were free to come and go—the males being a little freer—provided no publicity arose. The scale of female prostitution was enormous, and it provided an alternative to starvation for girls who were exploited in the needle trades or who could find no work at all. One of the saddest anecdotes was provided by Thomas deQuincy (1821), who in the extremity of his addiction to opium was looked after by an orphan girl who was less than sixteen years old. Ann of Oxford Street lived by prostitution and already had acquired a chronic cough. In later days of restored health, deQuincy frequented Titchfield Street in hopes of finding her, presumably to thank her for her kindness by rescuing her from the streets. Sad to relate, deQuincy did not find her, and, in his *Confessions,* tells how he sought her for years, but to no avail. Less at the mercy of harsh necessity were the young girls called at the time, "Dolly-mops," young girls out for a good time and not reticent to share their favors. The implicit consensus which produced the spectacle of demimondaines riding in Rotten Row also resisted reforms. Within this social system there flourished a substantial trade in child prostitution. Pearsall's (1969) "Sin Map" of London includes two child brothels which operated east of the Tower in Dock Street and Betty Street.

In understanding this tragic aspect of Victorianism it is ironic to recall the Cult of the Little Girl, in which adult males sighed and photographed preadolescent females, sometimes with a bare shoulder evident and always insisting on a higher, nonmaterial interest in their ethereal qualities. Lewis Carroll and John Ruskin were two votaries of the cult.

Between child prostitution at one extreme and simpering over nymphs at the other, the Victorian male's interest in the opposite sex had ample outlet. Slowly, reform made headway against the abuse of children, although the problem existed well up to the end of the century. Organizations which sought to eliminate the vice were the Rescue Society, the Society for the Protection of Young Females, the Vigilance Societies of various counties, and the Society for the Prevention of Cruelty to Children. In addition, there were the crusading individuals, such as Dr. Thomas Barnardo, William Booth and his Salvation Army, and Mary Carpenter. The journalist Henry Mayhew and the Liverpool investigator Charles Booth did their part to arouse the public conscience against abuses of all kinds and especially involving children as victims of crime.

Young Offenders

The size of a problem is always a matter of scale. In the case of delinquency at all ages, the number of crimes rises in significance when the total population is comparatively small. Juvenile delinquency understood as crime associated with a given age group varies according to the proportion of the entire population below a given age. In Victorian times, the proportion of the population below ages defined by statute— for example, fourteen or twenty one—was always high, because life expectancy above these ages was lower than today. Juveniles were a larger proportion of the total population and so their offenses were numerically important. The architect and reformer George Godwin (1859) spent an hour and a half at the Bow Street Police Court. Of fifteen cases dealt with, five were juveniles. Two girls aged fourteen and sixteen were drunk; three boys, of whom two were thirteen and fifteen, were charged with theft. Godwin added to the account his memory of the sternness and impassivity of the judge who, it appears, averaged one case every six minutes, adult or juvenile.

The most trivial form of delinquency was that of children engaged in salvaging scrap whose ownership was contested. Mayhew (1851) gives endless examples of the unskilled foragers who picked up anything they might sell. When lost objects—for example, those found in sewers by scavengers and known in Victorian slang as "tosh"—were identified, a charge of theft was always possible. Less organized and impulsive acts were equally liable to have unfortunate consequence. Octavia Hill (1875) describes two children whose adult guardian she had never encountered when collecting her rents.

> In one room a handsome, black, tangle-haired ragged boy and girl, of
> about nine and ten, with wild dark eyes, were always to be found. . . .
> For months I never saw these children in the open air . . . at night . . .
> the boy would creep like a cat along the roofs of the outbuildings to
> steal lumps of coal from a neighboring shed.

Stealing in this sense of foraging in the immediate vicinity can be
distinguished from organized burglary. For that, ex-climbing boys were
highly prized because they could enter buildings through the smallest
openings and had a working knowledge of houses that was not otherwise available to people outside the household. One such boy, born in
London in 1825, is recorded on the manifest of the convict ship, *Lord
Goderich,* which reached Tasmania on November 16, 1841. Sixteen-
year-old William Harwood had a ruddy complexion, a long sharp nose,
and scars on his right thumb and right forefinger. We have no knowledge
of how he turned out after his term was served. We know more, however,
about young Richard Boothman transported for participating in the
murder in Colne of Constable Joseph Halstead. He left an estate of £559
in 1877. Storch (1975) observed that Halstead was probably innocent of
the crime.

DeMotte (1977) has described the career of the young ne'er-do-
well, John Jones of Manchester, who was sentenced in 1839. The offense for which he was arrested was taking four pennies from his
employer's till. In fact, this was the last of his depredations, for he had
begun a series of thefts some time before; in each instance, the victim
was his employer. At age eleven, he started working for a watchmaker
but was dismissed four months later for stealing. After five months with
a jeweller, he learned to shortchange customers and was dismissed.
Young John then worked for an accountant and stole petty cash regularly. It was in that job that his master, who neither saw nor heard very
well, finally detected the 4d. theft, and Master Jones was sentenced to
transportation for seven years.

A juvenile offender of greater skill, also in Manchester, was described by one of the *Morning Chronicle*'s correspondents, Angus B.
Reach (Aspin 1972). In the company of a subinspector of police, Reach
entered the Dog and Duck in Charter Street.

> As we were leaving the house a boy about thirteen or fourteen, smartly
> dressed, with a tassel dangling from his cap entered. 'Well, young 'un,'
> said my companion, 'whose pockets have your hands been in this eve-
> ning?'

> The boy stared coolly at the inspector. The light from a lamp fell on his face, and I never saw a worse one—little deep sunk eyes, and square bony jaws, with a vile expression. 'What do you mean talking about pockets to me? I don't know nothing about pockets,' and turning on his heel he entered the house. The boy had been twice convicted, and several times in trouble. He walked Market Street at night, often in partnership with a woman.

Here we see a youngster well-established in a way of life which undoubtedly led to Strangeways prison. Once imprisoned as a young person, he would increase his survival skills for the streets by picking up tricks from old lags. Only slowly did the public appreciate the lesson taught by Mary Carpenter and others that prisons did not reform, did not reduce crimes, and in selected ways contributed to the further delinquency of juveniles cast among their elder brethren in crime.

Towards the end of the nineteenth century, delinquent youths adopted the uniform of a belt with a large buckle, a neckchief, and a cap, and were named for Patrick Hooligan. While there are alternative explanations for the term "hooligan" (Pearson 1983), a journalist in the 1890s, Clarence Rook (1899), named the Lambeth criminal. Hooligan's residence near Lambeth Walk was visited by Rook in the company of young Alf. This particular hooligan was quick, alert, and not unwilling to use violence. However, he was clever, and he developed a technique for obtaining beer at the expense of the constable on the beat. It was customary, Rook reports, for policemen ending their tour to cadge a free beer by offering a penny which was always refused. Young Alf would walk into a pub, never the same one twice, and offer a penny on behalf of the policeman theoretically developing a thirst on the street outside. The penny was declined, the beer drawn, and an ostensibly compliant, helpful Alf took the gargle outside to the nonexistent copper.

Offenses

Consideration of youthful offenders begins with an attempt to understand who they are and what they did. In the case of their actions, there is the presumption that they did something quite wrong and that their subsequent fate, however harsh, was based on palpable offenses. On close inspection, this latter-day rationality dissolves, because the standard by which behavior is judged contrary to law is quite arbitrary. If a community has a law which makes it an offense for a person under age sixteen to be on the streets after, say, ten o'clock at night, twins born

TABLE 8.1
SIX CLASSES OF OFFENSES RECORDED BY THE METROPOLITAN POLICE*

First Class

Murder, Manslaughter, Shooting,
Stabbing, Poisoning
("Crimes affecting the Person")

Second Class

Burgulary, Embezzlement by
Servants, Frauds, Larceny
("Crimes affecting Property")

Third Class

Stealing Cattle, Horses, Sheep
("Cattle Stealing")

Fourth Class

Sexual Assaults
("Rape")

Fifth Class

Arson, Bigamy, Cattle Maiming
Child Stealing, Concealing
Birth, Game Laws, Piracy,
Treason, Slave Traffic
("Crimes of Rare Occurrence")

Sixth Class

Forgery of Coins and Bank Notes
("Offenses against the Currency")

*Report from the Select Committee on the Police of the Metropolis. *Parliamentary Papers*. 1828, 4.

just before and just after midnight on a given date are an offender on the one hand and a nonoffender on the other. Similarly, loitering may be distinguished from prayerful consideration merely by the attitude of the Police Constable or the dress of the pedestrian. Our consideration of juvenile offenses in the nineteenth century ranges from the acts of habitual criminals, junior in years only—e.g., the hardcore offenders who set Parkhurst Prison on fire in 1850—to abandoned children who looked suspicious because they were shabbily dressed.

The early Victorians constructed their empirical picture of crime, its taxonomy, in a variety of ways. In 1828, the Metropolitan Police recorded six classes of offenses, as Table 8.1 shows. The fifth class is noteworthy because it is an odd mixture, but also because it includes child stealing. With regard to the severity with which offenses were regarded, the parliamentary committee which provided the six classes of offenses also reported sentences. In the 1820s, nineteen people were executed for forgery, eighty-three were executed for property crimes, and only eleven for murder. Compared to the previous decade, executions had dropped by nearly two-thirds in the 1820s for murder, doubled for crimes against property, increased greatly from none for stealing cattle, remained stable for sexual offenses, dropped from seven to one for rare crimes, and were halved for forgeries. In 1816, London had three thousand prisoners under age twenty, of whom one-half were under age seventeen (Griffiths 1896). Executions were public in those days, and one of James Burn's earliest memories in Scotland was of being taken to see a hanging, an event he recalled clearly fifty years later in his memoirs. In the 1816 report on crimes and sentences, there is no apparent discrimination by age or sex.

Ten years later, the status of juveniles was clearly recorded in Newcastle-upon-Tyne by William Cargill (1838). He reported for the years 1836–38 that eleven boys and eleven girls under age twelve were sentenced to the Newcastle prison. Nineteen boys and six girls were imprisoned at age twelve to fourteen, and sixty-five boys and twenty-six girls between ages fourteen and seventeen were imprisoned. Out of 1,264 prisoners, 138 were under age seventeen. The youth of these offenders was sufficiently important for Mr. Cargill to have investigated their level of education; but, unfortunately, he did not report it by age. One-third of the twelve hundred adults and children could neither read nor write, and only thirty could do both well.

From the 1830s, we have a consideration of young persons "brought before the Magistrates" in Leeds in the period 1833–38 (Statistical Committee 1839). Of fifteen thousand persons before the bench, just over one-third were under age twenty-one; of those approximately six thousand, 10% were under age fifteen, so that the under fifteen group was about one in thirty of the whole group of offenders. In 1865, J. Thackray Bunce thought Leeds quite the average of five large towns, with Sheffield and Birmingham more crime-ridden, and Manchester and Liverpool the least of the five towns. The ratio of police to population obviously enters in. For the whole of England there was one policeman per 906 people. Liverpool was most policed, with one policeman per 431 people. Bunce gives the order of towns most successful at arresting lawbreakers as Birmingham, Manchester, Liverpool, Leeds, and Sheffield. He thought Sheffield quite the worst place on several grounds. In Birmingham, Bunce's special interest, the bulk of offenses were larcenies and burglaries; violence was a component of very few crimes in the years 1858–64. In the mid-century there were, according to Mr. Turner (1851), 14,569 males and 2,557 females under age seventeen in prisons, two-fifths of whom were in one town, London.

An overview of contemporary pictures of juvenile crime across the nineteenth century provides a picture of how juvenile offenses were described at mid-century. Joseph Fletcher (1852) classified the offenses of 8,787 juvenile males and 1,466 females under the Acts and Laws they had transgressed. For the males, indictment under the Vagrancy Act accounted for 2,259 cases, and was followed by 1,544 breaches of the Juvenile Offender Act; these two classes account for about one-half of the total. For the females, 590 were convicted for vagrancy and 155 were thieves; these two classes also account for nearly one-half of the total.

Our last view of the nature and scope of juvenile crime comes from Oxford in 1890. Gillis (1975) cites twenty-six offenses, all of which were—fortunately for the juveniles—nonindictable, including twelve instances of willful damage, four instances of "dangerous play," and seven instances of malicious mischief. Of course, these examples bring us to the fringes of violations. In all periods there were, as now, judges inclined to severity and leniency. Lest the picture seem one of unremitting prosecution, we cite the following instance in which Edward Gould, a lad of twelve, was brought up before Mr. Alderman Lainson for passing a bad check in the premises of Mr. Dickens, a chemist of Holborn, in 1841.

> Mr. Wontner, who attended for the prisoner, said he was prepared to show that he was a boy of good character, who had been tempted by the offer of a shilling by some stranger who accosted him in the street, to carry a letter to Mr. Dickens, and wait for an answer. This letter enclosed the check, and purported to be written by a neighbour, who wanted cash for it. The only suspicious circumstances was that the boy

attempted to run away when Mr. Dickens said he would get his hat and accompany him; but he accounted for this very naturally, by saying he was frightened on overhearing Mr. Dickens speak of sending for the police. Mr. Wontner also proposed to show that the stranger had employed other boys in presenting similar checks.

The boy's employer and his brothers were examined as to his habits and conduct.

Humberstone, a city policeman, deposed that he had a boy in custody for presenting a check from the same book on the 20th of February, at Mr. Holmes's, a butcher, in Fore-street, who gave cash for it. It then appeared that cash had been obtained by a third boy upon a similar check from a butcher in Kennington-lane; and another had been passed in Clerkenwell. The police had now obtained a good description of the man.

William Marks, a clerk from Sir Charles Price's bank, stated that a check-book had been obtained by a person who had used the name of a customer. The clerk thought he remembered having seen him before, and taking his signature in the check delivery book gave him a book.

Mr. Alderman Lainson being satisfied the boy had been made a dup of, gave him up to his friends, and expressed a hope that the circumstances would make tradesmen careful how they cashed checks for pretended neighbours.

The prisoner was discharged.

Ships

When Sara Martin visited Yarmouth Prison in 1818, she found prisoners ranging in age from nine to eighty years. The prisoners were "filthy, confined, unhealthy . . . infected with vermin and skin disease" (Stratta 1970). Prisons were brutal places where chains were worn and old lags trained young offenders in all the skills of gambling, breaking and entering, and assault. Some young offenders were transported, but not all ships associated with juvenile prisoners sailed the seas. One of the consequences of the end of the Napoleonic Wars was a surplus of battleships. Britannia ruled the waves, and they were peaceful once more. The domestic scene was turbulent, and the combination of dismissed soldiers and sailors and an economic recession resulted in an increase in crime. Ships of the line like the *Fighting Temeraire* in Turner's picture were decommissioned, dismasted, and turned into floating prisons. *Bellerophon* was the first hulk for juveniles, and around 1825, the smaller hulk *Euryalus* at Chatham was assigned as a segregated prison for juveniles. Roughly four hundred young prisoners were the complement to those in county gaols. Prior to segregation in *Euryalus*, boys as young as age nine were held in Newgate, where, according to Mr. John Wontner, the Keeper, there was "a regular system of nurture by the old thieves of the young lads" (Wontner 1828). Assignment of boys to the *Euryalus* was an innovation in 1825 and was intended to protect those under age sixteen from the influence of old lags and to provide an occasion for reform.

Mr. Capper reported to the House Select Committee on the Police of the Metropolis on St. Patrick's Day in 1828 on life aboard *Euryalus*.

TABLE 8.2
TOTAL NUMBER OF JUVENILE PRISONERS
SENTENCED TO TRANSPORTATION AT ASSIZES AND
QUARTER SESSIONS IN ENGLAND AND WALES, IN 1849*

TERMS	Males	Females	Total
For 7 and under 10 years	145	9	154
For 10 and under 15	61	1	62
For 15 and under 20	4	1	5
For 20 years and upwards	1		1
For Life	3		3
Total	214	11	225

Total of both Sexes and all Ages—3,099

*Report from the Select Committee on Criminal and Destitute Children. *Parliamentary Papers.* 1853, 23, Appendix I.

Monday, at half-past five in the morning, all hands called, ports opened, hammocks lowered and rolled up, boys washed, and hammocks got on deck and stowed; at six, boys sent into chapel, the morning hymn sung, and a prayer read by the schoolmaster, (an adult convict) the officers and guards being present; after the prayers, breakfast is served, under the inspection of the first mate and officers, consisting of "one half of the daily allowance of oatmeal boiled," and "one third of the daily allowance of bread;" after breakfast, the boys confined in one deck, are sent on the main deck for air and exercise; those on the other decks after the mess tables, kids &c. are cleared away, are sent to their respective trades; at half-past six, beef generally received for the day's consumption, inspected by the overseer and officers, and weighed by the steward, under the inspection of the first mate; at seven, main and quarter decks washed and chapel cleaned; at nine, the boys progress at work, and ship generally inspected by the overseer and first mate; boilers, kids &c. cleaned and inspected; at half-past nine, the surgeon generally attends; one division of the boys got on deck, their hammocks, bedding and cloaths examined, hair trimmed, and persons washed in a cistern of salt water. Day's supply of bread received about eleven o'clock, and inspected; weighed by the steward under the inspection of the first mate; at half-past eleven, boys leave their work, clean their wards, wash themselves, dinner served, consisting of "one-third of the daily allowance of bread, seven ounces of meat, twelve ounces of potatoes, and about one pint of soup." At twelve, the boys belonging to one deck, sent to school in the chapel, to learn reading, writing, arithmetic, catechism, and hymns. And those belonging to another deck, are sent on the main deck for air and exercise; mess tables cleaned and stowed away; wards swept. At half-past one boys sent from school, &c. to work; at half-past two, clothes, bedding &c. examined, as in the morning. At five, boys leave work, sweep the wards, wash themselves, and their suppers served to them, consisting of "one-third of the daily allowance of bread, and one-half of the daily allowance of oatmeal boiled;" at half-past five, the boys of one deck sent to school, and those of another sent on the main deck for air and exercise; and hammocks sent below; at half-past seven, the school over; previous to the boys being dismissed, they sing the evening hymn, and prayer is read by the schoolmaster. Boys mustered into their respective wards, and secured for the night. At half-past eight the watch set.

Each succeeding day is the same, with the exception of Saturday, when one-third of the allowance of bread, and three ounces of cheese only are served for dinner, and the day is devoted to general washing and cleaning of the ship; packing and sending to store the articles made by the boys during the week. No school is held at noon, but in the evening all the boys are sent into chapel, and those boys who committed hymns to memory recite them, which closes with the evening hymn and prayer, as on the other nights. At seven, boys mustered into their wards, clean shirts, handkerchiefs, &c. served to them, and secured for the night.

Sunday morning commences as on other days; at eight o'clock, boys let on deck by divisions, and inspected; at a quarter before eleven they are sent into the chapel, at which time the chaplain attends, and reads a part of the morning service, and delivers an extemporaneous discourse, which generally occupies from fifty minutes to one hour; dinner served when the service is over, under the superintendence of the officers; after dinner the boys of one deck sent on the main-deck for air; at half-past two sent below, and the boys at each ward assembled at their tables to hear the Scriptures read by boys selected for that purpose; at half-past three another division of the boys sent on deck for air; at five, supper service, at six, all hands sent to chapel, evening service read by the schoolmaster, and the boys catechized; at eight, mustered and secured for the night, and watch set.

Of 345 boys on *Euryalus,* 62 entered able to read and write; 70 could read, and about 200 could not read. In the first two years of the program, 112 boys had learned to read, 116 boys had learned to write, and 24 boys were "put in arithmetic." Capper's account made no reference to the boys ever leaving, an experience hulk inmates generally had in the form of going ashore to work.

Parallel to the reforming goals of *Euryalus* was the work of the *Solebay,* a smaller ship owned by the Marine Society and moored at Greenwich. The Society took boys who were fifty-seven inches or more in height, regardless of age, with a view to providing one to eight months of training as seamen. The plan was to take one hundred "poor, distressed boys" and eventually place them in the navy or on merchant ships. A private philanthropy, the Marine Society's committee of gentlemen, merchants, and an occasional elder Brother of Trinity House met on Thursdays to select applicants. Started in the eighteenth century, the Marine Society is an example of private philanthropy in an age of increasing social disorganization. In the earliest decades it played a unique role by clothing and placing boys. It did not seek delinquents, but the *Solebay* acquired them. Its Master, John Byers, reported to the Select Committee of 1828 that he flogged boys—on the bottom, he was quick to point out—but preferred confinement for infractions of rules. Boys did not leave the *Solebay* because they had completed a course of preparation; rather, a captain needing crew selected the healthiest and literate from a line-up of the full complement of boys. Accordingly, a boy might stay a week or several months before leaving the *Solebay* for an East Indiaman or a fishing boat working the Dogger Bank. The Marine Society continues its work today, having commissioned the seagoing training ship, *Jonas Hanway,* in 1986.

Some fifty years before the Select Committee of 1828 looked into the *Euryalus,* Dr. Johnson had observed that there was little difference between being in the navy and in prison. In the case of ships—human agencies we now class as "total institutions," which control all aspects of living—the worst features of both conditions of servitude were evident. Some delinquent boys moved to sailing ships and were transported to Cape Town, Canada, Bermuda, or Australia. An example is seventeen-year-old William Butler of Birmingham, who sailed on the prison ship *Frances Charlotte* arriving in Van Diemen's Land on May 15, 1833 (Description 1833). Ships continued as model institutions well into the twentieth century. Such an establishment, its teachers in quasi-naval uniforms, was established at Blythe, Northumberland. Strict discipline, control of all phases of life, and a nominal sense of a life on the rolling wave were obvious aspects of boys' education.

Penal Reform

The 1828 inquiry into conditions on *Euryalus* showed that life on hulks provided segregation from adult convicts, but that was merely

TABLE 8.3
CRIME AND PUNISHMENT IN THE EIGHTEENTH AND NINETEENTH CENTURIES

NAME	AGE	YEAR	INCIDENT	SENTENCE	SOURCE
Branham, Mary	17	1785	". . . feloniously stealing . . . two stuff petticoats value, 20s. one pair of stays, value 18d. four and a half yards of cloth, value 5s . . ."	Transported to Africa for 7 years	Cobley, 1970
Hudson, John	13	1783	"burglarously and feloniously breaking and entering the house of William Holsworth"	Transported for 7 years. "I think it would be too hard to find a boy of his tender age guilty of the burgulary; one would wish to snatch the boy from destruction."	Cobley, 1970
Hughes, John	18	1784	"feloniously assaulted on the King's Highway Edward Halfhide and stole from him one watch . . value of £5 . . ."	Sentenced to be hanged. Reprieved. Transported to Africa for 6 years.	Cobley, 1970
Williams, John (alias 'Black Jack')	15	1784	Stole a "wooden cask of the value of three shillings, Six quarts of a certain liquor called Geneva . . ."	To be hanged. Reprieved. 7 years transportation.	Cobley, 1970
2 Boys	14	1791	Robbed a 12 year old boy	Hanged	Shaw, 1966
George Crow	15	1818	Stole £3.3 6d. Lincolnshire	Sentenced to death	Aldington, 1948
Thomas Young	17	1818	House-breaking, Lincolnshire	Sentenced to death	Aldington, 1948
Boy	9	1839	Set a building on fire, Chelmsford	Hanged	Behlmen, 1982
Boy	10	1869	Took threepenny worth of turnips from a pile laying in a field, Dorset	10 days at hard labour plus 5 years in a reformatory	Walvin, 1982

modification of a bad plan. A former naval Captain, Edward Brenton, opened an asylum for delinquent boys in Hackney and a similar agency for girls at Chiswick a little later. Public provision caught up with private philanthropy a few years later with the establishment of Parkhurst Prison as the agency for delinquent youth. Progress in treatment of delinquents on dry land was little advanced. It was not until two years after opening Parkhurst that Whitehall removed leg irons from the young inmates, some of whom had relatively short sentences to serve. Innovation also came in the form of better classification and grouping of boys. In contrast, continental thinking had evolved in the direction of distinguishing criminals from pauper children and towards establishing farm schools where hard work and country air could prevail.

TABLE 8.4

TERMS OF IMPRISONMENT OF THE TOTAL NUMBER
OF JUVENILE PRISONERS, AFTER TRIAL AT ASSIZES
AND QUARTER SESSIONS, IN ENGLAND AND WALES, IN
ENGLAND AND WALES, IN THE COURSE OF THE YEAR 1849*

Terms	Males	Females	Total
Under 14 days	168	32	200
14 days and under 1 month	182	59	241
1 month and under 2 months	319	65	384
2 months and under 3 months	287	40	327
3 months and under 6 months	386	84	470
6 months and under 1 year	271	35	306
1 year and under 2 years	55	9	64
2 years and under 3 years	7	2	9
3 years and upwards	2	1	3
Whipped, fined, or discharged on sureties	25	2	27
Sentence deferred		1	1
Total	1702	330	2032

*Report from the Select Committee on Criminal and Destitute Children. *Parliamentary Papers.* 1853, 23, Appendix I.

The practice of sentencing criminals to transportation, usually for no less than seven to fourteen years, provided a model. Noncriminal, pauper children had been sent to Virginia in the seventeenth century because they cluttered the streets of the metropolis. Very little of benefit came of indenturing them as servants; many died, a few prospered, and others made their way back from the wilderness of Virginia to England. Australia, in contrast, was a more hospitable climate in the early nineteenth century; the natives were gone in many places—displaced in some, shot like vermin in others. The climate was salubrious, and superior individuals would thrive (Cawte 1986). In some respects, the plan paralleled the French practice of shipping orphan boys to populate Algeria. Return from the Antipodes was unlikely, and when given a modicum of rehabilitation within the mailed fist of character training by close discipline, seemed unnecessary. Some lessons had been drawn from placement of children in South Africa by the Children's Friend Society, so that the enterprise was better conceived (Jordan 1985b).

A special colony was established near Hobart, Tasmania, at that time still known as Van Diemen's Land, and recalled from the days of convicts as recently as 1962 by Carrie James at age ninety-four (Farson 1986). Point Puer's name means "boy," so that the colony there was planned as a separate facility, however barbaric the more fundamental matter of transporting children seems today. The colony was established by the Governor across the bay in order to segregate juveniles. A visitor, found it "a wretched, bleak, barren spot without water, wood for fuel or an inch of soil that is not for agricultural purposes absolutely valueless" (Hooper 1954). However, it was an improvement over life in hulks, and the boys learned trades. One of the benign aspects of the colonial service at that time was that it had, in Sir William Denison, one of the great administrators. He looked after his charges in Australia, and his despatches to Whitehall read well. That is, schooling was planned, and boys were well supervised. Even the adults were treated well; for example, one of the more preposterous of Victoria's restless Irish subjects, William Smith O'Brien (Touhill 1981), survived his experience of transportation and returned to live out his life quietly in Ireland.

Point Puer was an opportunity to start a new life for boys judged "incorrigible" at Parkhurst. Under twenty-nine rules established by William Crawford, James Kay-Shuttleworth, and J. Webb the first group of boys set sail to be apprenticed in New Zealand and Western Australia, and to finish sentences in Van Diemen's Land. In 1843, there were 143 boys at Point Puer, out of a total of about seven thousand males in Van Diemen's Land. Mr. M. Forster's report of October 20, 1845, on Point Puer shows that about one-fourth of the six to eight hundred boys were Catholic, an unusual proportion for the times in the general population. There were Anglican and Catholic chaplains, and a classification system based on age and conduct was operated. A few years later, the annual report stated that the behavior of the boys was splendid; they manufactured their own shoes and clothes "which were made by sheepskins"

(Correspondence 1847). They attended school for seventeen and a half hours each week and learned trades. The report for 1847 urged that those who had learned to "read, write and cipher," and had acquired a trade, be given conditional pardons.

It seems likely that some boys prospered in their new setting. We know that the Point Puer boys were very short (Jordan 1985a); evidence suggests that males did not attain their full height until their early twenties in the nineteenth century. We trust that the younger convict boys improved physically. However, there remained the following problem identified by Mr. Forster:

> Up to the present period I fear that much of the positive good effected at Point Puer has been rendered of little or no avail, by the lads on emergence being associated with the old convicts, especially in barracks, when not able to obtain service or wages.

Even with improvements in penology and in management, Point Puer was subsequently held to be a failure because many Australian adults found to be criminals turned out to have spent some time there as boys. The colony was allowed to decay and, when coupled with Whitehall's abandonment of transportation for children, fell into complete disuse. The name persists as an echo of an attempt at penal reform prior to the 1854 Act which established reformatories. Marcus Clarke weaved it into his novel of early Australia, *His Natural Life* (1874), and Farson referred to it in his novel of Tasmania, *Swansdowne* (1986).

Not many boys went to Point Puer, but its significance lies in the attempt to provide a rational disposition of young offenders. When assessing the transportation of juveniles, an act which is destestable to the contemporary observer, it is helpful to keep in mind the harshness of children's lives in nineteenth-century Britain. There were worse fates; and for some children, transportation was the lesser evil. In 1849, the barrister, Mr. Michael O'Shaugnessy, reported from Mayo instances of destitute youngsters committing crimes out of desperation. The Ruddy family was one of the most respectable on Clare Island. Famine led young John, Austin, and Charles, aged eight, twelve, and fifteen, to steal a sheep. The were imprisoned, where they probably received an improved diet.

Martin McGunty, John M. Grone, and John English, each about seventeen, told the court that they had no way to earn a living and would steal again if freed. Martin and the two Johns requested transportation. All three were transported, even though the offense was the first for John

English. Owen Eady requested transportation, although he didn't know what it meant. O'Shaugnessy reported to the Poor Law Committee:

> I asked him if he knew what transportation was; he said he knew he would be kept at work for seven years and that at the end he would have his liberty in another country, which would be better than starving and sleeping out at night; he was told he might have chains on his legs. 'If I have,' he said, 'I will have something to eat' (O'Shaugnessy 1849).

Of course, not every Irish boy was a victim. In 1859, Mullingar in County Westmeath saw the trial of three young rascals named Bryan, Flanagan, and Lawless. In successive forays from their Mullingar Workhouse residence, they stole a ram and ate it over a period of three days. They set fire to the workhouse, and stole a clock, twenty brass pins, and a pistol. In addition, they failed in an attempt to steal clothes from the fever hospital. Chief Justice Monahan expressed astonishment that such things could happen in a civilized country.

In the case of Ireland, it is interesting to note that the number of juveniles sent to prison in 1851 was 12,283. In the years 1861, 1871, and 1881, the numbers averaged 1,100, or less than 10% of the number when the effects of the Famine were evident (Barrett 1902).

In England, there remained the problem of other youngsters. Table 8.5 contains information developed by Captain J.R. Groves, the Governor of Milbank prison. Of significance is the age of these "criminals" and the savagery of the sentences under laws which, within memory, had hanged children of tender years with some regularity. The materials in Table 8.5 were submitted by Captain Groves to the House of Lords (First Report 1847). Here we see that Dominick and John, who probably were six and seven years old at the time of arrest, each received sentences of seven years transportation for petty theft. Time and again, one reads of heavy sentences imposed on children for minor crimes. What is noteworthy is that the materials in Table 8.5 show that the authorities were sensitive to the social context of these little boys, although the judgment on Dominick Rafferty is quite unenlightened. Mary Carpenter presented the boy's bad family background in 1851. Even the most humane of judges faced problems which defied solution in an age before probation and other social services. One can only wonder about the proper course of action for a magistrate in the case of the boy reported by Beggs in 1849. The offender was a pickpocket, seven years old, who stood two feet ten inches at his fullest. This lad, barely old enough to enter school by our standards, was already engaged in a life of crime and regularly

TABLE 8.5
RETURN OF TWO BOYS SENT TO MILBANK PRISON UNDER SENTENCE OF TRANSPORTATION

NAME	AGE	CRIME	SENTENCE	WHEN AND WHERE TRIED	REMARKS BY JUDGE	WHETHER BEFORE CONVICTED	TIME SUPPOSED TO HAVE LIVED UPON CRIME	CHARACTER OF PARENTS	CHAPLAIN'S REMARK	REMARKS
John Nicholls	7	Stealing Monies	7 Years	12th June 1846, at Warwick.	None	Not known	Not known	Bad; Connexions bad.		Sent to House of Correction, Warwick, 19th Jan. 1847, under the Provisions of a conditional Pardon. This prisoner was little more than Six Years of Age.
Dominick Rafferty	8	Stealing Ninepence in Copper	7 Years	21st Oct. 1846, at Preston.	"Must be separated from his family and Connexions."	Not known	Lived by Crime from the Moment he was capable of committing it.	Thieves and Vagabonds. Father tramps about the Country; an elder Brother transported; another, 12 Years old, who has been Eight Times in Prison.	"The Habits and Society in which this poor Child has lived render it almost impossible to develope, in his short Stay here, any good Tendency in his Feelings or Disposition.	This Prisoner was not supposed to be more than Six Years of Age from his Appearance, and was rejected by Order of the Secretary of State as unfit to be received.

J. R. GROVES, Governor

engaged in the hazardous task of stealing from his elders. Such children were frequently put to the trade by their parents. To the situation of children living by their wits, abandoned by drunken, irresponsible parents, Mary Carpenter brought evangelical zeal, personal experience with the poor in Bristol and a tendency to call a spade a spade. In that style she believed that the Parkhurst experiment was incorrectly formulated, an opinion she was not loath to share with unimaginative officials.

Mary Carpenter established her own reformatory for girls in Bristol in 1854 at an improbable site, the beautiful and historic Red Lodge. She acted as superintendent, coping with the everyday crises which agency social workers in any age encounter. By 1857, there were sixty girls in residence, and the Red Lodge was operating with good days and bad—runaways, episodes of acting-out behavior by the girls, and crises of management. A series of matrons were tried and some found the job too difficult. A superintendent much addicted to physical punishment was hired in 1858, and the reformatory oscillated from Miss Carpenter's genial style to the physical assault favored as a means of management by the newcomer, who left in 1859. From that year on, Mary Carpenter handled fewer of the day-to-day problems presented by her charges and devoted herself to education of the public and advocacy for the children of the street (Manton 1976).

In 1851, Mary Carpenter published *Reformatory Schools for the Children of the Perishing and Dangerous Classes and for Juvenile Offenders*. In it, she explains that the perishing classes consist of "those who have not yet fallen into actual crime, but who are almost certain from their ignorance, destitution, and the circumstances in they are growing up, to do so." The dangerous were those "who unblushingly acknowledge that they can gain more for the support of themselves and their parents by stealing than by working . . . they know not that any man is their brother." James Greenwood (1881) reported the following conversation between the warden and an adolescent about to be released from prison:

"How many times have you been in trouble, 99?"

99 gave the splinter a reflective turn in his mouth, nibbled off a little bit, and spat it out ere he made an answer.

"Oh, I don't know; what's the good of keepin' count?—Wot odds how many?"

"Twenty times at least I'll be bound?"

99 drew the splinter into his mouth an chewed and swallowed it with a snort of sulky defiance.

"So you might be bound if you made it thirty times—five and thirty;" said he. "I ain't pertickler—wot's the odds?"

"Well, as I often tell you, 99, the way you seem bent on going can have but one ending. You think of what I tell you, and of the good advice you are wickedly deaf, when it is too late." At this 99 uttered a short laugh.

"Allright, Guv'nor, don't you bother, I'm good for the end whatever it is."

Largely as a result of the efforts of Mary Carpenter, Annie MacPherson, Sidney Turner, Matthew Davenport Hill, and others, penal reform for juveniles made progress. Wills (1971) points out that the imagination of reformers was not unlimited, for they espoused three convictions. The first was social stratification—classes—which they thought immutable; at its worst, this premise associated riches with virtue and the lack of riches with vice. The second was the conviction that misbehavior was a

TABLE 8.6
NINETEENTH-CENTURY SLANG

Beak	Justice of the Peace, Magistrate	*Hoisting*	Shop-lifting
Betty	Pick-lock	*Jemmy*	Iron Bar
Blow	Betray, inform	*Jug*	Jail
Boat	Transported	*Kid Ken*	Lodging for Juvenile thieves
Bughunter	One who robs drunks	*Knob-stick*	Non-striking working
Bull	Second brew from tea-leaves	*Lady Green*	Prison chaplain
Bulls-eye	Lantern	*Lag*	Convict
Chunk	School-Board Officer	*Little snakesman*	Boy who enters houses for thieves
Cush	Club	*Meg*	Halfpenny
Cocker-up	Give a person ideas about their station	*Peter*	Safe, strongbox
Crusher	Policeman	*Ponce*	Pimp
Dip	Pickpocket	*Shoot the crow*	Order drink without paying

Table 8.6 (Continued)

Dollymop	Promiscuous young woman	*Shoot the moon*	Move without paying rent
Drum	House for burgling	*Slavey*	Young general servant
Esclop	Police	*Stir*	Prison
Flash house	Establishment patronized by crooks	*Stretch*	Three year imprisonment
Gaff	Entertainment	*Swag*	Loot
Gammon	Ruse, Deception	*Tain-piece*	Three months imprisonment
Get a seat	Obtain work as a bootmaker	*Topped*	Hanged
Going snowing	Stealing linens from clothes-lines	*Tosh*	Valuables found in sewer
Grass	Inform police	*Walker!*	An expression of incredulity from the improbable stories of John "Hookey" Walker.

moral failure rather than a behavioral accommodation to circumstances. In his report to the Select Committee of 1852–53, the Rev. G.H. Hamilton of Durham reported the causes of imprisonment of 192 boys and girls. After neglect, he put ignorance, idleness, covetousness, bad temper, and total depravity. His list included twenty-six cases he could only report as "comparatively respectable." No psychological or social phenomena here, only moral failings. In Greenwood's report, the governor speaks of the good advice to which the boy is "wickedly deaf." The third was the belief that a mode of life best described as spartan was essential for moral reform. In this regard, there is the view of Jelinger C. Symons, well-known for his efforts on behalf of children in factories, who disagreed with the notion that "juvenile offenders are little errant angels who require little else than fondling" (May 1973).

The first important step forward was the Summary Jurisdiction Act of 1847, which allowed separate arraignment and disposition of boys and girls under age fourteen. In 1850, the age was raised to sixteen. It was in that stream of events that the Youthful Offenders Act of 1854 was moved by Mr. C.B. Adderley. The Act provided for segregation by age, with those convicted under age sixteen segregated and treated in a different manner. As with many Victorian innovations, this one was by fiat, so that the same governors and prison officers, with their own sense of what was good penology, filled in the gaps in the legislation. Today, people realize that Bills need guidelines to implement their intent, and it is guidelines or operating principles which really determine the consequences of making laws. Under the 1854 Act, a boy convicted of a crime went to prison for fourteen days and then went to a reformatory. Parents were expected to contribute to the cost of confinement. Birmingham Gaol was notorious in the 1850s, and a fifteen-year-old boy, Edward Andrews, committed suicide (Allday 1853). A few years later, in 1857, legislation enabled local government to fund schools, and other laws in 1861 and 1866 dealt with some of the neglected details, for example, children who were vagrants.

Reform had a long way to go even after several bills followed the 1854 Act. Reformatory and industrial schools were not Borstal institutions. Indeed, penology seems to have taken some retrograde steps for a time with tighter security.

Eventually, positive results from the continent could not be ignored (Fletcher 1852). The progressive penology at Elmira, New York, was especially influential. At the end of the nineteenth century, in 1895, the Gladstone Committee prepared a separate institution for boys aged sixteen to twenty-one. First introduced at Bedford, the new system directed by Sir Evelyn Ruggles-Brise eventually opened at Borstal. It maintained the tradition of close discipline and hard work. Not until 1922 did the system undergo a modest relaxing of its spartan style.

It is worth noting that the nineteenth-century reformers did an excellent job of appealing to the public's breadth of motive. While pious in their private convictions, they saw themselves as controlling a dangerous segment of the population for the general good. Mary Carpenter's arguments were not restricted to moral appeals, although in her 1851 book on reformatory schools for the children of the perishing and dangerous classes she warned against "the Idolatry of figures"—statistics and indicators of reforming methods which were cheaper than imprisonment. She did a good job of showing that reforming as opposed to punishing could be both more effective and cheaper; addressing the National Society for the Promotion of Social Science in 1864, she put the cost of maintenance in reformatories at one-half that of prisons, or about twenty pounds per year.

Drinking

A vice whose indirect effect on children worked through intoxicated and abusing parents was misuse of alcoholic beverages. Writing as "Alfred" in 1857, S.H.G. Kydd recorded

> I have seen a little boy, only this winter, who works at a mill, and who lives within two hundred or three hundred yards of my door; he is not six years old, and I have seen him, when he had a few coppers in his pocket, go to a beer shop, call for a glass of ale, and drink as boldly as any full grown man.

The scope of abuse of alcohol in the nineteenth century was enormous, and it merits consideration as a family problem because its most focused impact was on the lives of those most involved with the drinker. Antecedent to the problem in the nineteenth century was abuse of gin and related spirits in the eighteenth century. We need not look to industrialization or urbanization as a cause because the problem of excessive drinking was an old one. "Drunk for a penny, dead drunk for tuppence," was the byword as the eighteenth century came to a close. In 1828, a great deal of gin was consumed. The type called by drinkers "Blue Ruin" was a shilling a pint (Report 1828). In the 1880s, "Old Tom" sold for fourpence a quartern (Greenwood 1881). Dickens gave us Sara Gamp, in *Martin Chuzzlewit*.

> In her drinking, too, she was very punctual and particular, requiring a pint of mild porter at lunch, a pint at dinner, half a pint as a species of stay or holdfast between dinner and tea, and a pint of the celebrated staggering ale, or Real Old British Tippler, at supper.

By 1885, the national expenditure on alcohol was 76 million pounds, and it doubled to 122 million by 1880. More significantly, per capita expenditure rose from £2.14.6 in 1855 to £4.7.3. in 1875 (Shelley 1969). In the case of a particular place—one hesitates to use the word "community"—the mining town of Bilston in Staffordshire, the *Morning Chronicle*'s correspondent reported in 1851 that "it is calculated that 5,000 miners spend annually £50,000 in ale; at Moxley there is one beer shop to every twelve dwellings." One drinker would consume eleven quarts at a time. Drink was easy to get in Dumfries, which had twelve bakeries and seventy-nine whiskey shops (Flinn 1965). Even at the end of the century, the problem was acute. The average York worker's family budget assigned one-sixth of the weekly income to drink (Anderson

1971). Not surprisingly, there was an enormous impact on collective health. Bourne (1882) estimated annual mortality directly attributable to drink at 40,500 deaths each year. To that number, however, he added "two innocents," or about eighty thousand deaths. Sixty-five thousand of them were infant deaths attributed by Bourne to "deficient nutrition and attention."

The ranting against drink, and the temperance movements launched by clergymen of all persuasions, were more than exhortations for the godly to become godlier. They constituted a public movement to reduce an appalling problem, one which in the context of this work was a major threat to children, direct as well as indirect. An equally direct threat was that to the life of infants. Commentaries in the nineteenth century frequently referred to "overlaying" as a cause of death. This was frequently manslaughter, the accidental effect of an intoxicated mother smothering her baby by rolling over on it in the night.

Alcohol affected children in the form of abandonment by alcoholic parents. Many of the street children ministered to by Mary Carpenter were in their plight because parental intoxication never ended; children were simply not considered in the planning of the alcohol-addicted parent. Barnardo estimated that alcoholism was responsible for 85% of the abandoned children he cared for (Williams 1966). Although not abandoned, young James Dawson Burn (nee MacBurney) was frequently beaten by his stepfather William McNamee (Vincent 1982).

Children were introduced to alcohol early in life. At a time when cow's milk was not pasteurized, water was frequently undrinkable, and beer was a comparatively safe liquid—despite the risk of adulteration before 1860. An early mode of introduction was being dispatched to buy drink for parents from a beer shop or off-license establishment. Access was no problem, for there were over one hundred thousand public houses and beer shops by 1872. Street life and pub life were one, and Reach, the *Morning Chronicle*'s correspondent, wrote in his portion of the paper's 1850 series of articles on the poor:

> In returning last Sunday night by the Oldham road, from one of my tours among the druggists, I was somewhat surprised to hear the loud sounds of music and jollity which floated out from the public house windows. The street was swarming with drunken men and women; and with young mill girls and boys, shouting, ballooing, and romping with each other. Now, I am not one of those who look upon the slightest degree of social indulgence as a downright evil, but I confess that last Sunday night in the Oldham-road astonished and grieved me. In no city have I ever witnessed a scene of more open, brutal, and general intemperance. The public houses and gin-shops were roaring full. Rows, and

fights, and scuffles, were every moment taking place within doors and in the streets. The whole street rung with shouting, screaming, and swearing, mingled with the jarring music of half a dozen bands. A tolerably intimate acquaintance with most phases of London life enables me to state that in no part of the metropolis would the police have tolerated such a state of things for a single Sunday. I entered one of the musical taverns—one of the best of them. It was crowded to the door with men and women—many of them appearing to belong to a better station in life than mill-hands or mechanics. The music consisted of performances on the piano and seraphine. In the street I accosted a policeman, telling him of my surprise that music should be allowed in public houses on Sunday evenings. Such a thing was never dreamt of. . . .

Abuse of alcohol is a personal problem, but it is a community problem when we sum the individual offenses. Our picture of the aggregate social problem in the nineteenth century becomes clearer as the century progresses. In the 1870s, the House of Lords established a Select Committee to inquire into "the Prevalence of Habits of Intemperance." Their Lordships learned that illiteracy was common among public drunkards, that is, those charged with drunkenness. In Liverpool in 1876, only 1.3% of those charged could read and write well. Over a one-third, 35.1%, could neither read nor write. In Dublin in the same period, almost 150 people were arrested every week for being drunk, incapable, or disorderly. Examination of the statistics from Dublin shows that Saturday and Sunday were the peak days. Saturday night was the high point and Monday was the low. Mr. Dendy and Mr. Poynting of Manchester showed that inebriation was greater in the north and northwest regions of the country, laying above a line from the Bristol Channel to the Humber. Southampton, Gravesend, and Rochester, however, were above the average of the northern towns. However, there is a problem with these statistics, which is that they represent "persons proceeded against," and there is always the uncertainty with crime statistics that they can reflect vigor of prosecution rather than absolute rate of occurrence. In the case of the Liverpool statistics, it is possible that gentlemen were treated differently from the poor when in their cups. In either case, we see that inebriation was a substantial, visible problem. We add a final numerical item on the regional differences in public drunkenness. Dendy and Poynting (Fourth Report 1879) found little difference in the availability of public houses by region and still found prosecutions four times more frequent in northern towns. When counties were the geographical unit—i.e., towns plus villages and the countryside—northern regions exceeded southern regions by a rate three times higher per thousand people. The investigators found that the coal fields provided the highest rates of public drunkenness, and that density of population was highest where drunkenness was most frequently prosecuted. The highest number of public houses per ten thousand people, they report, was 110 in Carmarthen, and the lowest was 36 in Middlesborough and in Kendal. The usual rate of "apprehensions" was 49 in Congelton and the highest was 420 in Liverpool, per ten thousand people.

Drink suffused the workplace, and there are places even today where union contracts label the mid-morning and afternoon breaks as "beer breaks." At Bilston, the community's eleven chapels and churches were outweighed by 142 drinking places, according to the *Morning Chronicle,* whose correspondent added that there was one beer shop for every twelve dwellings in nearby Moxley. Not surprisingly, a good deal of the weekly wage did not reach home and family, but was deposited with the publicans on pay day.

An occupational group whose lives were inextricably bound up with alcohol were the Thames ballast heavers. Here, too, we turn to the investigative reporting of the *Morning Chronicle* in 1850, and probably to the work of Henry Mayhew in particular. Ballast heavers worked on coal boats, and mostly at night. Publicans and some grocers contracted with ships' captains to provide labor, and undertook hiring on their premises. They also paid wages there, and the heaver looking for work had to buy drinks before he was hired and before he was paid. One heaver reported:

> . . . I get to the public house for my money at six in the even, I'm forced to wait until eleven—until I'm drunk very often . . . (Labour 1850).

In the same article, a wife was reported as:

> . . . perfectly modest in manner, speech, and look, and spoke of what her husband was, and still might be, with much feeling. She came to me half-clad and a half-famished child in her arms.

Her problem was to intercept some of the money before it all returned to the publican so that she might buy food for the child and herself.

In general, people understood the problem, but heavy drinking was sanctioned by local custom and was a part of life. The groups combatting abuse of alcohol were in opposition to powerful forces. Breweries had everything to gain from an increase in consumption of beer; government drew revenue from beer and spirits in 1859 in the amount of 31% of revenues. In comparison, stamps generated 12% and income tax 15%

(Shelley 1979). Gladstone attributed the loss of the 1874 election to the role of spirits in the election; "a torrent of gin and beer," namely, the influence of the alcohol trade. Shelley points out that there were over three hundred thousand people engaged in various aspects of the production and sale of drink in 1871. The distracted wife and mother was up against powerful forces of custom and influence.

Denyer (1893) summarized the place of various beverages in the pattern of national consumption from approximately 1850 to 1890. In 1852, per capita consumption of beer was 23 gallons, peaking at 33.8 gallons in 1876, and declining to 30.13 gallons per capita in 1891. In 1852, consumption of spirits was 1.09 gallons per person, reaching a peak of consumption in 1875 at 1.30 gallons, and then declining steadily but slowly to 1.03 gallons in 1891. In the case of wine, consumption per person rose steadily from .23 gallons in 1852 to a peak of .56 in 1876 and declined to .39 in 1891. Consumption of tea per capita in 1852 was 1.99 pounds; and cocoa was .12 pounds. Tea gained steadily, reaching a high for the period of 5.35 pounds in 1891. Cocoa rose in parallel fashion to .57 pounds per capita in 1891. Clearly, the overall trend was the rise in the consumption of tea, with an equally positive and welcome increase in the taste for cocoa. If we broaden the concept of alcohol to include resort to additional noxious if popular consumables, we can offer a brief look at tobacco, ever a temptation to the young. In 1841, per capita consumption was thirteen ounces, and it rose to thirty ounces by 1901, according to Wilson (1940). Returning to drinks, the overall picture is that the total consumption of liquid refreshments rose after 1850. While the trend was to increased consumption overall, the domestic beverage, tea, established itself as a family drink. Those addicted to alcohol undoubtedly remained so, to the detriment of the family and to those whose lives were intertwined with them. For others, the rise of alternatives to spirits broadened the rage of alternatives.

For children, the rise of soft, fizzy drinks provided a needed alternative to a sip of the parents' beer. That innovation reduced the risk of premature introduction of alcohol into the lives of people whose temperaments we diagnose today as "addictive personalities," that is, people who are compelled, probably for reasons of biochemistry rather than the Victorian oversimplification of "moral weakness," to abuse spirits. In such cases there seems to be a role for the family, because research suggests a familial—e.g., genetic—susceptibility to alcohol addiction. The emergence of the beverages of moderation—tea, in particular— postponed the ravages of alcoholism if not entirely avoiding them. As an example, we read in many of the accounts of working-class diets that the modest breakfast consisted of food plus tea laced with alcohol. The slow supplanting of alcohol with nonalcoholic drinks was a triumph of merchandizing harmful only to the brewers and distillers. By 1878, the Licensed Victuallers National Defense League—a name suggesting a defensive posture—could say to the House of Lords, "we heartily hate intemperance," and argue for improved schools and libraries (Fourth Report 1878). Children were direct beneficiaries of the rise of the soft drink and tea industries.

Reform. In Ireland, there was a successful temperance movement in the 1840s led by Father Theobald Mathew, whose work has been fully presented by Malcolm (1986). Denyer (1893) points out that the national consumption of spirits in Ireland had been 12.3 million gallons in 1838, but had dropped to just under one-half that amount, 5.5 million gallons, by 1843. Of course, the stage was set by the respect given to the clergy by the Irish. For those less predisposed by religious heritage, the matter of ending abuse of spirits was slower to improve. In some, the matter was a hard-earned lesson. Young William Thompson awakened once too often in jail to enjoy the prospect of repeated visits. He told James Greenwood (1881) that before he was discharged from jail he decided to drink no more, and he had kept to his resolve. For other young persons, the effort was not to control themselves but others. The child who sang "Father, dear Father come home with me now, the clock in the steeple strikes" was trying to get an inebriated parent back to the bosom of his family. James Burn (1855) recalled his father's attack of delirium as they tramped across desolate moorland from Lander to Edinburgh. Burn's step-father began to see stage coaches passing.

> Some of the passengers were ugly demons of every possible shape and form, some were merry imps, and other mischievous rascals. . . . Some were for hanging him; others preferred the amusement of drowning; some suggested roasting. . . .
> I remember when these blue fellows held him in their hellish thrall for six days and nights . . . while we were being storm-staid in a lonely ferry-house in the Island of Skye.

Children were surrounded by public and private intoxication. For every child who was repelled by the sight there was probably another (or more) who internalized drinking as evidence of adult role-behaviour and sought to take it up as a way to exhibit an appearance of maturity, much like smoking.

Slowly, there appeared organized attempts to lead drunkards to see the error of their ways. The temperance movement begun in Bradford in 1830 is the first one about which much is known, and there were others in centers of population undoubtedly. By 1831, a national movement was apparent under the name, British and Foreign Temperance Society. It was followed in 1835 by the British Temperance Association. The former appears to have been Establishmentarian in connection, while the latter was a working class movement. The National Temperance Society followed in 1842, and we surmise that the titles must have been confusing to the already befuddled who gave thought to their straits. In 1853 the United Kingdom Alliance appeared. Less forbidding in name and more gregarious in style were the Rechabites, founded in 1835, and the Sons of Temperance who followed a little later. Both organizations were national, the Rechabites being the larger with 168,000 members by 1900. The Sons of Temperance were only about two thirds as numerous. Both the Rechabites and the Sons of Temperance had junior divisions.

An organization solely for juveniles was the Band of Hope sponsored by the Leeds Temperance Society and led by the formidable Jabez Tunnicliff and Anne Carlile (Shiman 1974). As with organizations for adults, the Band was evangelical in persuasion; its Catholic counterpart was the Children's Guild. The Band offered organized activities and promoted total abstinence among its working-class child-patrons. Unfortunately, there were children below that social stratum who needed help and were not reached. Even so, the Band of Hope made a positive contribution in northern towns. It was less successful in the south, however.

Both the adult and juvenile organizations worked in an unsympathetic climate. In part, they insisted that alcohol abuse be viewed as a moral failure, a view compatible with the religious zeal of nonconformists and other sects. They failed to attract or reform those whose drinking was less a moral insensibility than a physiological susceptibility. At the same time, the temptations to drink were all around. Pubs evolved into handsome establishments whose cut-glass and brass handles we still admire today. The public house became the 'local,' and so a social center for the neighbourhood. At the same time, there were the larger celebrations in various towns; in Nottingham, the annual gain in teetotallers was winnowed by the attractions of Goose Fair (Church 1966). In that week a lot of reformed people fell off the wagon and broke the pledges so earnestly made after last year's fair on practical and religious grounds.

Religion

Burnett (1982) records that the five-year-old Leonard Ellisdon was present when an old woman died. Leonard recalled in his later years that he looked out of a window so that he could see her soul go up to Jesus.

An equally direct view of death was held in the family of Patrick McGill. His brother Daniel died and their mother opened a window for young Daniel's soul to ascend. With a high rate of mortality, the next world and God were very close to people who had religious convictions. In November 1856, young Mabel Wellan of Tunbridge Wells was in her bedroom when God distinctly said to her, "be prepared." As a consequence, she became a missionary and spent forty of her adult years in North Africa (Nicholson 1932). Victorians took their Bible seriously and turned to it for consolation amidst the crises of life. However, the role of religion was more than passive, for it galvanized individuals into good works, and children were the frequent beneficiaries of religious motives. Religious knowledge required the ability to read, although not necessarily to write, and education for literacy frequently began for religious motives. Two early educational reformers, Hannah More of Bristol and Edmund Lancaster, were explicitly using the education of children for a religious end. Hannah More's program at Cheddar employed parables for children, and she developed tracts for the children and an adaptation of the catechism. In her own words, "To tend the poor to read without providing them with 'safe' books, has always appeared to me as improper" (Aspinall and Smith 1959). To Hannah More, education of children and the poor had to be approached very carefully. It carried within it the risk of people reading Voltaire and Tom Paine, and literacy could lead to a loss of religion—infidelity—as well as to Jacobinism. Religion was to educate children towards religious truths but not towards a social gospel. In understanding this, it is well to recall that Hannah More lived a very long and active life in the nineteenth century. As a girl, she had been accepted by Dr. Samuel Johnson and had roots firmly in the eighteenth century. For Lancaster, a Quaker, literacy was the key to the scriptures, and piety could only be based on a reasoned grasp of biblical evidence.

Of course, religion motivated people to good ends besides literacy. On that point the Dissenters broke new ground, for they shrewdly saw that the poor were approachable through their emotions as well as reason. Writing in 1865, J.R. Green expressed his distaste for the color and pagentry of William Booth's Salvation Army; "By the mouth of such persons as Booth the poor are not tempted to worship God by the bait of a breakfast and a coal-ticket," he observed. And yet the campground meeting of the Methodists and the revivalism of the American preachers Sankey and Moody won converts to the Lord. Children were not immune to such influences, for the imagery of the Pit was vivid and the emotions evoked were strong. In his autobiography, Thomas Cooper, who apparently taught himself to read around age four, records that he gave up the Chapel because Primitive Methodism forbad all but religious books.

One of Burnett's (1982) people recalling childhood, John Bezar, recalled his religious conversion as a child. However, when a little older, he revolted against the idea of a vengeful God and stopped going to church entirely. Marianne Farningham's life with parents who taught in the Baptist Sunday School excluded fairy tales; we recall that the Reverend Mr. Bronte burned his children's shoes because he thought them too colorful. Within this tradition were people who clearly could not distinguish major from minor transgressions. Reporting to the Statistical Society in 1839, Mr. William Felkin tabulated the offenses of the Gray's Inn poor on Sundays; "Early and excessive dram-drinking and Sabbath-breaking, are practiced to an awful extent." Such Puritanism did not sit well with many people for whom, in Thomas Wright's (1873) words, "a beefsteak, a flagon of porter, a pipe, and a sporting newspaper form their chief joys." To E.P. Thompson, Methodism spilled over into the practices of factory owners and explained how one could justify employing child laborers in factories for merciless hours at low wages and also be devoutly Methodical.

At the level of children's daily lives, religion was a set of family practices to follow, hymns to sing, and doctrines to absorb. On closer examination, children in any given decade were acquiring the formulations of a given church at a particular time. What children would not appreciate until they were adults was that they were absorbing Anglicanism at a given moment, Catholicism of a decade, or Millenianism of a day. For, one of the major aspects of social change in the nineteenth century, surely as earth-shaking as the explosion of manufacturing and the spread of red on the map of the world, was the upheaval in the world of religion. Within the confessions, the analytic found their tranquil faith turned into a minefield of dissent and innovation.

From our twentieth-century viewpoint, the major event was the impact of the new scholarship on accepted, unquestioned belief. Wallace and Darwin demolished the history of a world only four thousand years old according to Bishop Ussher in the preceding century, and dissolved the certainty of a man-centered—if not helio centered—world. Man was demonstrable as the by-product of impersonal, subrational forces; indeed, he was descended from brutes and was susceptible to replacement by higher-order beings in the processes of nature; she herself was less the handmaid of the Infinite and a little above a Bawd who played games with the Universe. The changes—so quietly discussed at first as a consequence of fossil remains—altered the sense of the times, the world outlook. Religious conviction fell on the defensive assaulted by empirical observations on the one hand and biblical scholarship within on the other. In this process, the historical fusion of science and religion, evidenced in the tradition of Parson-Naturalists from the eighteenth century, fell apart. Only Tennyson's *In Memoriam* was capable of catching the writhings of impaled rationalism and spreading doubt.

For those within the Established Church it was a century of surprises. Wesleyanism early in the century had established itself as a successful suitor for the neglected working class. In 1829, the beleagered Catholic minority content to live outside the public life of the nation, disenfranchised, unable to enter Oxford and Cambridge, had some of their disablements removed by the Emancipation Act. In the 1840s, the Tractarian movement saw its fulfillment as John Henry Newman strode from Canterbury through Rome's Flaminian gate. The sects flourished as Joseph Smith's Latter-Day Saints gathered in Merthyr Tydfil and Lancashire's towns on their way to Nauvoo and then to Salt Lake City in many cases. Reform swept away plural, absentee livings, and a zeal to reclaim the urban poor was ignited.

But the Established Church was not alone in this regard. The quiet, semisecret "old religion," which grew from under seventy thousand adherents outside of Ireland in 1870 to a quarter of a million at mid-century, also underwent shocks. The influx from Ireland overran the native Catholic laity and set a stamp upon the Church in England. This Catholicism was that of the urban poor, a caste unrecognizable to a gentry inured to invisibility, silence, and to a comparatively constricted liturgy. A mere three decades after emancipation, the Tractarians spilled over into Catholicism, bringing a sense of high drama to the liturgy and a missionary drive to reclaim those lost by neglect. The mission was largely successful among the urban Irish and was accomplished by a cadre of priests numbering less than six hundred in 1851 (Clark 1965). With the establishment of an English episcopacy, Catholicism became a militant presence whose leaders, Newman and Wiseman, combined oratorical technique with a sense of the aesthetic which was largely retrospective and fevered. The Church had a brilliant, mannered leadership and a poor, semiliterate laity at mid-century. Over a half-century, a new Church was forged by a dedicated clergy and laity. It did not evangelize its non-Catholic audience, and it raised turmoil only the twentieth century could begin to lower. Not the least of the crises was that precipitated by Pius IX, whose doctrinal absolutism confirmed the worst fears of thoughtful men inside and out his own confession.

Among the Dissenters, dissension and hair-splitting lead to proliferation of the sectaries. The Church of Scotland was a radical improvisation. The Methodists had crises of doctrine and organization with offshoots and secessions. As in the early Church, those in command smote the disloyal, and Jabez Bunting expelled dissidents without mercy.

Armstrong (1973) estimates that one hundred thousand members were lost in this fashion between 1849 and 1855. Swedenborgians, Agape-monites, and Sandemanians arose in the tradition of Southcottians and Puritan scrupulosity. One sect reported in the 1851 religious census was the (Calvinist) "Countess of Huntingdon's Connexion," indicating that groups as large as the Methodists were still effervescent. Millenianism flourished and sects subdivided on whether music should be played dur-ing services. The result was that religion was as dynamic as any other segment of life in the nineteenth century. In contrast, the Quakers met and sat in contemplation in their congregations, alert to the inner promptings only the still can hear. The Jews, established in London's East End and in some larger cities (Leeds, for example), gave thanks for escaping Czarist pogroms and observed the law of Moses in respectful, closeted poverty. However, not all chose to cultivate their own gardens; among the more colorful people in the nineteenth-century world of reli-gion was Charles Newdigate Newdegate of Birmingham. A pleasant enough looking fellow, he became inflamed about the transfer of a nun to a convent on the continent. Given the emergence of Catholicism and its episcopacy, Mr. Newdegate's worst fears were fanned. Anti-Catholicism appeared as the Murphy riots in large towns and pandered to the imaginings of the credulous and affrighted. Of course, anti-Semitism had its turn too. But religious hostility was less of a problem for the nation as a whole than the religious indifference which left churches empty. Clark (1965) thought Bethnal Green quite the worst example of religious indifference; only six of ninety thousand people attended church there. The zeal of evangelism came none too late, as the alienation of people from the organs of society proceeded apace.

Finally, Secularism arose from the clash of science and dogma, producing a de-mythologized Christ and, eventually, a secular Human-ism in which cultural relativity was the eventual, bankrupt theme. The most curious of the secular theologies was that of Fourier, whose system "unites spiritualism with materialism and explains in harmony all the leading views of Doctrine and of party in Religion and Politics" (London Phalanx 1968). Hell and Heaven were on earth, each the product of harmony or the lack of it. Whatever the theological points which gener-ated heat, and some light, religion generally flourished and congrega-tions grew. Table 8.7 shows data over the last half of the nineteenth century on the growth of church in counties and towns between 1851 and 1911.

Knowledge of 1851 comes from the remarkable religious census of that year. Its findings were important, for it showed that about one-third of the population did not attend any church, and that one-half of the

TABLE 8.7
CHURCHES AND PEOPLE 1851 AND 1911*

Place	Year	N Churches	Growth	Proportion of People/Churches	Growth
Counties					
Lancashire	1851	1627	2637	1248	-54
	1911	3994		1194	
Devonshire	1851	1297	250	437	15
	1911	1547		452	
Shropshire	1851	679	62	338	44
	1911	741		382	
Cumberland	1851	389	125	503	14
	1911	514		517	
Bedfordshire	1851	327	92	381	83
	1911	419		464	
Towns					
London	1851	1097	933	2153	74
	1911	2030		2227	
Leeds	1851	137	15	1257	9
	1911	152		1266	
Tynemouth	1851	22	30	1326	-195
	1911	52		1131	

*Developed from Census 1911 (1917).

churchgoers did not attend the Established Church; indeed, slightly
more attended the Nonconformist churches. Of those in church on the
census day, 49% were Nonconformist, 47% were Anglican, and 4%
were Catholic (Best 1971). Anglican attendance in proportion to the
population was highest in a belt from south of the Bristol Channel to
south of the Wash. Nonconformist attendance was highest in Wales, and
Catholic attendance was highest in Lancashire. An effect of the presence
of Irish Catholics in the industrial work force was to delay labor solidarity through sectarianism and so to delay social reform (Kirk 1985). Centers of population tended to have the lowest levels of attendance for all
denominations. No equally sustained effort to conduct a national religious census was made until 1911, although there were local efforts. In
1881, for example, Sheffield conducted a census; of a population of
284,410 the number in church was 87,745, and 33,835 of them were in

Anglican churches. With the exception of 5,000 Catholics, the rest were in the chapels, of which the majority was the 4,000 people who attended the services of Charles Booth's Salvation Army (Wickham 1957).

In the case of the new religious associations, they became institutionalized in the form of respectable congregations of what were once sects. The Muggletonians and followers of Joanna Southcott did not make the transition to institutionalized, respectable forms—there is scarcely time for such temporal preoccupations when the Millenium is at hand—but the Mormons made the transition and so did the followers of John Wesley. In the case of the Mormons, the Church of Latter-Day Saints of Jesus Christ, the family became a much stronger institution as a consequence, once the problem of polygamy was settled. All ideologies which look beyond the moment grasp that the family is the agency to perpetuate the values of the collective through education of the young. In the case of the early followers of John Wesley, a Sunday School teacher was accused of teaching Jacobinism; his orderly conduct of the young from chapel to school building was misrepresented as drilling his charges for collective military action; the "evidence" was that they walked in columns and were quiet and obedient. The children's fellowship of the Methodist Church was an example of how new organizations ensured their institutional future. But even Methodists were not beyond criticism in their early days.

In some instances, churches sponsored organization of groups intended to help the children, and the Scouting movement for boys and girls founded by Baden-Powell at the turn of the century is the best example. Prior to that remarkable innovation, there were other benign movements whose objectives were child-centered. The reverend Jabez Tunnicliff and Anne Jane Carlile of the Temperance Society in Leeds established the Band of Hope for children in 1847. Its object was to promote abstinence, and it was fairly successful in Yorkshire, Lancashire, and Cheshire. It had a working-class origin and in the north kept that orientation. The Band of Hope usually met for about an hour once a week. Prayers and singing hymns were important, and a massed choir of one thousand children sang in 1862. Nominally nonsectarian, the Band was closer to chapel than to church, Anglican or Roman. Shiman (1974) points out that the Band reached children of the operator-level of workmen. With its lower-middle-class values, it failed to reach the children of the desperately poor, who, more than other segments of society, were likely to turn to drink for solace in an unspeakable way of life. This problem is perennial because Scouting reaches those whose responsiveness makes scouting important but not critical; the problem is always to reach the unreachable, a mission conducted by the middle class who bring middle-class solutions and mechanisms to nonmiddle-class children. Indeed, the very notion of organization as a mode of approaching problems is beyond the grasp of the most desperate whose sense of isolation is a critical element in their dilemmas. The test for children, however, is not whether a technique is perfect, or whether it encompasses all the years of childhood and the subsequent years. It is enough that caring adults offered help and supportive social structures. Such innovations may be contrasted with the evils of children's agricultural work gangs, for example, which offered a sense of identity with a group but at the price of exploitation in many forms. Church membership provided an otherwise absent marginal literacy through Sunday Schools to poor children.

9.

ADVOCACY AND REFORM

Scope

In this chapter, I step back from the detail of children's lives and their own words as the perspective within which to examine childhood in Victorian Britain. In that watershed era, mortality fell, education spread, and the working place stole fewer and fewer children. None of these events occurred as a natural reaction to the abuses of the earliest decades. In Coketown, cited by Dickens in *Hard Times,* "facts" prevailed, and whatever was reflected the inevitable order of things. In a society spared the upheavals of Napoleon's brief new order, and trembling before the respectable Chartists forty years later, there was little natural yeast to leaven the whole. Men had glimpsed change, but they had not lived through the process of forging a new society by righting accumulated wrongs. Such abrupt changes, as thoughtful people conceived, do great harm, and social change based on political radicalism sets afoot changes not glimpsed by the innovators. In postrevolutionary periods, radicals are likely to be as dismayed, in their own way, as those whose world they sought to turn upside-down.

In the absence of a general social upheaval, a situation which Britain escaped in the long peace from Waterloo to Sarajevo, change sprang from no overarching sociopolitical imperative. There was no lack of ideological movements in the century which saw the appearance of Owenism, Marxism, Fourierism, and Phrenology. Theologies proliferated from the finer shadings of Methodism to Mormonism and the visions of Joanna Southcott and Immanuel Swedenborg. Children had a minor place as a movement; for example, reform of factory life included child-workers. The move to dis-establish the Anglican Church incorporated the question of who would indoctrinate little Christians. Accordingly, advocacy on these two fronts encountered resistance from cost-conscious industrialists, and from the seats of episcopal privilege. Neither establishment was antichild, but child advocacy evoked highly effective resistance among powerful, entrenched interests.

The advocates themselves were often of two minds. To be concerned about "the children" meant other people's children to those in a position to make a difference. Other people's children, numerically speaking, meant the poor, and they were an alien race. In his great work on the English constitution, Walter Bagehot (1872) characterized the general population as, "narrow-minded, unintelligent, incurious." Writing in 1841 of his native Manchester, Robert Parkinson asserted that industrialization had polarized the classes; "there is no town in the world where the distance between the rich and the poor is so great, or the barrier between them so difficult to be crossed." Early advocates such as Hannah More wanted the status quo in the sense of the social order; she wanted pious, literate children saved from infidelity but in no way less respectful to their betters who chose to lift them up. This shading of reform to the point that it did not disturb the personal lives of reformers and others in general was evident in several ways. One of the more concrete examples of advocating elevation-without-propinquity was the staircase episode. Russell (1983) reports that the Lecture Theatre of the Royal Institution originally had a separate entrance leading via a staircase to a segregated gallery from which mechanics could observe demonstrations and hear lectures. As a result of objections from regular patrons who did not wish to advance dangerous political ideas such as separate and unequal intellectual training for artisans, the staircase from a sidestreet was pulled down at considerable expense. In this anecdote we see educational reform discounted by class prejudice. Writing of her work with the deserving poor in need of housing, as opposed to the undeserving who needed but did not merit it, Octavia Hill could write patronizingly of her dependents that "they are easily governed by firmness, which they respect much" (Hill 1875). Of course, situations varied from place to place. Then as now, social-class gradients decreased as one moved away from the home counties towards the provinces. That vigorous man of public affairs, Lyon Playfair, later Baron Playfair of St. Andrews, could record his sense of social ease with the schoolmates of his Scottish youth; they met as friends in later years despite his eminence, and he wrote in 1870:

> . . . the son of the minister, the doctor, and the tradesman sit on the same bench with the son of a ploughman. I have just left a Scotch town in which I was at a parochial school, and many a friendly grip of the hand did I get from working men and tradesmen who were schoolfellows with me. Neither of us had lost our respect for the other. . . .

Playfair felt that English elementary schools chose to

> inculcate—humility, obedience, give unto Caesar the things that are Caesar's; pay your taxes and above all things your tithes; touch your hat to the parson, the squire and his lady, and these, in a temporal sense, form the chief end of man. And so village schools became things of small temporal use, but well fitted, as the old phrase went, to keep men satisfied with the sphere in which they were born.

The vigorous Lancashire physician James Kay-Shuttleworth, whose public life lasted about twenty years, was a most effective advocate for education, and the school inspectors he trained and supervised in the 1840s were singularly vigorous and influential. On close inspection Dr. James Kay of the 1832 report on Manchester and the covert manipulator of Privy Council power we know as Sir James Kay-Shuttleworth were not inconsistent. In Kay-Shuttleworth's more discursive writings (Kay-Shuttleworth 1862) we see a grave, unremitting indictment of ordinary people. Schools were antidotes to irresponsible families, and so upheld public order. This is quite different from education as a process of human development or the realization of human potentials; it is a conservative's way of preserving order amidst the unhinging of affairs in the age of steam. In this light, Kay-Shuttleworth's preoccupation with teacher training schemes was the way to perfect the mechanism he substituted for the disreputable, irreligious workingman's family. Education was not the goal, but the means to socialize the rising generation into God-fearing compliance with the ordnances of their betters. One reads in vain within Kay-Shuttleworth's lengthy, thoughtful writings for a glimpse of the child-centeredness he admired in Pestalozzi and the continental reformers; it is Bentham rather than Rousseau who shows the way.

Still loftier was the vision of Lord Ashley, to be styled Lord Shaftes-bury, and recorded for us by Trollope as Mr. Palliser, who succeeded the Duke of Omnium. Shaftesbury was an Evangelical Tory with a deeply religious approach to life. He entered public affairs as an M.P. for Dor-setshire in 1831, a dignified figure who at no time abandoned his con-servative beliefs. In 1840, as Lord Anthony Ashley, he wrote of "the two great demons in morals and politics, Socialism and Chartism." The mass of people he viewed, in the same article titled *Infant Labour,* as "vast multitudes, ignorant and excitable in themselves . . . surrendered . . . to the experimental philosophy of infidels and democrats." Shaftesbury en-tered the world of reform when he responded to Parson Bull's invitation to join the reformers following Michael Sadler's defeat when running for the House of Commons in Leeds. Most of Shaftesbury's knowledge of the evils of factory life and child labor was indirect. In one episode, he paid the writer William Dodd, The Factory Cripple, forty-five shillings per week plus expenses to travel around the country and provide him with vivid reports of egregious conditions. After John Bright attacked his credibility, Dodd left for Massachusetts, but Shaftesbury remained the great advocate. The *Illustrated London News* in 1842 described "this tall and commanding figure, with strongly marked features, intelligent and pleasant in their expression." Summing up Lord Ashley, the future Lord Shaftesbury, the *Illustrated London News* prophetically described him as one "altogether independent of party considerations or party conflicts; he has appealed to broader principles, to more general sympathies; he has advocated the cause of common and general humanity."

In Shaftesbury there is the power of religious conviction turned to the ends of philanthropy and reform. At mid-century, religion was a culture complex of great power, a medium analogous to television today. That is, the pulpit was a source of influence on many matters, and preaching addressed a wide range of social evils as well as doctrinal topics. Victorians were amenable to the words of religious figures, and preachers were a powerful influence on the public mind. Through Shaf-tesbury, the religious impulse reached further expression in the form of his public life. Religion also combatted alcoholism and excessive drink-ing. Father Theobald Mathew of Cork brought his rhetorical skill to this grievous problem and, in an age of sectarian strife, Cardinal Manning joined Protestant speakers on behalf of temperance later in the century. In its own way, this was also child advocacy, for Thomas Barnardo con-cluded that the plight of more than eight of every ten of his early wards was due to parents' abuse of alcohol (Williams 1966). Here too we see that children were indirect beneficiaries of reform, whose primary target was drunken adults.

TABLE 9.1
MID-NINETEENTH-CENTURY RELIGIOUS EDUCATION
SOCIETIES AND THE YEAR OF THEIR FOUNDATION*

Book Society for Promoting Religious Knowledge among the Poor (1750). 7938 volumes issued, many of which were *lent* to the poor.

Stranger's Friend Society (1785). Paid 35,000 visits mostly to the 'destitute sick poor'.

Religious Tract Society (1799). Annual circulation is twenty five million

British and Foreign Bible Society (1804). Issued 26 million bibles ad hoc in 148 languages and dialects. In 1852 the Society issued 1.1 million bibles.

Christian Instruction Society (1825). Visits the poor in hospitals, workhouses, prisons, etc. 814 children induced to attend Sunday schools.

British Reformation Society (1827). Sold 799 books, and gave away 79. Sold 20,666 tracts. Gave away 46,430.

London City Mission (1835). Has 297 agents who made 1.2 million visits to people, and distributed 1.7 million tracts. "236 couples, who had been cohabiting, were induced to marry", in 1852.

Town Missionary and Scripture Readers Society (1837). Has 58 missionaries: induced 886 children to attend Sunday schools.

Weekly Tract Society (1847). Distributed a half million tracts in 1853.

*Adapted from, 1851 Census Great Britain. Report and Tables on Religious Worship England and Wales. *Parliamentary Papers*. 1853.

Personal Philanthropy

Not every advocate for childhood in the nineteenth century led a national movement or became a public figure. As the century opened, Peter Bedford, the Spitalfields philanthropist, conducted his efforts among the poor, a contribution not greatly remembered today. Also early in the century was the benevolent and occasional employer of the bootmaker, John O'Neill. For many years Mr. Moxhay gave O'Neill a shoulder of mutton for Christmas. O'Neill (1869) also records that Moxhay spontaneously gave him a good suit of clothes on the occasion of going to meet a publisher. Still more private was the dedication of William Busfield. Described in 1862 by J.T. Ward as the "heir to two squirearchical families," Busfield recalled:

> I had found a little factory slave half-buried in a snow drift, fast
> asleep . . . the icy hand of death had congealed its blood and paralyzed
> its limbs. I aroused it from its stupor and saved its life. From that day I
> became a 'Ten Hours Bill' man.

In his memoirs, Lyon Playfair (Reed 1899) recorded his patronage of a
deaf and blind girl, Edith Thomas, at the Perkins Institute for the Blind
in Boston, Massachusetts, in the 1880s. Playfair was greatly moved by
the plight of the child and gave her presents. He visited her over several
years and engaged in correspondence.

Perhaps the most common form of philanthropy was the practice
of domestic visitation. Conducted by the middle-class churchgoers for
the most part, it consisted of visits to the homes of the poor in order to
promote churchgoing and other religious practices. Secondarily, it provided an opportunity for instruction in sobriety, polite manners, and
sound parenting. The Christian Instruction Society and the Home Mission Society were two prominent organizations. Rack (1973) reported
that the C.I.S. had over 2,500 home visitors reaching 60,000 homes by
1840. In the secular sphere, the Ladies Sanitary Association was active
and produced pamphlets and verse through which they stressed the value
of fresh air, cleanliness, and clean clothes.

Influenced by his own poverty-stricken youth in the West County in
the 1820s and 1830s, J. Passmore Edwards used his wealth in later years
to help bookish, ambitious young people. In memoirs published posthu-
mously, Edwards (1906) presented a list of which he was most proud; it
was the names of communities in which he had founded libraries.
Equally firm in his intent to help educate the young, "Hole of Leeds"—
James Hole—designed boxes to protect books as they circulated among
Yorkshire villages. By this mechanism, village readers had access on a
circulating basis to large numbers of books. The books came to the
readers, unlike the more conventional form of readers coming to libraries. In Passmore Edwards and James Hole we see the love of books
translated into philanthropy made accessible in a routine way to young
and old. It seems quite unlikely that village readers had heard of either
man, their philanthropy and advocacy being discreet as well as pervasive.

In order to convey the range of reforming zeal, we need to move
from the reality of reform and advocacy into the realm generally known
as Utopianism. While Hole and Carpenter strived to make society more
effective now, there were people who chose to speculate on the form that
a thoroughly radical approach, one built on no existing foundation,
might take. Utopians began with Plato's Republic and continue today. In

1849, James Buckingham published his version of his model town, *Victoria,* and proposed the following:

> Education also to be given to all the children in the community, without individual cost, from the earliest age up to fifteen; during which, for a certain number of hours every day, in the intervals between the short period of their labour in light work suited to their ages, and the open air exercise necessary for the full development of their health, every child, male and female, to be taught at the least, reading, writing, arithmetic, the outlines of geography, botany, geology, mineralogy, natural history, and chemistry; with the addition of the French language, as the most available for foreign literature and travel; also as much of drawing as to give them facility in committing to paper forms of objects, and views of nature, all which is eminently conducive to accuracy of perception and correctness of taste; and so much of music as to be able to perform on at least one instrument, or to join, at sight, in any vocal composition in parts, either for devotion, or enjoyment. Beyond this, care to be taken to watch the development of peculiar aptitudes or capacities or tastes for certain arts and sciences, in order that the children possessing them, may have their faculties cultivated to the highest point of perfection to which they can attain—for their own happiness and the benefit and honour of the community to which they belong.

It is hard to quarrel with Utopianists, especially those who do not take concrete steps to form communities. In this regard, Buckingham stands in contrast to Robert Owen, who tried and failed at New Harmony, but left a charming community which thrives on his memory today, and where Owen is a common name amongst the townspeople. Buckingham can also be contrasted with Mary Carpenter and Thomas Barnardo, who moved in the realm of everyday events to build a better world.
Mary Carpenter (1807–1877). Appropriately described by Manton (1976) as the quintessential Victorian spinster, Mary Carpenter worked in her father's school and served a period of two years as a governess. In 1846, she founded a ragged school in Bristol and, subsequently, founded a reformatory school at Kingswood, which led to her Red Lodge in 1854. Relatively early in this phase of her career she published her book on the perishing and dangerous classes, in 1851. With Matthew Davenport Hill, she organized the first major conference on delinquency two years later. Mary Carpenter was bright and could be acerbic in her comments, especially towards the work at Parkhurst (Schupf 1971). She made one trip to the United States and Canada, and made two trips to India. The striking feature of Mary Carpenter's work is that she worked on a daily basis with perishing, dangerous, and delinquent young people

personally (and not always with great success), while also addressing the broader policy issues of what society as a whole needed to do.

Thomas Barnardo (1845–1905). At the age of twenty-one, he left Dublin and trained as a medical missionary for a life of service in China. Barnardo taught in a ragged school for a period, and encountered the problems of poor children first-hand. In 1870, he opened his first home for children, an enterprise now in its second century. Barnardo became a public figure; he dined with Lord Shaftesbury and attracted a good deal of support. In Barnardo's case, religious conviction in the broadest sense disposed him to a life of service. However, like William Busfield, it was an encounter with the reality of children's lives which goaded him into a particular style of child advocacy. Barnardo prowled the alleys behind main streets and found homeless children. He sheltered them and fed them and sent thousands to Australia and Canada under schemes still active in the middle of the twentieth century. In the period 1867–1910, Barnardo is credited with assisting the emigration of over twenty thousand children (Johnson 1913)—by methods not always legal—however moral the purpose. The years have not been kind to philanthropic emigration from Britain, and the literature on the fate of the children in their new homes, especially Canada, has not been as salutary in local eyes as it was in the benign plans of Barnardo and his colleagues (Jordan 1985b).

In the last three decades of the nineteenth century, the "ever-open door" of Dr. Barnardo's homes sheltered nearly eight thousand children under his National Waif's Association, and generally had about one thousand babies in care. In Dr. Barnardo's Homes we see today a living link to one of the original and enduring Victorian philanthropists. Often overlooked is Thomas Barnardo's effective campaigning against alcoholism and excessive drinking. In the early 1870s, he purchased the Edinburgh Castle gin palace and converted it into a social center for the district run on temperance lines. There, he also gave his Waif's Suppers, free meals for children by means of tickets given out by teachers and others who knew deserving children (Williams 1966).

Royal Society for the Prevention of Cruelty to Children. Much of the endemic violence of Victorian life was aimed at spouses and at animals; children were not excluded, but their situation was hidden behind the front door and behind the fright of children whose complicity was obtained by the threat of further beatings. This oppressed minority had no voice, constituting a province whose subjects were abused and exploited by violent adults. Such behavior towards horses, whose floggings were evident in the streets, had led to societies opposed to cruelty to animals and, in 1832, to laws proposed to protect them. From that precedent, the Liverpool merchant Thomas Agnew founded a society for the prevention of cruelty to children in 1883. In the course of the next decade, other large towns also established societies and, eventually, the London society, under the Rev. Benjamin Waugh became the chief agency. With Queen Victoria's patronage in 1890, and royal charter in 1895, the association of societies evolved into a single society whose local activities were controlled by Waugh. The society's journal, *The Child's Guardian,* had a monthly circulation of twenty thousand, according to Behlmer (1982). Benjamin Waugh is not widely known, but he was a superb organizer. In some respects, Waugh and Barnardo were in competition for the largesse of the same London-based philanthropists. To his credit, Waugh created an organization whose activities outlasted his own personal efforts. Laws punishing cruelty to children were enacted, and thousands of abusive adults were successfully prosecuted.

Voluntarism. Not every organization which benefitted children did so directly. In some instances, children became beneficiaries of movements intended to promote other causes. In 1833, Manchester and Oldham Radicals, some of them mill owners led by John Fielden, formed the National Regeneration Society to promote an eight-hour day (Gadian 1978). Success came in the next decade with passage of the Ten Hour legislation. Leeds, forty miles to the east, was a cauldron of radical thoughts; there, James Hole and colleagues formed the Leeds Redemption Society, in 1845, aimed at reducing ignorance of all kinds—academic and sanitary, crime and poverty—among the working classes (Harrison 1954). This approach to change by constructive association of thoughtful people continued. Later, Leeds saw the birth of the Band of Hope temperance movement for children.

Social Science Association. In the twenty-nine years of its existence, (1857–1886), the National Association for the Promotion of Social Science met annually. Members discussed papers on a variety of subjects from law, where many of its suggestions were enacted into legislation, to childhood, a topic on which reformers thundered for decades. Women were active in founding the Association (Cobb 1861) and were especially effective in three subordinate organizations, the Ladies Sanitary Association, the Workhouse Visiting Association, and the Society for the Employment of Women. The Association eventually dissolved owing to some internal problems but also owing to the rise of narrower associations less global in scope. However, prominent and distinguished people addressed the Association, and the transactions of annual meetings present the names of virtually all the great figures of the second half of the nineteenth century identified with philanthropy and the welfare of children. Goldman (1986) has described how the Association became the vehicle for mid-Victorian liberal thought.

The Royal Statistical Society. In the 1830s, the statistical section of the British Association, known to Dickens as the "Mudfog Association for the Advancement of Everything" (Howarth 1922), was home to the "statists." They were a group of men whose goal was to describe in empirical rather than theoretical terms the nature of society. Here, too, the object of study was not children, but they were inescapable to statists drawing up pictures of communities. John Heywood's study of the village of Miles Platting near Manchester showed that three-fifths of the children had no schooling whatsoever (Heywood 1839). In his paper in the first volume of the *Statistical Society of London,* Heywood set forth the objective of the Statists

> The minute analysis of the internal structure of society appears to the author to constitute the leading object of statistical sciences; and the investigation of the physical, moral, intellectual and religious condition of the human race is the chosen occupation of the statistical enquirer.

Until the 1890s, the journal was the repository of a broad range of papers, most of which we would call public health, all sharing a penchant for descriptive statistics. It was only with the last decade of the century that specifically mathematical papers began to appear. Then, for a considerable period, they were paralleled by highly detailed descriptive papers on, for example, the wage structure of various occupations by A.L. Bowly. Also, some of the papers provided excellent retrospective summaries of data over several decades of the nineteenth century. We note, in passing, the same kind of valuable information in the Census reports, especially that of 1911. By turning to the extensive tables in the journal, we grasp the intensity of the Statists. Cullen (1975) has pointed to urbanization as the theme which preoccupied them, with the working class being the persistent object of inquiry. As one reads papers in the journal over the course of the nineteenth century, the now-familiar confusion of concomitants with causes is apparent, especially in the relationship between illiteracy on the one hand and crime and alcoholism on the other. Lacking inferential statistical tests, the reports strike today's reader as overstating conclusions. And yet without the statistics on social and, to employ a word used with ease by the statists, *moral* problems of the times, reform would have been delayed even longer. In that sense, much of the reforming zeal of the Statistical Society was propagandizing, but it was also irreplaceable. Comparative infant mortality rates by occupational level were in the Gradgrind tradition of "Facts," and could not be refuted.

Emigration of Children. Not every effort to help children in the nineteenth century was successful. Evolution of Parkhurst Prison to provide special training for young delinquents became something of a dead-end because planning failed to include placement after discharge. Transportation to Point Puer near Hobart, Tasmania, helped some Parkhurstians, but transportation was itself an abusive public policy. In the private sector of Victorian affairs, philanthropy was not necessarily more effective and, occasionally, the best of intentions led to harm to the benefactors. The best example is the ill-fated work of the Children's Friend Society.

In 1831, Captain Edward Pelham Brenton and friends established a small program of agricultural training for boys. Three years later, they moved the program to Hackney Wick and incorporated the Children's Friend Society "for the reclamation of the destitute and vagrant young of the metropolis, scarcely one in 100 of whom ever heard anything of their duty to God or man," in the words of Mr. Serjeant Adams (Children's Friend Society 1840). Their major strategem, beyond opening institutions at Chiswick and Hackney Wick, was to send children to the Cape of Good Hope for apprenticeship and education.

In 1838, young William Henry Bay wrote the following to his mother at Walham Green from Great Constantia, about twelve miles from Capetown:

> . . . learning no trade, but am only a servant . . . and have not the best of masters. I am neither found in caps or shoes . . . I am placed among a parcel of slaves . . . there is no difference made between us. I would not advise you to make any complaint . . . it will only make bad worse, and it will be of no use . . . and will cause me to be treated worse. . . .

One year later, there was an inquiry under police auspices in Marylebone, and the following exchange was recorded between the Magistrate and the boys' mother.

> Mr. RAWLINSON.—What steps did you take on receiving the letters I have read?

> Mrs. BAY.—I . . . laid the letters before the Children's Friend Society's committee; but Captain Brenton, on looking at them, treated me with contempt.

> Inspector Tedman, of the D division, here addressed the magistrate, setting forth that one of his sergeants, named Hardy, had, upon the

flattering promises held out to him by the Society referred to, sent his
son to the Cape about four years ago. He had repeatedly written to him,
but could gain no tidings as to where he was, nor the name of the person
by whom he was employed (Police April 9, 1839).

Subsequently, the British public expressed indignation, it being generally
supposed that, first, boys were sold into slavery in South Africa for
profit, and second, that they were invariably ill-used by their masters.
The situation in South Africa has been elucidated by Bradlow (1984),
whose examination of local documents shows that influential people at
the Cape saw boys and girls as cheap labor vital to development of the
colony. They and others did not discriminate the poor and respectable
from juvenile, hardened delinquents. All were "appropriate," a term
which, on closer examination, might mean little more than bondage, in
view of the superficial mode of supervising their life on remote laagers.
As cheap labor, the children would have been doubly-appealing; they
represented a savings on the investment in labor, and they were used to
close supervision and discipline from their days at sea. Having no one
else to turn to in South Africa, they were scarcely likely to cause trouble
for the farmers who took them in.

Eventually, letters from children such as that written by William
Bay, and the prior case of young Edward Trubshaw, led to an outcry in
London. The entire affair was hard on the elderly Captain Brenton, who
died from a heart attack attributed by his Society colleagues to the harassment he had received in the streets and in the newspapers. On May
25, 1841, in a general meeting at Exeter Hall the Society discussed its
diminished income, its responsibility for two institutions, and the plight
of the children in South Africa. On a motion by Mr. Gally Knight, the
Society voted to dissolve itself. Thus ended a philanthropic movement
whose demise was the result of a lack of common purpose agreed to in
London and in Capetown. At the Antipodes, the problem was compounded by the Dutch-English conflict, and by the Black-White difference, both of which led to dissimilar views of why the children were at
Capetown in the first place.

Undoubtedly, Captain Brenton died an unhappy, disappointed
man, not the first or the last to see good intentions confounded by the
realities of human nature and by disharmony of purpose and means. The
highest and loftiest of motives need efficient, enlightened bureaucracies
to reach fruition. Such resources were uncommon in the nineteenth century, and would have been compromised at best by the immense distance
involved. In the 1830s, the world's cities were as far apart as they had
been at any time in recorded history. Only in the distant future were fast

ships to carry messages and people by steam and screw, and communication by electrical impulses over wire was even more remote. The fiasco of the children sent to Capetown has some similarity to the Point Puer episode in Van Diemen's Land a few years later. A further link is that some of the Children's Friend Society boys left South Africa for Australia, an instance of being thrown out of the frying pan for something not demonstrably better.

In the following decades there was no shortage of Britons advocating emigration of children. With zeal, which seemed to some of their Millenarian fellow pietists to exceed God's plan, they interfered in the "natural" course of events. Children were rounded up and, even when they had adult relations, were sometimes shipped abroad with an arrogance we can only view with amazement. Through the efforts of Maria Rye, Annie McPherson, and Thomas Barnardo, thousands of children found themselves off to a new life in a place they had scarcely heard of. Canada alone took in eighty thousand juveniles in the half-century ending around 1925.

What tends to be slighted in this expression of Victorian and Edwardian high-handed altruism are two elements. First, there is the fact that emigrants become immigrants and an entirely new episode begins, one which has its own hagiology and history. In the case of Australia, there is the story of Caroline Chisholm, who reached New South Wales from India in 1838. Through her efforts hundred of single females and entire families began to build modern Australia. Unlike the zealots, she saw that young people needed family life. She concentrated her efforts around that theme calling wives and children "God's police" (Shann 1930).

In the case of the third depository for emigrant children, Canada, events began later. They entered the final decades of the century when high-handedness was less tolerated and public policy was open to dispute by a literate, experienced, and well-travelled public. For this aspect of advocacy and reform, the smaller distance to Canada and the comparative experience of the United States led to a shrewder appraisal of child emigration. In 1884, Forster had argued, Stay and Starve; Go and Thrive. However, thriving was not automatic, and life from the sender's end is not the same as life experienced by the immigrant and, increasingly, by his host. It was also a case of chickens coming home to roost.

The second aspect of Victorian child emigration began with the fact that Mary Carpenter and her fellow reformers had painted a dark picture of childhood in order to arouse the slumbering Victorian conscience. She spoke movingly of the children of the perishing classes to middle-class Britons, and she painted a garish picture of starving, delinquency-prone children. Her recital of their problems was harrowing, if only because it was true in so many cases. Her listeners were galvanized by the reformers' catalogue of skinny, near-criminal, alcohol-prone young proletarians sympathetic to Chartism, republicanism, and religious indifference. In less lurid colors, the children were also undersized city dwellers, plagued by skin and eye problems, of undeveloped musculature, pleasure-prone, and ignorant. Their intended Canadian homeland was bitterly cold in winter, largely rural, and conformist. When we put the characteristics of hosts and young emigrants side by side, the scene was ripe for misunderstanding. The Canadian farmer found the young immigrant one more mouth to feed while not knowing one end of a scythe from the other. Into the self-contained farm families of Saskatchewan and Ontario came street-arabs with unfathomable accents and a taste for city lights. When adopted, they were unpaid servants; when indentured on a farm they were proposed for a lifestyle they wished to flee. The Canadian social welfare leader, Charlotte Whitton, is described by Rooke and Schnell (1981) as documenting the argument, by selective use of case histories, that young immigrants from Britain were undermining Canadian stock with their bad blood, criminal taint, and other traits, which, in the world of the Eugenics movement, would bring Canada to pandemic idiocy in a few generations. Of course, the core concepts were Mary Carpenter's, and the decades of the nineteenth and twentieth centuries heard them on both sides of the Atlantic.

What was a good reason for sending children abroad was a poor reason for accepting them in Canada. Late nineteenth-century Canada was not the empty, docile colony which Australia had been. A shrewd, self-contained Canadian yeomanry had no wish to share its bounty with just anyone. Over time, Canadian laws and regulations imposed order and justice on a process which had good motives but frequently replaced lack of supervision in British towns with a lack of supervision on the Canadian Prairie. Slowly, Canadian procedures imposed controls and children received protection from the abuses which had led to their emigration originally. Of course, most children were well-received and cared for in Canada, but many were not. To the clash of cultures, a world of mild climates and town dwellings replaced by the long night of a prairie winter, was added exploitation of bewildered children. Not uncommonly, the clash of a city child fresh from London streets with farm families, whose youngest could gather eggs and play an economically useful role, turned into outright rejection. Young girls were exploited, and when pregnant, expelled from the family as demonstrably corrupt. Parr (1980) reported cases of children shipped back to Britain as incorrigible. Others returned in order to exorcise demons of lost parents and families. Of course, many stayed, and their descendents are found all over Canada.

As one looks at the entire process of child emigration, several things stand out. There is the political theme of empty colonies in New Zealand, Canada, and Australia as a handy dumping-ground for surplus or dangerous sectors of the population. However, it was a largely negative vision because it denied the central role of family in forming mature men and women. In the case of children, there was the discontinuity of reformers' words coming home to roost as colonists became articulate and saw danger to their hard-won achievements in the very traits calling for child emigration. Finally, in all places deemed hospitable there was failure to provide much beyond biblical aphorisms from which children cast among strangers could seek comfort. The resulting maladjustment, for good reason, led to problems and clashes with hosts. Better screening of would-be emigrants before and after the voyage and supervision of homes used for placement were steps which increased the success of an idea which changed the lives of children irrevocably.

From the point of view of child welfare, the failure to select discrete groups of problem children begat the confusion. Much of the difficulty had its origin in the failure to discriminate delinquents from other youngsters, and to view literate, respectable children from poor but moral homes in the same way as young career criminals. Accordingly, their mentors in South Africa and Canada saw much to be wary of in the appearance and manner of their immigrant children. Under the best of circumstances it takes very little to give a bad name to a group; in this instance, young people who were undesirables in London were no less undesirable on the frontier. Police Sergeant Hardy's boy was undoubtedly conventional and moral. However, he probably did not appear particularly fetching to people in Cape Town after the long voyage across the equator in a sailing ship. The Society's collaborators there would have been more struck by junior delinquents than by the moiety of respectable, earnest lads meriting a fresh start and more education. We may suppose that written characters accompanied the young immigrants; however, their subsequent treatment suggests that such hypothetical documentation meant little in regions needing workers to run farms. One can only speculate on the inner damage to children by displacement, cultural alienation, and occasional cruelty. It seems likely that there were resilient children who turned out well despite their placement in unsympathetic homes. However, there appear to have been many whose psychological makeup was scarred or deformed in a migratory process whose founders perceived a clear beginning but gave little thought to the end of the hegira.

TABLE 9.2
ESTIMATED CHILD EMIGRATION, AGES 0–14 YEARS, IN
DECENNIAL YEARS TO EXTRA-EUROPEAN DESTINATION*

Year	British N. America	United States	Australia, N. Zealand	Total
1820	6,327	2,382	—	8,709
1830	10,793	8,782	438	20,013
1840	11,400	14,346	5,594	42,740
1850	11,635	78,768	5,662	96,065
1860	3,464	30,974	8,603	43,041
1870	12,494	69,410	6,040	87,944
1880	10,387	91,076	9,005	110,468
1890	11,292	82,666	7,635	101,593

*From Jordan (1985b).

The volume of children fourteen years and under who emigrated to other countries in the nineteenth century was enormous. Beginning as a trickle, as best we can tell from less than complete statistics, in 1820 North America was the major objective. The proportion going to the United States was always the largest by far, reaching the rate of seventy-eight thousand in 1840. Two decades later, after the Civil War in the United States had ended, it recovered to a rate of sixty-nine thousand per year. The rate to Canada fluctuated around an annual rate of ten thousand. Emigration to Australia and New Zealand was even less, a fact which is not surprising considering the enormous distance and proportionate expense and travel time. Much of the vigor of emigration to the colonies in southeast Asia did not occur until the end of the nineteenth century and the first decade of the twentieth.

Government Action

In the face of traditional distaste for laws inhibiting John Bull's personal liberty, the idea of inquiry into problems by Select Committees and Royal Commissions came slowly. Across the nineteenth century, parliamentary bodies looked into a variety of problems affecting children. Armed with authority to summons, the reformers could count on compulsion when the network of like-minded people could not quite do the job. In the massive volumes of Parliamentary Papers are found facts and opinions, and masses of propaganda for good ends tied to particularly favored means. In the case of Commissioners and Sub-Commissioners, they ranged far and wide gathering information and providing rich appendices for exploration. Tremenheere, testy and lacking tact, would file his detailed reports. The Rev. J.C. Clay would provide documentary evidence, and Kay-Shuttleworth would weave his Inspectors' report into a seamless garment. In these early bureaucrats and allies we see the beginning of a powerful establishment. Together with the medical-social reformers, they constituted an effective force for good. Once information had accrued and hearings were conducted, reform could count on its friends to speak up. Shaftesbury's oratorical powers on behalf of remedies for demonstrated evils were substantial.

And so, as Table 9.3 illustrates, the topics followed each other across the decades. In the table, we refer to education, but in other spheres there were the apprentices acts, the factory acts, the infant registration act, the food acts, and the penal reform acts. All became permanent reforms through the agency of laws. Government, consequently, grew as employees were needed to collate surveys and to enforce regulation. Some laws distributed funds and others abolished obsolete laws such as those requiring capital punishment. Many of the actions of government turn out to have been piecemeal and not thought through. In the case of the factory acts intended to protect children, it was possible to split work shifts and so evade the spirit of the law while observing its letter. Another example from the same set of laws was the early practice of restricting laws to factories engaged using a particular fabric—e.g., cotton—and leaving untouched identical abuses in factories using other fabrics. Even when all fabrics were encompassed, the child laboring for long hours in brickyards was left unprotected.

As we look at the pieces of legislation in a series, we see gross problems solved and, subsequently, finer discriminations used. In the case of the young, a persistent problem was treating all children as hardened criminals. It is true that many were, but people who should have recognized generalizations when they saw them tended to make broad indictments of children. When coupled with incomplete planning, as at Parkhurst, well-meant training led to nothing in the way of supervision or placement for boys released but only nominally rehabilitated. With Forster's 1870 Education Act, we begin to see action at a national level. Not every child went to school after 1870, but the Act set the stage for subsequent refinements, all of which assumed some rather modern concepts of education as a national responsibility to be met in several ways acceptable to local citizens and religious bodies.

TABLE 9.3
ADVOCACY AND REFORM IN EDUCATION

YEAR	MECHANISM	TOPIC
1816–18	Parliamentary Committee	Education of the lower orders in the Metropolis
1834	Parliamentary Committee	The State of Education
1839	Privy Council	Creation of the Education Committee
1846	Education Committee	Minute on Pupil Teachers
1847	Parliamentary Committee	Education in Wales
1861	Newcastle Report	Education in England
1862	Education Committee	Revision of the criteria for reimbursement by Lowe
1864	Clarendon Report	Revenues and administration of Public Schools
1868	Taunton Report	Condition of endowed schools
1870	Forster's 1870 Act	Education as a National function
1872	Devonshire Report	Science Education
1881	Aberdare Report	Higher Education in Wales
1882–84	Samuelson Report	Technical Education
1888	Cross Report	Elementary Education
1895	Bryce Report	Secondary Education

Scotland and Ireland

Scotland. Perhaps the most interesting example of initiatives on behalf of children is the development of programs for poor children in Aberdeen after 1840. Our grasp of the stages of development of services for poor and neglected children is due largely to the writings of Alexander Thomson of Banchory (1852). A firm believer in strict observance of the Sabbath and of the evils wrought by drink, Thomson showed great sympathy for children. He credited Mr. Sheriff Watson with founding the "Aberdeen Industrial Feeding Schools," but noted that the originality of the system resided in coordination of elements to be found severally and separately in various schools and workhouses. The salient elements of the "Aberdeen Experiment," as Thomson styled it, were food, training, and religious instruction; to a lesser extent, clothing was supplied.

In 1840, Watson counted 280 children under age fourteen who maintained themselves by begging; 77 of them had spent some time in prison in that year. In October 1841, a room and a teacher were retained after a public subscription raised one hundred pounds in Aberdeen. Twenty poor boys were admitted for five and a half days to undergo four hours of instruction, five hours of work and three meals per day. On Sunday mornings, there was a short session of breakfast and a brief religious service, and there was an evening service and supper. By 1844, there were sixty-nine boys, of whom four were under seven years, sixty between seven and twelve years, and the oldest five were thirteen. Thirty-six boys were fatherless and four were motherless. By 1845, twenty-four of seventy-two boys enrolled had attended for two years or more. In the years 1841–51, the peak of success was 1848, when twenty-eight of sixty-six boys found employment. Thomson made the point that the pupils were from the poorest circumstances and not merely sons of working people.

In 1843, a school for very poor girls was opened with three pupils, and the enrollment later rose to sixty. Operations ran along the lines of the boys school, although the costs were higher due to less income from the work performed by the girls. In 1847, the sponsors had a falling out and a second girls school appeared; the original was known as "Sheriff Watson's Female Industrial School," and the new school was styled the "Girl's Industrial School of Aberdeen."

Enrollment of about 130 boys and girls, two-thirds of whom were between eight and eleven years old, left many deserving children uncared for. In particular, the prevalence of begging children, proscribed by law but still much in evidence on the streets, remained a problem. A third school associated with a soup kitchen opened in 1845, when the police rounded up seventy-five children. All of them, Thomson states, were below the level of those attending the three schools, and only four of them could read. Writing in 1852 Thomson concluded that

> a few years ago there were 20 such children in Aberdeen, who had no visible means of subsistence but by begging and stealing. A begging child is now seldom to be seen in our streets or in the county.

Ireland. On John Bull's Other Island, in Bernard Shaw's phrase, the situation was unique. The machinery of government had been held firmly by the Protestant minority, and public welfare was used for sectarian ends. The tradition of schooling for ordinary people's children had been extinguished by the penal laws and there was no operating system of schools supported by central and local funds. Hedge schools provided some schooling in the early decades, and Bible societies provided instruction designed to turn Catholic children into Protestants. Of course, in the history of Ireland, poverty and hunger made schooling less fundamental than shelter, food, and clothing. These necessities were provided by orphan societies of all religious persuasions.

The most significant social agency affecting children was the Dublin Foundling Institution, a name and organization grafted on to an existing workhouse in the eighteenth century. The early history summarized by Robins (1980) was tragic, and for decades consignment to this institution was a virtual death sentence. In some instances, this was because infants died of neglect; and in others, death followed neglect by foster parents with whom children were placed. Fundamental was the discrepancy between the number of children to be cared for and the administration of the program. Managers ranged from incompetent to cruel, and boards of supervisors were consistently negligent. With a second, smaller institution at Cork we encompass virtually all of the public provisions for institutional care of foundlings in Ireland.

A parallel track lay within the workhouse movement and the Houses of Industry. These public institutions required work for food and generally resembled their English counterparts. However, they were strained beyond tolerance by the Famine in the years 1845–49, the result of which was one of the world's massive displacements by death, migration, and wandering of a people. In the process, parents died and left children to be tended; but children were abandoned, among whom the more fortunate were formally committed at the workhouse door. We use the term relatively because workhouses were overcrowded, and infections raged through them. Robins (1980) reported that there were 68,402 children in workhouse care in 1852; interestingly, only 4,431 of them were illegitimate, a rate of 6%. Some of the workhouse children were sent to Australia, where girls were in great demand.

The progress of the last half of the nineteenth century began on the reality of Irish life. The people were at odds with the Pale and with Westminster. Religious questions created malicious legislation and, proportionately, lowered public confidence in State-sponsored schemes. The Famine unhinged the rural economy, and the welfare of children was submerged in the general question of the survival of the population. The few towns of any size were overrun by desperate people, and children were lost in the sea of the demoralized and starving. For them, government action, meaning Dublin or Westminster, was too little and too late.

In general, the care of children in Ireland improved in the decades after the Famine. An infusion of ideas crossed the Irish Sea with a version of the Great Exhibition, a meeting of the Social Science Association, and establishment of the Statistical and Social Inquiry Society. From Ireland came Dr. Thomas Barnardo, whose nineteenth-century zeal was to be felt on behalf of children in many parts of the world. A second Irishman whose zeal did much to prevent abuse of children occasioned by drunkenness, in an earlier period, was Father Theobald Matthew of Cork.

Dynamics of Change

Our subject is children, but an understanding of the ways in which this powerless minority slowly moved from the squalor of the early years of the century to the recognizable outlines of the imminent welfare state requires that we alter the focus. Princess Victoria's England had institutions such as a central bank, constitutional government, and a sense of identity, all of which were to prove instruments of national progress in the decades to come. Within that matrix, the actors took their places. Progressive legislators were elected to the Commons and were aided by sympathetic figures in another place. A burgeoning middle class, especially the medical and legal professions, applied science to social problems by defining them and by measuring their costs. Evangelical enthusiasms influenced all classes and brought a sense of personal responsibility into public questions. The combined efforts of middle-class reformers and evangelicals created legislation. In time, reformed institutions, especially education, created a new, literate working class who demanded political and social privilege based on personal achievement.

Increasingly, well-organized ordinary people extracted further reform as the price of support at the ballot box.

But change was not uniformly welcome or invariably positive. The reformed Poor Law produced terrible hardships, and economic growth spawned evil practices. The workhouse became the repository for those who failed in the grim struggle to earn a living. Class tensions persisted, and the rancor may be glimpsed in the title of Michael Sadler's pamphlet (1834), "A Letter to those Sleek, Pious, Holy and Devout Dissenters, Messrs. Get-All, Keep-All, Grasp-All, Scrape-All, Whip-All, Gull-All, Cheat-All, Cant-All, Work-All, Sneak-All, Lie-Well, Swear-Well, Scratch-'em and Company . . ." Among enlightened people the problem was felt to be a lack of noblesse oblige, a moral failure of the privileged, to supervise the great mass of humanity. The great popularity of social reforms reported from Elberfeld was that they institutionalized control of the poor by the middle classes. Writing in the *Saturday Review* in 1839, J.R. Green urged his readers to modify for insular use, but then apply vigorously, the Elberfeld practice by which the bourgeois supervised several poor families. The latter would have their morality restored by the paternal supervision of their betters who, in turn, would have their position and status buttressed, and the proper order of things would prevail as ordained by an English God. Not everyone agreed that the German model of reform from above was suitable. Indeed, a product of the *gymnasium* in Elberfeld, Friedrich Engels of Barmen, was to influence twentieth-century history to the extent that an all-excluding State would tolerate no philanthropic or ideological rival from the private sector. The brothers James Kay-Shuttleworth and Joseph Kay saw Swiss and Dutch reforms as suitable to the Briton's temperament, but they still looked to continental models modified by a national tradition of voluntarism and private association of philanthropists and public-minded people. Hugh Seymour Tremenheere noted in 1869 that popular education required social consensus in order to be effective. He reported that schooling was successful in Frankfort because popular culture supported it.

The missing element was the absence of a strong central government, in the continental tradition of a powerful bureaucracy implementing clear national policy. Victoria's Britain absentmindedly gathered a second empire after losing a continent in 1776. The prevailing color red on the globe was as much the accident of events turning out better than expected as the expression of a relentless bureaucratic will in Whitehall. In contrast, centralized Prussia had model legislation on child welfare as early as 1828, but for nonhumanitarian reasons. General-Leutnant Von Horn had pointed out to Friedrich Wilhelm III that army conscripts from

factory districts were more likely to be unfit for service than those from
the country. As a result, Minister Von Rochow promulgated ten regulations on factory work for children which prescribed educational and
religious training (Anton 1953). After the Franco-Prussian war, physical
training entered the elementary curriculum of British schools, and sometimes it came nakedly as military training; the lessons were absorbed
slowly but inevitably as the "degeneracy" problem weighed on the minds
of thoughtful people.

While it took the pressure of trade and geopolitical considerations
to bring a sense of urgency to building a national agenda for social
reform, children being its implicit beneficiaries, there had been consensus among thoughtful men on how to formulate public policy empiri-
cally since the 1830s. Samuel Hare, President of the Leeds Statistical
Society in 1838, presented a Benthamite proposal for inquiries to be
conducted by other local statistical societies for the British Association.

I.   Physical Statistics; relating to Topography, and etc.
II. Vital Statistics; relating to the Physical Being of Man.
III. Mental Statistics; relating to the Intellectual and Moral Being of
     Man.
IV. Economic Statistics: relating to the Social Condition of Man.
V.   Miscellaneous.

(Hare 1839)

The value of social statistics was evident in the same year, when the army
concluded that it should reduce the period of service in the West Indies
from ten to three years, and decreased use of food salted for preservation. The Editor of the Statistical Society's journal pointed out:

> It is thus that statistical investigations may be rendered available to the
> best of all purposes, that of improving the condition, increasing the
> health, and diminishing the sufferings and mortality of our countrymen
> (Note 1839).

One year later, Thomas Tooke, T. Southwood Smith, Leonard Horner,
and Robert J. Saunders could assert for the Children's Employment
Commission to their Sub-Commissioners:

> Childhood is no less essentially the period of the development of the
> mental faculties, on the culture and development of which, at this tender
> age, the intellectual, moral, and religious qualities and habits of the
> future being almost wholly depend . . . You have undertaken the task of

collecting, from the various sources which will be pointed out to you, the information necessary to arrive at a just conclusion on these deeply interesting and important subjects . . . (Appendix 1841).

The information referred to acquired clarity. In the Factory Inspectors' reports in the 1830s and 1840s, children's measurements had been lumped together in a fashion which reduced their impact. By the 1880s, the physical measurement of children—for example, data reported to the British Association in 1883—is quite recognizable to the modern student of development. By the 1860s, the army had reduced the mortality rate of soldiers in Britain from 17.5 to 8.5 per thousand men (Hole 1866). In 1899, numerical description and mathematical analysis assumed its modern form. In that year, G. Udney Yule published "An Investigation Into the Causes of Changes in Pauperism in England, Chiefly During the Last Two Intercensal Decades." In this model paper, Yule assembled data from workhouse Unions and proceeded to undertake the laborous task of generating regression equations in order to test explicit, quantified changes in local practices. The paper reads well to the modern mind, for whom the calculations by Yule are accomplished by software and computers in mere moments. In Yule's paper we see culmination of the trend since the 1830s to describe things numerically. However, Yule added regression equations, thereby ushering in the modern age of policy studies on social questions. The development of factor analysis (Cattell 1953) and multiple linear regression (McNeil, Kelly and McNeil 1975) expanded the study of social questions in the twentieth century.

In the social sphere, the Victorians grouped the poor into deserving and undeserving; this was an irrelevance based on the pervasive idea that the poor merited social services on the basis of character. Today, we see our own interests at stake, if only indirectly, in helping families in distress. In the early decades, reformers and child advocates saw only children in general needing help. Hardened young criminals were lumped together with the children of respectable but unemployed mechanics. Similarly, the lad who stole from the Squire's apple tree was treated as an old lag. As late as 1860, and despite the influence of Mary Carpenter, the Dean of Ely described the class of juvenile criminals as

> boys who play at pitch-farthing at street-corners, or hang about railway stations, or sweep crossings, or beg for coppers . . . the disease is fundamentally idleness; the cure is industry . . . (Dean 1860).

The degree of depravity in Cambridgeshire clearly shocked the Dean, but it would have seemed innocuous in the metropolis. Slowly, the reforms in treatment of juvenile offenders became more effective as juveniles were separated from adults, first-offenders from recidivists, and the offenses themselves were grouped into rational aggregations. Similarly, crimes against children were distinguished; death due to "rolling over" by the mother came under closer scrutiny to detect infanticide. Death while under care of a paid care-giver was no longer inevitable. However, the problem of baby-farming persisted into the last decade. The related abuse of death for the insurance money was isolated and reduced by regulations listing age as eligibility for coverage. In the field of education, performance was discriminated by levels or standards which children of various ages were expected to reach. The ritual of taking attendance acquired an almost sacramental form as funding moved from block grants to the niceties of payment by results, and per capita and per diem.

The question of how change occurred in public opinion is interesting below the level of people and laws; the latter tends to be the codification of change already agreed to, although sometimes providing surprises in the subsequent phase of implementation. In addition to concepts becoming more analytic, new concepts were added to old. The public mind added costs to piety as a basis for forming political and social opinions. In his book intended for the general public in 1866, James Hole could offer sanitary reform as good public policy. His argument was that one hundred thousand annual deaths were due to bad sanitation. Calculating an economic loss of £50 per death cost the nation five million pounds per year. This generalized, fairly abstract idiom is not always accepted today, and it shows that Hole, a practical man, believed his readers would follow his argument for efficient public sanitation. In education, literacy providing access to the Bible evolved into a utilitarian combination of training for work and general application. In time, secondary education and specialized instruction for the sciences appeared. In each case, the new propositions built on the old, and illustrations and facts illuminated the problems.

However, evidence and logic were not enough. As with Chadwick's sanitary research and the reports of factory Commissioners, the evidence was inescapable. Moral fervor was a critical component and the reports of the Statistical Society were necessary but not quite sufficient. To Carlyle in 1829, the basis of personal happiness was all in the mind; external circumstances could be changed but the alteration would not bring happiness. Given Carlyle's reputation, reform was not universally popular because his words gave comfort to those tolerant of the status quo. For Mary Carpenter (1851) reports and surveys suggested "idolatry of figures," while to Shaftesbury, undisturbed by personal encounters with the lives of the poor but motivated by strong piety and firm principle, facts were useful illustrations for his hortations.

Towards the end of the century, Walter Besant put forward the general case for promoting the welfare of children in terms of enlightened self-interest of the nation:

> We may readily conceive of a time when—our manufactures ruined by superior foreign intelligence and skill, our railways earning no profit, our carrying trade lost, our agriculture destroyed by foreign imports, our farms without farmers, our houses without tenants—the boasted wealth of England will have become even as the children of the poor; all this may be within measurable distance, and may very well happen before the death of men who are no more than middle-aged. Considering this, as well as other points . . . before us, it may be owned that it is best to look after the boys and girls while it is yet time (Besant 1886).

In this passage, we glimpse the agenda of the twentieth century, as well as a prescience of lamps going out in 1914 and the end of an era. The century which has seen the loss of British economic hegemony has seen the rise of services to children and the family.

After Besant's farsighted observations, General William Booth of the Salvation Army published *In Darkest England and the Way Out* (1890). To the evolving formulation, Booth offered a reversal of the traditional view of poverty institutionalized in the Benthamite new poor law of 1834 and later expressed by the Charity Organization Society. Booth asserted that personal distress, the "moral" failure of early formulations, was a consequence rather than the cause of social distress. Thus, the family living on the edge of catastrophe at best was thrown into disorganization and short-term tactics by hard times. Economic recession and industrial strife were society's collective problem and required collective solutions. Booth's view was not original, but it was compelling when expressed by one whose life was spent amid the poor. Booth sought relief through city, rural, and overseas settlements for social problems. In some respects, it was a formulation in the Utopian tradition of Robert Owen, James Buckingham, and Robert Pemberton. In all three formulations, schooling was important; in the secular cities of Buckingham and Pemberton, school buildings were central considerations in their respective square and circular model towns. In General Booth (1890), the century ended with theory and practice combined; utopianism was evident in the proposed system of city, rural, and overseas colonies to be populated by wretches snatched from the sea of drink and waves of despair. General Booth argued that people's minimum level of welfare be raised to that of the London cab horse, leading to the reminder that the society to protect children was formed after that for the welfare of animals; a discrepancy of appalling significance, it demonstrates how oppressed a minority Victorian children could be. The welfare of the family was placed at the center of the Salvation Army agenda. Unlike the Benthamite calculus of pleasure and pain a century before, Booth tempered the wind to the shorn lamb. In place of the utilitarian equation which abstractly put the poor in the scales, Booth contrived a clinical formulation of poverty within a larger perspective; he leavened the whole with the message of the Gospel.

With Bentham at its opening and Booth at its closing, the Victorian century spanned the working-out of the Industrial Revolution and the rise of public sensitivity. Children evolved from labor cheaper and more docile than that of their mothers to Besant's perception that world was heading down Tennyson's "ringing grooves of change," and that childhood would play no small part in the future.

I now return to the theses of this work and conclude that children were, in the language of today, an oppressed minority, collectively subject to a great deal of stress. Children must inevitably be less powerful than those who are taller, stronger, and more experienced. But in Victorian days childhood became more rather than less vulnerable at a time when, overall, economic and social progress was steady. Across the century we begin with tired, frail factory children and end with adolescents rejected for military service in the Boer War in large numbers.

At the same time education lagged behind the general pace of social change as the sectaries fought to a standstill over control of education at mid-century. Forster's Act of 1870 was late and did far less than it might. It took the Education Act of 1902 to introduce efficiency into the system of schooling by replacing school boards with local education authorities. Only the factory system benefitted, as children entered the work force semi-literate and wholly tractable.

And yet it might have been worse; Britain escaped the full and direct expression of Jeremy Bentham's ideas. Had his proposal for a National Charity Company been adopted, the condition of childhood would have been truly terrible. In 1797, on the verge of the nineteenth century, Bentham proposed for poor children's food that "the smallest allowance is preferable," and urged experiments intended to remove meat from the diet. In one passage, we see refracted the potentials of his utilitarianism as he urged that

> in the article of diet, no unsatisfied longings, no repinings:—Nothing within knowledge that is not within reach (Bentham 1816).

Had this cold doctrine prevailed as national policy, instead of appearing randomly through the acts of ignorant, cruel men, children would have been even more oppressed. Fortunately, Bagehot's observation (1872) that Englishmen are influenced by facts rather than ideas prevailed.

A second example of potential oppression of children is the fortunate delay in the innovation we know as the mental testing movement. In 1885 Dr. Sophie Bryant reported to the Anthropological Institute her explorations of children's perceptions and recall of a classroom and of pictures. She tried to develop, "definite tests of mental operations of a higher kind" but found that they were "apt to produce no appreciable result at all." Two years later, Mr. Joseph Jacobs (1887) reported data on what we now refer to as memory for nonsense syllables and digit span. In data from boys at the Jews Free School in Bell Lane, London, and from girls at the North London Collegiate School there was a clear increase in the ability to repeat syllables and numbers as age increased. Jacobs saw the value of developing norms, observing that,

> "if that were done we should obtain a *standard* span for the various ages and conditions just as we do for height . . . enabling us to ascertain whether a boy or girl were above or below the average." (*Jacobs, 1887*)

The hazard was that these early studies made no mention of culture and social class as major influences, although the digit span task has stood the test of time fairly well.

Mental testing did not assume great importance in the remaining years of Victoria's century. It remained for Cyril Burt in this century to emphasize mental test in research now scarcely credible. Burt's research influenced British education, but the times were less rigid than the last decades of the nineteenth century. The impact of the mental testing movement was less harmful that it would have been had Bryant's and Jacob's promising studies launched a vigorous testing movement. Still greater would have been the harm had testing data on children's abilities been available when Forster's 1870 education bill was debated. It seems likely that working class children would have been 'scientifically' demonstrated to be inherently less worthy of education by virtue of socially created, but genetically transmitted, defect. Langdon-Down's (1865) comments quoted in Chapter One are evidence of the attitudes and convictions of those times. There are fleeting and tantalizing references to diagnosis of learning ability in the literature of the times on teaching. Had Karl Pearson's preoccupations with race and eugenics been augmented by the tests of Alfred Binet and Theodore Simon in France in their earliest days, the plight of poor children would have been frozen by recourse to "scientific" evidence that the poor and illiterate were innately so. Pearson's fulminations against immigrant Jewish children are unpleasant reading. We find some solace in the fact that the pace of innovation in developing mental tests and diffusing their use was slow in Great Britain.

When we review the evidence on childhood, the cumulative picture of *stress* emerges. From the 1780s and the beginning of the Industrial Revolution, children evolved from relatively unproductive figures within the family circle into docile and inexpensive factory workers. Less independent than women workers and far more malleable, children extended the evolution of the industrial worker to its logical end with the realization that still lower wages, and occasionally none, in the guise of an entry-level position, could be paid for child labor. At the same time, stress increased in new forms. Urban housing grew more concentrated, bringing the attendant ills of poor sanitation and communicable disease. The evidence of stress became apparent and visible in the form of rising mortality rates for children and declining height and weight among the children of the working classes. The problems of child mortality and ill health grew across most of the nineteenth century, although the economic ascendency of Great Britain raised the standard of living at all levels.

By the end of the century, child health had improved, although extreme stress existed in pockets. For example, at the Johanna Street School in Southwark, Dr. David Eicholz found physical disorders in 92% of the children in 1903 (Interdepartmental Committee 1904). Stress also declined as alcoholism slowly receded as a source of family discord and child abuse. The end of involuntary emigration reduced the stress attendant to separation from familiar people and culture, and from exposure to the unfamiliar societies of the new world.

In tracing the nature of stress as an implicit theme in the lives of children across the nineteenth century, we note that relief came slowly. Persistence of subpopulations in stress, such as the children attending the Johanna Street school, may be explained by the search for macrosolutions, innovations which would clear up a lot of problems, in the middle third of the century. Chadwick's reforms best exemplify remediation of the collective problems of society by erecting a barrier of clean water and effective sewage for the community as a whole. Thirty years later, in 1870, we see in Forster's Act an approach to individual children through education. However, the fruits of education—i.e., discipline, postponement of rewards, and other implicit elements of the Board School curriculum—were fully gathered only later in adulthood. Forster's children in the 1870s became parents in the 1880s and 1890s. Had the bickerings of religious factions in the 1840s not delayed educational reform, there might have been a faster leavening of Bagehot's "cake of custom." Events were to the contrary, however, and so the infusion of individualized reform through elementary education came after an interval of several decades. Stress in the lives of children persisted in the absence of personal services to needy children provided by nurses and other specialists as supplements to schooling; at a later date, those individualized forms of relief appeared, for example, in school lunch programs and provision of dental services in the twentieth century.

In the case of the second thesis, the discontinuity of public indifference to children and the passion of individual reforms, the evidence lies in the march of great men and women across the canvas of nineteenth-century life. From Robert Owen to General Booth, men and women larger than life took up the cause of childhood. Some stood on private platforms, as in the case of Mary Carpenter and Thomas Barnardo, while James Kay-Shuttleworth and Lord Shaftesbury occupied the engine room and bridge of Whitehall and Westminster. In Bagehot's (1872) language, they occupied, respectively, the "dignified" and "efficient" parts of government. The discontinuity of government's ineffectiveness through fragmentary laws and disinterest stood in contrast to the passion of the reformers. When goaded by scandalous tales from the coal mines and embarrassed by an absent minded public's fleeting attention, Westminster made fitful advances. Political leaders paid scant attention to childhood as national policy, leaving an agenda to be worked out in the more progressive twentieth century in what Searle (1971) called, "The Quest for National Efficiency." Few men had the vision of Walter Besant, who saw that time was running out for the Victorians and that the themes and variations of Victorian childhood required immediate attention. It remained for twentieth-century Britain, energized by the fiery power of war, to address in a continuous and sustained blend of social policy and diminished national resources the heritage of Victorian childhood.

REFERENCES

Accidents in Coal Mines. 1862. *British Medical Journal* 2:374.

Adshead, J. 1842. *Distress in Manchester: Evidence (Tabular and Otherwise) of the State of the Labouring Classes in 1840–42.* London: Henry Hooper. In Carpenter, K. (ed.). *Conditions of Work and Living: The Reawakening of the English Conscience.* New York, Arno Press, 1972.

Adult Female Education. 1856. *Irish Quarterly Review* 6:165–182.

Advice to Railway Travellers. May 14, 1842. *Illustrated London News.*

Aldington, R. 1948. *Four English Portraits 1801–1851.* London: Evans Brothers.

Alfred (S. H. G. Kydd). 1857. *The History of the Factory Movement from the Year 1802, to the Enactment of the Ten Hours Bill in 1847.* London: Simpkin, Marshall and Co.

Allday, J. (ed.). 1853. *True Account of the Proceedings Leading to, and a Full and Authentic Account of, the Searching Inquiry into the Horrible System of Discipline Practiced at the Borough Gaol of Birmingham.* London: Pitman.

Altick, R. D. 1957. *The English Common Reader: A Social History of Mass Reading 1800–1900.* University of Chicago Press.

Anderson, M. 1971. *Family Structure in Nineteenth Century Lancashire.* Cambridge University Press.

Angus, J. 1854. Old and New Bills of Mortality: Movement of the Population: Death and Fatal Diseases During the Last Fourteen Years. *Journal of the Statistical Society of London* 17:117–138.

Anton, G. K. 1953. *Geschichte der Preussischen Fabrikgesetzegeburg bis Zu ihrer Aufnahme durch die Reichsgewerbeordnung.* Berlin: Rutten and Leoning.

Antonov, A. N. 1947. Children Born During the Siege of Leningrad in 1942. *Journal of Pediatrics* 30:250–259.

Appendix. 1841. First Report of the Commissioners on the Employment of Children. *Parliamentary Papers.*

Archer, J. H. G. 1982. A Civic Achievement: The Building of Manchester Town Hall. Part One: The Commissioning. *Transactions of the Lancashire and Cheshire Antiquarian Society* 81:3–41.

Aries, P. 1962. *Centuries of Childhood.* New York. Vintage Books.

Armstrong, A. 1973. *The Methodists and Society 1700–1850.* Rowman and Littlefield, Totowa, New Jersey.

Armstrong, W. A. 1981. The Trend of Mortality in Carlisle Between the 1780s and the 1840s: A Demographic Contribution to the Standard of Living Debate. *Economic History Review* 34:94–114.

Arnott, N. 1840. (Testimony) Minutes of Evidence. Select Committee on Health of Towns. *Parliamentary Papers, 37.*

Ashley, A. Infant Labour. 1840. *Quarterly Review* 171–181.

Ashton, T. 1844. (Testimony) *Parliamentary Papers 332.*

Ashton, T. S. 1925. The Records of a Pin Manufactory 1814–1821. *Economica* 5:281–292.

Aspin, C. (ed.). 1972. *Manchester and the Textile Districts in 1849.* Manchester: Helmshore Local History Society.

Aspinall, A., and E. A. Smith (eds.). 1959. *English Historical Documents 1783–1832.* Oxford University Press.

The Assistant Commissioners and Scotch Morals. April 3, 1871. *Pall Mall Gazette.*

"Author." 1831. *Plain Sense and Reason. Letter to the Present Generation on the Unrestrained Use of Modern Machinery . . .* Norwich, Wilkins and Fletcher. In Carpenter, K. (ed.). *Conditions of Working and Living: The Reawakening of the English Conscience.* New York. Arno Press, 1972.

Autobiography of a Navvy. 1861. *MacMillan's Magazine* 5:140–151.

Avery, G. 1970. *Victorian People in Life and Literature.* New York. Holt, Rinehart and Winston.

Babbage, C. 1851. *The Exposition of 1851.* London: John Murray.

Baber, R. 1842. (Testimony) Minutes of Evidence. *Select Committee on the Health of Towns.*

Baber, R. S. 1868. The Social Results of the Employment of Girls and Women. *Transactions of the National Association for the Promotion of Social Science* 12:537–549.

Bacon, E. E. Gesellschaft. In Gould, W., and W. L. Kilb (eds.). *A Dictionary of the Social Sciences*. The Free Press, 1964.

Bagehot, W. 1872. *The English Constitution*. 2d ed. Garden City, New York, Doubleday, 1962.

Bamford, S. 1849. *The Autobiography of Samuel Bamford: Volume I. The Early Days*. London.

Bamford, S. 1959. Recollections of Manchester Free Grammar School. In Aspinall, A., and E. A. Smith (eds.). *English Historical Documents 1783–1832*. Oxford University Press, 1959.

Barr, R. I., and A. G. Mettler. 1983. The Artificial Feeding of Young Infants in Britain. *Journal of the Royal Society of Health* 103:131–134.

Beames, T. 1840. *The Rookeries of London: Past, Present, and Prospective*. London: Bosworth.

(Beddoe, J.) 1870. Miscellanea. VII. The Stature and Bulk of Man in the British Isles. *Journal of the Royal Statistical Society* 33:278–280. (a)

Beddoe, J. 1870. On the Anthropology of Lancashire. *Report of the Fortieth Meeting of the British Association for the Advancement of Science*. Liverpool. (b)

Beddoe, J. 1870. *On the Stature and Bulk of Man in the British Isles*. London: Asher and Co. (c)

Beddoe, J. 1871. On the Anthropology of the Merse. *Report of the Forty First Meeting of the British Association for the Advancement of Science*. Edinburgh.

Beggs, T. 1849. *An Inquiry into the Extent and Causes of Juvenile Delinquency*. London: Gilpin.

Beets, F. C. 1869. (Testimony) Evidence on Agricultural Gangs Collected by Mr. J. E. White. *Sixth Report of the Commissioners on the Employment of Children and Young Persons*.

Behan, B. (ed.) 1967. *The Autobiography of a Working Man: Alexander Somerville*. London: MacGibbon, and Kee.

Behlmer, G. K. 1982. *Child Abuse and Moral Reform in England 1870–1908*. Stanford University Press.

Bell, Lady. 1907. *At the Works: A Study of a Manufacturing Town*. London: Nelson.

Benoiton de Chateauneuf, L. 1830. De La Durée de la Vie Chez le Riche et Chez la Pauvre. *Annales d'Hygiene Publique et de Medicine Legale* 3:5–15.

Benson, J. 1985. *The Penny Capitalists: A Study of Nineteenth Century Working-Class Entrepreneurs*. New Brunswick, NJ: Rugters University Press.

Bentham, J. 1797. Tracts on Poor Laws and Pauper Management. In Bowring, J. (ed.). *The Works of Jeremy Bentham*. Volume 8. London, 1816.

Beresford, M. W. The Back-To-House in Leeds 1787–1937. In S. D. Chapman (ed.). *The History of Working Class Housing: A Symposium*. London: Rowman and Littlefield, 1971.

Berridge, V. 1978. Victorian Opium Eating: Responses to Opiate Use in Nineteenth Century England. *Victorian Studies* 21:437–461.

Berridge, V. 1979. Opium in the Fens in Nineteenth Century England. *Journal of the History of Medicine and Allied Sciences* 34:293–313.

Berridge, V. and Edwards, G. 1981. *Opium and the People: Opiate use in Nineteenth Century England*. London: Allen Lane and St. Martin's Press.

Besant, W. 1886. From Thirteen to Seventeen. *Contemporary Review* 49:413–425.

Best, G. 1971. *Mid-Victorian Britain 1851–1875*. London: Weidenfeld and Nicholson.

Boas, F. 1897. The Growth of Toronto Children. *Report of the Commissioner of Education*. Washington, DC.

Booth, C. 1886. Occupations of the People of the United Kingdom, 1801–1881. *Journal of the Royal Statistical Society* 49:314–435.

Booth, C. 1888. Conditions and Occupations of the People of East London and Hackney, 1887. *Journal of the Royal Statistical Society* 51:276–331.

Bott, A. 1972. *Our Fathers (1870–1900)*. New York: Blom.

Boulton, P. 1880. On the Physical Development of Children; Or, the Bearing of Anthropometry to Hygiene. *Lancet* 2:502–504.

Bourne, S. 1882. The National Expenditure upon Alcohol. *Journal of the Royal Statistical Society* 45:297–323.

Bowley, A. L. 1898. Comparison of the Changes in Wages in France, the United States and the United Kingdom from 1840 to 1891. *Economic Journal* 8:474–489.

(Bowditch, H. P.) 1872. Comparative Rate of Growth in the Two Sexes. *Boston Medical and Surgical Journal* 87:434–435.

Bowman, M. J. et al. 1968. *Readings in the Economics of Education*. Paris: UNESCO.

Bowman, M. J., and C. A. Anderson. Concerning the Role of Education in Development. In Bowman, M. J. (ed.). *Readings in the Economics of Education*. Paris: UNESCO, 1968.

Boyson, R. 1970. *The Ashworth Cotton Enterprise*. Oxford: The Clarendon Press.

Brabazon. 1887. Decay of Bodily Strength in Towns. *The Nineteenth Century* 21:673–676.

Bradlow, E. 1984. The Children's Friend Society at the Cape of Good Hope. *Victorian Studies* 27:155–177.

Bradshaw's Railway Manual, Shareholder's Guide and Director 1869. London: W. J. Adams, Manchester: Bradshaw and Blackloch, 1869.

Braudel, F. 1975. *Capitalism and Material Life 1400–1800.* New York. Harper Colophon.

Breach of Promise. Saturday, September 17, 1853. *The Times.*

Bremner, J. A. 1866. By What Means Can the Impediments to the Education of the Children of the Manual-Labour Class . . . be Most Effectively Removed? *Transactions of the National Association for the Promotion of Social Science* 10:307–317.

Breschi, M., and Bacci, M. L. 1986. Saison et Climat comme Contraints de la Survie des Enfants. l'Expérience Italienne au XIXe Siècle. *Population* 41:9–36.

Briggs, A. 1968. *Victorian Cities.* London. Pelican Books.

Brown, C. M. 1986. Copley School and the Ackroyd Family. *History of Education Society Bulletin* 36:?–31.

Brown, J. 1832. *A Memoir of Robert Blincoe.* Manchester: Doherty.

Brown, K. D. 1982. *The English Labour Movement. 1700–1951.* New York. St. Martin's Press.

Bryant, S. 1885. Experiments in Testing the Character of School Children. *Journal of the Anthropological Institute of Great Britain* 15:338–349.

Buchan, W. 1797. *Domestic Medicine.* 2d ed. Philadelphia: R. Aitken.

Buckingham, J. S. 1849. *National Evils and Practical Remedies.* London: Jackson.

Bunce, J. T. 1865. On the Statistics of Crime in Birmingham as Compared with other Large Towns. *Journal of the Statistical Society* 28:518–526.

Burn, J. D. 1855. *Autobiography of a Beggar Boy.* London: Tweedie.

Burnett, J. (ed.) 1974. *Annals of Labour: Autobiographies of British Working Class People 1820–1920.* Indiana University Press.

Burnett, J. 1979. *Plenty and Want: A Social History of Diet from 1815 to the Present Day.* London: Scolar Press.

Burnett, J. 1982. *Destiny Obscure: Autobiographies of Childhood, Education and Family from the 1820's to the 1920's.* London: Allen Lane.

Burns, J. 1906. *Presidential Address.* National Conference on Infant Mortality. London.

Burritt, E. 1847. *A Journal of a Visit of Three Days to Skibbereen and its Neighborhood.* London: Gilpin.

Cadogan, W. (December 1765). Some of the Causes that Occasions the Mortality of Children Under Two Years of Age. *Gentlemen's Magazine* 547–548.

Cameron, N. 1979. The Growth of London Schoolchildren 1904–1966: An Analysis of Secular Trend and Intra-County Variation. *Annals of Human Biology* 6:505–526.

Cannadine, D. 1980. *Lords and Landlords: The Aristocracy and the Towns 1774–1967.* Leicester University Press.

Cannadine, D., and D. Reeder (eds.). 1982. *Exploring the Urban Past: Essays in Urban History by H. J. Dyos.* Cambridge University Press.

Cantlie, J. 1885. *Degeneration Amongst Londoners.* London: Field and Tuer.

Capper, H. 1828. (Testimony) Report from the Select Committee on the Police of the Metropolis with Minutes of Evidence and Appendix. *Parliamentary Papers* 4:103–104.

Carlyle, T. 1829. Signs of the Times. *Edinburgh Review* 439–459.

Cargill, W. 1838. Educational, Criminal and Social Statistics of Newcastle-upon-Tyne. *Journal of the Statistical Society* 1:356–361.

Carlyle, T. 1843. Past and Present. In Traill, D. H. (ed.) *The Works of Thomas Carlyle.* Volume X. London: Chapman and Hall, 1897.

Carpenter, M. 1864. On the Non-Imprisonment of Children. *Transactions of the National Society for the Promotion of Social Science* 8:247–255.

Carpenter, M. 1851. *Reformatory Schools for the Children of the Perishing and Dangerous Class and for Juvenile Offenders.* London: Methuen.

Cattell, R. B. 1953. A Quantitative Analysis of the Changes in the Culture Pattern of Great Britain 1837–1937, by P. Technique. *Acta Psychologica* 9:99–121.

Caulfield, E. 1930. The Infant Movement in the Eighteenth Century. *Annals of Medical History* 2:480–494, 660–696.

Cawte, M. 1986. Craniometry and Eugenics in Australia: R. J. A. Berry and the Quest for Social Efficiency. *Historical Studies* 22:35–53.

Census of England and Wales. 1911. General Report with Appendices. London: T. Fisher Unwin, 1917.

Chadwick, D. 1860. On the Rate of Wages in Manchester and Salford, and the Manufacturing Districts of Lancashire, 1839–59. *Journal of the Royal Statistical Society* 23:1–36.

Chadwick, E. 1842. Report on the Sanitary Condition of the Labouring Population of Great Britain. *Parliamentary Papers*.

Chadwick, E. 1844. (Testimony) First Report of the Commissioners on the Health of Towns. *Parliamentary Papers*.

Chadwick, E. 1844. On the Best Modes of Representing Accurately, by Statistical Returns, the Duration of Life, and the Pressure and Progress of the Causes of Mortality Amongst Different Classes of the Community, and Amongst the Populations of Different Districts and Counties. *Journal of the Statistical Society of London* 7:1–40.

Chaloner, W. H. 1940. The *Social and Economic Development of Crewe 1780–1923*. Manchester: Manchester University Press.

Children's Friend Society. November 13, 1840. *The Times*.

Chinn, S. and Rona, R. J. 1984. The Secular Trend in the Height of Primary School Children in England and Scotland from 1972 to 1980. *Annals of Human Biology* 11:1–16.

Christison, J. 1832. Effects of Opium-Eating. *London Medical Gazette* 9:553–557.

Church, R. A. 1966. *Economic and Social Change in a Midland Town: Victorian Nottingham 1815–1900*. London: Cass.

Clark, D. 1981. *Colne Valley: Radicalism to Socialism*. London. Longmans.

Clark, G. K. 1982. *The Making of Victorian England*. London: Methuen.

Clarke, M. 1874. *His Natural Life*. Melbourne, Australia: George Robertson.

Clarke, A. 1923. *The Story of Blackpool*. London: Palatine Books.

Clay, J. 1844. Borough of Preston. Report on its Sanitary Condition. *First Report of the Commissioners for Inquiring into the State of Large Towns and Populous Districts*. Appendix.

Cobbe, F. P. 1861. Social Sciences Congresses, and Women's Part in Them. *MacMillan's Magazine* 5:81–94.

Cobley, J. 1970. *The Crimes of the First Fleet Convicts*. Sydney, Australia: Angus and Robertson.

Cole, P., and W. A. Dean. 1967. *British Economic Growth 1688–1959: Trends and Structure*. Cambridge University Press.

Coleman, J. 1968. *The Railway Navvies*. London. Pelican Books.

Collett, C. E. 1891. Women's Work in Leeds. *Economic Journal* 1:460–473.

Collier, F. 1964. *The Family Economy of the Working Classes in the Cotton Industry 1784–1833*. Manchester University Press.

Collins, E. J. T. 1975. Dietary Change and Cereal Consumption in Britain in the Nineteenth Century. *Agricultural History Review* 23:97–115.

Commission on the Employment of Children. 1842. First Report of the Commissioners. *Parliamentary Papers*.

Conley, C. 1984. Crime and Community in Victorian Kent. Unpublished Ph.D. dissertation, Duke University.

Cook, D., and B. Keith. *British Historical Facts 1830–1900*. London. MacMillan, 1975.

Cook, E. T., and A. Wedderborn (eds.). 1908. *The Works of John Ruskin*. Volume 35. London: Allen.

Cooke-Taylor, W. 1840. On the Moral Economy of Large Towns. *Bentley's Miscellany* 7:470–478.

Cooke-Taylor, W. 1842. *Notes of a Tour in the Manufacturing Districts of Lancashire*. 2d ed. London: Duncan and Malcolm.

Cooper, A. A. (Shaftesbury) Children in Mines and Collieries (1840). In Kessen, W. (ed.). *The Child*. New York: Wiley, 1965.

(Cooper, Astley). 1824. Surgical Lectures: Lecture 48. *Lancet* 1:33–41.

(Cooper, Astley). 1824. Surgical Lectures: Lecture 54. *Lancet* 1:169–179.

Cooper, T. 1872. *The Life of Thomas Cooper, Written by Himself*. London: Hodder and Stoughton.

Cope, C. H. 1891. *Reminiscences of Charles West Cope R.A.* London: Bentley and Son.

Copelman, D. M. 'A New Comradeship Between Men and Women': Family, Marriage and London's Women Teachers, 1870–1914. In Lewis, J. (ed.). *Labour and Love: Women's Experience of Home and Family 1850–1940*. Oxford: Blackwell, 1986.

Coroners Inquests. July 9, 1842. *Illustrated London News*.

Correspondence and Papers Relating to Convict Ships, Convict Discipline, and Transportation 1843–45. 1847. *Parliamentary Papers* vol. 7.

Coulhart, J. R. 1844. (Testimony) Ashton Under Lyne. Health of Towns Commission. *Parliamentary Papers* 17:Appendix, 77–78.

Cowan, R. 1840. Vital Statistics of Glasgow: Illustrating the Sanatory Condition of the Population. *Journal of the Statistical Society of London* 3:257–292.

Cowell, J. W. 1833. (Evidence) First Report. Factory Inquiries Commission. *Parliamentary Papers*.

Cowgill. 1970. The People of York 1538–1812. *Scientific American* 222:104–122.

Cowlard, K. A. 1979. The Identification of Social (Class) Areas and their Place in Nineteenth Century Urban Development. *Institute of British Geographers* 4:239–257.

Crawford, E. M. 1984. Dearth, Diet, and Disease in Ireland, 1850: A Case of Nutritional Deficiency. *Medical History* 28:151–161.

Creighton, C. 1894. *A History of Epidemics in Britain. Volume Two: From the Extinction of the Plague to the Present Time.* Cambridge University Press.

Crook, J. M. 1973. *The Reform Club.* London: Reform Club.

Crook, J. M. 1981. *William Burges and the High Victorian Dream.* University of Chicago Press.

Crouzet, F. 1985. *The First Industrialists: The Problem of Origins.* London: Cambridge University Press.

Cruickshank, M. 1981. *Children and Industry: Child Health and Welfare in North-West Textile Towns During the Nineteenth Century.* Manchester: Manchester University Press.

Cullen, M. J. 1975. *The Statistical Movement in Early Victorian Britain.* London: Harvester Press.

Cunyghame, H. Railways. In Oliver, T. (ed.). *Dangerous Trades.* London: John Murray, 1902.

Daly, A., and B. Benjamin. 1964. London as a Case Study. *Population Studies* 17:249–262.

Daly, M. The Development of the National School System, 1831–1840. In Cosgrove, A., and D. McCartney (eds.). *Studies in Irish History.* University College, 1979.

Danford, J. E. 1977. Robert Lowe and Inspectors' Reports. *British Journal of Educational Studies* 25:155–169.

Danson, J. T. 1862. Statistical Observations Relative to the Growth of the Human Body (Males) in Height and Weight, from Eighteen to Thirty Years of Age. As Illustrated by the Records of the Borough Gaol of Liverpool. *Journal of the Royal Statistical Society* 24:20–26.

Davey, B. J. 1983. *Lawless and Immoral: Policing a Country Town 1838–1857.* Leicester University Press.

Davies, J. Aristocratic Town-Makers and the Coal Metropolis: The Marquis of Bute and the Growth of Cardiff 1776 to 1947. In Cannadine, D. (ed.). *Patricians, Power and Politics in Nineteenth Century Towns.* London: St. Martin's Press, 1982.

Dawson, C. 1901. The Housing of the People, with Special Reference in Dublin. *Journal of the Statistical and Social Inquiry Society of Ireland* 81:45–56.

Deane, P. and Cole, W. A. 1967. *British Economic Growth 1688–1959: Trends and Structure.* Cambridge: Cambridge University Press.

Dean of Ely. 1860. Annals of an Industrial School. *MacMillan's Magazine* 4:13–18.

Debates in the House of Commons on the Factory Bill, 19 and 23 February, and 27 April, 1818. In Aspinall, A., and E. A. Smith (eds.). *English Historical Documents 1783–1832.* Oxford University Press, 1959.

De Motte, C. M. The Dark Side of Town: Crime in Manchester and Salford 1815–1875. Unpublished Ph.D. dissertation, University of Kansas, 1977.

Denyer, C. H. 1893. The Consumption of Tea and Other Staple Drinks. *Economic Journal* 3:33–51.

deQuincy, T. 1821. Confessions of an English Opium Eater. *London Magazine.*

Description of Convicts, H. M. S. "Frances Charlotte," 1833. Microfilm #95220 (ASTAL 20, Roll 33) Genealogical Archives, Church of Jesus Christ of Latter Day Saints, Salt Lake City, Utah.

Dickson, R. W. On Housing Conditions in Lancashire (1815), In Aspinall, A., and E. A. Smith (eds.). *English Historical Documents 1783–1832.* Oxford University Press, 1959.

(Dickens, C.) June 30, 1860. The Uncommercial Traveller. *All the Year Round* 274–278.

Dillon, T. 1974. The Irish in Leeds, 1851–1861. *Thoresby Society Publications Miscellany* 54:1–28.

Dodd, W. 1841. *A Narrative of the Experience and Sufferings . . .* London: L. G. Seeley and Hatchard and Son.

Dosing Infants with Drugs. 1882. *Lancet* i:923.

Drummond, J. C. and Wilbraham, A. 1939. *The Englishman's Food: A History of Five Centuries of English Diet.* London: Jonathan Cape.

Dunae, P. A. 1983. *Gentlemen Immigrants: From the British Public Schools to the Canadian Frontier.* Manchester University Press.

Duncan, M. 1866. *Fecundity, Fertility, Sterility and Etc.* Edinburgh: A. & C. Black.

Duncan, W. H. 1844. On the Physical Cause of the High Rate of Mortality. Health of Towns Commission. *Parliamentary Papers* Appendix, 17–19.

Dunlop, O. J. 1912. *English Apprenticeship and Child Labour: A History.* Macmillan.

Dunning, E. and Sheard, K. 1979. *Barbarians, Gentlemen and Players,* New York University Press.

Dyhouse, C. 1977. Good Wives and Little Mothers: Social Anxieties and the Schoolgirl's Curribulum, 1890–1920. *Oxford Review of Education* 3:21–35.

Dyos, H. J. 1957. Social Costs of Railway Building in London. *Journal of Transport History* 3:1–30.

Dyos, H. J. 1961. *Victorian Suburb: A Study of the Growth of Camberwell.* Leicester University Press.

Eason, C. 1899. The Tenement Houses of Dublin. Their Condition and Regulation. *Journal of the Statistical and Social Inquiry Society of Ireland* 79:383–398.

Eden, F. M. On the State of the Poor in 1797. In Aspinall, A., and A. E. Smith (eds.). *English Historical Documents 1783–1832.* Oxford University Press, 1959.

Edmonds, T. R. January 30, 1836. On the Mortality of Infants in England. *Lancet* 692–694.

Edwards, J. P. 1906. *A Few Footprints.* London: Watts and Company.

Effect of Interment of Bodies in Towns. 1842. *Report from the Select Committee on the Health of Towns. Parliamentary Papers.*

Elliot, A. Municipal Government in Bradford in the Mid-Nineteenth Century. In Fraser, D. (ed.). *Municipal Reform and the Industrial City.* St. Martin's Press, 1982.

Engles, F. 1845. *Condition of the Working Class in England.* Moscow. Progress Publishers.

Engels, F. The Position of England. The British Constitution. In *Karl Marx and Frederic Engels: Articles on Britain.* Moscow: Progress Publishers, 1975.

England. 1865. Infanticide Among the Poor. *Nation* 1:270–271.

Eveleth, P. B. Population Differences in Growth: Environmental and Genetic Factors. In Falkner, F., and J. Tanner (eds.). *Human Growth: 3. Neurobiology and Nutrition.* Plenum Press, 1979.

Eversley, Lord. 1907. The Decline in Number of Agricultural Labourers in Great Britain. *Journal of the Royal Statistical Society* 70:267–306.

Extreme Distress in Spitalfields and its Vicinity. London: *The Morning Chronicle,* January 4, 1817.

The Factory Act of 1819. In Aspinall, A., and E. A. Smith (eds.). *English Historical Documents 1783–1832.* Oxford University Press, 1959.

Factory Inquiries Commission. 1833. First Report of the Central Board. *Parliamentary Papers.*

Factory Inquiries Commission. 1834. Second Report of the Central Board. *Parliamentary Papers.*

(Farr, W.) 1856. Miscellanea. I. Mortality at Different Stages of Life. *Journal of the Statistical Society of London* 28:403–413.

Farr, W. 1865. The Mortality of Infants. *Journal of the Statistical Society* 28:403–413.

Farr, W. 1866. Mortality of Children in the Principal States of Europe. *Journal of the Royal Statistical Society* 29:1–35.

Farson, D. 1986. *Swansdowne*. London. Arrow Books.

Finlayson, G. B. A. M. 1981. *The Seventh Earl of Shaftesbury.* London: Eyre Methuen.

Finnegan, F. 1979. *Poverty and Prostitution: A Study of Victorian Prostitutes in York.* New York: Cambridge University Press.

Finnegan, F. 1982. *Poverty and Prejudice: Irish Immigrants in York, 1840–1875.* Cork: University Press.

Finnegan, F., and E. Sigsworth. 1978. *Poverty and Social Policy: An Historical Study of Batley.* York University.

First Report of the Commissioners. 1842. Children's Employment Commission.

First Report of the Commissioners on the Employment of Children, Young Persons, and Women in Agriculture. 1868. *Parliamentary Papers* vol. 10.

First Report from the Select Committee of the House of Lords . . . Juvenile Offenders . . . Parliamentary Papers vol. 1.

First Report from the Select Committee on the Act for Regulation of Mills and Factories. 1840. *Parliamentary Papers* vol. 7.

Fishman, W. J. 1973. *East End Jewish Radicals 1875–1914*. London: Duckworth.

Fletcher, J. 1842. Abstract from a Register of Accidents in the Coal Mines of the Camber and Werneth Company, at Oldham, During the Year Ended October, 1841. *Journal of the Statistical Society of London* 5:222–225.

Fletcher, J. 1852. Statistics of the Farm School System of the Continent, and of its Application to the Preventive and Reformatory Education of a Pauper and Criminal Children in England. *Journal of the Statistical Society* 3–49.

Flinn, M. W. (ed.). 1965. *Report on the Sanitary Condition of the Labouring Population of Gt. Britain by Edwin Chadwick*. Edinburgh University Press.

Forbes, J. D. 1837. On the Result of Experiments on the Weight of Height and Strength of above 8000 Individuals. *Proceedings of the Royal Society of Edinburgh* 1:160–161.

Forbes, T. 1971. *Chronicle from Aldgate*. Yale University Press.

Forrest, D. W. 1974. *Francis Galton: The Life and Work of a Victorian Genius*. New York: Taplinger Publishing Co.

Forster, J. 1884. *Stay and Starve; Or, Go and Thrive.* London.

Fourth Report from the Select Committee of the House of Lords on Intemperance, 1878. 1879. *Parliamentary Papers* 4:Appendix.

France, R. S. 1953. The Diary of John Ward of Clitheroe, Weaver, 1860–1864. *Transactions of the Historical Society of Lancashire and Cheshire* 105:137–185.

Fry, A. A. 1839. Report of the Inspector of Factories on the Effects of the Educational Provisions of the Factories Act. *Journal of the Statistical Society of London* 1:173–181.

Fuchs, R. 1984. *Abandoned Children: Foundlings and Child Welfare in Nineteenth Century France.* Albany, New York: State University of New York Press.

Gadian, D. S. 1978. Class Consciousness in Oldham and Other North West Industrial Towns, 1830–1850. *Historical Journal* 21:161–172.

Gallagher, T. 1982. *Paddy's Lament: Ireland 1846–1847.* New York. Harcourt Brace Jovanovich.

Galton, F. et al. 1884. Final Report of the Anthropometric Committee . . . Report of the Fifty Third Meeting of the British Association for the Advancement of Science. London: John Murray.

Gammage, R. G. 1969. *History of the Chartist Movement 1837–1854.* London: Holyoake, 1854. New York: Kelley.

Gandevia, B. 1977. A Comparison of the Heights of Boys Transported to Australia from England, Scotland, and Ireland c. 1840, with Later British and Australian Developments. *Australian Paediatric Journal* 13:91–97.

Gardner, P. 1984. *The Lost Elementary Schools of Victorian England. The People's Education.* Dover, New Hampshire: Croom Helm.

Gardner, R. The Economy of Shorter Hours. Letter from Gardner of Preston to the Chairman of the Meeting in the Corn Exchange, Manchester, April 22, 1845. In Young, G. M., and W. D. Handcock (eds.). *English Historical Documents 1833–1874.* Oxford University Press, 1956.

Gaskell, E. C. 1907. *The Life of Charlotte Bronte (1863).* Edinburgh: Grant.

Gatliff, C. 1825. On Improved Dwellings and their Beneficial Effect on Health and Moods, with Suggestions for their Extension. *Journal of the Royal Statistical Society* 38:33–54.

Gayer, A. D., W. W. Rostow, and A. J. Schwartz. *The Growth and Fluctuation of the British Economy 1790–1850.* Oxford. Clevendon Press, 1953.

Gibbon, C. 1878. *The Life of George Combe.* London: Macmillan.

Gibbs, J. A. 1903. *A Cotswold Village, or Country Life and Pursuits in Gloucestershire.* London: John Murray.

Gibson, C. B. 1859. A Visit to the Cork Union Workhouse. A Letter to the Editor of the Cork Constitution. *Irish Quarterly Review* 9:90–103.

Giffen, R. 1883. The Progress of the Working Classes in the Last Half Century. *Journal of the Royal Statistical Society* 46:593–622.

Gilbert, B. B. 1969. Health and Politics: The British Physical Deterioration Report of 1904. *Bulletin of the History of Medicine* 39:143–153.

Gilbert, E. W. 1949. The Growth of Brighton. *Geographical Journal* 114:30–52.

Gillis, J. R. 1975. The Evolution of Juvenile Delinquency in England 1890–1914. *Past and Present* 67:96–126.

Glass, D. V. 1940. *Population, Policies and Movements in Europe.* London Arnold.

Glen, R. A. 1979. The Manchester Grammar School in the Early Nineteenth Century: A New Account. *Transactions of the Lancashire and Cheshire Antiquarian Society* 80:30–42.

Godwin, G. 1859. *Town Swamps and Social Bridges.* London: Routledge, Warnes and Routledge.

Goffman, I. 1962. *Asylums: Essays on the Social Situation of Mental Patients and Other Inmates.* Chicago: Aldine.

Goldman, L. 1986. The Social Science Association, 1857–1886: A Context for Mid-Victorian Liberalism. *English Historical Review* 101:95–134.

Gordon, H. 1923. Mental and Scholastic Tests among Retarded Children. *Board of Education Pamphlet #44.* London.

Gourvish, T. R. 1972. *Mark Huish and the London and North Western Railway: A Study of Management.* Leicester University Press.

Granville, A. B. 1860. On Certain Phenomena, Facts, and Calculations, Incidental to or Connected with the Power and Act of Propagation in Females of the Industrial Classes of the Metropolis. *Transactions of the Obstetrical Society of London* 2:139–196.

Granville, A. B. 1841. *The Spas of England.* London.

Graunt, J. 1662. *Natural and Political Observations Mentioned in a Following Index and Made upon the Bills of Mortality.* London.

Greaves, G. 1863. Observations on Some of the Causes of Infanticide. *Journal of the Manchester Statistical Society* 10:2–22.

Green, J. R. January 23, 1869. Benevolence and the Poor. *Saturday Review.* (*Stray Studies: Second Series.* London, 1900).

Greenhow, Dr. Privy Council Medical Reports 1861, No. 4. In Pike, E. R. *Golden Times: Human Documents of the Victorian Age.* New York. Schocken Books, 1972.

Greenwood, J. 1881. *Low-Life Deeps: An Account of the Strange Fish to be Found There.* London: Chatto and Windos.

Greenwood, J. 1869. *The Seven Curses of London.* London: Stanley Rivers.

Greg, S. 1840. *Two Letters to Leonard Horner, Esq. on the Capabilities of the Factory System.* London: Taylor and Walton.

Gregory, D. 1982. *Regional Transformation and Industrial Revolution: A Geography of the Yorkshire Woollen Industry.* London: MacMillan.

Gregson, M. 1817. *Portfolio of Fragments Relative to the History of Antiquities of the County Palatine and Duchy of Lancaster.* Liverpool.

Griffin, D. 1841. An Enquiry into the Mortality among the Poor in the City of Limerick. *Journal of the Statistical Society* 4:316–330.

Griffiths, A. 1896. *The Chronicles of Newgate.* London: Chapman and Hall.

Grindrod, R. B. 1844. *The Slaves of the Needles: An Exposure of the Distressed Condition Moral and Physical of Dress-Makers, Milliners, Embroiderers, Shop-Workers, etc.* London: Britain and Gilpin. In Carpenter, K. (ed.). *Conditions of Working and Living: The Reawakening of the English Conscience.* Arno Press, 1972.

Guy, W. A. 1881. On the Temperature and its Relation to Mortality: An Illustration of the Application of the Numerical Method to the Discovery of Truth. *Journal of the Royal Statistical Society* 44:235–262.

Guy, W. A. 1882. Two Hundred and Fifty Years of Smallpox in London. *Journal of the Royal Statistical Society* 45:399–457.

Hack, M., A. A. Fanaroff, and I. R. Merkatz. 1979. The Low-Birth-Weight Infant-Evolution of a Changing Outlook. *New England Journal of Medicine* 301:1162–1165.

Hale, William to Patrick Colquhoun (1800). In Aspinall, A., and E. A. Smith (eds.). *English Historical Documents 1783–1832.* Oxford University Press, 1959.

Halley, E. 1693. An Estimate of the Degrees of the Mortality of Mankind Draw from Curious Tables of the Births and Funerals of the City of Breslaw; With an Attempt to Ascertain the Price of Annuities upon Lives. *Philosophical Transactions* 17:596–610.

Hammond, J. L., and B. Hammond. 1923. *Lord Shaftesbury.* London: Methuen.

Hammond, J. L., and B. Hammond. 1925. *The Rise of Modern Industry.* London: Methuen.

Hancock, W. M. 1861. The Aberdeen Industrial Schools Contrasted with Irish Workhouses; Family Ties being Cherished in the Schools, and Violated in the Workhouse. *Journal of the Statistical and Social Inquiry Society of Ireland* 18:6–19.

Hancock, W. N. 1862. The Mortality of Children in Workhouses in Ireland. *Journal of the Statistical and Social Inquiry Society of Ireland* 20:193–198.

Hare, S. 1839. Abstract of Outline of Subjects for Statistical Enquiries. *Journal of the Statistical Society of London* 1:426–427.

Harley, C. K. 1982. British Industrialization Before 1841: Evidence of Slower Growth During the Industrial Revolution. *Journal of Economic History* 42:267–285.

Harrison, B. 1971. *Drink and the Victorians.* University of Pittsburgh Press.

Harrison, J. F. C. 1954. *Social Reform in Victorian Leeds: The Work of James Hole 1820–1895.* Leeds: Thoresby Society.

Harrison, J. F. C. 1971. *The Early Victorians 1832–1891.* London: Weidenfeld and Nicholson.

Hart-Davis, R. (ed.). 1962. *The Letters of Oscar Wilde.* New York: Harcourt Brace.

Harvie, C., G. Martin, and A. Scharf (eds.). 1970. *Industrialization and Culture 1830–1914.* London: MacMillan.

Head, F. 1851. *A History of the English Railway.* London: Longman, Brown, Green, and Longmans.

Head, F. B. 1849. *Stokers and Pokers: Or, the London and North Western Railway, the Electric Telegraph, and the Railway Clearing House.* London: John Murray.

Head, G. 1836. *A Home Tour Through the Manufacturing Districts of England, in the Summer of 1835.* London: John Murray.

The Health and Morals of Apprentices Act, 1802. In Aspinal, A., and E. A. Smith (eds.). *English Historical Documents 1783–1832.* Oxford University Press, 1959.

Her Majesty's First Trip by Railway. June 18, 1842. *Illustrated London News.*

Hewitt, M. 1975. *Wives and Mothers in Victorian Industry.* Westport, Connecticut. Greenwood Press.

Heywood, J. 1839. Report of an Enquiry, Conducted from House to House, into the State of 176 Families in Miles Platting, Within the Borough of Manchester, in 1837. *Journal of the Statistical Society of London* 1:34–36.

Higgs, E. 1983. Domestic Servants and Households in Victorian England. *Social History* 8:201–210.

Hill, O. 1875. *Homes of the London Poor*. London: MacMillan.

Hillyard, P. A. R. et al. 1972. Variations in the Standards of Housing Provisions in Northern Ireland. *Regional Studies* 6:393–399.

Hilton, K. J. (ed.). 1967. *The Lower Swansea Valley Project*. London: Longmans.

Hird, F. 1898. *The Cry of the Children*. London: James Bowden.

The History of a Hospital. 1862. *MacMillan's Magazine* 5:252–260.

Hobhouse, C. 1937. *1851 and the Crystal Palace* London: John Murray.

Hobsbawm, E. J. 1964. *Labouring Men: Studies in the History of Labour*. New York. Anchor Books.

Hoffer, P. C., and N. E. H. Hull. 1981. *Murdering Mothers: Infanticide in England and New England 1558–1803*. New York University Press.

Hohenburg, P. 1968. *A Primer on the Economic History of Europe*. New York. Random House.

Hole, J. 1850. *'Light, More Light!' On the Present State of Education Amongst the Working Classes of Leeds*. London: Longmans.

Hole, J. 1866. *The Homes of the Working Classes*. London: Longmans.

Hollingsworth, T. H. Illegitimate Births and Marriage Rates in Great Britain 1841–1911. In Dupaquier, J. et al (eds.). *Marriage and Remarriage in Populations of the Past*. Academic Press, 1981.

Hooper, F. C. *The Point Puer Experiment: A Study of the Penal and Educational Treatment of Juvenile Transportees in Van Diemen's Land 1830–1850*. University of Melbourne, Unpublished M.Ed. Thesis, 1954.

Hopkins, E. 1969. A Charity School in the Nineteenth Century: Old Swinford Hospital School, 1815–1914. *British Journal of Educational Studies* 17:177–192.

Hopkins, E. 1986. Working-Class Housing in Birmingham During the Industrial Revolution. *International Review of Social History* 31:80–94.

Horn, P. 1979. Child Workers in the Pillow Lace and Straw Plait Trades of Victorian Buckinghamshire and Bedfordshire. *Historical Journal* 17:779–796.

Horn, P. 1974. *The Victorian Country Child*. Kineton: Hornwood Press.

Horner, L. Factory Inspectors' Special Reports on the Practicability of Legislation for the Prevention of Accidents (1841). In Young, G. M., and W. D. Handcock (eds.). *English Historical Documents 1831 1874*. Oxford University Press, 1956.

Howarth, O. J. R. 1922. *The British Association for the Advancement of Sciences: A Retrospect 1831–1921.* The British Association.

Hughes, M. V. 1977. *A London Child of the 1870s.* Oxford University Press.

Hume-Rotheny, M. C. 1871. *Women and Doctors: Or Medical Despotism in England.* London: T. W. Grattan.

Hunt, E. H. 1981. *British Labour History 1815–1914.* London: Weidenfeld and Nicholson.

Hunter, H. J. Report on the Excessive Mortality of Infants in Some Rural Districts of England. Medical Reports of the Privy Council No. 6, Appendix 14, 1864. In Pike, E. R. *Golden Times: Human Documents of the Victorian Age.* Schocken, 1974.

Ikin, J. I. 1864. On the Undue Mortality of Infants in Connection with the Questions of Early Marriages, Drugging Children, Bad Nursing, and Certificates of Death, etc. *Transactions of the National Association for the Promotion of Social Sciences* 4:509–511.

Illick, J. E. 1974. Child Rearing in Seventeenth Century England and America. In deMause, L. (ed.). *The History of Childhood.* New York. Harper Torchbooks.

Illingworth, R. S., and E. M. Illingworth. 1966. *Lessons From Childhood: Some Aspects of the Early Life of Unusual Men and Women.* Edinburgh: E. and S. Livingstone.

Index to British Parliamentary Papers on Children's Employment. 1973. Limerick. Irish University Press.

Innes, J. W. 1938. *Class Fertility Trends in England and Wales 1876–1934.* Princeton University Press.

J. July 5, 1849. *The Times.*

Jacobs, J. 1887. Experiments in Prehension. *Mind.* 12: 75–79.

Jeffreys, J. 1840. Observations on the Improper Use of Opium in England. *Lancet* 1:382–383.

Jenkins, B. G. 1879. On a Probable Connection Between the Yearly Death-Rate and the Position of the Planet Jupiter in his Orbit. *Journal of the Royal Statistical Society* 42:330–331.

John, V. 1883. The Term 'Statistics.' *Journal of the Statistical Society* 46:656–679.

Johnson, R. 1970. Educational Policy and Social Control in Early Victorian England. *Past and Present* 49:96–119.

Johnson, S. C. 1913. *A History of Emigration from the United Kingdom to North America 1763–1912.* London: Cass.

John O'London. 1912. *London Stories.* London and Edinburgh: T. C. and E. C. Jack.

Jones, R. E. 1976. Infant Mortality in Rural North Shropshire. *Population Studies* 30:305–317.

Jones, G. S. 1971. *Outcast London*. Oxford: Clarendon Press.

Jones, H. R. 1894. The Perils and Protection of Infant Life. *Journal of the Royal Statistical Society*. 57: 1–98.

Jordan, T. E. (ed.). 1966. *Perspectives in Mental Retardation*. Carbondale, IL: Southern Illinois University Press.

Jordan, T. E. 1976. *The Mentally Retarded*. 4th Edition. Columbus, Ohio: Merrill Books.

Jordan, T. E. 1980. *Development in the Preschool Years*. New York: Academic Press.

Jordan, T. E. (ed.). 1982. *Child Development, Information, and the Formation of Public Policy: An International Perspective*. Springfield, IL: Thomas.

Jordan, T. E. 1982. Lancashire Lasses and Yorkshire Lads: Childhood in the Early Nineteenth Century. *Journal of the Royal Society of Health* 102:14–20.

Jordan, T. E. 1985. Transported to Van Diemen's Land: The Boys of the *Frances Charlotte* (1832) and *Lord Goderich* (1841). *Child Development* 493–516. (a)

Jordan, T. E. 1985. Stay and Starve or Go and Prosper! Juvenile Emigration from Great Britain in the Nineteenth Century. *Social Science History* 9: 145–166. (b)

Jordan, T. E. 1986. *Technical Report 43: Percentiles for Height and Weight from Birth to Age Fifteen Years in White Children Born in St. Louis*. University of Missouri-St. Louis.

Jordan, T. E. 1987. The Keys of Paradise: Godfrey's Cordial and Children in Victorian Britain. *Journal of the Royal Society of Health* 107, 19–22.

Jordan, T. E. and Silva, P. A. 1987. Height and Weight in the First Decade of Life: A Comparative Study of Prospective Data from New Zealand and the United States.

Jordan, T. E., and S. D. Spaner. 1981. Effects of Age at Delivery and Other Maternal Traits on the Cognitive Development of Children: An Application of Interaction Regression Analysis to a Policy Complex. *Multiple Linear Regression Viewpoints* 11:1–60.

Journeyman Engineer. (Wright, T.) 1867. *Some Habits and Customs of the Working Classes*. London: Tinsley Brothers. (New York: Kelley, 1967).

Journeyman Engineer. 1868. *The Great Unwashed*. London. Tinsley Brothers.

Joyce, T. 1869. The Pharmacy Act and Opium Eaters. *Lancet* 1:150.

J. R. Notice. 1828. Doses of Opium. *London Medical Gazette* 2:320.

Kay, J. 1850. *The Social Condition and Education of the People in England and Europe.* Volume I and II. London: Longmans Brown. (New York: Kelley, 1973).

Kay, J. P. 1832. *The Moral and Physical Condition of the Working Classes Employed in the Cotton Manufacture in Manchester.*

Kay-Shuttleworth, J. 1862. *Four Periods of Public Education as Reviewed in 1832, 1839, 1846, 1862.* London: Longmans.

Kellett, J. R. 1969. *The Impact of Railways on Victorian Cities.* London: Routledge and Kegan Paul.

Kirby, P. G., and A. E. Musson. 1975. *The Voice of the People, John Doherty 1798–1854.* Manchester University Press.

Kirk, N. 1985. *The Growth of Working Class Reformism in Mid-Victorian England.* London: Croom Helm.

Knodel, J. 1968. Infant Mortality in Three Bavarian Villages: An Analysis of Family Histories from the Nineteenth Century. *Population Studies* 22:297–318.

Knox, W. 1986. Apprenticeship and de-Skilling in Britain, 1850–1914. *International Review of Social History* 31:166–184.

Kohlberg, L. 1972. A Cognitive-Developmental Approach to Moral Education. *Humanist* 32:13–16.

Korr, C. 1978. West Ham United Football Club and the Beginnings of Professional Football in East London, 1895–1914. *Journal of Contemporary History* 13:211–232.

Korr, C. P. 1986. *West Ham United: The Making of a Football Club.* London: Duckworth.

Kuczynski, J. 1946. *Labour Conditions in Great Britain: 1750 to the Present.* London: International Publishers.

Labour and the Poor: The Manufacturing Districts. The Staffordshire Collieries. Letter XXIII. *The Morning Chronicle.* January 3, 1850.

Labour and the Poor: The Manufacturing Districts. *The Morning Chronicle.* (Supplement) January 4, 1850.

Lacqueur, T. W. Working Class Demand and the Growth of English Elementary Education 1750–1850. In Stone, L. (ed.). *Schooling and Society: Studies in the History of Education.* Johns Hopkins University Press, 1976.

Lambertz, J. 1985. Sexual Harassment in the Nineteenth Century English Cotton History. *History Workshop Journal* 19:29–61.

Langdon-Down, J. H. 1866. Observations on an Ethnic Classification of Idiots. *Reports and Observations of the London Hospitals*

3:259–262. In Jordan, T. E. Perspectives in Mental Retardation. Southern Illinois University Press, 1966.

Langdon-Down, J. H. 1865. On the Same. *Transactions of the National Association for the Promotion of Social Science* 9:345–350.

Lankester, E. 1864. Infant Mortality. *Transactions of the National Association for the Promotion of Social Science* 8:588–590.

Lankester, E. 1866. Infanticide with Reference to the Best Measures of its Prevention. *Transactions of the National Association for the Promotion of Social Science* 10:216–224.

Lasker, G. W., and D. F. Roberts. 1982. Secular Trends in Relationship as Estimated by Surnames: A Study of Tyneside Parish. *Annals of Human Biology* 9:299–307.

Law Report. February 22, 1823. *The Times.*

Laycock, T. 1844. The City of York. Health of Towns Commission. *British Parliamentary Papers* Appendix, Table 8.

Lee, C. H. 1979. *British Regional Employment Statistics 1841–1971.* Cambridge: Cambridge University Press.

Lee, C. H. 1984. The Service Sector, Regional Specialization, and Economic Growth in the Victorian Economy. *Journal of Historical Geography* 10:139–155.

Lentzner, H. R. 1985. Adult Mortality Estimates from Successive Censuses: England and Wales in the Nineteenth Century. *Historical Methods* 18:51–62.

Leon, D. 1949. *Ruskin, the Great Victorian.* London: Routledge and Kegan Paul.

Levine, D. 1979. Education and Family Life in Early Industrial England. *Journal of Family History* 4:368–380.

Levitt, I., and C. Smout. 1979. *The State of the Scottish Working Class in 1843.* Edinburgh. Scottish Academic Press.

Lewes, C. L. 1887. How to Ensure Breathing Spaces. *Nineteenth Century* 21:677–682.

Lewis, R. A. 1952. *Edwin Chadwick and the Public Health Movement 1832–1854.* London. Longmans Green.

Liddle, J. Estate Management and Land Reform Politics: The Hesketh and Scarisbrick Families and the Making of Southport, 1842 to 1914. In Cannadine, D. (ed.). *Patricians, Power and Politics in Nineteenth Century Towns.* London: St. Martin's Press, 1982.

Litchfield, R. B. The Family and the Mill: Cotton Mill Work, Family Work Patterns, and Fertility in Mid-Victorian Stockport. In Wohl, A. S. (ed.). *The Victorian Family: Structure and Stresses.* St. Martin's Press, 1978.

Little, W. J. 1862. On the Influence of Abnormal Parturition, Difficult Labours, Premature Birth, and Asphyxia Neonatorum, on the Mental and Physical Condition of the Child, Especially in Relation to Deformities. *Transactions of the Obstetrical Society of London* 3:293–320.

Lockhead, M. 1956. *Their First Ten Years: Victorian Childhood.* London: John Murray.

London Phalanx: Numbers 1–57, 1841–1842. 1968. New York: Greenwood Reprint Corporation.

Longstaff, G. B. 1893. Rural Depopulation. *Journal of the Royal Statistical Society* 56:380–433.

MacGill, P. 1914. *Children of the Dead End: The Autobiography of a Navvy.* London: Jenkins.

Madoc-Jones, B. Patterns of Attendance and their Social Significance: Mitcham National School 1830–1839. In McCann, P. *Popular Education and Socialization in the Nineteenth Century.* London: Methuen, 1977.

Malcolm, E. 1986. *"Ireland Sober, Ireland Free": Drink and Temperance in Nineteenth Century Ireland.* Syracuse, NY: Syracuse University Press.

Malcolmson, Robert W. 1973. *Popular Recreations in English Society 1700–1850.* Cambridge: Cambridge University Press.

Manchester. August 20, 1842. *Illustrated London News.*

Manchester As It Is: Or, Notices of the Institutions, Manufactures, Commerce, Railways, etc. Manchester: Love and Barton, 1839.

Mangan, J. A. 1981. *Athleticism in the Victorian and Edwardian Public Schools.* Cambridge University Press.

Mann, J. 1898. Better Houses for the Poor—Will They Pay? *Proceedings of the Philosophical Society of Glasgow* 30:83–124.

Mann, H. 1853. Education. England and Wales. Report and Tables. *Parliamentary Papers* 40.

Manning, H. E., and B. Waugh. 1886. The Child of the English Savage. *Contemporary Review* 49:687–700.

Manton, J. 1977. *Mary Carpenter and the Children of the Streets.* London: Heinemann.

Mapother, E. D. 1866. The Unhealthiness of Irish Towns and the Want of Sanitary Legislation. *Journal of the Statistical and Social Inquiry Society of Ireland* 30:250–271.

Marchant, P. 1954. Early Excursion Trains. *Railway Magazine* 100:426–427, 429.

Matheson, R. E. 1903. The Housing of the People of Ireland during the

Period 1841–1901. *Journal of the Statistical and Social Inquiry Society of Ireland* 83:196–212.

Matossian, M. K. 1985. Death In London, 1750–1909. *Journal of Interdisciplinary History* 16:183–197.

May, M. 1973. Innocence and Experience: The Evolution of the Concept of Juvenile Delinquency in the Mid-Nineteenth Century. *Victorian Studies* 17:7–29.

Mayer, J. P. (ed.) de Tocqueville, A. 1968. *Journeys to England and Ireland*. Garden City, New York: Anchor Books.

Mays, J. O'D. 1983. *Mr. Hawthorne Goes to England*. Ringwood, Hants: New Forest Leaves.

Mayhew, H. 1851. *London Labour and the London Poor*. London. Methuen.

McBride, T. "As the Twig is Bent": The Victorian Nanny. In Wohl, A. S. (ed.). *The Victorian Family: Structure and Stresses*. New York: St. Martin's Press, 1978.

McCleary, G. F. 1932. *The Early History of the Infant Welfare Movement*. London: H. K. Lewis.

McCleod, R. M. 1966. Social Policy and the Floating Population 1877–99. *Past and Present* 35:101–132.

McCord, N. 1972. Some Aspects of North East England in the Nineteenth Century. *Northern History* 7:73–88.

McGregor, O. R. 1957. Social Research and Social Policy in the Nineteenth Century. *British Journal of Sociology* 8:146–157.

McKenzie, J. C. 1962. The Composition and Nutritional Value of Diets in Manchester and Dukinfield. *Transactions of the Lancashire and Cheshire Antiquarian Society* 72:123–140.

McKeown, T., and R. G. Brown. 1955. Medical Evidence Related to English Population Changes in the Eighteenth Century. *Population Studies* 9:119–214.

McKeown, T., and R. G. Record. 1962. Reasons for the Decline in Mortality in England and Wales During the Nineteenth Century. *Population Studies* 16:94–142.

McLaughlin, M. M. 1974. Survivors and Surrogates. In deMause, L. (ed.). *The History of Childhood*. New York. Harper Torchbooks, 1974.

Mearns, A. 1883. *The Bitter Cry of Outcast London*. London: James Clark.

Meindl, J. L., and C. O. Meindl. March 6, 1982. Tuberculous Meningitis in the 1830s. *Lancet* 554–555.

Meller, H. 1981. *London Cemeteries: An Illustrated Guide and Gazeteer*. Amersham: Avebury.

Menefee, S. R. 1981. *Wives for Sale.* Oxford: Blackwell.

Meredith, H. V., and E. M. Meredith. 1944. The Stature of Toronto Children Half a Century Ago and Today. *Human Biology* 16:126–131.

Miller, J. H. Temple and Sewer: Childbirth, Prudery and Victoria Regina. In Wohl, A. S. (ed.). *The Victorian Family: Structure and Stresses.* St. Martin's Press, 1978.

Millin, S. S. 1909. The Duty of the State toward the Pauper Children of Ireland. *Journal of the Statistical and Social Inquiry Society of Ireland* 89:249–262.

Mills, D. R. 1978. The Quality of Life in Melbourne, Cambridgeshire, in the Period 1800–1860. *International Review of Social History* 23:382–404.

Mintz, S. H. 1979. Studies in the Victorian Family. Unpublished Ph.D. dissertation, Yale University.

Miscellanea: V. 1865. Infanticide and Illegitimacy. *Journal of the Statistical Society* 28:420–423.

Mitchell, B. R., and P. Dean. 1962. *Abstract of British Historical Statistics.* Cambridge University Press.

Mitchison, R. 1970. *British Population Change Since 1860.* London: MacMillan.

Morgan, J. E. 1865. The Danger of Deterioration of Race from the Too Rapid Increase of Great Cities. *Transactions of the National Association for the Promotion of Social Science* 9:427–429.

Mowat, R. B. 1929. *The Life of Lord Pauncefoote.* New York: Houghton Mifflin.

Muffang, M. H. 1899. Ecoliers et Etudiants de Liverpool. *l'Anthropoligie.* 10: 21–41.

Muller, P. 1969. *The Tasks of Childhood.* New York: World University Library.

Neale, A. V. 1964. *The Advancement of Child Health.* London: The Athlone Press.

Neff, W. F. 1929. *Victorian Working Women: An Historical and Literacy Study of Women in British Industries and Professions 1832–1851.* London: Frank Cass.

Neild, W. 1841. Comparative Statement of the Income and Expenditure of Certain Families of the Working Classes in Manchester and Dukinfield, in the Years 1836 and 1841. *Journal of the Royal Statistical Society* 4:320–324.

Newman, G. 1907. *Infant Mortality.* London. Dutton.

Nicholson, H. Pure in Heart. In Pryce-Jones, A. (ed.). *Little Innocents: Childhood Reminiscences.* London: Cobden-Sanderson, 1932.

Note by the Editor. 1839. *Journal of the Statistical Society in London* 1:444.

O'Connell, D. On the State of the Irish Peasantry, 1825. In Aspinall, A., and E. A. Smith (eds.). *English Historical Documents 1783–1832.* Oxford University Press, 1959.

Odling, W. 1857. On the Composition of Bread. *Lancet* 1:137–138.

O'Hanlon, W. M. 1853. *Walks Among the Poor of Belfast, and Suggestions for Their Improvement.* Belfast: Henry Greer.

O'Neil, J. 1869. Fifty Years Experience of an Irish Shoemaker in London. *St. Crispin* 1 and 2 (passim)

Opiates to Children. Varieties. 1862. *British Medical Journal.* 2:374.

Opie, I. and P. Opie. 1959. *The Lore and Language of School Children.* Oxford University Press.

O'Shaugnessy, M. 1849. Minutes of Evidence Taken Before the Select Committee on Poor Laws (Ireland). *Parliamentary Papers.* Part 1, 38–39.

O'Shaugnessy, M. D. 1861. The Education and Other Aspects of the Statistics of Crime in Dublin. *Journal of the Statistical and Social Inquiry Society of Ireland* 19:61–70.

O'Tuathaigh, N. A. G. The Irish in Nineteenth Century Britain: Problems of Integration. In Swift, R. and Gilley, S. (eds.). *The Irish in the Victorian City.* London: Croom Helm, 1985.

Outside Opinions: Opium in the Nursery. *Chemist and Druggist.* 1879, 15 September, page 398.

Palmer, D., and G. Pincetl (eds.). 1980. *Flora Tristan's London Journal, 1840.* Charleston, Massachusetts: Charles River Books.

Pankhurst, S. 1932. Those Elfin Days. In Pryce-Jones, A. (ed.) *Little Innocents: Childhood Reminiscences.* London: Cobden-Sanderson.

Papers Relating to Proceedings for the Relief of Distress and the State of the Unions and Workhouses in Ireland. *Parliamentary Papers,* 1847–48.

Parkinson, R. 1841. *On the Present Condition of the Labouring Poor in Manchester.* London: Simpkin Marshall.

Parr, J. 1980. *Labouring Children: British Immigrant Apprentices to Canada, 1869–1924.* Montreal: McGill-Queen's University Press.

Parsinnen, T. M. 1983. *Secret Passions, Secret Remedies: Narcotic Drugs in British Society 1820–1930.* Philadelphia: Institute for the Study of Human Issues.

Pearsall, R. 1969. *The Worm in the Bud: The World of Victorian Sexuality.* London: MacMillan.

Pearson, G. 1983. *Hooligan: A History of Respectable Fears.* London: Methuen.

Peel, R. Debate in the House of Commons on the Factory Bill, 1818. In Aspinall, A., and E. A. Smith (eds.). *English Historical Documents 1783–1832*. Oxford University Press, 1959.

Pemberton, R. 1854. *The Happy Colony*. London: Saunders and Otley.

Perkin, H. 1976. The "Social Tone" of Victorian Seaside Resorts in the Northwest. *Northern History*. 11:180–194.

Piersman, P. et al. 1977. *Law and Tactics in Juvenile Cases*. Philadelphia, Pennsylvania: American Institute.

Pim, J. 1876. Address at the Opening of the Thirtieth Session. *Journal of the Statistical and Social Inquiry Society of Ireland* 50:1–26.

Pinchbeck, I., and M. Hewitt. 1973. *Children in English Society. II. From the Eighteenth Century to the Childrens Act 1948*. London: Routledge and Kegan Paul.

Pitter, J. 1864. The Employed Dressmakers and Milliners. *Transactions of the National Society for the Promotion of Social Science* 7:769.

Playfair, L. 1870. Address on Education. *Transactions of the National Association for the Promotion of Social Science* 14:41–62.

Police. April 9, 1839. *The Times*.

Police. Saturday, April 3, 1841. *London Phalanx*.

Pollard, M. 1984. *The Hardest Work Under Heaven. The Life and Death of the British Coal Miner*. London: Hutchinson.

Pooley, C. G. 1977. The Residential Segregation of Migrant Communities in Mid-Victorian Liverpool. *Institute of British Geographers* 2:364–382.

Porley, C. G. 1977. The Residential Segregation of Migrant Communities in Mid-Victorian Liverpool. *Institute of British Geographers* 2:364–382.

Popular Portraits—No. VI. Lord Ashley M. P. 1842. *Illustrated London News* 173.

Porter, W. T. 1894. The Relation Between the Growth of Children and their Deviation from the Physical Type of their Sex and Age. *Transactions of the Academy of Science of St. Louis* 6:233–250.

Postans, T. 1831. *Letter to Sir Thomas Baring, Bart. M. P. On the Causes Which Have Produced the Present State of the Agricultural Poor*. London: Staunton.

Potter, B. 1888. Pages from a Work-Girl's Diary. *Nineteenth Century* 24:301–314.

Potter, B. 1888. East London Labour. *Nineteenth Century* 29:161–183.

Price-Williams, R. 1880. On the Increase of Population in England and Wales. *Journal of the Royal Statistical Society* 43:462–496.

Quennell, P. (ed.). 1969. *Mayhew's London*. London: Hamlyn Publishing Group.

Quennell, P. 1972. *Samuel Johnson: His Friends and Enemies.* London: Weidenfeld and Nicholson.

Quetelet, Ad. 1871. *Anthropometrie: Ou Mesure des Differentes Facultes de l'Homme.* Brussels: G. Muquardt.

Rack, H. D. 1973. Domestic Visitation: A Chapter in Early Nineteenth Century Evangelism. *Journal of Ecclesiastical History* 24:357–376.

Ragsdale, H. 1980. *Detente in the Napoleonic Era: Bonaparte and the Russians.* Regents Press of Kansas.

Ramasubban, R. 1982. *Public Health and Medical Research in India: Their Origin Under the Impact of British Colonial Policy.* Sarec Report R4. Stockholm.

Ratcliffe, B. M., and W. H. Chaloner (eds.). 1977. *A French Sociologist Looks at Britain: Gustave D'Eichthal and British Society in 1828.* Manchester: Manchester University Press.

Rawson, R. A. 1883. Proceedings of the 20th November, 1883. *Journal of the Royal Statistical Society* 46:623–625.

Razzell, P. E., and R. W. Wainwright (eds.). 1973. *The Victorian Working Class: Selections from Letters to the Morning Chronicle.* London: Cass.

(Redgrave, A.) 1865. Reports of the Inspectors of Factories. *Parliamentary Papers.*

Redgrave, A., and R. Baker. 1877. Reports of the Inspectors of Factories, 1876. *Parliamentary Papers* 17:522–524.

Reid, D. A. 1976. The Decline of St. Monday. 1776–1876. *Past and Present* 71:76–101.

Reid, W. (ed.). 1899. *Memoirs and Correspondence of Lyon Playfair.* London: Harper and Brothers.

Report of the Committee for the Relief of Distressed Districts in Ireland. 1823. London: Phillips.

Report of a General Plan for the Promotion of Public and Personal Health, Devised, Prepared and Recommended by the Commissioners Appointed under a Resolve of the Legislature of Massachusetts, Relating to a Sanitary Survey of the State. 1850. Boston: Dutton and Wentworth.

Report of Her Majesty's Commissioners Appointed to Inquire into the Revenues and Management of Certain Colleges and Schools. 1864. Volume II. Appendix. *Parliamentary Papers.*

Report from the Commissioners on Employment of children. 1843. *Parliamentary Papers* 14:5–61.

Report from the Committee on Parish Apprentices (Hansard, 1815). In

Aspinall, A. and E. A. Smith (eds.). 1959. *English Historical Documents 1783–1832.* Oxford University Press.

Report from the Select Committee on Criminal and Destitute Children. 1853. *Parliamentary Papers* vol. 3.

Report from the Select Committee on the Police in the Metropolitan Area. 1828. *Parliamentary Papers* 21:7.

Report from the Select Committee on the Police of the Metropolis. 1828. *Parliamentary Papers* 21:Appendix.

Report from the Select Committee on the Police of the Metropolis with Minutes of Evidence and Appendix. 1828. *Parliamentary Papers* vol. 4.

Report of the Education Committee of the Statistical Society of London on the Borough of Finsbury. 1843. *Journal of the Statistical Society of London* 6:78–140.

Report of the Minutes of Evidence Taken Before the Select Committee on the State of Children Employed in the Manufactories of the United Kingdom. 1816. House of Commons.

Report of the Interdepartmental Committee on Physical Deterioration. 1904. *House of Commons Sessional Papers.* vol. 32.

Report of Leonard Horner (1847). Reports by Inspectors of Factories Made to the Government 1847–48 to 1852. 1848. *Parliamentary Papers.*

Reports of Lunatic Asylums Published During 1857 and 1858. 1859. *Journal of Medical Science* 5:157–200.

Reports of the Assistant Commissioners Appointed to Inquire into the State of Popular Education in England. 1861. Volume II. *Parliamentary Papers.*

Report on the Sanitary Condition of Agar Town and Other Parts of the Metropolis. 1849. Report by the General Board of Health, H. M. S. O.

Report upon the Condition of the Town of Leeds and its Inhabitants. 1839. *Journal of the Statistical Society of London* 3:397–424.

Reveley, G. 1817. (Testimony) *Report from the Committee on Employment of Boys in Sweeping Chimneys.* House of Commons.

Review of A. B. Granville's Catechism of Health. 1832. *London Medical Gazette* 9:551–553.

Reynolds, T. 1870. Smoking in Relation to Physical and Mental Culture. *Transactions of the National Association for the Promotion of Social Sciences* 14:448–449.

Rimmer, W. G. 1960. *Marshalls of Leeds. Flax-Spinners 1788–1886.* Cambridge: Cambridge University Press.

Ritchie, R. B. *Observations on the Sanatory Arrangements of Factories* . . . London: John Weale, 1844. In Carpenter, K. (ed.). *Conditions of Working and Living: The Reawakening of the English Conscience.* New York. Arno Press, 1972.

Ritt, L. *The Victorian Conscience in Action: The National Association for the Promotion of Social Science 1857–1866.* Unpublished Ph.D. dissertation, Columbia University, 1959.

Robert, P. Rumont (1720–1790). 1970. *Annales de Demographie Historique 1869.* Paris: Editions Sivey.

Roberts, C. 1876. The Physical Requirements of Factory Children. *Journal of the Royal Statistical Society* 39:681–733.

Roberts, D. The Paterfamilias of the Victorian Governing Classes. In Wohl, D. (ed.). *The Victorian Family: Structure and Stresses.* New York: St. Martin's Press, 1978.

Roberts, H. 1858. The Dwellings of the Labouring Classes, Their Improvement Through . . . As well as by Individual Efforts. *Transactions of the National Association for the Promotion of Social Science: Transactions* 2:583–620.

Roberts, R. 1973. *The Classic Slum: Salford Life in the First Quarter of the Century.* London. Pellican Books.

Roberts, R. Leasehold Estates and Municipal Enterprise: Landowners, Local Government and the Development of Bournemouth c. 1850 to 1914. In Cannadine, D. (ed.). *Patricians, Power, and Politics in Nineteenth Century Towns.* London: St. Martin's Press, 1982.

Robins, J. 1980. *The Lost Children: A Study of Charity Children in Ireland 1700–1900.* Dublin: Institute of Public Administration.

Robinson, N. 1861. Dwellings of the Poor in Dublin. *Transactions of the National Association for the Promotion of Social Science: Transactions* 5:594.

Rolt, L. T. C. 1970. *Isambard Kingdom Brunel.* London. Pellican Books.

Rook, C. H. 1899. *The Hooligan Nights.* London: Grant Richards.

Rooke, P. T., and R. L. Schnell. 1981. The Kings' Children in English Canada: A Psychohistorical Study of Abandonment, Rejection, and Colonial Response (1869–1930). *Journal of Psychohistory* 8:387–420.

Rose, P. 1984. *Parallel Lives: Five Victorian Marriages.* New York: Vintage Press.

Rosenbaum, S. 1905. A Contribution to the Study of Vital and Other Statistics of the Jews in the United Kingdom. *Journal of the Royal Statistical Society* 68:526–556.

Ross, E. Labour and Love: Rediscovering London's Working-Class Mothers, 1870–1918. In Lewis, J. (ed.). *Labour and Love: Women's Experience of Home and Family, 1850–1940.* Oxford: Blackwell, 1986.

(Routh, Dr.) 1857. On the Mortality of Infants in Foundling Institutions, and Generally as Influenced by the Absence of Breast Milk. *Lancet* i:420–421.

Rowntree, S. 1901. *Poverty: A Study of Town Life.* London: MacMillan.

Ruger, H. and Stoessiger, B. 1927. On the Growth Curves of Certain Characteristics in Man (Male). *Annals of Eugenics.* 2: 76–110.

Rumsey, H. W. 1871. On a Progressive Physical Degeneracy of Race in the Town Populations of Great Britain. *Transactions of the National Society for the Promotion of Social Science* 15:466–472.

Ruskin, J. 1886. *Praeterita.* Orpington, Kent. George Allen.

Russell, C. A. 1983. *Science and Social Change in Britain and Europe 1700–1900.* New York: St. Martin's Press.

Russell, J. C. 1937. Length of Life in England, 1250–1348. *Human Biology* 9:528–541.

Sala, G. A. 1857. Fishers of Men: Or Recruiting for her Majesty's Forces in London. *Illustrated Times* 5:379–381.

Sala, G. A. 1872. *Gaslight and Daylight, with Some London Scenes they Shine Upon.* London: Tinsley Brothers.

Salisbury, H. 1969. *The Nine Hundred Days.* New York. Avon Books.

Samuel, R. 1981. *East End Underworld: Chapter in the Life of Arthur Harding.* London: Routledge and Kegan Paul.

Sanderson, M. 1967. Education and the Factory in Industrial Lancashire, 1780–1840. *Economic History Review* 20:266–279.

Sandiford, K. A. P. 1983. Cricket and the Victorian Society. *Journal of Social History* 17:303–317.

Sandys, E. 1899. Letter to Sir Robert Naunton Concerning the Poor Children to be Sent to Virginia. *Virginia Magazine of History and Biography* 6:232.

Sauer, R. 1978. Infanticide and Abortion in Nineteenth Century Britain. *Population Studies* 32:81–93.

Schools and Scholars in Massachusetts, 1837. 1839. *Journal of the Statistical Society* 1:173–174.

Schools Inquiry Commission. 1868. Minutes of Evidence. *Parliamentary Papers* vol. 20.

Schools Inquiry Commission. 1868. Report of the Commissioners 1867–68. *Parliamentary Papers* vol. 26.

Schupf, H. W. *The Perishing and Dangerous Classes: Efforts to Deal with the Neglected Vagrant and Delinquent Juvenile in England,*

1849–1875. Unpublished Ph.D. dissertation, Columbia University, 1975.

Scola, R. 1975. Food Markets and Shops in Manchester, 1770–1870. *Journal of Historical Geography* 1:153–168.

Scott, J. 1982. *The Upper Classes: Property and Privilege in Britain*. London: MacMillan.

Searle, G. R. 1971. *The Quest for National Efficiency*. London: Oxford University Press.

Second Report of the Commissioners. 1843. Children's Employment Commission, *Parliamentary Papers*.

Second Report of the Health of Towns Commission. 1845. *British Parliamentary Papers* 18: Appendix, 66.

Second Report of the Commissioners on Children's Employment. 1864. *Parliamentary Papers* vol. 14.

Second Report from the Commissioners on the Employment of Children, Young Persons and Women in Agriculture. 1869. *Parliamentary Papers* 11: pt. II.

Seymour Tremenheere's Account of the Miners and Ironworkers of Bedwelty and Merthy Tydfil in 1839. In Young, G. M. and W. D. Handcock (eds.). *English Historical Documents 1833–1874*. Oxford University Press, 1956.

Shaftesbury. Children in Mines and Collieries. In Kersen, W. (ed.). *The Child*. Wiley, 1965.

Shaftesbury. 1858. On Public Health. *Transactions of the National Association for the Promotion of Social Sciences* 2:84–95.

Shann, E. 1930. *An Economic History of Australia*. Cambridge University Press.

Shapter, T. 1850. (Testimony) *Second Report of the Commissioners on the Health of City, Town, and Country Bills of Mortality*. London. Longmans.

Shaw, A. G. L. 1966. *Convicts and the Colonies*. London: Faber and Faber.

Shelley, R. M. *From Free Trade to Local Option: The Scope of Parliament's Activities Affecting Drinking and the Liquor Trade, 1860–1880*. Unpublished M. A. Thesis, University of Missouri-St. Louis, 1979.

Shepperd, F. 1971. *London 1808–70: The Infernal Wen*. Berkeley, California: The University of California Press.

Sherrard, O. A. 1966. *Two Victorian Girls*. London: Frederick Muller.

Shiman, L. L. 1974. The Band of Hope Movement: Respectable Recreation for Working Class Children. *Victorian Studies* 18:49–74.

(Shimmin, H.) 1856. *Publicity the True Core of Social Evils. Liverpool*

Life: Its Pleasures, Practices and Pastimes. Liverpool: Egerton Smith.

Silva, P. A. et al. 1982. Some Developmental and Behavioral Problems Associated with Bilateral Otitis Media with Effusion. *Journal of Learning Disabilities* 15:417–421.

Sims, G. R. 1889. *How the Poor Live.* London: Chatto and Windus.

Simpson, A., and M. Simpson (eds.). 1977. *I Too am Here: Selections from the letters of Jane Welsh Carlyle.* Cambridge University Press.

Sixth Report of the Commissioners on the Employment of Children and Young Persons in Trades and Manufacturers. 1867. *Parliamentary Papers* vol. 15.

Slugg, J. T. 1881. *Reminiscences of Manchester Fifty Years Ago.* Manchester: J. E. Cornish.

Smith, E. 1864. *Practical Dietary for Families, Schools, and the Laboring Classes.*

Smith, G. 1870. The Employment of Children in Brick and Tile Making Considered in Relation to the Factory and Workshop Acts. *Transactions of the National Association for the Promotion of Social Science* 14:537–540.

Smith, G. 1875. Our Canal Population. *Fortnightly Review* 97:233–242.

Smith, G. 1876. On the Inspection of Brick and Tile Yards and Canal Boats. *Transactions of the National Association for the Promotion of Social Sciences* 20:614–615.

Smith, H. L. (ed.). 1934. *The New Survey of London Life and Labour. Volume I: Forty Years of Change.* London. P. S. King and Sons.

Smith, J. H. Ten Acres of Deansgate in 1851. 1979. *Transactions of the Lancashire and Cheshire Antiquarian Society* 80:43–59.

Special Correspondent. January 3, 1850. Labour and the Poor: The Manufacturing Districts. The Staffordshire Collieries. Letter XXIII. *The Morning Chronicle.*

Springlett, J. 1982. Landowners and Urban Development: The Ramsden Estate and Nineteenth Century Huddersfield. *Journal of Historical Geography* 8:129–144.

Stanley, L. (ed.). 1984. *The Diaries of Hannah Cullwick, Victorian Maidservant.* London: Virago Press.

Statement of the Size of Men in Different Counties of Scotland, Taken from the Local Militia. 1817. *Edinburgh Medical and Surgical Journal* 13:260–264.

Statistical Committee of the Town Council. Report upon the Condition of the Town of Leeds and its Inhabitants. 1839. *Journal of the Statistical Society of London* 2:392–424.

Statistical Society of Manchester. 1839. Report on the Condition of the Population in Three Parishes in Rutlandshire, in March, 1839. *Journal of the Statistical Society* 2:297–302.

Steckel, R. H. 1979. Slave Height Profiles from Coastwise Manifests. *Explorations in Economic History* 16:363–380.

Stevenson, J. 1979. *Popular Disturbances in England 1700–1870.* London: Longmans.

Stieb, E. W. 1966. *Drug Adulteration: Detection and Control in Nineteenth Century Britain.* University of Wisconsin Press.

Storch, R. D. 1975. The Plague of Blue Locusts: Police Reform and Popular Resistance in Northern England, 1840–57. *International Review of Social History* 20:61–90.

Strange, K. H. 1982. *Climbing Boys: A Study of Sweeps' Apprentices 1773–1875.* London: Allison and Bushy.

Stratta, E. 1970. *The Education of Borstal Boys.* London: Routledge and Kegan Paul.

Stuart-Wortley, J. 1887. The East End as Represented by Mr. Besant. *Nineteenth Century* 28:361–377.

Sutherland, G. 1971. *Elementary Education in the Nineteenth Century.* London: The Historical Association.

Swift, R. Another Stafford Street Row: Law, Order and the Irish Presence in Mid-Victorian Wolverhampton. In Swift, R. and Gilley, S. (eds.). *The Irish in the Victorian City.* London: Croom Helm, 1985.

Symons, G. J. 1880. Some Deficiences in our Knowledge Respecting Health Resorts. *Transactions of the Sanitary Institute of Great Britain* 2:245–252.

Symons, J. C. 1842. Appendix C. Height of Colliery Boys. *Commission on the Employment of Children: First Report.* House of Commons.

Symons, J. C. 1842. Appendix H. Yorkshire Coalfield. Average of Wages and Consumption of Food for Eight Weeks in the Families of Six Colliers in Flockton, a Parish in Yorkshire Chiefly Composed of Colliers. Appendix to the First Report to the Commissioners, Children's Employment Commission. House of Commons, *Parliamentary Papers.*

Tanner, J. M. 1981. *A History of the Study of Human Growth.* Cambridge University Press.

Tanner, J. M., Whitehouse, R. H., and Takaishi, M. 1966: Standards from Birth to Maturity for Height, Weight, Height Velocity, and Weight Velocity: British Children, 1965, Part II. *Archives of Diseases of Childhood.* 41:613–635.

Tarn, J. 1966. The Peabody Donation Fund: The Role of a Housing Society in the Nineteenth Century. *Victorian Studies* 10:7–38.

Taylor, W. The Awful Sublimity of the Victorian City: Its Aesthetic and Architectural Origins. In Dyos, H. J., and M. Wolff (eds.). *The Victorian City: Images and Realities*. London: Routledge and Kegan Paul.

The London Shoe Black. 1855. *Ragged School Union Magazine* 7:35–36.

Thomson, A. 1852. *Social Evils: Their Causes and Cure*. London: Nisbett.

Thompson, B. Infant Mortality in Nineteenth Century Bradford. In Woods, R., and J. Woodward (eds.). *Urban Disease and Mortality in Nineteenth Century England*. London: Botsford, 1984.

Thompson, C. J. S. 1929. *The Mystery and Art of the Apothecary*. New York. Lippincott.

Thompson, F. 1973. *Lark Rise to Candleford*. London: Penguin Books.

Thompson, W. J. 1913. The Census of Ireland, 1911. *Journal of the Royal Statistical Society* 76:635–662.

Thorne, W. 1925. *My Life's Battles*. London: Newnes.

Tod, I. S. M. 1878. Boarding Out Pauper Children. *Journal of the Statistical and Social Inquiry Society of Ireland* 54:293–299.

Tomes, N. 1978. A "Torrent of Abuse": Crime of Violence Between Working Class Men and Women in London, 1849–1875. *Journal of Social History* 11:328–345.

Touhill, B. M. 1981. *William Smith O'Brien and His Irish Revolutionary Companions in Penal Exile*. Columbia, Missouri: University of Missouri Press.

Toynbee, J. 1844. (Testimony) Report of the Commissioners on the Health of Towns. *Parliamentary Papers, 335*.

Treble, J. H. 1971. Liverpool Working-Class Housing, 1801–1851. In Chapman, S. D. (ed.) *The History of Working Class Housing*. London: Rowman and Littlefield.

Tuchman, B. 1978. *A Distant Mirror*. New York. Ballantine Books.

Turner, E. S. 1968. *Roads to Ruin*. London: Penguin Books.

Turner, S. 1851. Juvenile Delinquency. *Edinburgh Review* 94:207–220.

Turner, S., and T. Paynter. 1846. *Report on the System and Arrangements of 'La Colonie Agricole' at Mettray*. London: Philanthropic Society.

Unwin, G. 1924. *Samuel Oldknow and the Arkwrights: The Industrial Revolution at Stockport and Marple*. Manchester University Press.

Unwin, T. F. (ed.). 1906. *The Hungry Forties*. London: Unwin.

Ure, A. 1835. *The Philosophy of Manufactories: Or, an Exposition of the Scientific, Moral and Commercial Economy of the Factory System of Great Britain.* London: Charles Knight.

The Vegetarian Society. 1862. *British Medical Journal* 2 374.

Urlin, R. D. On the Dwellings of Working Men in Cities, and the Efforts that have been made to Improve Them. *Journal of the Statistical and Social Inquiry Society of Ireland.* 1865, 29, 158–164.

Villermé, L. R. 1840. *Tableau de l'etat Physique et Moral des Ouvriers Employees dans les Manufactures de Coton, de Laine, et de Soie.* 2 vols. Paris: Renouard.

Villermé, L. R., and H. Milne-Edwards. 1829. De l'Influence de la Temperature sur la Mortalité, des Enfans Nouveau-Nés. *Annales D'Hygiene Publique et de Medecine Legale.* Paris: Gabon.

Vilquin, E. 1978. La Mortalité Infantile Selon les Mois de naissance. Le Cas de la Belgique au XIXe Siècle. *Population* 6:1137 1153.

Vincent, D. 1982. *Bread, Knowledge and Freedom: A Study of Nineteenth Century Class Autobiography.* London: Methuen.

Walker, B. 1981. Meat Preservation in Scotland. *Journal of the Royal Society of Health* 101:19–28.

Walker, G. 1839. *Gatherings from the Graveyards: Particularly those of London.* London. Longmans.

Walker, G. A. 1846. *Burial Ground Incendiarism. The Last Fire at the Bone House in the Spa Fields Golgatha.* London: Longman, Brown, Green, and Longmans.

Walton, J. K. 1979. Railways and Resort Development in Victorian England: The Case of Silloth. *Northern History* 15:191–209.

Walton, J. K. Social Development of Blackpool 1788–1914. Unpublished Ph.D. Dissertation. University of Lancaster, 1974.

Walvin, J. 1975. *The People's Game.* London: Allen Lane.

Walvin, J. 1978. *Leisure and Society 1830–1950.* London: Longmans.

Walvin, J. 1982. *A Child's World: A Social History of English Childhood 1800–1914.* London: Pelican Books.

Ward, J. T. 1962. *The Factory Movement 1830–1855.* London: MacMillan.

Ward, J. T., and J. H. Treble. 1969. Religion and Education in 1843: Reaction to the 'Factory Education Bill.' *Journal of Ecclesiastical History* 20:79–110.

Waugh, B. 1890. Baby-Farming. *Contemporary Review* 57:700–714.

Weeks, W. S. 1918. Proverbs and Proverbial Phrases of the Clitheroe District. *Transactions of the Lancashire and Cheshire Antiquarian Society* 36:32–64.

Weightman, G., and S. Humphries. 1983. *The Making of Modern London 1815–1914*. London: Sidgwick and Jackson.

Weld, C. R. 1840. Minutes of Evidence, March 30, 1840. Select Committee on the Health of Towns. *Parliamentary Papers* 68.

Weld, C. R. 1842. On Accidents upon the Railways in Great Britain. *Journal of the Statistical Society of London* 5:226–228.

Werner, E., J. M. Bierman, and F. E. French. 1971. *The Children of Kauai*. University of Hawaii Press.

West, E. G. 1975. *Education and the Industrial Revolution*. New York: Barnes and Noble.

West, G. M. 1893. Worcester School Children.—The Growth of the Body, Head, and Face. *Science* 21:2–4.

Whyman, J. A. Hanoverian Watering Place: Margate before the Railway. In Everett, A. (ed.). *Perspectives in English Urban History*. London: MacMillan, 1973.

Wickham, E. R. 1957. *Church and People in an Industrial City*. London: Lutterworth Press.

Wilde, O. May 28, 1897. The Case of Warder martin. London. *Daily Chronicle*.

Wilkinson, R., and E. M. Sigsworth. 1963. A Survey of Slum Clearance Areas in Leeds. *Yorkshire Bulletin of Economic and Social Research* 15:25–51.

William Cargill, esq., and a Committee of the Educational Society of Newcastle. 1838. Educational, Criminal, and Social Statistics of Newcastle upon Tyne. *Journal of the Statistical Society of London* 1:356–361.

Williams, G. 1966. *Barnardo: The Extraordinary Doctor*. London: MacMillan.

Williams, W. J. 1853. (Testimony) *Parliamentary Papers* 28:200–201.

Wills, W. D. 1971. *Spare the Child: The Story of an Experimental Approved School*. London: Penguin Books.

Wilson, C. 1968. *The History of Unilever. A Study in Economic Growth and Social Change*. Volume I. New York: Praeger.

Wilson, G. B. 1940. *Alcohol and the Nation*. London: Nicholson and Watson.

Wontner, J. 1828. (Testimony) Report from the Select Committee on the Police of the Metropolis with Minutes of Evidence. *Parliamentary Papers* vol. 4.

Woodbridge, G. 1978. *The Reform Club 1836–1978*. Lonon: Clearwater Publishing Company.

World's Children Data Sheet. 1979. Washington, D.C.: Population Reference Bureau.

Wrigley, E. A. Mortality in Pre-Industrial England: The Example of Colyton, Devon, Over Three Centuries. In Glass, D. and Revelle, R. (eds.) *Population and Social Change*. London: Arnold, 1972.

Wright, T. 1873. *Our New Masters*. London: Strahan and Co.

Yeats, J. 1855. On our National Strength: Tested by Numbers, the Ages, and the Industrial Qualifications of People. *Journal of the Statistical Society of London* 18:367–377.

Yeats, J. 1864. On Human Growth in Towns. *Transactions of the National Association for the Promotion of Social Science* 7:536–547.

Yule, G. U. 1906. On the Changes in the Marriage- and Birth-Rates in England and Wales During the Past Half-Century; With an Inquiry as to their Probable Causes. *Journal of the Royal Statistical Society* 69:88–132.

Yule, G. U. 1899. An Investigation into the Causes of a Change in Pauperism in England, Chiefly During the Last Two Intercensal Decades (Part I). *Journal of the Royal Statistical Society* 63:249–268.

Zangwill, I. 1892. *Children of the Ghetto*. London: MacMillan.

1851 Census Great Britain. 1854. Reports and Tables on Education England and Wales and on Religious Education and Worship Scotland. *Parliamentary Papers* 11.

NAME INDEX

SUBJECT INDEX

PLACE NAMES